Rites of Power

*Published under the auspices of
the Shelby Cullom Davis
Center for Historical Studies,
Princeton University*

Rites of Power
Symbolism, Ritual, and Politics Since the Middle Ages

SEAN WILENTZ,
Editor

upp

University of Pennsylvania Press
Philadelphia

Library of Congress Cataloging in Publication Data

Main entry under title:

Rites of power.

   Collection drawn from the essays presented to and
discussed by the Shelby Cullom Davis Center seminar from
1980 to 1982.
   Includes bibliographies and index.
   1. Symbolism in politics—History—Addresses, essays,
lectures. 2. Power (Social sciences)—History—Addresses,
essays, lectures. I. Wilentz, R. Sean. II. Shelby
Cullom Davis Center for Historical Studies.
JA74.R56 1985   306'.2   84-20937
ISBN 0-8122-7948-4

Printed in the United States of America

To Kenneth Burke and Family

Contents

Acknowledgments

Collecting, editing, and revising these essays has deepened my admiration for the Davis Center and its unique combination of freewheeling inquiry and scholarly fellowship. As director, colleague, and friend, Lawrence Stone has helped me in countless ways, with wise counsel and unflagging good cheer. Joan Daviduk, the Davis Center's secretary and all-around troubleshooter, pretended to be unperturbed whenever I arrived with a long list of new chores and incipient crises. Without their suggestions and tireless efforts this book never would have appeared.

The essays come from a much longer series of papers presented to the Davis Center on the general topic of politics and ideology. Not all of those papers spoke to the specific theme of this book; nevertheless, almost all of the scholars who addressed and attended the Center's seminars in some way helped to shape and improve its discussions of political symbolism. I am especially grateful to Davis Center fellows Baruch Knei-Paz, Richard L. McCormick, Gary Puckrein, Gerald Sider, and Elizabeth Traube for their lively conversation and astute criticism, in and out of seminar. Thanks also to Bernard Cohn, Natalie Zemon Davis, and Orest Ranum for their splendid contributions to a Davis Center symposium on political symbolism, held way back in March 1981.

Several editors, current and former, at the University of Pennsylvania Press shepherded the book through some difficult terrain. I am particularly obliged to John McGuigan, who acquired the manuscript, and to Ingalill Hjelm, who saw it safely home. Robert Brown of Princeton, New Jersey, copy-edited the book with precision and creativity. Helen Wright typed and retyped the introduction and several essays with an uncommon mixture of blinding speed and extraordinary patience. Françoise Harisclur-Arthapignet and Marta Petrusewicz were extremely helpful in translating portions originally written in French. Christine Stansell offered her formidable editorial talents and some cogent criticisms.

The dedication is a token repayment of an old personal debt. While editing *Rites of Power*, I kept Kenneth Burke's works close to hand, for inspiration and instruction. But long before then, over several childhood summers in Andover, New Jersey, the irrepressible example of assorted Burkes, Chapins, Leacocks, and others taught me more than they can possibly realize. To them all, my belated thanks.

S. W.

Princeton, New Jersey
December 1984

NOTE

The essays by Hanley, Agulhon, Isaac, and Lüdtke were originally written while the authors were fellows-in-residence at the Davis Center. Those by Giesey and Wortman were originally presented to the Center's symposium, "Symbolism, Ritual, and Political Power," held on March 14, 1981, as was Hanley's. Ruiz, Elliott, and Cannadine offered their papers to the Center's seminar for criticism and discussion. Geertz's essay, first published in 1977, contains some of the thoughts Geertz developed at the Center's symposium. It was also a touchstone for many of the seminar's formal and informal conversations. This collection would not have been quite complete without it.

Editorial regularization has been kept to a minimum, in order to preserve the authors' diverse styles and vocabulary. All spellings, outside of quoted material, have been put into American. Punctuation has been standardized, except where variations have been justified by the authors' substantive arguments (e.g., Hanley's use of *lit de justice* and *Lit de Justice*).

SEAN WILENTZ

Introduction
Teufelsdröckh's Dilemma: On Symbolism, Politics, and History

> Often in my atrabiliar moods, when I read of pompous
> ceremonials, Frankfort Coronations, Royal Drawing-rooms,
> Levees, Couchees; and how the ushers and macers and pursuivants
> are all in waiting; how Duke this is presented by Archduke that,
> and Colonel A by General B, and innumerable Bishops, Admirals,
> and miscellaneous Functionaries, are advancing gallantly to the
> Annointed Presence; and I strive, in my remote privacy, to form a
> clear picture of that solemnity,—on a sudden, as by some
> enchanter's wand, the—shall I speak it?—the Clothes fly-off the
> whole dramatic corps; the Dukes, Grandees, Bishops, Generals,
> Annointed Presence itself, every mother's son of them, stand
> straddling there, not a shirt on them; and I know not whether to
> laugh or weep.
>
> Teufelsdröckh, in Carlyle, *Sartor Resartus*

Like Herr Doktor Teufelsdröckh, current historians are fascinated by political ritual and symbolism. Like him, and like Carlyle, they have been
looking through the clothing of power, to see how it expresses some
deeper ordering of political and social relations. And at times, the historians have not known whether to laugh or weep.

This collection, drawn from the essays presented to and discussed by
the Shelby Cullom Davis Center seminar from 1980 to 1982, includes ten
examples of the most recent scholarship on symbolism and politics. The
authors have already contributed greatly to our understanding of the subject; here, they offer either reflections on previous work or, in most cases,

1

the first fruits of new projects. Together, their essays provide a broad thematic and chronological survey ranging from tenth-century France to Great Britain in 1977. Each makes intriguing suggestions about how the historian's craft might be joined with the interpretive methods used by anthropologists, art historians, and literary critics. Each breaks through the usual bounds of political history to turn the study of politics, social relations, and cultural creation into a single endeavor.

Why this shattering of conventions? What accounts for the recent interest in the history of political symbols and ritual? Several factors come to mind: the recurrent and shifting influences of Freud, Jung, and their followers on historians' awareness; the abiding shock and curiosity attached to seemingly irrational political movements and official acts; the erotic pull of visual imagery in our own time; the movie-palace politics of the age of Reagan. Above all, though, these studies should be understood as one of several reactions to an acknowledged, long-term, and continuing crisis in historical scholarship, a crisis that began more than a decade ago and has deepened in recent years.

Into the 1970s, three broad, sometimes overlapping influences shaped the most innovative historical work undertaken in the United States, Great Britain, and on the Continent: The *Annales* school (with its numerous subschools), social science history (a branch of which was dubbed "cliometrics"), and Marxism. Each ran into difficulties at different times and in different circumstances, but to a remarkable degree the same issue reappeared; namely, the tendency of each of these approaches to neglect politics or to interpret political consciousness and power in mechanistic and reductionist ways. For *Annalistes*, politics and political ideology remained the least interesting of subjects, banished to the tertiary significance of *histoire événmentielle* and "mere" narrative, superseded by the study of social structures and *mentalités*. Social science historians imputed models of power and motivation from the statistics of historical behavior, as if historical causes could be divined from historical effects, and as if social and political history could be understood without direct study of social relations, ideas, politics, and culture. Marxists, with some important exceptions, still could be heard discussing these matters with hackneyed allusions to "base" and "superstructure." With the great boom in social and cultural history of all kinds, political history—especially the history of formal politics and institutions—began to be pushed to the sidelines, as a "traditional" subject of dubious relevance. To make matters worse, some provocative but at times belligerently ahistorical approaches to the study of power—notably structuralism and semiotic deconstructionism—began to gain considerable intellectual prestige, first among literary critics and political scientists and then in the tone-setting reviews and journals. Historians, especially political historians, started to feel either impotent or irate. The search began for more satisfying historical interpretations of authority, power, and social perception.

The study of political ritual has been one of the more promising outcomes of that search. Its practitioners form no new school; as this volume indicates, they draw upon an eclectic range of intellectual traditions. On certain fundamental issues—the relations between class and politics, for example—they often disagree. Nevertheless, these scholars share both a frustration at attempts merely to correlate social history with politics, consciousness, and ideas, and a desire to begin looking at politics as a realm of social experience and action in its own right—a realm partly (but never entirely) independent of other social realms. They have focused on the symbols and conventions of political life, and on the interpretation of those dramas of political expression—sometimes contrived, sometimes spontaneous—that reflect and help determine the boundaries of power.

There have been, to be sure, important forerunners in this kind of work, and their writings inform current historical studies: the art historians Ernst Gombrich and Erwin Panofsky on iconology, the literary critic Kenneth Burke on rhetoric and symbolism, the philosopher Ernst Cassirer on the myth of the state, as well as the historians Marc Bloch, Percy Ernst Schramm, and Ernst Kantorowicz.[1] Some recent French structuralist and poststructuralist writers—Michel Foucault most of all—have expanded and improved the historians' working assumptions, despite their often cavalier regard for the discipline of historical context.[2] But to the extent that any single body of scholarship has influenced recent historians of political ritual, it has been the cultural anthropology of contemporary writers like Mary Douglas, Clifford Geertz, and Marshall Sahlins.[3] Anthropology, unlike *Annales* materialism, functionalist sociology, and orthodox Marxism, has given historians ways of seeing politics as a form of cultural interaction, a relationship (or a set of relationships) tied to broader moral and social systems. Political symbols and acts of persuasion, in this view, carry with them complex networks of social customs, aspirations, and fears. Whereas previous historians interpreted politics either as a narrative with a logic of its own, or as the conjunctural outcome of economic and demographic indicators, those influenced by the anthropologists interpret political ceremonies and insignias as minidramas or as metaphors, upon which are inscribed the tacit assumptions that either legitimize a political order or hasten its disintegration. By reading these "metaphorical" acts, symbols, and pronouncements, much as an anthropologist reads everyday events and rituals, the historians hope to fuse our understanding of power, cultural expression, and political consciousness. Of course, there are differences in the ways the historians approach their tasks and the ways the anthropologists approach theirs—differences, incidentally, which were the subject of sometimes fractious debate in the Davis Center. Above all, establishing a historical context in which to study politics and consciousness and establishing an ethnographic context in the field involve different kinds of intellectual operations. Still, the similarities are much more obvious than the differences, at least with respect to the three basic axioms that guide the historians' research and interpretations.

Of utmost importance is the idea, discussed by Geertz in his influential essay on charisma (reprinted here), that all polities are ordered and governed by "master fictions" as well as by the threat of official or sanctioned force.[4] Certain fictions—the divine right of kings, the ceremonial charisma of Geertz's Indic Negara, the Nazi Aryan cult—may seem like sheer fantasy to later generations and alien cultures. Others—like American ideals of the virtuous yeoman or of equality and popular sovereignty—may seem to partake of a mixture of fact, myth, and wishful thinking. In all cases, they operate as the unchallenged first principles of a political order, making any given hierarchy appear natural and just to rulers and ruled. By exploring how these fictions, and the rhetoric that sustains them, are invented and perpetuated, historians of political ritual look for the ideological lineaments of authority and consent in a particular historical context.

A second axiom concerns the character of political rhetoric. Historians are accustomed to studying rhetoric only in its public verbal forms, in the texts of speeches, sermons, parliamentary debates, and the like. In the recent literature, however, all kinds of signs and rhetoric—public and private, verbal and nonverbal—are open for interpretation. Indeed, as historians have begun to understand, both nonverbal public displays and "private" rhetoric—political spectacle, public art, everyday gestures and remarks—can carry far more meaning and significance for contemporaries than the most eloquent, but often unread, political treatises.[5] Thus, as J. H. Elliott argues in his essay on Spain under Philip IV, an appreciation of the powers and limitations of seventeenth-century absolutism might begin with an interpretation of the effectiveness of royal portraiture and court drama as propaganda. So, as Rhys Isaac demonstrates, personal diary jottings about recalcitrant slaves, disobedient children, and mired cattle can tell us things about political relations in colonial Virginia not to be found in the most impassioned pamphlet on natural law. And so, according to Maurice Agulhon, the changing political iconography of nineteenth-century French statuary reveals an interplay of official ideology and popular perceptions missing in the voluminous writings on that country's revolutions.

Finally, while historians now look at all sorts of rhetoric, they also assume that different groups and individuals attach different meanings to the same rhetoric. In stable political orders—like the United States through most of its history—this shared rhetoric helps to harmonize or at least keep in check otherwise divergent interests and ideologies, shrouding them all in what Kenneth Burke calls a "eulogistic covering." When harmony dissolves—as during the American Civil War—the common rhetoric can serve as the ideological rallying points for opposing causes. At all events, political rhetoric carries a multitude of contradictory meanings. The art of interpreting the many meanings of a single rhetoric or symbolic event has been closely associated with Geertz and his exercises in "thick description," but the technique will be familiar to any reader of William Faulkner or Gabriel García Márquez.[6] Historians, comparative novices at literary innovation, have yet to find an agreed form with which to order their evidence and interpretations while still capturing the subtlest dynamics of assent and disagreement. They have, however, taken single events, symbols, and rituals and successfully sorted out their various levels of rhetorical meaning—as, in this volume, in Sarah Hanley's rereading of the *lit de justice*, in Richard Wortman's interpretation of the clashing meanings of tsarist rituals, and in Alf Lüdtke's essay on *Eigensinn* and political protest by German factory workers.

Working with these axioms, historians have advanced on several fronts, in each case stressing different historical processes. If the essays in this book are any indication, the uses of symbolic interpretation can vary considerably according to country, region, and historical era.

No Western nation has been more self-conscious—some might say pompous—in the propagation of political rituals and symbols than France; it was, for instance, flattering but not surprising for scholars to learn that after the Socialist victory in 1981, François Mitterand consulted historians of the fêtes of the French Revolution to help choreograph his own inauguration ceremonies. Ralph Giesey and Sarah Hanley trace the origins of this French fixation, from medieval times through the long reign of Europe's most splendid absolutist, Louis XIV. Taking what he calls a semiotic approach, Giesey shows how changes in court ceremonial bespoke fundamental shifts in rulership and constitutional theory, culminating in the personalized kingship of *le Roi Soleil*. Hanley blends symbolic analysis with a tight historical rendering of constitutional discourse in order to overturn some old myths about the *lit de justice*, one of the grandest political occasions in all of early modern Europe.

Teofilo Ruiz and J. H. Elliott find very different trends in this history of Spanish ritual over roughly the same period covered by Giesey and Hanley. The monarchs of medieval Castile inherited some precedents for royal ceremonial, but as Ruiz shows, they generally made little use of them. Ruiz's conclusions remind us that the threat of physical force and terror may lie just beneath the rhetorical surface of symbolic spectacle. Elliott likewise sees the limitations as well as the possibilities of what he calls the propaganda of seventeenth-century Spanish absolutism. At least in the case of the reforming minister *manqûe* Olivares, the deployment of pomp only created illusions that could not be sustained, leading to the minister's downfall—a sobering lesson to present-day absolutists and their ambitious servants.

If the creation of political charisma remained troublesome in the age of absolutism, the problem of ceremonial legitimation lasted long after the enlightened revolutions of the modern era. Recent monographs on Robespierrist France and on the Soviet Union have shown how revolutionary regimes consolidated support through rituals and quasi-religious cults; other studies have examined how late-nineteenth-century aristocrats and monarchs, pressed by movements for popular democracy, literally invented traditions of their own in order to buttress their privileges and authority.[7] Three essays here survey the fate of official political imagery in the nineteenth and twentieth centuries. Maurice Agulhon picks up his impressive studies of French republican symbolism, extends his period of investigation to cover the years after 1880, and explores the controversial thesis that political symbolism became increasingly transparent (and, by implication, egalitarian) over the nineteenth century. David Cannadine's detailed study of England follows the sometimes hilarious ceremonial history of what British loyalists still boast of as the world's oldest monarchy. He discovers that a succession of factors—political, commerical, technological, and cultural—all contributed to the elevation of the monarchy from its degraded status of the 1820s to its exalted position of the Victorian age and after. Richard Wortman looks at the public ceremonies of a tsarist dynasty that was slipping into its final years; beneath the attempts at majesty, Wortman finds those cultural schisms that were to help bring the Romanovs' downfall.

The book's final section includes two essays that depart from the conventions of both political history and what Ralph Giesey calls "ceremonial studies." A major preoccupation of recent social historians has been what they loosely refer to as everyday life, in particular the daily lives of ordinary people. Although these investigations have done a great deal to recapture the experiences of the lowly and to restore a sense of popular agency to historical studies, they have sometimes slighted the political dimension. At its weakest, the study of popular history has contented itself with celebrations of the hitherto uncelebrated: Political history is left to the historians of the state; early attempts to get at the politics of ordinary life and their connection to formal politics—once advanced with the slogan, "The personal is the political"—remain underdeveloped. It is, in part, to resist such trends that Rhys Isaac and Alf Lüdtke investigate how everyday symbols and rituals expressed and reinforced political relationships, in and out of political institutions. Isaac, inspired by the work of sociolinguists as much as by anthropology, takes soundings in the rich diary of the eighteenth-century Virginia planter Landon Carter, and finds forms of paternalist communication and control even more complex than those emphasized by recent historians of the nineteenth-century slave South. Lüdtke examines the horseplay and other forms of sometimes brutal camaraderie that occasionally broke out on the shop floor, in order to explore a highly ritualized world of struggle between workers and employers and among workers themselves; in the end, Lüdtke forces us to reconsider the common distinctions between "public" and "private" forms of political expression.

Given such variety, it would be unwise to fix only one label on all of these essays. Indeed, since the Davis Center series on politics and ideology ended in 1982, the variety of approaches to the subject has grown, especially in art history and literary criticism.[8] If anything, this book will have accomplished one of its aims if it encourages historians to look for as-yet-untried methods of interpretation in other historical contexts. This said, it is important to raise a cautionary note. Despite their diversity, all of these essays point out a vexing problem common to any history of political symbolism, one that raises serious questions about the limitations and significance of symbolic interpretation—and the limits of *verstehen* in any scholarly enterprise—a problem that even the historians' shared assumptions cannot remove. The problem is as old as Plato's cave. Let us call it Teufelsdröckh's dilemma.

Teufelsdröckh, we will recall, fantasized the disrobing of the potentates only when he was in one of his irreverent, atrabiliar moods. Most of the time, he was trying to figure out how to maintain respect for his rulers in all their ridiculous regalia. Much to his chagrin, Teufelsdröckh—like his contemporary Karl Marx—came to decide that society was virtually founded on cloth. Yet whereas this discovery goaded the real-life German Hegelian to demystify the political order (and trace its origins to the *manufacture* of cloth and attendant class relations), Carlyle's philosopher ran into trouble. Could it be, he reasoned, that if people find some sort of meaning in the symbols of power, the clothing, then these mystifications might truly represent the deeper human reality that they are supposed to mask? And if this is so, he continued, should we not treat these mystifications with respect, even reverence, instead of scorn?[9]

Historians face a version of the same dilemma in their own studies of symbols and rituals, although they usually pose it differently, as the opposition between rhetoric and reality. If, as is commonly assumed, all political orders are governed by master fictions, is there any point in trying to find out where historical rhetoric and historical reality diverge? Can historians of the symbolic even speak of objective "reality" except as it was perceived by those being studied, and thereby transformed into yet another fiction? Once we respect political mystifications as both inevitable and worthy of study in their own right—once we abandon crude and arrogant explanations of the origins of "false consciousness" and vaunt the study of perception and experience—is there any convincing way to connect them to the social and material characteristics of any hierarchical order without lapsing into one form or another of mechanistic functionalism? Some historians insist that it is still possible—indeed imperative—to make these connections, and they warn of the rise of an "anthropologized" idealism, disrespectful of historical contexts, in which a new fetish of elegant presentation replaces the old fetish of sociological abstraction and cumbersome prose. Others respond that such fears, although justified, need not block the historical study of perception and political culture in ways influenced by the anthropologists' insights.[10]

The important thing about such questions, however, is not that they are troublesome. Nor is it likely that historians may someday arrive at an amicable consensus. The point is that historians are asking such questions at all: By confronting their own version of Teufelsdröckh's dilemma, historians may well be ending their long-term crisis. For years, it seemed as if politics and the life of the mind had been driven to the margins of innovative historical scholarship, as if social scientism and a preoccupation with the inexorable forces and weighty inheritances of material and mental life had become the premier virtues of any historical study. The recent work on political symbolism has helped restore those missing elements whose absence has led to an intellectual impasse—a restoration that has involved, not the revival of an older discredited history of ideas or of narrative political history, but instead an effort to rethink the history of power, perception, social relations, and cultural expression in new ways. As the essays presented here indicate, such rethinking demands far more than the analysis of structural data or the telling of a story, as essential as these endeavors are. It demands an exercise of the moral imagination. With this task before them, historians may finally stop thinking of their discipline as a kind of retrospective social science, or as any merely academic enterprise. They may begin to practice their own art and mystery as the most exemplary writers and critics practice theirs, interpreting political meanings and perceptions as well as causes and events, studying the past with a sensitivity to humanist dialectics.

Notes

1. E. H. Gombrich, *Art and Illusion* (New York, 1961); Gombrich, *Symbolic Images* (London, 1972); Erwin Panofsky, *Meaning in the Visual Arts* (new ed., Chicago, 1982); Panofsky, *Studies in Iconology* (New York, 1972); Kenneth Burke, *Language As Symbolic Action* (Berkeley, 1966); Ernst Cassirer, *The Myth of the State* (New Haven, 1946); Marc Bloch, *Les rois thaumaturges* (Strasbourg, 1924); Percy Ernst Schramm, *Herrschaftszeichen und Staatssymbolik*, 3 vols. (Stuttgart, 1954–56); Ernst Kantorowicz, *The King's Two Bodies* (Princeton, 1957).

2. One needs only to note the ubiquity of the term *discourse* in the present collection, and many other places, to get a sense of Foucault's direct and indirect influence on historians. How thorough and lasting the influence will be remains to be seen given current fluctuations in academic fashions. But certainly historians in the foreseeable future are likely to shun the kind of "common-sensical," face-value, apolitical reading of texts that Foucault's work did so much to discredit.

   Social and political historians have displayed less interest to date in semiotics and the more purely literary textual analyses of Jacques Derrida and his school. This may change. Note, for example, Ralph Giesey's attempt in this volume to take a "semiotic" approach to royal ceremonies. Note, too, Jacques Rancière's challenge to nineteenth-century social and labor historians, *La nuit des proletaires. Archives du rêve ouvrier* (Paris, 1981), in which Rancière deconstructs various texts by radical French workers.

3. Mary Douglas, *Purity and Danger* (London, 1966); Clifford Geertz, "Ideology as a Cultural System," in David E. Apter, ed., *Ideology and Discontent* (New York, 1964); and Geertz, *The Interpretation of Cultures* (New York, 1973);

Marshall D. Sahlins, *Stone Age Economics* (Chicago, 1972); Sahlins, *Culture and Practical Reason* (Chicago, 1976). See also Max Gluckman, *Politics, Law, and Ritual in Tribal Society* (Oxford, 1965); Victor W. Turner, *The Forest of Symbols* (Ithaca, 1967); Turner, *The Ritual Process* (Chicago, 1969). Of somewhat less abiding influence owing to its ahistorical bias—but influential nevertheless—has been the structural anthropology of Claude Lévi-Strauss. See especially his *Structural Anthropology*, 2 vols. (New York, 1963–76); and Lévi-Strauss, *The Raw and the Cooked* (New York, 1969).

4. Edmund S. Morgan has more recently developed this idea with respect to the political fictions of early America. See his "Government by Fiction: The Idea of Representation," *Yale Review*, 72 (1983): 321–39.

5. Although, to be sure, the interpretation of texts remains an important part of the history of rhetoric and political fictions. Quentin Skinner is one of many recent intellectual historians who have tried to alter their methods in ways that bear resemblance to the work on political symbolism. See Skinner's overview of political theory, *The Foundations of Modern Political Thought*, 2 vols. (Cambridge, 1978).

6. Geertz, *Interpretation of Cultures*, pp. 3–30.

7. Mona Ozouf, *La fête révolutionnaire* (Paris, 1976); Nina Tumarkin, *Lenin Lives!* (Cambridge, Mass., 1983); E. J. Hobsbawm and Terence Ranger, eds., *The Invention of Tradition* (Cambridge, 1982).

8. See for example the recent work in the journal *Representations* as well as the essays collected in Robert M. Berdahl, Alf Lüdtke, Hans Medick, and Gerald Sider, *Klassen und Kultur. Sozialanthropologische Perspectiven in der Geschichtschreibung* (Frankfurt, 1982).

9. This analysis is heavily indebted to Kenneth Burke, *A Rhetoric of Motives* (1950; reprinted, Berkeley, 1969), pp. 114–23.

10. For criticisms, see E. P. Thompson, "Rough Music: Le Charivari Anglais," *Annales E. S. C.*, 27 (1972): 285–312; Thompson, "Anthropology and the Discipline of Historical Context," *Midland History*, 1 (1972): 41–55; Elizabeth Fox-Genovese and Eugene D. Genovese, "The Political Crisis of Social History," in Fox-Genovese and Genovese, *Fruits of Merchant Capital* (New York, 1983). See also Felix Gilbert's review of Richard C. Trexler, *Public Life in Renaissance Florence*, in *New York Review of Books*, January 21, 1982. For further reflections on the affinities between history and anthropology, see the contributions by Bernard S. Cohn, John N. Adams, Natalie Z. Davis, and Carlo Ginzburg, in *Journal of Interdisciplinary History*, 12 (1981): 227–79.

PART I

An Anthropological Overview

———————————

1

CLIFFORD GEERTZ

Centers, Kings, and Charisma: Reflections on the Symbolics of Power

Like so many of the key ideas in Weber's sociology—*verstehen*, legitimacy, inner-worldly asceticism, rationalization—the concept of charisma suffers from an uncertainty of referent: does it denote a cultural phenomenon or a psychological one? At once "a certain quality" that marks an individual as standing in a privileged relationship to the sources of being and a hypnotic power "certain personalities" have to engage passions and dominate minds, it is not clear whether charisma is the status, the excitement, or some ambiguous fusion of the two. The attempt to write a sociology of culture and a social psychology in a single set of sentences is what gives Weber's work its orchestral complexity and harmonic depth. But it is also what gives it, especially to ears less attuned to polyphony, its chronic elusiveness.

In Weber, a classic instance of his own category, the complexity was managed and the elusiveness offset by his extraordinary ability to hold together warring ideas. In more recent and less heroic times, however, the tendency has been to ease the weight of his thought by collapsing it into one of its dimensions, most commonly the psychological, and nowhere has this been more true than in connection with charisma.[1] Everyone from John Lindsay to Mick Jagger has been called charismatic, mainly on the grounds that he has contrived to interest a certain number of people in the glitter of his personality; and the main interpretation of the rather more genuine upsurge of charismatic leadership in the New States has been that it is a product of psychopathology encouraged by social disorder.[2] In the general psychologism of the age, so well remarked by Phillip Rieff, the study of personal authority narrows to an investigation

13

of self-presentment and collective neurosis; the numinous aspect fades from view.[3]

A few scholars, among them prominently Edward Shils, have, however, sought to avoid this reduction of difficult richness to neo-Freudian cliché by facing up to the fact that there are multiple themes in Weber's concept of charisma, that almost all of them are more stated than developed, and that the preservation of the force of the concept depends upon developing them and uncovering thereby the exact dynamics of their interplay. Between the blur produced by trying to say too much at once and the banality produced by dismissing mysteries there remains the possibility of articulating just what it is that causes some men to see transcendency in others, and what it is they see.

In Shils's case, the lost dimensions of charisma have been restored by stressing the connection between the symbolic value individuals possess and their relation to the active centers of the social order.[4] Such centers, which have "nothing to do with geometry and little with geography," are essentially concentrated loci of serious acts; they consist in the point or points in a society where its leading ideas come together with its leading institutions to create an arena in which the events that most vitally affect its members' lives take place. It is involvement, even oppositional involvement, with such arenas and with the momentous events that occur in them that confers charisma. It is a sign, not of popular appeal or inventive craziness, but of being near the heart of things.

There are a number of implications of such a glowing-center view of the matter. Charismatic figures can arise in any realm of life that is sufficiently focused to seem vital—in science or art as readily as in religion or politics. Charisma does not appear only in extravagant forms and fleeting moments but is an abiding, if combustible, aspect of social life that occasionally bursts into open flame. There is no more a single charismatic emotion than there is a single moral, aesthetic, or scientific one; though passions, often enough distorted ones, are undeniably involved, they can be radically different from case to case. But my concern here is not to pursue these issues, as important as they are to a general theory of social authority. It is to probe into another matter Shils's approach causes to appear in a novel light: the inherent sacredness of sovereign power.

The mere fact that rulers and gods share certain properties has, of course, been recognized for some time. "The will of a king is very numinous," a seventeenth-century political divine wrote; "it has a kind of vast universality in it"—and he was not the first to say so. Nor has it gone unstudied: Ernst Kantorowicz's extraordinary *The King's Two Bodies*—

that magisterial discussion of, as he put it, "medieval political theology"—traced the vicissitudes of royal charisma in the West over two hundred years and a half-dozen countries, and more recently there has been a small explosion of books sensitive to what now tends to be called, a bit vaguely, the symbolic aspects of power.[5] But the contact between this essentially historical and ethnographic work and the analytical concerns of modern sociology has been weak at best, a situation the art historian Panofsky once analogized, in a different context, to that of two neighbors who share the right to shoot over the same district, but one of them owns the gun and the other all the ammunition.

Though still very much in process, and cast sometimes on too apodictic a level, Shils's reformulations promise to be of enormous value in overcoming this unuseful estrangement because they encourage us to look for the vast universality of the will of kings (or of presidents, generals, führers, and party secretaries) in the same place as we look for that of gods: in the rites and images through which it is exerted. More exactly, if charisma is a sign of involvement with the animating centers of society, and if such centers are cultural phenomena and thus historically constructed, investigations into the symbolics of power and into its nature are very similar endeavors. The easy distinction between the trappings of rule and its substance becomes less sharp, even less real; what counts is the manner in which, a bit like mass and energy, they are transformed into each other.

At the political center of any complexly organized society (to narrow our focus now to that) there is both a governing elite and a set of symbolic forms expressing the fact that it is in truth governing. No matter how democratically the members of the elite are chosen (usually not very) or how deeply divided among themselves they may be (usually much more than outsiders imagine), they justify their existence and order their actions in terms of a collection of stories, ceremonies, insignia, formalities, and appurtenances that they have either inherited or, in more revolutionary situations, invented. It is these—crowns and coronations, limousines and conferences—that mark the center as center and give what goes on there its aura of being not merely important but in some odd fashion connected with the way the world is built. The gravity of high politics and the solemnity of high worship spring from liker impulses than might first appear.

This is, of course, more readily apparent (though, as I shall eventually argue, not any more true) in traditional monarchies than in political regimes, where the ingenerate tendency of men to anthropomorphize power is better disguised. The intense focus on the figure of the king and the frank construction of a cult, at times a whole religion, around him make the symbolic character of domination too palpable for even Hobbesians and Utilitarians to ignore. The very thing that the elaborate mystique of court ceremonial is supposed to conceal—that majesty is made, not born—is demonstrated by it. "A woman is not a duchess a hundred yards from a carriage," and chiefs are changed to rajahs by the aesthetic of their rule.

This comes out as clearly as anywhere else in the ceremonial forms by which kings take symbolic possession of their realm. In particular, royal progresses (of which, where it exists, coronation is but the first) locate the society's center and affirm its connection with transcendent things by stamping a territory with ritual signs of dominance. When kings journey around the countryside, making appearances, attending fêtes, conferring honors, exchanging gifts, or defying rivals, they mark it, like some wolf or tiger spreading his scent through his territory, as almost physically part of them. This can be done, as we shall see, within frameworks of expression and belief as various as sixteenth-century English Protestantism, fourteenth-century Javanese Hinduism, and nineteenth-century Moroccan Islam; but however it is done, it is done, and the royal occupation gets portrayed as being a good deal more than merely hedged with divinity.

Elizabeth's England: Virtue and Allegory

On 14 January 1559, the day before her coronation, Elizabeth Tudor—"a daughter, whose birth disappointed her father's hopes for succession, and thus, indirectly, caused her mother's early demise; an illegitimized Princess whose claim to the throne was, nevertheless, almost as valid as those of her half-brother and half-sister; a focus of disaffection during Mary's reign; and a survivor of constant agitation by Imperial and Spanish emissaries to have her eliminated"—rode in a great progress (there were a thousand horses, and she sat, awash in jewels and gold cloth, in an open litter) through the historical districts of the City of London. As she moved, a vast didactic pageant unfolded, stage by stage, before her, settling her into the moral landscape of the resilient capital that five years earlier had done as much, or tried to, for Philip of Spain.[6]

Starting at the Tower (where she aptly compared her seeing the day to God's delivery of Daniel from the lions), she proceeded to Fenchurch

Street, where a small child offered her, for the town's sake, two gifts—blessing tongues to praise her and true hearts to serve her. At Gracechurch Street she encountered a *tableau vivant* called "The Uniting of the Houses of Lancaster and York." It took the form of an arch spanning the street, covered with red and white roses and divided into three levels. On the lowest, two children, representing Henry VII, enclosed in a rose of red roses, and his wife Elizabeth, enclosed in one of white, sat holding hands. On the middle level there were two more children, representing Henry VIII and Ann Boleyn, the bank of red roses rising from the Lancaster side and the bank of white ones from the York converging upon them. And at the top, amid mingled red and white, perched a single child, representing the honored (and legitimate) Elizabeth herself. At Cornhill, there was another arch with a child on it representing the new queen, but this one was seated on a throne held up by four townsmen dressed to represent the four virtues—Pure Religion, Love of Subjects, Wisdom, and Justice. They, in turn, trod their contrary vices—Superstition and Ignorance, Rebellion and Insolence, Folly and Vainglory, Adulation and Bribery (also impersonated by costumed citizens)—roughly under foot. And lest the iconography be too oblique, the child addressed an admonitory verse to the sovereign she mirrored, spelling out its message:

> While that religion true, shall ignorance suppresse
> And with her weightie foote, break superstitions heade
> While love of subjectes, shall rebellion distresse
> And with zeale to the prince, insolencie down treade
>
> While justice, can flattering tonges and briberie deface
> While follie and vaine glory to wisedome yelde their handes
> So long shall government, not swarve from her right race
> But wrong decayeth still, and rightwisenes up standes.[7]

Thus instructed, the queen moved on to Sopers-Lane, where there were no less than eight children, arranged in three levels. These, as tablets hung above their heads announced, represented the eight beatitudes of Saint Matthew, which a poem recited there described as grained into the character of the queen by the hurts and perils she had surmounted en route to the throne ("Thou has been viii times blest, O quene of worthy fame / by meekness of thy spirite, when care did thee besette").[8] From there she passed on to Cheapside, confronting at the Standard painted likenesses of all the kings and queens arranged in chronological order down to herself; receiving at the Upper End two thousand marks in gold from the City dignitaries ("Perswade you selues," she replied in thanks, "that for the safetie and quietness of you all, I will not spare, if nede be to spend my blood");[9] and arriving, in the Little Conduit, at the most curious image of all—two artificial mountains, one "cragged, barren and stony," representing "a decayed commonweal"; one "fair, fresh, green, and beautiful," representing "a flourishing commonweal." On the barren mountain there was a dead tree, an ill-dressed man slumped disconsolately beneath it; on the green one a flowering tree, a well-appointed man standing happily beside it. From the branches of each hung tablets listing the moral causes of the two states of political health: in the one, want of the fear of God, flattering of princes, unmercifulness in rulers, unthankfulness in subjects; in the other, a wise prince, learned rulers, obedient subjects, fear of God. Between the hills was a small cave, out of which a man representing Father Time, complete with scythe, emerged, accompanied by his daughter, Truth, to present to the queen an English Bible ("O worthy Queene . . . words do flye, but writing doth remain"), which Elizabeth took, kissed, and, raising it first above her head, pressed dramatically to her breast.[10]

After a Latin oration by a schoolboy in Saint Paul's churchyard, the queen proceeded to Fleet Street, where she found, of all people, Deborah, "the judge and restorer of the house of Israel," enthroned upon a tower shaded by a palm tree and surrounded by six persons, two each representing the nobility, the clergy, and the commonalty. The legend inscribed on a table before them read, "Deborah with her estates consulting for the good gouerment of Israel." All this, its designer writes, was to encourage the queen not to fear, "though she were a woman; for women by the spirite and power of Almyghtye God have ruled both honorably and pollitiquely, and that a great tyme, as did Deborah."[11] At Saint Dunstan's Church, another child, this one from Christ's Hospital, made another oration. Finally at Temple Bar, two giants—Gogmagog, the Albion, and Corineus, the Briton—bore a tablet on which were written verses summarizing all the pageants that had been displayed, and the progress ended.

This progress. In 1565 she goes to Coventry; in 1566 to Oxford; in 1572 she makes a long journey through the provinces, stopping for "masques and pageants" at a whole host of noble houses. She also enters Warwyck in that year, and the next she is in Sandwich, greeted with gilt dragons and lions, a cup of gold, and a Greek Testament. In 1574 it is Bristol's turn (there is a mock battle in which a small fort called "Feeble Policy" is captured by a large one called "Perfect Beauty"). In 1575 she visits the earl of Kenilworth's castle near Coventry, where there are Triton on a mermaid, Arion on a dolphin, the Lady of the Lake, and a nymph called Zabeta who turns lovers into trees; and later she enters Worcester. In 1578 the red and white roses and Deborah reappear in Norwich, accompanied by Chastity and Philosophy putting Cupid to rout. And they go on, "these endless peregrinations, which were so often the despair of her ministers"—in 1591 to Sussex and Hampshire, in 1592 to Sudeley, and, once again, Oxford.[12] In 1602, the year before she dies, there is the last one, at Harefield Place. Time emerges, as he had that first day in Cheapside, but with clipped wings and a stopped hourglass.[13] The royal progress, Strong remarks of Elizabeth—"the most legendary and successful of all [its] exponents"—was "the means by which the cult of the imperial virgin was systematically promoted."[14] The charisma that the center had (rather deliberately, as a matter of fact) fashioned for her out of the popular symbolisms of virtue, faith, and authority she carried, with a surer sense of statecraft than those pragmatical ministers who objected, to the countryside, making London as much the capital of Britain's political imagination as it was of its government.

That imagination was allegorical, Protestant, didactic, and pictorial; it lived on moral abstractions cast into emblems. Elizabeth was Chastity, Wisdom, Peace, Perfect Beauty, and Pure Religion as well as queen (at an estate in Hertford she was even Safety at Sea); and being queen she was these things. Her whole public life—or, more exactly, the part of her life the public saw—was transformed into a kind of philosophical masque in which everything stood for some vast idea and nothing took place unburdened with parable. Even her meeting with Anjou, possibly the man she came closest to marrying, was turned into a morality; he entered her presence seated on a rock, which was drawn toward her by Love and Destiny pulling golden chains.[15] Whether you want to call this romanticism or neo-Platonism matters little; what matters is that Elizabeth ruled a realm in which beliefs were visible, and she but the most conspicuous.

The center of the center, Elizabeth not only accepted its transformation of her into a moral idea, she actively cooperated in it. It was out of this—her willingness to stand proxy, not for God, but for the virtues he ordained, and especially for the Protestant version of them—that her charisma grew. It was allegory that lent her magic, and allegory repeated that sustained it. "How striking and meaningful it must have been to the spectators," Bergeron writes of that gift of an English Bible from the daughter of Time, "to see Truth in visible union with their new sovereign. . . . Morally Truth has chosen between good—the flourishing hill, the future,

Elizabeth—and evil—the sterile mount, the past, false religion and a false queen. Such is the path to salvation."[16]

Hayam Wuruk's Java: Splendor and Hierarchy

There are other ways of connecting the character of a sovereign to that of his realm, however, than enveloping him in pictured homilies; as moral imaginations differ, so do political, and not every progress is that of a Pilgrim. In the Indic cultures of classical Indonesia the world was a less improvable place, and royal pageantry was hierarchical and mystical in spirit, not pious and didactic.[17] Gods, kings, lords, and commoners formed an unbroken chain of religious status stretching from Siva-Buddha— "Ruler over rulers of the world . . . Spirit of the spiritual . . . Unconceivable of the unconceivable"—down to the ordinary peasant, barely able to look toward the light, the higher levels standing to the lower as greater realities to lesser.[18] If Elizabeth's England was a swirl of idealized passions, Hayam Wuruk's Java was a continuum of spiritualized pride. "The peasants honor the chiefs," a fourteenth-century clerical text reads, "the chiefs honor the lords, the lords honor the ministers, the ministers honor the king, the kings honor the priests, the priests honor the gods, the gods honor the sacred powers, the sacred powers honor the Supreme Nothingness."[19]

Yet even in this unpopulist a setting, the royal progress was a major institution, as can be seen from Indic Java's greatest political text, the fourteenth-century narrative poem *Negarakertagama*, which is not only centered around a royal progress but is in fact part of it.[20] The basic principle of Indonesian statecraft—that the court should be a copy of the cosmos and the realm a copy of the court, with the king, liminally suspended between gods and men, the mediating image in both directions— is laid out in almost diagrammatic form. At the center and apex, the king; around him and at his feet, the palace; around the palace, the capital, "reliable, submissive"; around the capital, the realm, "helpless, bowed, stooping, humble"; around the realm, "getting ready to show obedience," the outside world—all disposed in compass-point order, a configuration of nested circles that depicts not just the structure of society but, a political mandala, that of the universe as a whole:

The royal capital in Majapahit is Sun and Moon, peerless;
The numerous manors with their encircling groves are halos around the
    sun and moon;
The numerous other towns of the realm . . . are stars and planets;
And the numerous other islands of the archipelago are ring-kingdoms,
    dependent states drawn toward the royal Presence.[21]

It is this structure, the deep geometry of the cosmos, which the poem celebrates and into which, half as rite and half as policy, it fits the royal progress.

It opens with a glorification of the king. He is at once Siva in material form—"The Daymaker's Equal," upon whose birth volcanoes erupted and the earth shook—and a triumphant overlord who has vanquished all the darkness there is in the world ("Exterminated are the enemies . . . Rewarded, the good . . . Reformed, the bad").[22] Next, his palace is described: North, the reception areas; East, the religious shrines; South, the family chambers; West, the servants quarters; in the center, "The Interior of the Interior," his personal pavilion. Then, with the palace as center, the complex around it: East, the Sivaite clergy; South, the Buddhist clergy; West, the royal kinsmen; North, the public square. Then, with the complex as center, the capital in general: North, the chief ministers; East, the junior king; South, the Sivaite and Buddhist bishops; West, though not in fact mentioned, probably the ranking commoners.[23] Then, with the capital as center, the regions of the realm, ninety-eight of them, stretching from Malaya and Borneo on the North and East to Timor and New Guinea on the South and West; and, finally, the outermost ring, Siam, Cambodia, Campa, Annam—"Other countries protected by the Illustrious Prince."[24] Virtually the whole of the known world (later parts of China and India are mentioned as well) is represented as turned toward Java, all of Java as turned toward Majapahit, and all of Majapahit as turned toward Hayam Wuruk—"Sun and Moon, shining over the earth-circle."[25]

In cold fact, hardly more than the eastern part of Java was so oriented, and most of that in an attitude not properly described as either helpless or humble.[26] It was to this region, where the kingdom, however invertebrate, at least was more than a poetic conceit, that the royal progresses were directed: west to Pajang, near present-day Surakarta, in 1353; north to Lasem on the Java Sea in 1354; south to Lodaya and the Indian Ocean in 1357; east to Lumajang, nearly to Bali, in 1359.[27]

Only the last of these, which was probably the greatest, is described in detail, however—more than four hundred lines being devoted to it. The king left the capital at the beginning of the dry season, visiting no less than 210 localities scattered over about ten thousand to fifteen thousand square miles in about two and a half months, returning just before the west monsoon brought the rains. There were about four hundred ox-drawn, solid-wheel carts; there were, more for effect than anything else, elephants, horses, donkeys, and even camels (imported from India); there were swarms of people on foot, some carrying burdens, some displaying regalia, some no doubt dancing and singing—the whole lurching along like some archaic traffic jam a mile or two an hour over the narrow and rutted roads lined with crowds of astonished peasants. The core section of the procession, which seems to have come in the middle, was led by the cart of the chief minister, the famous Gajah Mada. Behind him came the four ranking princesses of the realm—the sister, mother's sister's daughter, mother's sister, and mother of the king—together with their consorts. And behind them, seated on a palanquin and surrounded by dozens of wives, bodyguards, and servants, came the king, "ornamented with gold and jewels, shining." Since each of the princesses represented one of the compass points (marked on her cart by traditional symbols and on her person by her title, which associated her with the quarter of the country in the appropriate direction from the capital), and the king represented the center in which they all were summed, the very order of the march conveyed the structure of the cosmos—mirrored in the organization of the court—to the countryside.[28] All that was left to complete this bringing of Heaven's symmetry to earth's confusion was for the countryside, struck with the example, to shape itself, in turn, to the same design.

The stops this lumbering caravan made—at forest hermitages, sacred ponds, mountain sanctuaries, priestly settlements, ancestral shrines, state temples, along the strand (where the king, "waving to the sea," composed some verses to placate the demons in it)—but reinforce the image of a metaphysical road show.[29] Everywhere Hayam Wuruk went, he was showered with luxuries—textiles, spices, animals, flowers, drums, fire drills, virgins—most of which, the last excepted, he redistributed again, if only because he could not carry them all. There were ceremonies everywhere, crowded with offerings: in Buddhist domains Buddhist, in Sivaite ones Sivaite, in many places both. Anchorites, scholars, priests, abbots, shamans, sages, entered into his Presence, seeking contact with sacred energies; and in virtually every town, sometimes at mere encampments, he held public audiences, also largely ceremonial, for local authorities, merchants, and leading commoners. When there were places he could not reach—Bali, Madura, Blambangan—their chieftains journeyed to meet him, bearing gifts, "trying to outvie each other" in the forms of deference. The whole was a vast ritual seeking to order the social world by confronting it with magnificence reaching down from above and a king so exactly imitative of the gods that he appeared as one to those beneath him.

In short, instead of Christian moralism, Indic aestheticism. In sixteenth-century England, the political center of society was the point at which the tension between the passions that power excited and the ideals it was supposed to serve was screwed to its highest pitch; and the symbolism of the progress was, consequently, admonitory and covenantal: the subjects warned, and the queen promised. In fourteenth-century Java, the center was the point at which such tension disappeared in a blaze of cosmic symmetry; and the symbolism was, consequently, exemplary and mimetic: the king displayed, and the subjects copied. Like the Elizabethan, the Majapahit progress set forth the regnant themes of political thought—the court mirrors the world the world should imitate; society flourishes to the degree that it assimilates this fact; and it is the office of the king, wielder of the mirror, to assure that it does. It is analogy, not allegory, that lends the magic here:

> The whole of Java is to be as the capital of the King's realm;
> The thousands of peasant huts are to be as the courtiers' manors
>   surrounding the palace;
> The other islands are to be as the cultivated lands, happy, quiet;
> The forests and mountains are to be as the parks, all set foot on by Him,
>   at peace in His mind.[30]

Hasan's Morocco: Movement and Energy

It is not necessary, of course, that power be dressed up in virtue or set round with cosmology to be perceived as more than force in the service of interest: its numinousness can be symbolized directly. In traditional Morocco, "the Morocco that was," as Walter Harris called it, personal power, the ability to make things happen the way one wants them to happen—to prevail—was itself the surest sign of grace.[31] In a world of wills dominating wills, and that of Allah dominating them all, strength did not have to be represented as other than what it was in order to suffuse it with transcendent meaning. Like God, kings desired and demanded, judged and decreed, harmed and rewarded. *C'est son métier:* one did not need an excuse to rule.

One, of course, did need the capacity, and that was not so easily come by in a vast and shifting field of literally hundreds of political entrepreneurs, each concerned to build a smaller or larger configuration of personal support about himself. Morocco did not have either the hierarchism of medieval Hinduism or the salvationism of Reformation Christianity to canonize its sovereign; it had only an acute sense of the power of God and the belief that his power appeared in the world in the exploits of forceful men, the most considerable of whom were kings. Political life is a clash of personalities everywhere, and in even the most focused of states lesser figures resist the center; but in Morocco such struggle was looked upon not as something in conflict with the order of things, disruptive of form or subversive of virtue, but as its purest expression. Society was agonistic—a tournament of wills; so then was kingship and the symbolism exalting it. Progresses here were not always easy to tell from raids.

Politically, eighteenth- and nineteenth-century Morocco consisted of a warrior monarchy centered in the Atlantic Plain, a cloud of at least sporadically submissive "tribes" settled in the fertile regions within its immediate reach, and a thinner cloud of only very occasionally submissive ones scattered through the mountains, steppes, and oases that rim the country.[32] Religiously, it consisted of a sharifian dynasty (that is, one claiming descent from Muhammad), a number of Koranic scholars, jurists, teachers, and scribes (*ulema*), and a host of holy men, living and dead, possessed of miraculous powers, the famous marabouts.[33] In theory, Islamic theory, the political and religious realms were one, the king was caliph and head of both, and the state was thus a theocracy; but it was not a theory that anyone, even the king, could regard as more than a lost ideal in the face of a situation where charismatic adventurers were constantly arising on all sides. If Moroccan society has any chief guiding principle, it is probably that one genuinely possesses only what one has the ability to defend, whether it be land, water, women, trade partners, or personal authority: whatever magic a king had he had strenuously to protect.

The magic was perceived in terms of another famous North African idea: *baraka.*[34] *Baraka* has been analogized to a number of things in an attempt to clarify it—mana, charisma, "spiritual electricity"—because it is a gift of power more than natural which men, having received it, can use in as natural and pragmatical a way, for as self-interested and mundane purposes, as they wish. But what most defines *baraka*, and sets it off somewhat from these similar concepts, is that it is radically individualistic, a property of persons in the way strength, courage, energy, or ferocity are and, like them, arbitrarily distributed. Indeed, it is in one sense a summary term for these qualities, the active virtues that, again, enable some men to prevail over others. To so prevail, whether at court or in a mountain camp, was to demonstrate that one had *baraka*, that God had gifted one with the capacity to dominate, a talent it could quite literally be death to hide. It was not a condition, like chastity, or a trait, like pride, that shines by itself but a movement, like will, that exists in its impact. Like everything the king did, progresses were designed to make that impact felt, most particularly by those who might imagine their own to be comparable.

Rather than occasional or periodic—and therefore a schedule of set pieces—the Moroccan progress was very nearly continuous. "The king's throne is his saddle," one saying went, "the sky his canopy." "The royal tents are never stored," went another. The great late-seventeenth-to-early-eighteenth-century consolidator of the dynasty, the man who made its *baraka* real, Mulay Ismail, seems to have spent most of his reign "under canvas" (during the first half of it, a chronicler notes, he did not pass a single uninterrupted year in his palace); and even Mulay Hasan (d. 1894), the last of the old-regime kings of Morocco, normally spent six months of the year on the move, demonstrating sovereignty to skeptics.[35] The kings did not even keep a single capital but instead shifted the court restlessly among the so-called Imperial Cities—Fez, Marrakech, Meknes, and Rabat—in none of which they were really at home. Motion was the rule, not the exception; and though a king could not, like God, quite be everywhere at once, he could try, at least, to give the impression that he was: "No one could be sure that the Sultan would not arrive at the head of his troops on the morrow. During such times the most adamant peoples were ready to negotiate with [his] officials and reach terms which suited the sovereign."[36] Like its rivals, the center wandered: "Roam and you will confound adversaries," another Moroccan proverb runs, "sit and they will confound you."

The court-in-motion was referred to either as a *mehalla*, literally, "way station," "camp," "stopover," or as a *harka*, literally, "movement," "stirring," "action," depending upon whether one wanted to emphasize the governmental or military aspects of it. Normally the king would remain camped in an area for anywhere from several days to several months and would then move, by gradual stages, to another, where he would remain for a similar period, receiving local chieftains and other notables, holding feasts, sending out punitive expeditions when need be, and generally making his presence known. This last was hardly difficult, for a royal camp was an impressive sight, a great sea of tents, soldiers, slaves, animals, prisoners, armaments, and camp followers. Harris estimated that there were nearly 40,000 people in Mulay Hasan's encampment (a "strange mixture of boundless confusion and perfect order that succeeded each other in . . . quick succession") in the Tafilalt in 1893, and fifty or sixty tents within the royal compound alone. Even as late as 1898, when all this was more or less drawing to a close, Weisgerber speaks of "thousands of men and beasts" in Mulay Abdul Aziz's encampment in the Chaouia, which he also describes, less romantically, as a vast lake of infected mud.[37]

The mobility of the king was thus a central element in his power; the realm was unified—to the very partial degree that it was unified and was a realm—by a restless searching-out of contact, mostly agonistic, with literally hundreds of lesser centers of power within it. The struggle with local big men was not necessarily violent or even usually so (Schaar quotes the popular maxim that the king employed ninety-nine ruses, of which firearms were but the hundredth), but it was unending, especially for an ambitious king, one who wished to make a state—one scuffle, one intrigue, one negotiation succeeded by another.[38] It was an exhausting occupation, one only the tireless could pursue. What chastity was to Elizabeth, and magnificence to Hayam Wuruk, energy was to Mulay Ismail or Mulay Hasan: as long as he could keep moving, chastening an opponent here, advancing an ally there, the king could make believable his claim to a sovereignty conferred by God. But only that long. The traditional shout of the crowds to the passing king, *Allāh ybarak f-'amer Sīdī*—"God give you *baraka* forever, my Master"—was more equivocal than it sounds: "forever" ended when mastery did.

There is no more poignant example of the degree to which this fact dominated the consciousness of Morocco's rulers, and no bitterer witness to its truth, than the terrible last progress of Mulay Hasan. Frustrated by the failure of his administrative, military, and economic reforms to bear fruit, threatened on all sides by intruding European powers, and worn out by twenty years of holding the country together by the main force of his personality, he decided, in 1893, to lead a massive expedition to the shrine of his dynasty's founder in the Tafilalt, a desert-edge oasis three hundred miles south of Fez. A long, arduous, dangerous, expensive journey, undertaken in the face of what seems to have been nearly universal advice to the contrary, it was quite possibly the greatest mahalla ever made in Morocco—a dramatic, desperate, and, as it turned out, disastrous effort at self-renewal.

The expedition, of thirty thousand men drawn from the loyal tribes of the Atlantic Plain, mounted mostly on mules, left Fez in April, crossed the middle and high Atlases in the summer and early autumn, and arrived in the Tafilalt in November.[39] Since only one European, a French doctor, was permitted to go along, and he was an indifferent observer (there do not seem to be any native accounts), we do not know much about the trip except that it was grueling. Aside from the simply physical obstacles (the highest passes reached nearly eight thousand feet, and the road was hardly more than a trail scratched across the rocks), the burden of baggage, tents, and armaments (even cannons were dragged along), and the logistical problems involved in feeding so many people and animals, the whole area was dotted with contentious Berber tribes, who had to be prevented, half with threats and half with bribes, occasionally with force, from "eating the caravan." But though there were some difficult moments and the expedition was seriously delayed, nothing particularly untoward seems to have happened. The sheikhs came, accompanied by dozens of tribesmen; royal hospitality was extended; and, amid flamboyant riding and shooting displays, gifts were exchanged, tea drunk, bulls sacrificed, taxes gathered, and loyalty promised. It was only after the shrine had been reached and the prayers accomplished that the trouble began.

It is likely that the king, his timetable disrupted by the slowness of the Atlas passage and his army fevered and malnourished, would have preferred to remain in the oasis through the winter, but a combination of factors caused him to stay less than a month. The Berber tribes were still a worry, particularly as the southern ones were even more belligerent; there was a fear of assassination by French agents directed from southern Algeria; and there were reports of severe fighting between Moroccans and Spaniards at the other, Mediterranean, end of the country. But perhaps the most important factor in the decision to try to make it back to the plains at so unsuitable a time was Mulay Hasan's own failing powers. Harris, who saw him at Tafilalt, found him terribly aged from only two years earlier (he was apparently in his mid-forties)—tired, sallow, prematurely gray; and the same sense of lost momentum that propelled him south apparently turned him north again when his journey to his origins failed to restore it.

In any case, the expedition, now but about ten thousand strong, left in December for Marrakech—three weeks' march over the High Atlas to the east, through a region even more forbidding, geographically and politically, than that through which it had already passed. In addition, it was winter now, and the whole affair soon turned into a retreat from Moscow:

By the time his army had reached the foothills the winter snows had begun; as they climbed higher into the main massif more and more of the camels, mules and horses, weak with starvation, stumbled into deep snowdrifts and died. Little but their carcasses stood between the remnants of the *harka* and starvation, and the surviving beasts staggered on and upwards laden with what little meat could be salvaged from the corpses of their companions. The army was attended by clouds of ravens, kites and vultures. Hundreds of men died daily, they were left unburied in the snow, stripped of whatever rags they had still possessed.[40]

By the time Marrakech was reached, more than a third of the already reduced army had been lost; and the himself rather mobile Harris (he was the London *Times* correspondent), who was on hand for the arrival, found the king no longer merely aging but dying:

What was noticeable at Tafilet was doubly apparent now. The Sultan had become an old man. Travel-stained and weary, he rode his great white horse with its mockery of green-and-gold trapping, while over a head that was the picture of suffering waved the imperial umbrella of crimson velvet. Following him straggled into the city a horde of half-starved men and animals, trying to be happy that at last their terrible journey was at an end, but too ill and too hungry to succeed.[41]

The king remained in Marrakech until spring, attempting to regather his powers; but then, renewed anxiety about the deteriorating situation in the North, and the need for his presence there, set him in motion again. He had got as far as Tadla, about a hundred miles from Marrakech, when he collapsed and died. The death was, however, concealed by his ministers. They were concerned that, with the king gone, the caravan would dissolve and the tribes fall upon it and that conspirators supporting other candidates would contrive to prevent the accession of Mulay Hasan's chosen successor, his twelve-year-old son, Mulay Abdul Aziz. So he was represented as being merely indisposed and resting privately, his corpse was laid in a curtained palanquin, and the expedition was launched into a forced march, brutal in the summer heat, toward Rabat. Food was brought to the king's tent and then taken away again as though consumed. The few knowledgeable ministers hurried in and out of his presence as though conducting business. A few local sheikhs, cautioned that he was sleeping, were even permitted to look in upon him. By the time that the progress neared Rabat, two days later, the king's corpse had so begun to stink that his death announced itself; but by then the dangerous tribes had been left behind, and Abdul Aziz, his backers informed of events by a runner, had been proclaimed king in the city. In two more days the company, largely reduced to the old king's ministers and personal bodyguard—the others having drifted away or straggled behind—limped into Rabat, engulfed in the stench of royal death:

It must have been a gruesome procession from the description his son Mulai Abdul Aziz gave me [Walter Harris wrote]: the hurried arrival of the swaying palanquin bearing its terrible burden, five days dead in the great heat of summer; the escort, who had bound scarves over their faces—but even this precaution could not keep them from constant sickness—and even the mules that bore the palanquin seemed affected by the horrible atmosphere, and tried from time to time to break loose.[42]

And so, its motion spent, the progress that had begun more than a year before ended, and with it two decades of rushing about from one corner of the country to another, defending the idea of religious monarchy. Indeed, this was more or less the end of the whole pattern; for the next two kings—one of whom reigned for fourteen years, the other for four—attempted only a few rather desultory *harkas* in a rapidly disintegrating situation, and the French, who took over after them, made palace prisoners of the two kings who followed. Immobilized, Moroccan kings were as dead as Hasan, their *baraka* impotent and theoretical. It was neither as embodiments of redemptive virtue nor as reflections of cosmic order but as explosions of divine energy that Moroccan kings recommended themselves to their subjects, and even the smallest explosion needs room in which to happen.

Conclusion

Now, the easy reaction to all this talk of monarchs, their trappings, and their peregrinations is that it has to do with a closed past, a time, in Huizinga's famous phrase, when the world was half-a-thousand years younger and everything was clearer. All the golden grasshoppers and bees are gone; monarchy, in the true sense of the word, was ritually destroyed on one scaffold in Whitehall in 1649 and on another in the Place de la Révolution in 1793; the few fragments left in the Third World are just that—fragments, relic kings whose likelihood of having successors diminishes by the hour.[43] England has a second Elizabeth, who may be as chaste—more so, probably—as the first, and who gets properly lauded on public occasions, but the resemblance rather ends there; Morocco has a second Hasan, but he is more a French colonel than an Arab prince; and the last of the great line of Javanese Indic kings, Hamengku Buwono IX, his royal office legally abolished, is (1977) the self-effacing, rather ineffectual, vaguely socialist vice-president of the Indonesian Republic, around whom not even the smallest planets revolve.

Yet, though all this is true enough, it is superficial. The relevance of historical fact for sociological analysis does not rest on the proposition that there is nothing in the present but the past, which is not true, or on easy analogies between extinct institutions and the way we live now. It rests on the perception that though both the structure and the expressions of social life change, the inner necessities that animate it do not. Thrones may be out of fashion, and pageantry too; but political authority still requires a cultural frame in which to define itself and advance its claims, and so does opposition to it. A world wholly demystified is a world wholly depoliticized; and though Weber promised us both of these—specialists without spirit in a bureaucratic iron cage—the course of events since, with its Sukarnos, Churchills, Nkrumahs, Hitlers, Maos, Roosevelts, Stalins, Nassers, and de Gaulles, suggests that what died in 1793 (to the degree that it did) was a certain view of the affinity between the sort of power that moves men and the sort that moves mountains, not the sense that there is one.

The "political theology" (to revert to Kantorowicz's term) of the twentieth century has not been written, though there have been glancing efforts here and there. But it exists—or, more exactly, various forms of it exist—and until it is understood at least as well as that of the Tudors, the Majapahits, or the Alawites, a great deal of the public life of our times is going to remain obscure. The extraordinary has not gone out of modern politics, however much the banal may have entered; power not only still intoxicates, it still exalts.

It is for this reason that, no matter how peripheral, ephemeral, or free-floating the charismatic figure we may be concerned with—the wildest prophet, the most deviant revolutionary—we must begin with the center and with the symbols and conceptions that prevail there if we are to understand him and what he means. It is no accident that Stuarts get Cromwells and Medicis Savonarolas—or, for that matter, that Hindenburgs get Hitlers. Every serious charismatic threat that ever arose in

Alawite Morocco took the form of some local power figure's laying claim
to enormous *baraka* by engaging in actions—*siba*, literally, "insolence"—
designed to expose the weakness of the king by showing him up as unable
to stop them; and Java has been continuously beset by local mystics emerging from meditative trances to present themselves to the world as its
"Exemplary Ruler" (*Ratu Adil*), corrective images of a lost order and an
obscured form.[44] This is the paradox of charisma; that though it is rooted
in the sense of being near to the heart of things, of being caught up in the
realm of the serious, a sentiment that is felt most characteristically and
continuously by those who in fact dominate social affairs, who ride in the
progresses and grant the audiences, its most flamboyant expressions tend
to appear among people at some distance from the center, indeed often
enough at a rather enormous distance, who want very much to be closer.
Heresy is as much of a child of orthodoxy in politics as it is in religion.

And both orthodoxy and heresy, however adept the secret police, are
universal, as we learn when workers explode in East Germany, Tolstoyan
romantics reappear in Russia, or, strangest of all, soldier-populists surface
in Portugal. The enfoldment of political life in general conceptions of how
reality is put together did not disappear with dynastic continuity and
divine right. Who gets What, When, Where, and How is as culturally
distinctive a view of what politics is, and in its own way as transcendental,
as the defense of "wisdom and rightwiseness," the celebration of "The
Daymaker's Equal," or the capricious flow of *baraka*. Nor is it any less
capable of yielding spectacle, center-praising or center-challenging:

I accompany the Humphrey press to one of Hubert's stops, a school for handi-
capped children, for the deaf and the retarded. He shakes hands with every single
Sister. Every one. And every child he can reach. Schedule allows for twenty
minutes. Thirteen used for shaking hands. The talk goes on for twenty minutes, *on*
for twenty-five, *on* for thirty. The hands of the poor priest who is trying to translate into sign language are wearing out . . . thirty-five minutes—another man
takes over as translator . . . "And some of the greatest men in history had handicaps"—he tries to think of one, his eyes flash, cheeks acquire that familiar beam-
ing, knowing look.—"Thomas Edison. We *all* have handicaps . . . " "What's the
most important word in the English language?" "Service!" "And the other most
important word is 'love!' " "And what are the last four letters in the word American? I CAN. Look at them. Spell it. I can. You *can*. You're great. You're wonderful.
God bless you." The tears are in the corners of his eyes, the tears that cause him
such grief on television. His head chucks up and down happily as he wades back
through the crowd of distracted, uncertain, uncomprehending kids.

In Madison Square Garden, then, on July 14, a celebration of moral purity is held. "Together with McGovern at the Garden," it is called. Its purpose is to raise funds. Mike Nichols and Elaine May come back together just for the event; so do Peter, Paul, and Mary; and Simon and Garfunkel. The contrast between such a rally and a Wallace rally—or, say, a gathering of Bob Hope and Billy Graham for Richard Nixon—explodes the circuits of the mind. Comparative liturgies! June 14 is Flag Day. But there are no flags on stage. No flags surround the Garden. The evening celebrates the resurrection of the youth culture. The liturgy of a new class is performed. Peter, Paul, and Mary, Dionne Warwick, Simon and Garfunkel in every song celebrate the mobile, lonely, vulnerable, middle-class life. Dionne Warwick warbles in blue-flowered, cottony, innocent, white gown: "Imagine!— No heaven—no hell—no countries—no religions! When the world will live as one." Simon and Garfunkel offer "Jesus loves you, Mrs. Robinson!" and the most revealing line: "I'd rather be a hammer than a nail." No Lawrence Welk. No Johnny Cash. No Benny Goodman. The music is singlemindedly sectarian. At 11:05, the entire cast gathers on stage, flashing peace signs. Then a great chant goes up: WE WANT MCGOVERN!" "It's a wonderful night of coming together," McGovern says. He tells them how he "loves this country enough to hold it to a higher standard, away from the killing, death, and destruction now going on in Southeast Asia." "I love this land and cherish its future. I want to set about making this country a great, decent, and good land . . . to be a bridge from war to peace . . . a bridge across the generation gap . . . a bridge across the gaps in justice in this country. . . . As the prophet wrote: 'Therefore, choose life . . . be on the side of blessing, not cursing' . . . on the side of hope, health, life. And peace for ourselves and peoples all around the globe."

At Racine, the rally is on again, this time in Memorial Hall, well after working hours and publicized through radio spots. The crowd assembles early; some are turned away at the door. 1200 sit inside, 330 in the balcony, standing room for 250. Excitement crackles. The loudspeakers are tuned just right, then turned up louder. "I've laid around and played around this ole town too long." Billy Grammer is singing, his blue eyes flashing. And: "Horseshoe diamond ring." Mr. Karl Prussian, twelve years a counterspy, is introduced by George Magnum, in the latter's high nasal best: "If you've been followin' the Conservative movement in the U.S., you'll know the man ah'm about to intr'duce to you." "George Wallace," Karl Prussian says, "is a man of God." "God bless you!" Goerge Magnum says. We're in Protestant territory now and the symbols are colliding, and sparks are shooting. It's meetin' time, and everyone's at ease. George Wallace, Jr., his hair as long as John Lennon's, swings out gently. He flourishes his dark electric guitar, tenderly, with restraint. No wild vulgar rock, no Mick Jagger here, but son of a man misunderstood, a young, patient, and determined Alabaman. "Gentle on my mind . . . " is his first number, and his second is: "I shot a man in Reno just to watch him die." Then the Governor, half-reluctant, half-jubilant, explodes across the stage. Pandemonium. He likes the crowd. His eyes begin to shine. Nervousness falls away and his movements become fluid, confident. Each gesture draws a response. "I tell you we're gonna give St. Vitus dance to the leadership of the Democratic party." "Ah'm sick of permissiveness in this society. Ah'm tired of false liberals!" "Ah'm sick'n' tired of giving up 50 percent of my income to the United States, to waste half of it overseas on nations that spit on us and half of it on welfare." "An' now they tell us Vietnam was a mistake. A mistake that cost the average citizen 50,000 lives, 300,000 wounded, 120 billion dollars down the drain. Ah don' call that a mistake. It's a tragedy." Like David Halberstam, he puts the blame upon the best and brightest—"them." *This* is how *they* run our lives.[45]

So the progresses continue. If the material were from Germany or France, India or Tanzania (to say nothing of Russia or China), the idiom would be different, as would the ideological assumptions upon which it rested. But there would be an idiom, and it would reflect the fact that the charisma of the dominant figures of society and that of those who hurl themselves against that dominance stem from a common source: the inherent sacredness of central authority. Sovereignty may rest now in states or even in the populations of states, as Humphrey, McGovern, and Wallace alike assume; but the "vast universality" that inheres in it remains, whatever has become of the will of kings. Neither nationalism nor populism has changed that. It is not, after all, standing outside the social order in some excited state of self-regard that makes a political leader numinous but a deep, intimate involvement—affirming or abhorring, defensive or destructive—in the master fictions by which that order lives.

Notes

This essay is from *Culture and Its Creators*, ed. Joseph Ben-David and T. N. Clark. © 1977 by The University of Chicago. Reprinted by permission.

1. For an excellent general review of the issue, see S. N. Eisenstadt's introduction to his collection of Weber's charisma papers, *Max Weber on Charisma and Institution Building* (Chicago, 1968), pp. ix–lvi. For the psychologization of "legitimacy," see H. Pitkin, *Wittgenstein and Justice* (Berkeley and Los Angeles, 1972); for "inner-worldly asceticism," D. McClelland, *The Achieving Society* (Princeton, 1961); for "rationalization," A. Mitzman, *The Iron Cage* (New York, 1970). All this ambiguity and even confusion of interpretation are, it should be said, not without warrant in Weber's own equivocalness.

2. For some examples, see "Philosophers and Kings: Studies in Leadership," *Daedalus*, Summer 1968.

3. P. Rieff, *The Triumph of the Therapeutic* (New York, 1966).
4. E. Shils, "Charisma, Order, and Status," *American Sociological Review*, April 1965; Shils, "The Dispersion and Concentration of Charisma," in *Independent Black Africa*, ed. W. J. Hanna (New York, 1964); Shils, "Centre and Periphery," in *The Logic of Personal Knowledge: Essays Presented to Michael Polanyi* (London, 1961).
5. E. Kantorowicz, *The King's Two Bodies: A Study in Medieval Political Theology* (Princeton, 1957); R. E. Giesey, *The Royal Funeral Ceremony in Renaissance France* (Geneva, 1960); R. Strong, *Splendor at Court: Renaissance Spectacle and the Theater of Power* (Boston, 1973); M. Walzer, *The Revolution of the Saints* (Cambridge, Mass., 1965); M. Walzer, *Regicide and Revolution* (Cambridge, England, 1974); S. Anglo, *Spectacle, Pageantry, and Early Tudor Policy* (Oxford, 1969); D. M. Bergeron, *English Civic Pageantry, 1558–1642* (London, 1971); F. A. Yates, *The Valois Tapestries* (London, 1959); E. Straub, *Repraesentatio Maiestatis oder Churbayerische Freudenfeste* (Munich, 1969); G. R. Kernodle, *From Art to Theatre* (Chicago, 1944). For a recent popular book on the American presidency in this vein, see M. Novak, *Choosing Our King* (New York, 1974). Anthropological studies, especially those done in Africa, have of course been sensitive to such issues for a long time (for an example: E. E. Evans-Pritchard, *The Divine Kingship of the Shilluk of the Nilotic Sudan* [Cambridge, England, 1948]), and both E. Cassirer's *Myth of the State* (New Haven, 1946) and M. Bloch's *Les rois thaumaturges* (Paris, 1961) have to be mentioned, along with Kantorowicz, as seminal. The internal quotation is from N. Ward, as given in the OED under "Numinous."
6. There are a number of descriptions of Elizabeth's London progress (or "entry"), of which the fullest is Bergeron, *English Civic Pageantry*, pp. 11–23. See also R. Withington, *English Pageantry: An Historical Outline*, vol. 1 (Cambridge, Mass., 1918), pp. 199–202; and Anglo, *Spectacle, Pageantry*, pp. 344–59. The text quotation is from Anglo, *Spectacle, Pageantry*, p. 345. The city was resplendent too: "The houses on the way were all decorated; there being on both sides of the street, from Blackfriars to St. Paul's, wooden barricades on which merchants and artisans of every trade leant in long black gowns lined with hoods of red and black cloth . . . with all their ensigns, banners, and standards" (quotation from the Venetian ambassador to London, in Bergeron, *English Civic Pageantry*, p. 14). For Mary and Philip's 1554 entry, see Anglo, *Spectacle, Pageantry*, pp. 324–43, and Withington, *English Pageantry*, p. 189.
7. Quoted in Bergeron, *English Civic Pageantry*, p. 17. The queen is supposed to have replied: "I have taken notice of your good meaning toward mee, and will endeavour to Answere your severall expectations" (ibid., p. 18).
8. Anglo, *Spectacle, Pageantry*, p. 349.
9. Bergeron, *English Civic Pageantry*, p. 15.
10. The quotation is given in Anglo, *Spectacle, Pageantry*, p. 350.

11. Grafton, quoted in ibid., p. 352. He was not unprescient: Deborah ruled for forty years, Elizabeth for forty-five.
12. The quotation is from Strong, *Splendor at Court*, p. 84.
13. For Elizabeth's progresses outside London, see Bergeron, *English Civic Pageantry*, pp. 25 ff.; Withington, *English Pageantry*, pp. 204 ff.
14. Strong, *Splendor at Court*, p. 84. The progress was, of course, an all-European phenomenon. Emperor Charles V, for example, made ten to the Low Countries, nine to Germany, seven to Italy, six to Spain, four to France, two to England, and two to Africa, as he reminded his audience at his abdication (ibid., p. 83). Nor was it confined to the sixteenth century: for fifteenth-century Tudor ones, see Anglo, *Spectacle, Pageantry*, pp. 21 ff.; for seventeenth-century Stuart ones, see Bergeron, *English Civic Pageantry*, pp. 65 ff., and Strong, *Splendor at Court*, pp. 213 ff.
15. Yates, *The Valois Tapestries*, p. 92.
16. Bergeron, *English Civic Pageantry*, p. 21.
17. Java was Hindu from about the fourth century to about the fifteenth, when it became at least nominally Islamized. Bali remains Hindu until today. Much of what follows here is based on my own work; see C. Geertz, *Negara: The Theatre State in Nineteenth-Century Bali* (Princeton, 1980). For Hindu Java generally, see N. J. Krom, *Hindoe-Javaansche Geschiedenis*, 2d ed. (The Hague, 1931).
18. T. Pigeaud, *Java in the 14th Century: A Study in Cultural History*, 5 vols. (The Hague, 1963), 1:3 (Javanese); 3:3 (English). The chain actually continues downward through animals and demons.
19. Ibid., 1:90 (Javanese); 3:135 (English). I have made alterations in the translation for clarity. Even then, "sacred powers" and "The Supreme Nothingness" (that is, Siva-Buddha) remain weak renderings of difficult religious conceptions, a matter not pursuable here. For an even more differentiated hierarchy, see the *Nawantaya* text, ibid., 3:119–28.
20. Ibid. (despite its title, the work is essentially a text, translation, and commentary of the *Negarakertagama*). Of the poem's 1,330 lines, no less than 570 are specifically devoted to description of royal progresses, and the bulk of the rest are ancillary to those. Literally, "Negarakertagama" means "manual for the cosmic ordering of the state," which is what it is really about rather than, as has so often been assumed, the history of Majapahit. It was written in 1365 by a Buddhist cleric, resident in the court of King Hayam Wuruk (r. 1350–89).
21. *Negarakertagama*, canto 12, stanza 6. I have again reconstructed Pigeaud's English, this time more seriously, to convey better what I take to be the sense of the passage. On the mandala concept in Indonesia, where it means at once "sacred circle," "holy region," and "religious community," as well as being a symbol of the universe as such, see J. Gonda, *Sanskrit in Indonesia* (Nagpur, 1952), pp. 5, 131, 218, 227; Pigeaud, *Java*, 4:485–86. On this sort of imagery

in traditional Asian states generally, see P. Wheatley, *The Pivot of the Four Quarters* (Chicago, 1971).

22. Cantos 1–7. The royal family is also praised, as the first circle outward from the king. "Daymaker" is, of course, a metonym for the sun, identified with Siva-Buddha, "The Supreme Non-Entity" in Indic Indonesia.

23. Cantos 8–12. There is much controversy here over details (cf. W. F. Stutterheim, *De Kraton van Magapahit* [The Hague, 1948]; H. Kern, *Het Oud-Javaansche Lofdicht Negarakertagama van Prapanca* [The Hague, 1919]), and not all of them are clear. The pattern has in any case been simplified here (it really is a 16-8-4-point system about a center, and of course it is cosmological, not exactly geographical). "Ranking commoners" is an interpolation of mine on the basis of knowledge of later examples. "Junior king" does not indicate a dauphin but refers to the second-ranking line in the realm. This "double-king" system is general in Indonesian Indic states but is too complex to go into here. See my *Negara* for a full discussion.

24. Cantos 13–16.

25. Canto 92.

26. On the exaggeration of the size of Majapahit, see, with caution, C. C. Berg, "De Sadèng oorlog en de mythe van Groot Majapahit," *Indonesie*, 5 (1951): 385–422. See also my "Politics Past, Politics Present: Some Notes on the Uses of Anthropology in Understanding the New States," in C. Geertz, *The Interpretation of Cultures* (New York, 1973), pp. 327–41.

27. Canto 17. Other minor progresses, for special purposes, are also mentioned for the 1360s; see cantos 61 and 70.

28. Cantos 13–18. The directional system was integrated with a color symbolism, the four primary colors—red, white, black, and yellow—being disposed about a variegated center. The five days of the week, five periods of the day, and five life-cycle stages, as well as plants, gods, and a number of other natural and social symbolic forms, were fused into the same pattern, which was thus extremely elaborate, a picture of the whole cosmos.

29. Cantos 13–38, 55–60. Four or five stops are described in detail; but there must have been ten or fifteen times that many.

30. Canto 17, stanza 3. Again I have altered the translation; in particular I have rendered *negara* as "capital" rather than "town." For the multiple meanings of this word, see my *Negara*.

31. W. B. Harris, *Morocco That Was* (Boston, 1921). The following discussion is confined to the period of the Alawite dynasty, that is, from the seventeenth to twentieth centuries (it still continues), with most of the material coming from the eighteenth and nineteenth centuries. Again, I have depended heavily on my own research (see C. Geertz, *Islam Observed: Religious Development in Morocco and Indonesia* [New Haven, 1968]); C. Geertz, H. Geertz, and L. Rosen, *Meaning and Order in Moroccan Society* (Cambridge, England, and New York, 1979).

32. The best study of the traditional Moroccan state is E. Aubin, *Morocco of Today*

(London, 1906). The term "tribe" is difficult of application in Morocco, where social groups lack stability and definition, See J. Berque, "Qu'est-ce qu'une 'tribu' nord-africaine?" in *Eventail de l'histoire vivante: Hommage à Lucien Febvre* (Paris, 1953).

33. See A. Bel, *La religion Musulmane en Berbérie* (Paris, 1938), vol. 1; E. Gellner, *Saints of the Atlas* (Chicago, 1969); C. Geertz, *Islam Observed*. Many of the ulemas and marabouts were also sharifs. On Moroccan sharifs in general, see E. Lévi-Provençal, *Les historiens des Chorfa* (Paris, 1922).

34. On *baraka*, see E. Westermarck, *Ritual and Belief in Morocco*, 2 vols. (London, 1926); C. Geertz, *Islam Observed*.

35. On Mulay Ismail's truly astounding mobility, see O. V. Houdas, *Le Maroc de 1631–1812 par Ezziani* (Amsterdam, 1969), pp. 24–55; text reference at p. 46. On Mulay Hasan, see S. Bonsal, *Morocco As It Is* (New York and London, 1893), pp. 47 ff.; cf. Harris, *Morocco That Was*, pp. 1 ff.

36. S. Schaar, "Conflict and Change in Nineteenth-Century Morocco" (Ph.D. diss., Princeton University, 1964), p. 72. The constant mobility also shaped, and similarly, the nature of the court: "The very life that the greater part of the members of the [court] must lead, uproots them and cuts them off from any contact with their tribe or their native town, and attaches them, to the exclusion of all other ties, to the institution on which they are dependent. The bulk of the [court] . . . centres around the Sultan, and becomes nomadic like him. Their life is passed under canvas, or else, at unequal intervals, in one of the imperial cities—constant change, in fact, and no ties anywhere. The horizon narrows, everything outside disappears, and the members of the [court] have no eye for anything but this powerful mechanism, mistress of their lives and their fortune" (Aubin, *Morocco of Today*, p. 183).

37. W. B. Harris, *Tafilet* (London, 1895), pp. 240–43; F. Weisgerber, *Au seuil du Maroc modern* (Rabat, 1947), pp. 46–60 (where one can also find a plan of the camp). On the move it was no less impressive; for a vivid description, complete with snake charmers, acrobats, lepers, and men opening their heads with hatchets, see Harris, *Morocco That Was*, pp. 54–60. The harkas were multitribal enterprises, the core of which was composed of the so-called military—*jaysh*—tribes, who served the court as soldiers in return for land and other privileges. One can't resist one more proverb here: *f-l-harka, baraka:* "There is blessing in movement."

38. Schaar, "Conflict and Change in Morocco," p. 73. The violence mostly consisted of burning settlements and cutting off the heads of particularly recalcitrant opponents (which, salted by the Jews, were then displayed over the entrance to the king's tent or palace). Meditation, which was more common, was conducted by royal officials or, often, various sorts of religious figures, specialized for the task. Schaar (ibid., p. 75) remarks that kings, or anyway wise ones, took care not to be overly harsh: "The ideal was to hit the enemy lightly, collect tribute payments, establish a firm administration in their midst, and move on to the next target."

39. Material on the Tafilalt mehalla can be found in Harris, *Tafilet*, pp. 213 ff.;
    R. Lebel, *Les voyageurs français du Maroc* (Paris, 1936), pp. 215–20;
    R. Cruchet, *La conquête pacifique du Maroc et du Tafilalet*, 2d ed. (Paris, 1934),
    pp. 223–41; G. Maxwell, *Lords of the Atlas* (New York, 1966), pp. 31–50;
    F. Linarès, "Voyage au Tafilalet," *Bulletin de l'Institut de la Hygiène du Maroc*,
    nos. 3–4 (1932). Cf. R. E. Dunn, *Resistance in the Desert* (Madison, Wisconsin,
    1977), who stresses the king's desire to stabilize the Tafilalt against French
    incursion as a motive for the trip. Ten women of the royal harem also accom-
    panied the king, and Cruchet estimates about 10,000 hangers-on, merchants,
    "et autres parasites qui sont la rançon d'une troupe, n'est pas une sinécure," as
    well (*La conquête pacifique*, p. 223).
40. Maxwell, *Lords of the Atlas*, pp. 39–40.
41. Harris, *Tafilet*, p. 333.
42. Harris, *Morocco That Was*, pp. 13–14; for a fuller description, see Harris,
    Tafilet, pp. 345–51.
43. For the argument concerning the ritual destruction of the monarchy, see
    Walzer, *Regicide and Revolution*. With Walzer's argument that the trials and
    executions of Charles and Louis were symbolic acts designed to kill not
    just kings but kingship, I am in agreement; concerning his further argument
    that they altered the whole landscape of English and French political life
    permanently and utterly—that is, that these rituals were availing—I am less
    convinced. The other wing of this sort of argument is, of course, that democ-
    racy makes the anthropomorphization of power impossible: "Die Repräsenta-
    tion [that is, of "majesty"] verlangt eine Hierarchie, die der Gleichheit des
    demokratischen Staates widerspricht, in der jeder Bürger Soverain ist und
    Majestas hat. So aber alle Könige sind, da kann keiner mehr als König auftre-
    ten, und die Repräsentation wird unmöglich" (Straub, *Repraesentatio Maies-
    tatis*, p. 10). But along with a number of other people, from Tocqueville to
    Talmon, I am not persuaded of this either.
44. For a description of some of the *siba* activities at the end of the Protectorate,
    see E. Burke, *Prelude to Protectorate in Morocco* (Chicago, 1976). On *ratu adil*,
    see Sartono Kartodirdjo, *Protest Movements in Rural Java* (Singapore, 1973).
45. Novak, *Choosing Our King*, pp. 211, 224–28, and 205–8. I have omitted, with-
    out indication, so as not to clutter the page with ellipses, large segments of
    these passages, and have repunctuated, reparagraphed, and even run some
    sentences together, both in the interests of brevity and to eliminate as many
    as possible of Novak's personal comments, some of which are extremely
    shrewd, others mere alternative clichés. Thus, though all the words are his
    (or those he is quoting), and nothing has been done to alter the meaning, these
    excerpts are better regarded as précis than as true quotations. For a similarly
    vivid view of 1972 presidential campaign theatrics from another part of the
    forest, see H. Thompson, *Fear and Loathing on the Campaign Trail*, '72 (San
    Francisco, 1973).

PART TWO

Ritual,
Kingship,
and Politics
in France,
c. 900–1715

2

RALPH E. GIESEY

Models of Rulership in French Royal Ceremonial

One of the classics of French royal ceremonial studies, Marc Bloch's *Les rois thaumatures*, is now sixty years old. That work did not stimulate studies of allied topics. Bloch himself turned away from them and devoted the last two decades of his life to the study of social and economic history. He was cofounder of the *Annales* school which, until recently, has given short shrift to things either royal or ceremonial. The same is true, in large measure, of social-scientific historiography in other countries.

The lively interest in ceremonial studies during the past few years does, however, owe a great deal to social scientists—not to those who practice it in history, but rather to those in anthropology and sociology. The new vogue for ritual studies relies heavily upon comprehension of the ineffable, semiotic element in ceremonial acts. Anthropologists have to be devoted to this element in order to understand rulership, since they usually lack the kinds of literary evidence historians of western society have in abundance. The theory and practice of kingship in France, for example, could be understood profoundly with scant recourse to ceremonial studies; indeed, nineteenth- and early twentieth-century scholars effectively accomplished this. The problem now, as I see it, is to maintain a congruence between long-established constitutional history (wherein I include not only legal and political but also theological and philosophical aspects) and the kind of affective comprehension of kingship that anthropologists apply so well when studying societies that have no thick transcription of their "constitution." For where, on one hand, detailed information about variations in successive performances of the same ceremony in western monarchies almost begs for the writing of an event-filled history that renders the enduring sense of the act tentative and changeful, the search for symbolical values in the same ceremonial demands, on the other hand, that the eventful sense be subjugated. If new methods are able to add to traditional understanding, let them not at the same time subtract from it.[1]

Centuries ago, in 1609, a Frenchman did try to portray the ceremonial of the French kings simultaneously as antiquarian history and sublime symbolism. The work is naive in both respects, the historical because antiquarian methods (in the good sense) were then still elementary, the symbolical because the author was a true believer in the phenomenon. The author, André Duchesne, wrote his essay on royal ceremonial as part of a comprehensive treatise on the "Grandeur and Majesty" of the kings of France.[2] This book has not caught modern scholars' fancy the way Jean du Tillet's treatment of royal ceremonial a generation earlier has, and let us allow that Duchesne does not push back very far the frontier of knowledge on this subject. Nor does Duchesne's persona as eulogist all by itself separate him notably from the chorus of heavenward praisers of the new Bourbon dynasty. It is the combination of history and eulogy that is intriguing. The analyst and the enthusiast, the detached scholar and the worshipful subject, are one. The ineffable quality of ceremony coalesces with its mundane history.

Four of the six chapters in Duchesne's discourse on the French king's majesty are devoted to ceremonials that we now regard as *the* state ceremonials of medieval and early modern times: the coronation, the funeral, the *entrée*, and the *lit de justice*. Duchesne sees them as varieties of just one model, Majestic Kingship. As an antiquarian of the new school, he commands an impressive array of historical facts, but the vision of majesty that pervades his work, and that he announces at the outset has motivated him to paint a "portrait" of majesty, always takes precedence over scholarly concerns.[3] In the picture that emerges, historical facts are like brushstrokes—as often as not applied with a real flair for anachronism—that impart realistic details to an otherwise idealized image. The affective impulse always wins over antiquarian scholarly restraint, for the canvas must capture the Majesty of the King in a holistic fashion. What emerges is at the same time a wonderful expression of the affectivity of royal ceremonial in the early seventeenth century and a model of what a scholar of the later twentieth century, trying to describe the same thing, should avoid doing.

Where Duchesne sees all four ceremonials as an integrated representation of Majesty, I shall stress the distinctness of their origins and the essentially different models of rulership to which they are related. Duchesne's transfigured Majesty will suffer deconstruction into elements that we can see had intrinsic (or contrived) compatibility. At least they

enjoyed a symbiotic relationship down to Duchesne's time, unless he himself bears false witness. Near the end of this essay, then, I try to show how
the system of traditional state ceremonials broke down not long after
Duchesne wrote about them, and in the final section I present in cameo
fashion the new species of royal ritual that effectively took their place.

Consecration—Coronation

The audacity of French claims regarding the superiority of their kings was
revealed already in the coronation ceremony of the Carolingian dynasty.
It is more appropriate to say "consecration," for besides the crowning
there also took place a sacring with holy oil. (The French overwhelmingly
prefer *sacre* to *couronnement* as a one-word designation for the two-part
ceremonial.) Some other nations had consecration of their kings, but none
built upon it an edifice such as the French.[4]

In the course of the ninth century a legend grew that the oil used to
anoint the French kings was the same oil, kept in the same holy vial, that
God had sent from heaven in the beak of a dove for the baptism of Clovis,
just after the year 500 (Fig. 2.1). Since Clovis' baptism had brought the
entire Frankish nation into the Christian faith, consecration of later kings
with Clovis' baptismal chrism linked them personally to the greatest event
in their nation's history, the adoption of the Christian faith, and at the
same time gained for them the grace of God that He had shown Clovis. In
the later Middle Ages the myth of the chosen people and the myth of the
providential sanction of Frankish kingship were reenacted at every new
king's consecration. The words "By the Grace of God" in the French
king's official title were in fact a *duplex dei gratia:* once for the moment in
his life when he became king by consecration, the other for the moment in
his nation's life when it became Christian by baptism. The same event was
performed in the same place, with the same holy oil, by the same cele-
brant, for nigh a thousand years.[5]

In practice, only a tiny bit of the precious Clovis oil was used each
time, mixed with a specially consecrated oil reserved for the investiture of
bishops. Consecration with this holy oil has led some historians to refer to
the Frankish royal cult as "sacerdotal kingship," but no king was ever
actually given the powers of a priest. He could not, for example, celebrate

Fig. 2.1. Baptism of Clovis.
Musée de Reims, Reims.

the sacraments as if he had been received in holy orders by ordination. This deficiency, however, was more than offset by the practice that arose early to speak of the French king's consecration as a separate sacrament of the church. It was a very special sacrament, indeed, since only one person could ever receive it! Even after the number of the sacraments was fixed at seven in the early 1200s, the French continued for centuries to refer to their king's consecration as the "eighth sacrament."[6]

Whatever the credibility of sacramental power imparted by the holy oil to the French king, he did finally acquire a unique magical power—unique, that is, until the English kings copied it—which made him, if not a priest-king, then surely a magic-working king. This happened when the myth of Clovis' balm joined forces with the legend of St. Marcoul and

Fig. 2.2. Henry II touching for the "King's Evil." Bibliothèque Nationale, Paris.

produced the miracle of "curing the king's evil." St. Marcoul, a local French saint whose shrine was not far from Reims, was believed to have had the power to cure a very disfiguring disease of the lymph gland, now identified as scrofula. In the course of the eleventh century this power was attributed to the French king as well, as an effect of his consecration with Clovis' holy balm. So, as a kind of appendage to the coronation at Reims, the consecrated kings of France traveled to the shrine of St. Marcoul, where all the afflicted who could come were assembled, "to touch (and cure) the king's evil" (Fig. 2.2).[7] The "royal touch" introduced a truly thaumaturgical element into the *sacré et couronnement* of the French kings, and so it allows us to designate the entire ceremonial as "sacral kingship." This is the senior member of four among the models of kingship in pre-

Bourbon France with which I shall deal, and also the longest-lasting in the sense that the others were born and died while the sacre was practiced down to 1825. Little public credibility remained in the royal touch at this last performance and probably not for some time before that. But there is no reason to doubt its efficacy during all the later Middle Ages.

Funeral

The coronation ceremony lost its legal force as the constitutive act of kingship during the course of the thirteenth century. Up to that time the king was not called king until crowned, and his reign was dated only from that moment, but in the year 1270, when St. Louis died while on a crusade in North Africa, his son Philip was with him and so obviously could not be crowned at Reims for months to come. The barons, therefore, hailed Philip III as king on the spot, and he immediately exercised the legal powers of king even though he was not crowned until over a year later. This practice of immediate assumption of effective legal power was followed by all kings thereafter. The exigencies of government had to prevail over ceremonial scruples. One could not countenance a "constitutional interregnum."

A "ceremonial" interregnum was, however, created. For if the new king's legal power was recognized at once but his inauguration was postponed for several weeks—or even longer—then during that period of time there would be no crowned and consecrated king of France. This deficiency was not easy to accept, for it suggested that to have an incumbent exercising the magical aura of sacral kingship was not really necessary. Over time, however, the French responded by creating a new state ceremonial, one that was bizarre yet sublimely suited to fill the "ceremonial interregnum" between the death of one king and the coronation of the next. At the same time it presented ingeniously a dramatic demonstration of the new ideal of kingship, which I shall refer to as "juristic kingship," that was to prevail during the later Middle Ages and Renaissance.

The ceremonial of which I speak is the royal funeral, and the psychedelic effect it imparts upon modern eyes comes from the display of a realistic effigy of the deceased king in full regalia (Fig. 2.3).[8] The French began to use the effigy upon the death of Charles VI in 1422, copying a

Fig. 2.3. Charles VI's fu-
neral effigy, 1422.
Bibliothèque Nationale,
Paris.

Fig. 2.4. Henry IV's funeral effigy. Musée Car-
navalet, Paris.

Fig. 2.5. Louis XII's funeral effigy. From *Le rozier
historical de France* (Paris,
1523).

practice that the English kings had employed on and off for a century. The effigy had one purely practical function: to substitute for (or "represent") the body when the period of lying in state for some reason had to be extended beyond the time the body itself could be decently preserved. The English used the effigy as long as the French, down to the seventeenth century, but never enhanced the treatment of it in the ways that the French did.[9]

At first the effigy represented the deceased king as deceased, but by the end of the century (in 1498, to be precise), the Parlement of Paris solemnly spoke of the effigy as if it were alive and of the ceremonial context as if it were attendance upon a living king.[10] To make this believable, the new king had to absent himself from his predecessor's funeral, for if he did attend there would be simultaneously two kings of France in the public eye: one alive but uncrowned, the other crowned but unalive. Circumstances had prevented some kings in earlier times from missing their predecessors' funerals; ceremonial exigencies now forced them to do so.

The funeral effigies of the French kings were made realistic by the use of death masks, which from 1498 were further enlivened by artistic doctoring of the wax visage to make the eyes appear open (Fig. 2.4).[11] The funeral manikin was garbed in full regalia, the only occasion after his coronation when the king's person was thus appareled.

Before 1515 the effigy was placed atop the encoffined body during the funeral procession, but in that year the effigy and corpse began to be carried separately. The body came first, in a black-draped hearse, the effigy after it, carried triumphantly under a canopy, a privilege reserved for royalty at this time (Fig. 2.5). The effigy no longer simply substituted for the dead body as originally it had; it now stood somehow for the live body. The king, therefore, had two bodies in his funeral procession: one, his encoffined body, soon to be enshrined at St. Denis, the royal necropolis; the other, a vividly lifelike image of himself, which represented the abstract royal dignity that never died.[12]

Contrasting display of coffin and effigy achieved its ultimate dramatic presentation at Francis I's funeral in 1547. For practical reasons the funeral had to be delayed, but the coffin and effigy had already been brought together in a palace in the suburbs of Paris, ready for the convoy to Notre Dame and then to St. Denis. To fill the days of waiting, a spectacular sequential display of the coffin and the effigy was contrived. First the effigy was displayed reclining on a bed of honor in the vividly bedecked *salle d'honneur*, where meals were served in its presence (Fig. 2.6).[13] One of the participants in Francis I's funeral tells us that "The three courses of the meal were carried out with the same forms, ceremo-

Fig. 2.6. Hall of Honor for the duke of Lorraine, 1608. From *Pompe funèbre de S.A.R. Charles III, Duc de Lorraine* (Nancy, 1608), as reproduced in Joseph Gregor, *Denkmäler des Theaters* (Munich, 1926), vol. 4, plate 3.

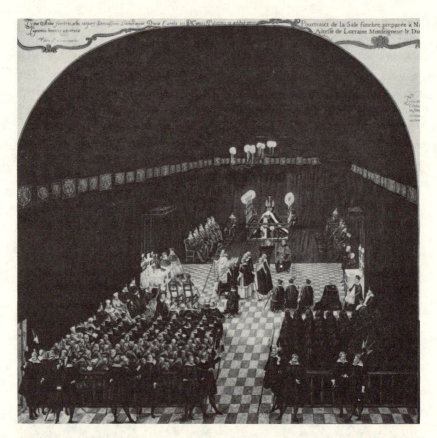

Fig. 2.7. Hall of Mourning for the duke of Lorraine, 1608. From *Pompe funèbre de S.A.R. Charles III, Duc de Lorraine* (Nancy, 1608), as reproduced in Joseph Gregor, *Denkmäler des Theaters* (Munich, 1926), vol. 4, plate 4.

nies and samplings as they were wont to be during the lifetime of the Seigneur, without forgetting those of wine, with the presentation of the cup at the places and times that the Seigneur had been wont to drink—twice at each meal."[14]

After this effigy ritual had been carried on for a week, the *mise-en-scène* was totally transformed overnight. The lively colored drapes were covered over with sombre black ones and the effigy abed replaced by the shrouded coffin in a *chapelle ardente;* the *salle d'honneur* had become a *salle de deuil* (Fig. 2.7).[15]

In French legal writings from these times the effigy is identified with Justice, the principal function of the royal office, which never dies. In the world of English jurists during the same era there arose the legal fiction of the "King's Two Bodies." In 1562 crown lawyers argued: "For the King has in him two Bodies, *viz.*, a Body natural, and a Body politic. His Body natural . . . is a Body mortal, subject to all Infirmities that come by Nature or Accident. . . . But his Body politic is a Body that cannot be seen or handled, consisting of Policy and Government, and constituted for the Direction of the People."[16] The English were the masters of legal fiction, the French of ritual symbolism. The body natural and body politic of English jurisprudence equal the corpse and effigy of French ceremonial.

English jurisprudence coined the enigmatic phrase "the king never dies" as a formulaic epitome of the notion of the King's Two Bodies. The French royal funeral ceremonial developed the equally paradoxical expression of this idea in the "The king is dead! Long live the king!" As the body was interred at St. Denis (the effigy having been taken away), the household officials' batons were lowered on the coffin and the cry went up (for the first time since the king's death) "Le roi est mort!" and then, a moment later, lifted up again to the cry "Vive le roi!"

Whether by legal fiction or funeral effigy, the same idea is present: the royal dignity, *dignitas regia*, is undying. Baldus, one of the princes of Italian jurisprudence in the fourteenth century, defined *dignitas* as "something intellectual, lasting forever miraculously, though not corporeally." Those words fit the then-current definition of an angel, even as Sir John Fortescue thought when he likened the king's greater-than-human powers to those of angels. It was second nature for jurists then to use the concepts of theologians, and the analogy between *angelus* and *dignitas* conveys vividly the symbolic values of everlastingness and unchangingness imparted to the state through the agency of kingship.[17]

It would not be simply levity, therefore, were we to describe the change in models of rulership from early medieval "sacral" kingship to later medieval "juristic" kingship as a descent in the cosmological order from the divine sphere to the angelic sphere. Nor would one be wrong to guess that the third stage, to which we now turn, will bring us down to the human sphere.

Entry into Paris

The characteristic feature of what I call "humanistic" kingship is the great authority provided by models derived from human history, especially classical antiquity, and from pagan mythology regarded as a historical (not religious) phenomenon. The passion for ancient prototypes found its expression in all ceremonials during the Renaissance, but the royal ceremonial best suited to the free expression of the humanistic model was the official entry and welcome of a king into a city.[18]

The evolution in style of the *entrée*, from medieval to modern, is clearly revealed in the French king's formal entry into his capital city after the coronation at Reims. In the fourteenth century, when the event became customary, the principal issue was constitutional: the citizens promised fidelity in exchange for the king's reaffirmation of the city's chartered privileges. Very early on, however, certain "stations" along the parade route became set places for gilds and corporations to decorate or to perform skits for the diversion and edification of the king as he passed by. Before 1500 the dominant element of these pictoral or dramatic scenes was religious: biblical models of kingship and other kinds of religious tableaux in the spirit of mystery plays. But regularly, too, the king was confronted with his own famous forebears: Clovis being baptized with the holy oil, Pharamond (Clovis' mythical ancestor) promulgating the Salic Law, and St. Louis, model of kingship for all time. Of these two themes, the scriptural and national-historical, the latter survived to a modest extent in Renaissance entries, but the former steadily receded until, by the early 1500s, it was completely replaced by pagan heroes and deities. This vogue for Roman and Greek antiquity brought forth naturally a humanistic ideal of kingship.

No finer rendering of French kingship *à l'antique* can be found than Henry II's entry into Paris in 1549.[19] The search for classical mirrors to hold up to modern princes had led to the invention, not long before, of the *Hercule Gaulois*, and a life-sized image of this fabulous figure was set atop the Porte St. Denis, the traditional entry gate, for Henry II to contemplate before he made his first public appearance in Paris since becoming king (Fig. 2.8).[20] The Gallic Hercules was based on a story from Lucan, who reported once having seen in Gaul the image of a deity that reminded him of Hercules even though the prowess involved was persuasion by speech rather than coercion by strength. Henry II saw Hercules with the features of his own father, Francis I, from whose mouth came four chains going to the ears of four figures representing different estates of the realm: clergy, nobility, magistrates, and workers. Francis I had been given the title "Father of the Arts and Sciences" during his lifetime, making him the perfect incarnation in France of the intellectualized god-hero in Gaul; Henry II was being propagandized by this scene—as well as by an inscription accompanying it that evoked the notion "like father, like son"—to carry forward the arts.[21] The ancient Gallic hero-god and the recent French king, each an exemplary patron of the arts in his time, exhort the new Francogallic king to emulate themselves.

Other stations on the parade way inside the city blended classical and modern themes in novel ways. A rhinoceros and obelisk device, adapted from recently learned Italian sources (Fig. 2.9),[22] perpetuates the theme set at the entry gate: the figure on high is a personification of France, the nation, and the inscription on the obelisk (given in Latin, Greek, and "Hieroglyphic") speaks of the glories of language and literature. Henry II did not encounter himself personified until he reached the bridge over the Seine, where his features are lent to the mythical hero Typhis, standing between Castor and Pollux (Fig. 2.10). Typhis had preserved the Argonauts' mission to find the Golden Fleece by piloting their ship in an emergency, aided by the star-twins, who symbolize safe navigation. Besides giving Henry the role of captain of the ship of state (the emblematic device Paris was a ship), the tableau also subtly invokes Henry's rivalry with the emperor, Charles V, who, as duke of Burgundy, was head of the chivalric Order of the Golden Fleece.[23]

Henry II himself rode into the city armed and caparisoned as it was imagined a Roman emperor would have been at a triumphal entry (Fig. 2.11).[24] The spirit of the late-medieval *entrée joyeuse* has been transformed into an ancient imperial *adventus*.

The *entrée*, like all other royal ceremonials, existed to honor the king, and he was the principal actor; but each performance of the event called for original theatrical creations that could be used to edify the king; he was therefore also the principal spectator. The scenario of 1549 established an admirable tension between classical ideas and national aspirations as the new French king, appareled *à l'antique*, had the leading role in a play that instructed him in classical models of rulership.

No other state ceremonial invited such expression of the subjects' sentiments—nor, as it turned out, did the *entrée* itself maintain the level it reached in 1549. For, were we to plot the themes of the scores of *entrées* and allied court festivals which entertained the king during the later sixteenth and early seventeenth centuries, we would find on one hand that themes out of French history become fewer and fewer, lessening the motif of ancestral piety that should inspire the king, while on the other hand classical themes are increasingly rigged to show what the king already *is*, not what he should become. Ceremonials of the festive variety become propaganda for the glory and power of the ruling monarch rather than representations of higher values that are the true source of all royal power. The same process of change, *mutatis mutandis*, can be observed in the fourth of the traditional state ceremonials of late medieval and Renaissance derivation, the *lit de justice*.

Fig. 2.8   Fig. 2.9   Fig. 2.10

Lit de Justice

As many different ways as the *lit de justice* served expedient political needs of the French crown from the fourteenth through the eighteenth centuries, it was (or should have been) always also a celebration of lofty constitutional principle: the monarch presiding in the highest court of the land, the Parlement of Paris (or, occasionally, a provincial one).[25] If the business of the court on the occasion of a *lit de justice* were judicial, such as treason trials of great persons where Parlement's numbers were augmented by high nobles so as to constitute a *cour des pairs*, as was often the case up into the sixteenth century, then the event was a ritual enactment of the highest purpose of rulership, justice. During the royal funeral the presidents of Parlement in their red robes marched alongside the king's lifelike effigy because they and it symbolized justice, the principal part of the crown, which never died. At a *lit de justice* in its judicial mode, the king came into Parlement so that he and they could actualize the principle of justice. The *lit de justice* was, in this sense, a variant of the model of "juristic" kingship.

The Parlement of Paris was also involved, however, in the legislative process insofar as it had to register royal edicts before they became effective as law. If Parlement procrastinated about registering an edict brought

Fig. 2.8. Hercule Gaulois, 1549. From *C'est l'ordre [tenu à l'entrée de] Henri deuxième [à Paris, le 16 juin 1549],* p. 5.

Fig. 2.9. Triagonal Obelisk, 1549. From *C'est l'ordre [tenu à l'entrée de] Henri deuxième [à Paris, le 16 juin 1549],* p. 11.

Fig. 2.10. Henry II as Typhis, 1549. From *C'est l'ordre [tenu à l'entrée de] Henri deuxième [à Paris, le 16 juin 1549],* p. 15.

Fig. 2.11. Henry II as Imperator, 1549. From *C'est l'ordre [tenu à l'entrée de] Henri deuxième [à Paris, le 16 juin 1549],* p. 19.

Fig. 2.11

to it from the king, typically by drawing up *remonstrances* against the "constitutionality" of the edict, or if the king anticipated that that might happen and wished to forestall it, he could then go into Parlement in person and willfully enforce the registration of his edict in what we might call the "legislative" mode of the *lit de justice.* This was the exclusive function of the *lit de justice* in the eighteenth century, upon which common historical recollection is based: a rancorous confrontation on the political level that could only depreciate the lofty celebration of high principles of rulership the *lit de justice* was wont to convey. If the eighteenth-century *lit de justice* deserves any place at all in the roster of state ceremonials, it might therefore best be called a model of autocratic kingship.

Establishing in this manner two different models of kingship that the *lit de justice* served at different times—one in which the king acted as *primus inter pares* championing justice, another in which he was a willful autocrat overriding the high court's objections—does not, however, exhaust the possibilities. The *lit de justice* also came to be used as a device to mark the moment of accession to power of the new king. The process may be said to have begun in 1568, when a *lit de justice* held in the Parlement of Rouen was used to announce Charles IX's attaining the age of majority, and to have been completed in 1610 when the eight-year-old Louis XIII, at dawn of the day after his father was assassinated, was enthroned at a *lit de justice* and an edict establishing his mother's regency was read in his name and thus given immediate force. If we recall that already in the late thirteenth century the new king's full legal power was recognized at once upon the death of his predecessor, then the "inaugural *lit*" of 1610 is but the ceremonial fulfillment of a tacitly accepted custom and only technically an expression of the "legislative" mode of enforcing the king's will upon Parlement. That the atmosphere in the chambers of Parlement that morning was charged with contention over the prize of regental power while the boy-king sat serenely enthroned like a puppet shows the remarkable power of the symbol of majesty inherent in the *lit de justice* to regulate the gravest of political situations.

Those who seized upon the *lit de justice* for purposes of legitimizing regency probably gave little thought to how this act would affect the symbolic force of two other state ceremonials, the coronation and the funeral. The coronation was affected, however, because, whenever it finally did take place, its investiture of the new king with royal robes, crown, and other emblems of kingship would have been preempted by the boy-king's having already been similarly endowed for his appearance in Parlement. The funeral's symbolism, too, was preempted, because of the role it assigned to the dead king-in-effigy, Henry IV, that of manifesting the principle that *le roi ne meurt jamais*, would have been personified already weeks earlier by the new king's live enthronement in Parlement. Those ceremonials had either to be modified or be made a travesty of.

A spectator at Louis XIII's inaugural *lit de justice* referred to the new young king as "the living image of the dead king." Unless he was referring simply to genetic resemblances of the bodies natural of the father and the son, this observation was a foretelling of the travesty that Henry IV's lifelike effigy had to have suffered some weeks later when it was displayed on a *lit d'honneur* and then conveyed in triumph in the funeral cortege as an emblem of the undying nature of the body politic. For if the make-believe that the dead king's effigy should be treated as alive required that the new king make no public manifestation of the royal dignity, then the inaugural *lit* of the new king made the dead king's effigy just a commemorative manikin. As the leading jurist of the time, Charles Loyseau, declared in this same year, "The instant the old king expires his last breath his successor is perfect king."[26] The king's everlasting body politic always has a living body natural in which to dwell; "angelic" effigies belong to a bygone age. So, not surprisingly, 1610 was the last occasion the effigy was used for a French king's funeral. At the next royal succession, in 1643, the new king was again just a child and an inaugural *lit de justice* was used again to affirm the powers of regency, but no thought seems to have been given to honoring the dead king in effigy.

The coronation of the boy Louis XIII, performed in the same year, 1610, was threatened by the same kind of loss of symbolic meaning that the funeral ceremony had suffered some months earlier. Some adjustment had to be made in this case, however, for the crowning and sacring of the king was the most hallowed of state rituals. And, indeed, the masters of ceremony came up with an embellishment of the coronation ceremony which ingeniously kept intact the fiction that the king's authority came from his coronation-consecration. On the morning of the ceremony, Louis XIII reclined on a bed of state in the "king's chamber" of the archiepiscopal palace attached to the cathedral at Reims. Two ecclesiastical peers, bishops, were sent to fetch him. At the door of the chamber they knocked; the chamberlain within asked: "Whom do you want?"; "Louis XIII, son of Henry the Great"; "He is sleeping." After the third knock, however, when asked whom they wanted, the bishops called for "Louis XIII whom God has given us for king." The door swung open at once, revealing the boy-king reclining on a bed, waiting for the bishops to come and help him up and lead him to the cathedral to be consecrated and crowned in the traditional fashion.[27]

The two conjoined bodies of Louis XIII responded differently when called: the body natural, Henry's son, slept; the body politic, the God-given king, was awake and waiting to be crowned. No new political power was gained in this ritual of the "sleeping king." It was, rather, an echo of the immediate succession acted out earlier at the inaugural *lit de justice*. By the kind of inversion of the proper order of things that ritual can effect, the de jure power which for centuries the new king was deemed to possess immediately upon his predecessor's death was made in 1610 to appear to have been only de facto, needful of the coronation to be made de jure. The "ceremonial interregnum" the funeral ceremonial had filled so marvelously by separating the king's two bodies and treating them differently was now filled by the same new king responding differently to questions addressed to his two bodies, one the son of Henry the Great, the other the God-given king.

The symbolic affiliation of the inaugural *lit de justice* and the coronation's sleeping king, contrived in 1610, happened to suit well the circumstances of the next two royal successions, in 1643 and 1715, when Louis XIV and Louis XV acceded as minors and needed regental direction. Then in 1775, the sleeping-king skit was kept even though Louis XVI acceded as an adult. The other three old state ceremonials, however, either died or went into full eclipse. We have seen that the funeral effigy ritual lapsed after 1610. The royal entry into Paris was practiced by Louis XIII and Louis XIV, but in the latter case it took place only eighteen years after his accession and served chiefly to celebrate his marriage and hopes for the renewal of the Bourbon dynasty. Louis XIII also had several grand entries into provincial cities during his reign, but Louis XIV had none such after the early years. The fact is that pompous civic entries went out of style everywhere in the seventeenth century as the art of creative entertainment by and for rulers moved from the streets of the city to the salons and gardens of the palace. Finally, the *lit de justice* (apart from its inaugural purpose) was utilized by Louis XIII very much in the spirit of Duchesne's vision of enthroned majesty. Parlement usually felt itself exalted by the royal presence, but toward the end of Louis XIII's reign the political element of forcing through unpopular legislation made the event more and more testy. Louis XIV, then, virtually abolished the *lit de justice* forever (he believed) in the early 1670s. His own last *lits de justice* in 1667 and 1673 forced Parlement to register decrees that established a process of registering future decrees without remonstrance, and for the last forty-odd years of his reign he never appeared before Parlement. As for the grandeur of enthronement, Louis accomplished that when *he* chose to, in the new throne room in Versailles, not as before when pressing affairs of state had forced him to go into the chambers of Parlement. Since his successor was a minor, an inaugural *lit de justice* was called, providing Parlement with the chance to trade approval of the regency for restoration of its right to remonstrate; eventually, this restoration of Parlement's right provoked the king, when a contretemps developed, to preside personally to enforce his will. Had Louis XV not been minor, however, there is no reason to suppose the *lit de justice* would ever have been revived and been able to play its famous role during the last decades of the old regime.

Seen in wide perspective, then, three of the four state ceremonials of medieval and Renaissance times were either abandoned (the funeral and the entry) or quashed (the *lit de justice*) just before or during the reign of Louis XIV, and the remaining one (the coronation) modified by the trick of the sleeping king in a way that vitiated its primal function of creating the king. This process of change began in the year 1610, but up to that time—indeed, until just the year before, when Duchesne published his treatise—the ceremonial practices of French kings held together as a unit, denoting compatible models of rulership. We turn now to what took their place.

The Sun King

If Louis XIV abandoned the traditional public state ceremonials of his predecessors, he created in their stead a private, palace-centered ceremonial life for himself as grandiose as any in the annals of western European history. The cult of the Sun King, elaborated in art and architecture at Versailles and Marly and acted out in a daily ritual lived by Louis XIV for several decades, has not yet received the comprehensive study it deserves, although we have enough details from literary accounts and artifactual remains to be sure of its main features.[28] I shall present it by imagining what a court chronicler of the year 1709 might have said had he tried to make a verbal portrait of "la Majesté du Roy" in counterpoint to what Duchesne had written exactly a century earlier. Gone are the traditional ceremonies that took place in the streets of the capital city, in cathedrals, and in the high court, that is, in public. Everything now takes place in the royal palace, performed in the presence of courtiers. My imaginary chronicler might have written something like this.

"The official emblem of His Majesty is a resplendent sun shining over a terrestrial globe with the device *Nec Pluribus Impar*, 'Not Unequal to Many,' which means to say His Majesty is equal to many kings. Examples of it can be found all over the palace: a stucco ornament in the throne room, on the woodwork of a door, on an urn in the garden. Others are found on frescoes and tapestries, porcelain, cutlery, and stained-glass windows. All the world knows the image of His Majesty as Sun King from the myriad of engravings that have been printed and the host of medals issued from the mint. His early life has been emblemized by a bundle of sun devices in medallic form; the central device, which is the obverse for all the others, reads *Deo Digna Facies*, 'a worthy face in the eyes of God.' In his youth His Majesty acted the role of Apollo in one of Monsieur de Benserade's pieces (Fig. 2.12).[29]

"The palace of Marly has marvelous images of Apollo on its facades, but I would like to point out a singular attachment of His Majesty to Apollo that is found at Versailles. It is not known by many because it is not immediately obvious, but it truly yields to no other artifice in the grandeur of its conception, since it involves the central axis of the gardens and the palace itself. If you place yourself behind the fountain of Apollo, as he rises in his chariot from the sea a thousand paces from the palace, and move along the line toward the middle of the palace, you will pass through the fountain of Latona, who was Apollo's mother, and on the palace facade between statues of Apollo and Diana (Diana is Apollo's sister, and in His Majesty's cultual family the queen is Diana), and inside arrive finally at His Majesty's bed. This bed has marvelous importance, as all the people of the court know. The king's rising in the morning, the *lever du roi*, is carried out with meticulous protocol dictating who can be present and who can assist him in getting dressed; and the *coucher du roi* in the evening is accomplished with the same exquisite detail as to where people stand in the room and the order in which they must retire—always backing away from His Majesty—until he is alone (except for a servant who sleeps in the corner).

"The day officially begins when His Majesty rises and it ends when he retires: sunrise equals kingrise, sunset equals kingset. No woman ever sleeps in this bed; His Majesty goes to the queen's room, or to his mistress's, if he seeks female companionship. Yet any lady of the court who happens to go through his bedroom during the day is obliged to curtsy toward His Majesty's bed.

"Each day's routine is regulated with ceremonial precision: the going to chapel, which His Majesty does every day, for he is a very devout Christian; the assembly of various administrative councils, which take place every weekday, for His Majesty is a very conscientious governor; the kinds of table settings, the rules of serving, and the persons who may be present at the various meals—and which of them might speak, and when; the evening gatherings where members of the court form circles around the king according to their status in the realm, with the princes of the royal blood seated closest to him.

"All these beautiful rites are carried on in a vast palace dedicated to classical mythology and history—and, of course, to His Majesty himself. Save in the chapel, there are no Christian religious images in the permanent decoration of the palace; only pagan deities are represented. As for mortals, there are heroes of antiquity, but none from French history except His Majesty of course. Each of the great chambers built in the sixteen-sixties is dedicated to a classical deity. The throne room, naturally—which was at first His Majesty's bedroom—is Apollo's. In the pendentives are scenes of Alexander, Caesar, and other great rulers, and on the walls are hung Gobelin tapestries. One of them faithfully copies the portrait of His Majesty by M. Rigaud (Fig. 2.13).[30] All who have seen this painting agree that it conveys the very ideal of Majesty, the more so because the person who in the picture personifies that idea is the one who, more than any other, has dramatized the ceremonial of Majesty, in a theatre he himself has built and according to a scenario he himself has composed."

The foregoing conceptualizing of the cult of the Sun King is, I confess, somewhat roguish. I have tried, in fact, to caricature the entirety of Louis XIV's ritualized existence in the spirit in which Thackeray once cartooned (Fig. 2.14)[31] the final element of my representation, Rigaud's painting. From the coign of vantage I have adopted in this essay, endeavoring to see

Fig. 2.12. Louis XIV as Apollo. From *Les oeuvres de M. de Bensserade* (Paris, 1697), vol. 2, p. 69 (above left).

Fig. 2.13. Rigaud's Louis XIV. From *Trésors du grand siècle: Louis XIV* (Paris, 1924), p. 110 (above right).

Fig. 2.14. Thackeray's satire of Louis XIV. From *Works of Thackeray*, Charter-house ed. (London, 1901), vol. 14, opposite p. 313 (bottom).

how various old royal ceremonials maintained a close relationship with constitutional principles of rulership, the Appolonic iconography of Louis XIV's cult amounts to little more than Thackeray's disembodied royal costume.

I find myself unable to respect the classical themes in the cult of the Sun King the way I do analogous elements in his predecessor's ceremonials—as, for example, in royal entries. Revival of the virtues of the pagan world during the Renaissance had meant a broadening of the base of *humanitas* in western society; Louis XIV made the pagan world seem to be an allegory of his own personal life. The cult of the Sun King postulated Louis's divinity on a colossal scale without risking the taint of sacrilege. Louis XIV emancipated himself from old royal ceremonials that had brought the ruler together with his subjects in public forums and created in their stead rites of personality carried out in his private dwellings. "L'état, c'est moi": whether or not Louis XIV ever uttered those words as a motto of his political conduct, they do catch the ineffable spirit of his ritual life.

Notes

1. An excellent example is Clifford Geertz, *Negara: The Theatre State in Nineteenth-Century Bali* (Princeton, 1980). Geertz has pungent criticism, with which I agree most emphatically, of the tendency of western historians to treat ceremonial studies frivolously, but I am not as sure as he that his techniques for analyzing Bali can be applied facilely to western European societies: cf. pp. 5–10, 121–25, 216.

2. André Duchesne, *Les antiquitez et recherches de la grandeur et maiesté des Roys de France* (Paris, 1609). We are concerned with Book 2, pp. 323–549, the first chapter of which, "De la Maiesté des Roys de France" (pp. 339–67) sets forth the overarching model; the five remaining chapters comprise four on state ceremonials (those I shall be dealing with) and one on royal dress at public church services. Throughout, costume is the capital component.

3. Ibid., p. 335.

4. In this section I draw freely upon Richard A. Jackson, *Vive le Roi! A History of the French Coronation from Charles V to Charles X* (Chapel Hill, 1984), also published in French as *Vivat Rex* (Strasbourg, 1983).

5. March Bloch, *Les rois thaumaturges* (Strasbourg, 1924; repr. 1961), pp. 185–224; in the English translation by V. E. Anderson, *The Royal Touch* (London, 1973), pp. 108–30. Fig. 2.1, showing the baptism of Clovis, is a detail of a tapestry of 1531 now in the Musée de Reims.

6. Bloch, *Rois thaumaturges*, pp. 224–29; in English, pp. 130–33.

7. Fig. 2.2 shows Henry II curing the scrofulous, from Bib. Nat. ms. lat. 1429, fol. 107ᵛ. The several other illustrations of this event found 'in Bloch's *Rois thaumaturges* have received new and immensely better reproduction in the English translation.

8. Fig. 2.3 shows Charles VI's effigy being carried on a litter, with the presidents of Parlement at the corners, from B.N. ms. fr. 5054, fol. 27ᵛ. Where not otherwise noted, everything in this section depends upon my *The Royal Funeral Ceremony in Renaissance France* (Geneva, 1960; reprinted in 1983).

9. To my knowledge, nothing has yet replaced the aged but exemplary work by Sir Wm. H. St. John Hope, "On the Funeral Effigies of the Kings and Queens of England," *Archaeologia*, 60, 2 (1907): 517–70. The remnants of these effigies are on display now in the Undercroft Museum in Westminster Abbey; my caveats about this exhibit are given in *Royal Funeral*, p. 204.

10. The circumstances of the 1498 debate over the lifelikeness of the effigy are spelled out more in my "The Presidents of Parlement at the Royal Funeral," *Sixteenth-Century Journal*, 7 (1976): 25–34, than they are in the *Royal Funeral*.

11. Fig. 2.4 shows a wax visage of Henry IV prepared in an artists' competition for the funeral effigy but not used. It is mounted in armor for display purposes at the Musée Carnavelet, in Paris. We know from literary evidence that after 1498 the effigies' eyes were opened.

12. The woodcut in Fig. 2.5 of Louis XII's effigy carried in procession is from *Le rozier historial de France* (Paris, 1523), reproduced in *Royal Funeral*, Fig. 15. How the French royal funeral dramatized the "two bodies" theme is ingeniously set forth in Ernst H. Kantorowicz, *The King's Two Bodies* (Princeton, 1957), pp. 419–37.

13. Fig. 2.6 is the best representation we have of any kind of the meal service in the presence of a funeral effigy, that of the duke of Lorraine in 1608 *(Pompe funèbre de S.A.R. Charles III, Duc de Lorraine* [Nancy, 1608]), as reproduced in Joseph Gregor, *Denkmäler des Theaters*, vol. 4 (Munich, 1926), pl. 3. The Lorraine ducal practice was borrowed directly from the French royal one, although we are sure that the meal service for the latter was physically more intimately related to the recumbent effigy than this engraving shows to have been the case in Lorraine. The effigy, barely visible at the far end of the hall in this engraving, is also awarded a separate, detailed engraving in the Lorraine funeral book.

14. Pierre du Chastel's account of Francis I's funeral, in *Royal Funeral*, p. 5.

15. Fig. 2.7 from the duke of Lorraine's funeral book (above, n. 13), ed. Gregor, pl. 4.

16. Kantorowicz, *King's Two Bodies*, p. 7, citing Plowden's *Commentaries*.

17. Ibid., p. 8 (Fortescue) and p. 400 (Baldus).

18. In this section I draw freely upon the forthcoming book by Lawrence M. Bryant, *The French Royal Entry Ceremony* (Geneva, 1985). The older standard work by Joseph Chartrou (Carbonnier), *Les entrées solennelles et triomphales à la Renaissance, 1484–1551* (Paris, 1928), illustrates well at least the main change in

mood from Christian to classical. Bryant's article, *"Parlementaire* Political
Theory in the Parisian Royal Entry Ceremony," *Sixteenth-Century Studies*, 7
(1976): 15–24, shows the dimensions for constitutional history far beyond
what I suggest here.

19. We now have a fine scholarly study of this entry, to which is appended a
photomechanical reproduction of the entry book itself, by I. D. McFarlane,
The Entry of Henri II into Paris, 16 June 1549 (Binghamton, N.Y., 1982).

20. Fig. 2.8 is from *C'est l'ordre [tenu à l'entrée de] Henri deuzième [à Paris, le 16 juin
1549]*, p. 5; also now in McFarlane, *Entry*. The full dimensions of the Hercule
Gaulois conceit has been set forth by Marc-René Jung, *Hercule dans la littéra-
ture française du XVIe siècle* (Geneva, 1966).

21. Not surprising, since the likes of Joachim du Bellay and Jean Goujon were
involved in the programming and embellishment of the event.

22. Fig. 2.9 from *C'est l'ordre*, p. 11; also in McFarlane, *Entry*.

23. Fig. 2.10 from ibid., p. 15; also in McFarlane, *Entry*.

24. Fig. 2.11 from ibid., p. 19; also in McFarlane, *Entry*.

25. In this section I draw freely from Sarah Hanley, *The Lit de Justice of the Kings
of France* (Princeton, 1983). Hanley's contribution to the present volume
spares me the need to provide scholarly annotations or illustrations of the *lit
de justice*.

26. *Du Droit des Offices*, I.x.58 (ed. *Les oeuvres de Loyseau* [Paris, 1666], p. 98).

27. Richard A. Jackson, "The Sleeping King," *Bibliothèque d'Humanisme et Renaissance*, 31 (1969): 527–51.

28. A flamboyant effort to penetrate the mythical décor of Versailles, using
Ovid's *Metamorphoses* as a touchstone, has been made by Edouard Guillou,
Versailles, le palais du soleil (Paris, 1963); the illustrations are lavish and the
scholarly apparatus (interlaced with the text and in endnotes) is creditable
although scanty. Ernst H. Kantorowicz, "Oriens Augusti—Lever du Roi,"
Dumbarton Oaks Papers, 17 (1963): 119–77, opens up the deep historical roots
of Louis's cult buried in classical and Byzantine ruler cults, which is a fruitful
line for future research if one believes (as do I) that Louis's cult was in part
contrived by humanists and antiquarians; see esp. § 4, "Lever du roi," pp.
162–77. By contrast, two recent efforts to penetrate the spirit of Louis's cult
(Louis Marin, *Le portrait du roi*, and Jean-Marie Apostolides, *Le roi-machine*,
both Paris, 1981) illustrate how the imagination can make order out of material for which no sturdy erudite construction exists.

29. Fig. 2.12 from *Les oeuvres de M. de Bensserade* (Paris, 1697), vol. 2, p. 69: "Le roi
représentant le Soleil levant."

30. Fig. 2.13: a Gobelin tapestry version of Hyacinthe Rigaud's portrait of Louis
XIV, from *Trésors du grand siècle: Louis XIV* (Paris, 1924), p. 110.

31. Fig. 2.14 from *Works of Thackeray*, Charterhouse ed. (London, 1901), vol. 14,
opp. p. 313.

3

SARAH HANLEY

Legend, Ritual, and Discourse in the Lit de Justice Assembly: French Constitutional Ideology, 1527–1641

Introduction

The most vexing and engaging task for historians is to unravel historical threads that have been woven over time into staid patterns of conventional wisdom. A study of the *Lit de Justice* of the kings of France—one of the most celebrated events of the ancien régime—presents such a challenge. Traditionally, historians have interpreted the *Lit de Justice* in light of late eighteenth-century events: as a ceremonial appearance of the king in Parlement used chiefly to exercise absolute royal power.[1] In the later decades of the eighteenth century, the *parlementaire* Louis-Adrien Le Paige propounded this view in his lively précis on French constitutional history.

You ask me what a *Lit de Justice* is? I will tell you! In its origins and according to its true nature, a *Lit de Justice* [assembly] is a solemn session of the king in the Parlement [of Paris] which is convoked to deliberate on important affairs of state. It is a tradition which originated in ancient general assemblies held in earlier times. . . . [But today] the convocation of a *Lit de Justice* [assembly] is an occasion of mourning for the nation.[2]

In his complaint that the perverted format of the *Lit de Justice* assembly betrayed the French constitution, Le Paige spoke from a political perspective already colored by quarrels between king and Parlement waged in *Lits de Justice* just preceding the French Revolution. In his mourning the loss of the pristine ancient *Lit de Justice*, he stood squarely on the historical legend about the medieval origins and constitutional prominence of the assembly propagated during the sixteenth and seventeenth centuries. Although Le Paige's view takes liberty with historical verities, modern scholars in the nineteenth and twentieth centuries have perpetuated both the legend about the *Lit de Justice* and its narrow political focus.[3] The time is at hand, therefore, to revise the standard accounts.[4]

This study is informed by a triad of interpretive propositions. The first proposition holds that the interaction of two historical processes, the repeated convocation of *Lit de Justice* assemblies and the invention of a legend about them, stimulated constitutional discourse and provided a public forum in which constitutional ideologies were articulated. Those intertwined processes are shown in table 3.1, which plots both the historical and legendary developments. The historical record of the *Lit de Justice* assembly is reconstructed vertically in Columns A to C, and its legendary life is charted horizontally across Columns D to Z. On the historical side of the picture, Column A lists by date appearances of the king in Parlement from the fourteenth through the mid-seventeenth centuries that were mentioned by historians and manuscript compilers of early modern times. Next, Column B cites the primary sources for these events, the registers of the Parlement of Paris (Series X1a in the Archives Nationales), and Column C gives the secondary sources, copies of the registers (Series U, Collection Le Nain, Archives Nationales) when the originals are missing. When the phrase *"lit de justice"* actually appears in conjunction with an event, the citation in Column B remains unbracketed; when the phrase does not appear, the citation is bracketed. Finally, when a dated session in Column A is adjudged a *Lit de Justice* assembly according to the criteria of this investigation, the date is set in italic type with an asterisk (*) to the left.

On the legendary side of the picture, Columns D to Z chart chronologically the published treatises and the anonymous manuscript compilations that listed *Lit de Justice* assemblies or commented on them between the sixteenth and eighteenth centuries. Those works identify royal visits to Parlement either as Royal *Séances* (✻) or as *Lit de Justice* assemblies (●) in agreement with or in opposition to the registers of Parlement.[5] When the commentators in Columns D to Z (who discussed the *Lit de Justice* over time) are compared with the sources in Columns A to C (which actually recorded the events themselves), the pattern that emerges gives form to two interesting phenomena. First, the table reveals the appearance in the sixteenth century of a historical fiction about the *Lit de Justice* which rooted its origins in medieval times, and it charts the subsequent steady growth in the seventeenth century of this legend, which firmly established the

TABLE 3.1

The Legend of the *Lit de Justice* Assembly

KEY

Dated Events (Column A): Those in italic type with an asterisk to the left (*) are adjudged as official *Lit de Justice* assemblies.

Primary Sources (Columns B and C): Those with bracketed dates cite no *lit de justice* apparatus or *Lit de Justice* assembly.

Secondary Sources (Columns D to Z):
❀ = Designated as a Royal *Séance*
● = Designated as a *Lit de Justice* assembly

	Primary Sources		Secondary Sources																							
	A	B	C	D	E	F	G	H	I	J	K	L	M	N	O	P	Q	R	S	T	U	V	W	X	Y	Z
		1315–1713		1563	1615	1616	1627	1632	1633	1634	1638	1641	1643	1643	1645	1649	1650	1662	1665	1673	1673	1680	1684	1723	1723	1725
	King in Parlement	Registers of Parlement (original accounts) A.N. X1a	Registers of Parlement (copies & notes) A.N. U (Le Nain)	Du Tillet	La Roche-Flavin	ms. fr. 2881	ms. fr. 18522	ms. fr. 18410	ms. n.a. 7231	ms. fr. 4346	U 425–426	ms. 2912	ms. fr. 16511	ms. fr. 23410	Dupuy and B.N. Dupuy mss. 513–514	Godefroy	Clairambault 715	ms. fr. 18411	ms. fr. suppl. 11737	C.P. ms. 5046	ms. fr. 16512	ms. fr. suppl. 10948–10949	KK 1441	ms. fr. n.a. 9749	ms. fr. n.a. 9750	A.N.
				Pub.	Pub.	B.N.	B.N.	B.N.	B.N.	B.N.	A.N.	Maz.	B.N.	B.N.	Pub.	Pub.	B.N.	B.N.	B.N.	B.V.P.	B.N.	B.N.	A.N.	B.N.	B.N.	
1	1315 4 July	[3]	2000																				●			
2	1353 4 Mar.		2005																				●	●	●	●
3	1358 10 Dec.		513																				●			
4	1364 12 Nov.	[1469][a]	2014														❀						●	*	●	●
5	1366 27 July	[1469] Saint-Pol.[b]	2014	❀																					●	

[a] Account inserted by Du Tillet in 1545.
[b] Session held in the Hôtel Saint-Pol, Paris.

67

TABLE 3.1 (cont.)

	Primary Sources			Secondary Sources																						
	A	B	C	D	E	F	G	H	I	J	K	L	M	N	O	P	Q	R	S	T	U	V	W	X	Y	Z
6	1369 9, 11 May	[1469]	2014 / 513	•	•			•		•	•	❋	•	•	•	•		•			❋	•	•	❋	•	•
7	1375 21 May	[1470] [8602]	2014 / 513	•	•									•		❋			❋	•	•	•
8	1378 9, 10 Dec.	[1471]	2014 / 513	•	•	•	•	•		•	•	•	•	•	•	•		•			•	•	•	•	•	•
9	1380 2 Oct.	[1471]	2014 / 513	❋	❋														❋			•	•
10	1387 2 Mar.	[1473]	2015 / 513	•	•	•	•	•		•	•	•	•	•	•	•		•		•	•	•	•	•	•	•
11	1392 3 Dec.	1477	2016 / 513	•	•										•							
12	1396 10 Apr.	4784	2170 / 513	•	•										•				•			
13	1407 26 Dec.	4784 8602	513	•	•										•							•
14	1413 26, 27 May	1479 4789	2018 / 513	•	•		•	•					•	•	•		•	•	•		•	❋	•	•	•
15	1413 5 Sept.	1479 4789 8602	2018 / 513	•	•	•	•						•	•			•	•	•		•	❋	•	•
16	1458 10 Oct.	Vendôme[c]	513[d]	❋	❋					•							•	❋					❋	
17	1484 20 July	4825	2175 / 513[e]														•					
18	1487 21, 22 Feb.	[1495]	513	•	•			•	•	•	•			•	•		•		•			•		•	•

[c]Trial held in the Château of Vendôme, Vendôme.
[d]A.N. U (Le Nain) mistakenly dates as 18 December.

TABLE 3.1 (cont.)

	Primary Sources			Secondary Sources																							
	A	B	C	D	E	F	G	H	I	J	K	L	M	N	O	P	Q	R	S	T	U	V	W	X	Y	Z
19	1493 8, 9, 11 July	[1500]	2024 513	✳	✳															●	✳	●		●		
20	1498 17 May	[1504]	513	✳	✳	●	✳					●	✳	●						✳	✳	●	✳	●	●	
21	1498 7 July	[1504]	2181^f 513^f	✳	✳								✳	●												
22	1499 13 June	[1504] [4840]	2024 2181 513	✳	✳									●						✳						
23	1515 14 Mar.	[1517]	2025 513	✳	✳		✳					●		●								●			●		●
24	1517 5 Feb.	[1519]	2026 513	✳	✳		✳			✳		●			●			●				✳	●	✳	✳	✳	●
25	1522 15 Feb.	[1524]	2168 513	✳	✳		✳					●				●		✳						✳	✳	✳	✳
26	1523 30 June	[1525]	2168 513	✳	✳		✳						●	●	✳			●						●	●	●	●
27	1524 8, 9 Mar.	[1526]	2168 513	✳	✳		✳			✳		✳	✳	●									●	●			●
*28	1527 24–27 July	1530	2029 513	●	✳	●	●	●	●	●	⊖	●	●	●	●	●	●	●	●	●	●	●	●	●	●	●	●
*29	1527 16, 20 Dec.	1531	2169 513	●	●		●	●		●	⊖	●		●		●		●	●								●
*30	1537 15 Jan.		2192 513	●	●			●	●	●	⊖	●	●	●				●	●				●		●	●	●
31	1549 2 July	[1565]	2038 2169 2196 513	✳	●	●	●	●	●	●	⊖	●	●	●	●	●	●	●	●	●	●		●	●	●	●	●

^f A.N. U (Le Nain) mistakenly dates as 5 July.

69

TABLE 3.1 (cont.)

		Primary Sources		Secondary Sources																							
	A	B	C	D	E	F	G	H	I	J	K	L	M	N	O	P	Q	R	S	T	U	V	W	X	Y	Z
32	1551 12 Nov.	[1571]	2039	✱	✱		●	●	●	●	●	●	●	●	●	●	●	●	●	●		●	✱	●	●	●
33	1552 12 Feb.	[1571]	513	✱	✱	●	●	●	✱	●	●	●	●	●	●	●	●	●	●			●	●	●	●	●
34	1558 5 Jan.	Salle Saint-Louis[g]	2046	✱								✱									✱	●	●	●	●	●
35	1558 15 Jan.	[1587]	2046	✱			●	✱		●	✱	●	●	●		✱		●					●	●	●	●
36	1563 17 May	[1605]	513	✱	●	●	●	✱	●	●	●	●	✱	●		●		●	●	●		●	●	●	●	●
*37	1563 17 Aug.	Rouen[h]	513	—	✱		●			●						✱	●					●	●			●
*38	1564 11 Apr.	Bordeaux[i]	513	—	●		●	●	●	●	●	●	●		●	●	●					●	●	●	●	●
*39	1565 1 Feb.	Toulouse[j]	513	—	●				●	●	●			●		●		●				●	●	●	●	●
40	1569 1 Aug.	5023[k]	2205	—																	✱					
41	1571 12 Mar.	[1631]	2205	—																						
42	1572 26 Aug.	[5039]	513	—																						
*43	1573 18 Sept.	1640	2063	—																			●			
44	1580 26 July	[1669][l]	513	—																			●			

[g] Session an Assembly of Notables which functioned as an Estates General, the first in Paris in that century, convoked in the Salle Saint-Louis, Palais de Justice.

[j] Convoked in the Parlement of Toulouse.
[k] X1a 5023 mistakenly denotes a Lit de Justice; not cited by any commentator except A.N. U (Le Nain).

TABLE 3.1 (cont.)

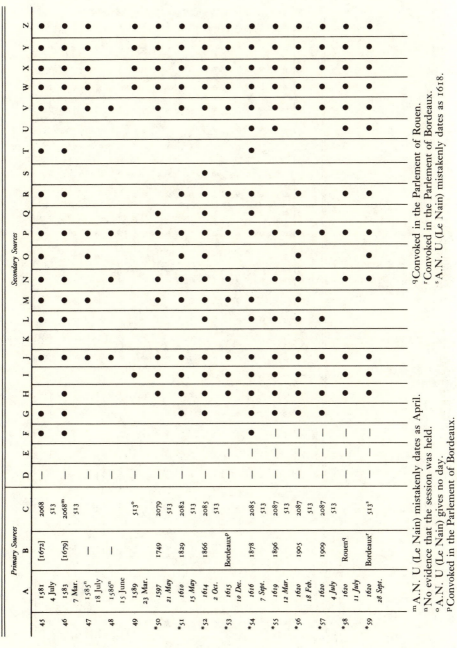

	Primary Sources			Secondary Sources																							
	A	B	C	D	E	F	G	H	I	J	K	L	M	N	O	P	Q	R	S	T	U	V	W	X	Y	Z
45	1581 4 July	[1672]	2068																							
46	1583 7 Mar.	[1679]	2068^m, 513																							
47	1585^n 18 July	—	513																							
48	1586^n 15 June	—																								
49	1589 23 Mar.		513°																							
*50	1597 21 May	1749	2079, 513																							
*51	1610 15 May	1829	2082, 513																							
*52	1614 2 Oct.	1866	2085, 513																							
*53	1615 10 Dec.	Bordeaux^p	513																							
*54	1616 7 Sept.	1878	2085, 513																							
*55	1619 12 Mar.	1896	2087, 513																							
*56	1620 18 Feb.	1905	2087, 513																							
*57	1620 4 July	1909	2087, 513																							
*58	1620 11 July	Rouen^q	513																							
*59	1620 28 Sept.	Bordeaux^r	513^s																							

^{m}A.N. U (Le Nain) mistakenly dates as April.
^{n}No evidence that the session was held.
^{o}A.N. U (Le Nain) gives no day.
^{p}Convoked in the Parlement of Bordeaux.
^{q}Convoked in the Parlement of Rouen.
^{r}Convoked in the Parlement of Bordeaux.
^{s}A.N. U (Le Nain) mistakenly dates as 1618.

71

TABLE 3.1 (*cont.*)

| | Primary Sources | | | Secondary Sources | | | | | | | | | | | | | | | | | | | | | | |
	A	B	C	D	E	F	G	H	I	J	K	L	M	N	O	P	Q	R	S	T	U	V	W	X	Y	Z
*60	*1621* *3 Apr.*	1918	2087 513	—	—	—	•	•	•	•		•		•	•	•	•	•			•	•	•	•	•	•
*61	*1622* *18 Mar.*	1929	2087 513	—	—	—	•	•	•	•		•		•		•		•		•	•	•		•	•	•
*62	*1626* *6 Mar.*	1967	2090 513	—	—	—	•			•		•		•	•	•		•		•	•		•	•	•	•
*63	*1627* *28 June*	1982	2089 513	—	—	—	•			•		•				•		•	•					•	•	•
*64	*1629* *15 Jan.*	2009	2089 513	—	—	—	—	•	•	•			•	•	•	•		•			•	•	•	•	•	•
*65	*1631* *13 Aug.*	2044	2091 513	—	—	—	—	•		•				•		•		•	•		•	•	•	•	•	•
*66	*1632* *12 Aug.*	2055	2091 513	—	—	—	—	•		•						•	•					•	•	•	•	•
*67	*1633* *12 Apr.*	2064	2091 513	—	—	—	—		•	•			•	•	•	•			•			•	•	•	•	•
*68	*1634* *18 Jan.*	2074	2094 513	—	—	—	—	—		•			•	•	•					•		•	•	•	•	•
*69	*1635* *20 Dec.*	2101	2094 513	—	—	—	—	—	—	—			•	•	•	•	•			•			•	•	•	•
*70	*1641* *21 Feb.*	8387	2096 513	—	—	—	—	—	—	—	—								•		•		•	•	•	•

assembly as a pillar of the French constitution. Second, the table reveals the existence of a mutual relationship between the events themselves (known correctly or incorrectly as *Lit de Justice* assemblies) and the legend developed about them. Keeping apace throughout the seventeenth century, the avid research of the new historians matched the growing prominence of the assembly.

The second interpretive proposition holds that the ritual (ceremonial configuration and procedural format) observed in *Lits de Justice* defined and disseminated precepts of French Public Law (or working axioms of government) in a national forum convoked for that purpose.[6] In the past the function of ceremony in French constitutional history has been treated with indifference, an attitude succinctly expressed by one historian who warned that "Nothing will be said about the solemn ceremonies in which the majesty of the monarch is manifested before the eyes of the crowd: Coronations, *Entrées* to cities, *Lits de Justice*, etc. The details are only of picturesque and anecdotal interest."[7] To the contrary, recent scholarship shows the French propensity to disseminate principles of Public Law through the agency of ceremony in the Royal Funeral, Coronation, *Entrée*, and *Lit de Justice*;[8] and the latter assembly provided the national forum most admirably suited for that purpose. In pertinent places throughout this study, therefore, the ceremonial ritual of the *Lit de Justice* is recapitulated in order to sort out the structures of significance, or levels of inference and implication,[9] through which constitutional axioms were articulated symbolically in the sixteenth and early seventeenth centuries. That ritual was manifested in two basic forms: first, the ceremonial configuration that was outlined by the archaeological disposition of the Grand-chambre (Palais de Justice) of the Parlement of Paris (reproduced on occasion in other locations), the type of seating plan employed there, and the particular habits worn by attendants; and second, the procedural format, which was organized by prescribed protocol, special privileges, and the order assigned for consultation. These underlying structures of meaning contained in the ritual of the *Lit de Justice* reveal a panoply of ceremonial symbols, or an alternative language molded from space, gesture, and symbol rather than word, which outlined the French constitution in the *Lit de Justice* assembly.

The third interpretive proposition holds that the modes of discourse, or vocabularies, encountered in the writings and speeches of kings, chancellors, *parlementaires*, and others at *Lits de Justice* and Royal *Séances* shed light on the *mentalité* of the participants and on the ties between constitutional practice and theory.[10] The evidence shows how innovative vocabularies were formulated (from private-law maxims, classical and juridical metaphors, biogenetic doctrines, popular proverbs, and historical legends) in order to express precise French constitutional precepts in *Lit de Justice* assemblies decades before such precepts were discussed in the writings of theorists. These modes of discourse coalesced in time to form a new language of French Public Law and diverged over time to propagate variants of constitutional ideology. Accordingly, this inquiry investigates the actual convocation of *Lit de Justice* assemblies and the invention of a legend legitimizing them; analyzes the modes of discourse and ceremonial rituals through which French constitutional precepts were articulated; and identifies the constitutional ideologies that were reflected in the language of French Public Law and of ritual during the sixteenth and early seventeenth centuries.[11]

Part One: Historical Overview and Case Studies in the Sixteenth Century

A. Historical Event and Antiquarian Fiction (1527–1597)

The *Lit de Justice* assembly and the legend that legitimized it developed in two stages during the sixteenth and early seventeenth centuries. The first stage from 1527 to 1597 marked the novel appearance and uneven growth of the *Lit de Justice* as a constitutional forum: kings convoked *Lits de Justice* rarely (eight times in seventy years) and distinguished them from Royal *Séances* on constitutional grounds. Rendered legitimate by the invention of tradition (supposed medieval origins), the assembly ranked as the fourth and major ceremony of French kingship (Funeral, Coronation, *Entrée*, and *Lit de Justice*). During those years the *Lit de Justice* served as a forum that publicly pronounced the separation of legislative (royal) and judicial (parlementary) powers, displayed the king primarily as legislator, secondarily as judge, and articulated constitutional axioms of juristic kingship, that is, precepts which defined kingship as an office, or *dignité*, conferred by French Public Law upon a hereditary successor. The events of the sixteenth century unfolded as follows.

The first three *Lit de Justice* assemblies in French history were convoked by Francis I in July and December 1527 and January 1537 to treat constitutional issues (that is, issues concerned with French Public Law) provoked by the bitter contest with Emperor Charles V in the early decades of the century.[12] The ritual of these assemblies and the discourse pronounced therein outlined a theory of the French constitution and subjected imperial power to French jurisdiction (see Case Study 1). Not long after the convocation of these innovative assemblies, they were defended ably as French custom. Historians in renaissance France, impressed by the nation's rich feudal past, retrieved and studied archival documents in order to reconstruct the ancient constitution. Early in the sixteenth century, Jean du Tillet, clerk of Parlement and historian, conducted the most formidable research project. He wrote a major historical treatise, *Recueil des roys de France, leurs couronne et maison*, which circulated first in manuscript from the 1540s through the 1570s and then as a posthumous publication in many editions between 1577 and 1618.[13] Convinced of the indigenous nature of French laws and institutions, Du Tillet pursued a scholarly course to decipher their origins. He scoffed at contemporary works which drew upon fabricated fables from chronicle lore and which emphasized text rather than context, appearance rather than reality. In contrast, he called attention to the unique historical method followed in his research, the citation of official documents which were signed, sealed, and preserved in archival repositories.[14] Founded on documentary proofs and historical ruminations, Du Tillet's compendium produced a critical typology of royal visits to the Parlement of Paris from the mid-fourteenth century, which divided sessions into Royal *Séances* (honorary visits) and *Lit de Justice* assemblies (constitutional sessions) and created in the process, despite his careful scholarship, a fictive medieval *Lit de Justice* assembly.[15] On the basis of that historical fiction, French constitutional history was divided into four stages: glorious decades when Royal *Séances* and *Lit de Justice* assemblies flourished (the 1360s to 1413) followed by a dark lull when the tradition was suppressed (from 1414 to 1483), interim decades when the Royal *Séance* was revived (1484–1526) followed by a French constitutional renaissance when the *Lit de Justice* assembly was "revived" (in 1527). The *Recueil des roys de France* provided a veritable handbook of French constitutional history which legitimized the *Lit de Justice* as a revival of French tradition, and it was consulted by virtually every commentator from the sixteenth century to our own time.

As might be suspected, however, when one turns to the original sources in registers of Parlement which supplied Du Tillet's evidence, the historical case for the medieval *Lit de Justice* vanishes along with the periodization based on it (consult table 3.1). The fact is that in the four-

teenth and fifteenth centuries there was no medieval *Lit de Justice* assembly
(a session distinguished from the Royal *Séance* on constitutional grounds),
even though commentators from the sixteenth through the twentieth centuries have accepted the feudal origins of that assembly. This point should
be emphasized because it challenges conventional wisdom which thus far
has escaped critical evaluation. In fact, the phrase *lit de justice* appeared
around the 1360s in the popular jargon of parlementary ushers who prepared the Grand-chambre for Royal *Séances*, and it was incorporated
briefly between 1387 and 1413 into the vocabulary of parlementary clerks
who wrote the minutes of those *Séances*. At that time, however, the phrase
signified nothing more than the royal drapery paraphernalia (canopy,
drapes, and pillows) left in Parlement's charge by Charles V in 1366 and
erected by ushers in the Grand-chambre of the Parlement of Paris to
cordon off royal space for the king.[16] The medieval term *lit de justice* thus
made an ephemeral appearance as a name for royal furnishings used in
parlementary *Séances*, not as a title for a constitutional assembly of ancient
origin; and the trivial nature of the term then, as compared to the constitutional import impressed upon it later, strikes an ironical chord. Indeed,
the appearance of the odd term *lit de justice* would not even elicit historical
interest except for the fact that early modern commentators interpreted it
as evidence for the medieval origins of the *Lit de Justice* assembly, be-
moaned the loss of that pristine institution, and invoked the fictive medieval *Lit de Justice* assembly as the prototype for its supposed renaissance
counterpart.

The auspicious debut of a *Lit de Justice* assembly clothed differently
from a Royal *Séance* in 1527 and 1537 did not go unchallenged. Vigorous
constitutional debate about the legitimacy of such a constitutional assembly took place during the 1540s and 1550s. The royal party culled
documentary evidence about the ancient constitution from Du Tillet's
compendium of sources and presented a radical historical argument for the
validity of the *Lit de Justice* and the separation of legislative and judicial
powers effected therein. Concentrating on archival texts in historical context, Chancellor François Olivier argued in 1549 that the Parlement of
Paris, institutionalized under Philip VI (1328–50), became a specialized
judicial body under Jean II (1350–64). Once the court was established as a
judicial institution with jurisdiction over private law, Olivier concluded,
the *Lit de Justice* assembly emerged as a constitutional forum with jurisdiction over French Public Law (that is, constitutional law).[17] Accordingly,
by the mid-fourteenth century a separation of powers had been pronounced: the monarch attended Royal *Séances* as the chief judge, but he

was enthroned in *Lits de Justice* as the legislator. Straightaway the *parlementaires* presented the opposing view of the ancient constitution, giving no quarter either to the notion of a historical separation of powers or to the existence of *Lit de Justice* assemblies that differed substantively from Royal *Séances*. Concentrating on the linguistic structure of parlementary orations, First President Pierre Lizet countered Olivier's assertions to show that the phrase *lit de justice* was simply a metaphor which evoked for the mind's eye a vision of the Parlement of Paris conjoined with monarch, princes, peers, and royal officers in the Grand-chambre; that is, an ordinary Royal *Séance* where all cases (legislative and judicial) were comprehended.[18] Since no *Lits de Justice* convened between 1537 and 1563, the polarized view of the French constitution expressed in this historical-rhetorical debate hung in abeyance. At the same time, however, Du Tillet's historical theory, strengthened by additional archival research commissioned between 1548 and 1559,[19] eventually stimulated the convocation of another *Lit de Justice* assembly in 1563.

When Charles IX came to the crown of France as a minor in 1560 (under the regency of Queen Catherine de Médicis), the royal party was stymied on the legislative front by Parlement's insinuation of itself as the legislative tutor of a minor king. Thoroughly out of patience with such parrying, Chancellor Michel de L'Hôpital organized a *Lit de Justice* assembly to publicize the king's newly attained majority and the royal theory of legislative kingship. Charles IX's Majority *Lit de Justice* was convoked in August 1563, but the assembly was located in the Parlement of Rouen, not Paris. The ceremonial ritual enacted in this unprecedented Majority *Lit de Justice* demonstrated the separation of legislative and judicial powers, and the mode of discourse adopted there defined the French Public Law of Succession in distinctly French constitutional terms (see Case Study 2). The event was dramatic for the royal party and the Parlement of Rouen, traumatic for the Parlement of Paris. The location of this important *Lit de Justice* in a provincial Parlement (contrary to Du Tillet's theory linking the assembly with the Parlement of Paris) unnerved the Parisian court which was struggling at the time to attain status as the supreme court in France. On the spot, therefore, the Parisian *parlementaires* reversed their position in the historical-rhetorical debate of yore. They adopted Du Tillet's historical theory and claimed the *Lit de Justice* as traditional Parisian parlementary procedure, publicly acknowledging the *Lit de Justice* assembly as a constitutional forum for the first time.[20] The crucial importance of this kind of ceremonial was borne out in the weeks that followed. The Parisian *parlementaires* fought bitterly with Charles IX over the legality of the Majority *Lit de Justice* of Rouen and lost that battle. The king then convoked two more *Lit de Justice* assemblies in the Parlements of Bordeaux and Toulouse in 1564 and 1565.[21]

Following these debuts in provincial Parlements, kings held *Lits de Justice* only twice more during the sixteenth century, both times in the Parlement of Paris.[22] Charles IX convoked the assembly in 1573 and Henry IV in 1597. The first was a legitimate assembly according to prevailing policy,[23] but the second was not.[24] Since the main architects of constitutional policy on the *Lit de Justice*, Chancellor L'Hôpital and the clerk Du Tillet, had departed from public life by the 1570s, it is not clear what official direction, if any, that policy took during the 1570s and 1580s. Still, by the 1580s a systematic body of information about the *Lit de Justice* had transcended narrow bounds. Du Tillet's historical treatise, *Recueil des roys de France*, was published six times between 1577 and 1588, and the formidable works of the new seventeenth-century antiquarian scholars were initiated not long after. During the first stage of the historical development of the *Lit de Justice* as event and legend, the assembly steered a narrow constitutional course and served as a public forum that confirmed juristic kingship in France. The two case studies outlined below show how ceremonial rituals and modes of discourse contributed to the making of that particular juristic brand of constitutional ideology.

B. Constitutional Ideology in Ritual and Discourse (1537 and 1563)

Case Study 1: The Lit de Justice assembly of 1537

On 15 January 1537 Francis I convoked a *Lit de Justice* in the Grand-chambre of the Parlement of Paris, a constitutional forum called to discuss disposition of the royal domain as regulated by French Public Law. The French king (as suzerain of Flanders and Artois) charged the emperor Charles V (as count of Flanders, vassal of the French crown) with the crime of "notorious felony" and called for deprivation of the domainal holdings in question.[25] The innovative ceremonial ritual (archaeological configuration and procedural pattern) employed there stressed important distinctions: first, the difference between the *Lit de Justice* as a constitutional assembly and the Royal *Séance* as an honorary session; second, the separation of the constitutional and legislative role of the king from the advisory and judicial role of Parlement in national affairs; and third, the emphasis upon the royal obligation to maintain the French constitution vis-à-vis imperial power in international affairs.

The archaeological configuration inside the Grand-chambre consisted of a diamond-shaped pattern that contained three hierarchical levels of seating. At the apex in royal space cordoned off, Francis I sat under a canopy of blue velvet embroidered with golden fleurs-de-lis on a dais elevated by seven steps and covered with the same material; and there were matching pillows around him and under his feet. On the steps leading down from the dais, the grand chamberlain, first chamberlain, and provost of Paris (holding a white baton) reclined. At the foot of the dais the chancellor sat in a chair decorated by an extension of the thronal drapery paraphernalia. At right and left angles from the thronal apparatus there were elevated tiers of seating: princes and lay peers sat in the highest seats to the right of the king, ecclesiastical peers and the archbishop of Paris to the left; crown officers and royal officers sat in seats just below to the right, red-robed presidents of Parlement just below to the left. The red-robed *parlementaires* sat on benches all around the parquet of the Grand-chambre, parlementary clerks and notaries at a desk, and behind them various royal household officers and royal guards sat or stood.[26] By contemporary standards this was an enormous entourage, around one hundred and fifty attendants, and the inordinately high enthronement of the king, flanked by princes and peers in the highest tiers, suggested superior rank for the royal party, inferior rank for the Parlement.

As the procedural pattern unfolded, there was bitter contention about the nature of the assembly: the royal party opted for a *Lit de Justice*, the *parlementaires* insisted on a Royal *Séance*. As a result, ceremonial innovations favoring the royal side caused a rising crescendo of concern among the *parlementaires*. Trouble surfaced even before the assembly opened. First, the presidents of Parlement commissioned a special report of the proceedings by placing a pleadings clerk, Pierre Le Maistre, in the Grand-chambre to record details of the ceremony. Then they sent the clerk of Parlement, Jean du Tillet, to the king protesting the order for red-robed habits (as opposed to black-robed habits for *Séances*) and were peremptorily rebuked. Francis I announced that the *Lit de Justice* would proceed according to a ceremonial plan designed to prevent precipitous or surprise moves. In a final attempt to raise Parlement's status, the presidents claimed access to the same high seats of the peers, but that ploy failed.[27]

The royal party figured most prominently in the proceedings. The dauphin (future Henry II, age eighteen) sat at the right hand of Francis I (somewhat lower), thus linked symbolically with the royal *dignité*; the dauphin and princes of the blood were provided with special footstools and consulted as a group (privileged status later written into law in 1576); and the queens attending the session sat on a special platform to the side. A delegation of *parlementaires* (several councilors and two presidents) escorted the royal retinue from Sainte Chapelle to the Grand-chambre. During the assembly, participants addressed the king with elaborate supplicatory gestures: the crimson-robed chancellor bowed and genuflected, the *avocats* and *parlementaires* bared their heads and knelt. Chancellor Antoine du Bourg, flouting parlementary protocol, entered the Grand-chambre accompanied by chancellery officials. Throughout the proceedings the chancellor sat on the special decorated chair at the foot of the throne and pronounced the guilty verdict against Charles V from there. The procedure denied the *parlementaires* time for separate deliberations as a body, required them to render an opinion in tandem with other groups, and placed the presidents last in the order of consultation.[28] All told, the ceremonial configuration spelled out relative ranks and provided Francis I with an exceedingly imperious, if not imperial, forum fit for discourse on the French constitution.

While contentious disagreement between king and Parlement marred the ceremonial surface of the *Lit de Justice,* the mode of discourse obtained there bespoke unanimity. The *avocat* Jacques Cappel argued the case in light of two legal traditions: feudal law, which mirrored the reciprocal tie between Francis I and Charles V; and French Public Law, which elevated French authority over imperial power on constitutional grounds. He invoked the familiar medieval legal proverb *Rex est imperator in regno suo* (The king is emperor in his kingdom), popular in French parlementary circles from the fifteenth century, to assert the ultimate sovereignty of the French king beholden to no other superior.[29] Cappel's main thesis focused on the French king's constitutional obligation. Fashioning a mode of discourse most extraordinary for the time, he made the following case.

By its nature the crown is inalienable . . . because according to the *Law of France,* which is called the *Salic* [*Law*], and customary, divine, and positive laws, the sacred patrimony of the crown, the ancient domain of the prince, cannot be divided among men. [Rather] it is transmitted to the king alone, who is the *husband and political spouse* of the *chose publique* which brings to him at his *sacre* and Coronation the said *domain as the dowry* of his crown. Kings swear solemnly at their *sacre* and Coronation never to alienate that dowry for any cause whatsoever, because it is itself inalienable. . . . Consequently, since [Public] Law not only forbids kings the right to alienate the domain but also prohibits the alienation of patrimonial or domainal property itself, and since such prohibition concerns the public welfare, it is obvious that contracts [treaties of Madrid and Cambrai] which contain clauses of alienation as heretofore mentioned are invalid from start to finish and cannot be validated by consent or oath.[30]

Repeating a constitutional concept introduced by President Jean (II) de Selve a decade earlier at the second *Lit de Justice* of December 1527,[31] Cappel invoked the marriage metaphor to describe the king's relation to the kingdom and then linked that constitutional adage to the *Law of France* (that is, French Public Law). Furthermore, he elaborated the adage first by appending the *dowry-domain* analogy to the metaphor, then by identifying the Coronation oath as the ceremonial expression of that patrimonial transfer.[32] There thus emerged in Jacques Cappel's pleading at the *Lit de Justice* of 1537 a two-pronged constitutional prohibition against alienation of the public domain, one tenet based on the definition of the inalienable nature of the domain itself, the other on the regulation of the king's relation to it through the marriage metaphor. It was this innovative constitutional praxis which demonstrated juristic kingship and provided a firm basis in French Public Law upon which to rest the case against imperial encroachment.

It has been assumed that in France the simplest formulation of the marriage metaphor, designating the king as the *spouse of the kingdom*, first appeared in a legal treatise of Charles de Grassaille (1538); that the metaphor then found its way into Coronation ceremonies (1547 and 1594) connected with the bestowal of the ring; and finally that its elaborate formulation, likening the *domain* of the kingdom to the *dowry* of the marriage, appeared in the late sixteenth century in writings of legists such as François Hotman and Jean Bodin.[33] Yet the first version of the metaphor (the king as spouse of the kingdom) actually emerged a whole decade earlier, not in a legal treatise but in a speech tendered by President De Selve in the *Lit de Justice* of December 1527; and the complex version of the metaphor (adding the equation of domain and dowry) also appeared decades earlier, not in the writings of legists of the late sixteenth century but in this speech set forth by Jacques Cappel in the *Lit de Justice* assembly of January 1537. There thus emerged early in the sixteenth century a formidable language of public discourse framed to discuss constitutional matters. The appearance of these rubrics at such an early date suggests that this juristic genre of French constitutional thought took root in the 1520s and 1530s within the purview of the *Lit de Justice* assembly.

Case Study 2: *The* Lit de Justice *assembly of 1563*

On 17 August 1563 the unprecedented Majority *Lit de Justice* of Charles IX convened in the Parlement of Rouen to celebrate the king's attainment of the legal age to rule the kingdom. The ceremonial ritual observed in 1537 (see Case Study 1) prevailed, although in 1563 Queen Catherine de Médicis as regent sat alongside the young king on the dais (see figure 3.1). Designed with precision, the procedural pattern separated legislative and judicial functions. The king acted as legislator with cognizance of French Public Law (constitutional) and private law (national and customary); the Parlement acted as a judicial body with jurisdiction over private law only. Charles IX issued a Majority Declaration affirming Public Law, then promulgated an ordinance creating national law; whereas in contrast the *parlementaires* argued a private case settled according to the customary law of Normandy.[34] The ritual of this *Lit de Justice* advanced the royal theory of government. The convocation of the assembly in a provincial Parlement and the pointed delineation of legislative and judicial powers substantiated allegations regarding legislative kingship already voiced in 1561 by the chancellor, Michel de L'Hôpital, in opposition to the claim of the Parlement of Paris to be colegislator with the king and the principal Parlement in France.[35]

In addition to the ritual demonstration of royal postulates of rulership, the mode of discourse propagated that day defined the French Public Law of Succession. Chancellor L'Hôpital's important speech used evidence from Du Tillet's treatise to trace the historical development of the French Law of Succession and to show its application to Charles IX.[36] L'Hôpital devised an innovative conceptual scheme for implementing the Law of Succession. He divided the process into two contiguous phases: first, the precise instant at which a successor legally assumed the office or "seized" the crown; and second, the later point (much later in minority kingship) at which the king actually undertook full "administration of the kingdom," that is, fully exercised the legislative prerogative. He identified two "laws," or precepts, which governed that time-bound sequence: the precept of *Saisine* (or *Seizure* of the kingdom), which regulated the initial phase, and the precept of *Majorité* (or *Majority* of the king) which regulated the second phase. L'Hôpital explained Seizure of the kingdom by recounting that

our wise rulers ordained as an immutable law *(loy perpetuelle)* [the precept] that *the kingdom is never vacant (le royaume n'est jamais vacant)*, because there is continuity from king to king so that *as soon as the king's eyes close [in death] [= mortuus aperit oculos viventis]* there is another king . . . without awaiting Coronation, unction, consecration, or any other ceremonies.[37]

The chancellor's discourse promoted the ideology of juristic kingship whereby nearest males in the royal line succeed to the *dignité* through French Public Law, not by virtue of personal inheritance,[38] and the con-

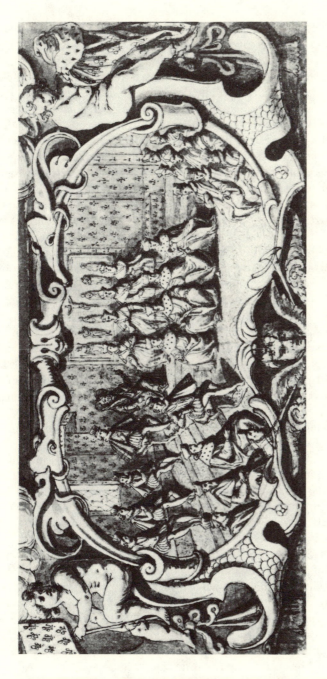

Fig. 3.1. Charles IX: Majority *Lit de Justice* held in the Parlement of Rouen, 1563. Bibliothèque Nationale, Paris.

ceptual vocabulary adopted to explain that ideology harked back to private law. L'Hôpital's reference to the king's eyes closed in death was derived from the medieval legal proverb *Mortuus aperit oculos viventis* (The dead opens the eyes of the living), which had been connected with another legal proverb, *Le mort saisit le vif* (The dead seizes [with respect to the inheritance] the living) and applied to cases in private law regulating inheritance. But L'Hôpital invested his statement with constitutional meaning by inventing for those precepts the first known French analogue *Le royaume n'est jamais vacant* (The kingdom is never vacant) to explain the concept of instant succession to the crown in terms of French Public Law. Reminiscent of the medieval maxim *Dignitas non moritur* (The *dignité* does not die), which illustrated the immortality of office, this vernacular maxim *Le royaume n'est jamais vacant* spelled out the perpetuity of royal office beyond the death of the individual incumbent in France.[39] By the mid-sixteenth century, therefore, a new French mode of discourse on Public Law surfaced to replace the older format, which depended on maxims from private inheritance law. Along these lines it has been argued that recourse to precepts of private law signaled a "proprietary" notion of kingship and the state.[40] But that suggestion does not take into consideration first, that the discussants at this time had no other appropriate vocabulary from which to draw; and second, that they succeeded in fashioning the best vocabulary available into a suitable language of Public Law. Chancellor L'Hôpital gave a legal definition of kingship in terms stressing continuity of office and the advanced new terms of discourse for this early constitutional discussion.

Following the exposition of the first precept, Seizure, which governed assumption of office, L'Hôpital turned to the second, Majority, which regulated full exercise of royal legislative prerogative during minority kingship. Citing evidence directly from Du Tillet's work, the chancellor provided the "Law of Majority" with historical roots: "The Law of Majority . . . considers our king a major at fourteen years of age and is unique [to France]. . . . [It] was promulgated by Charles V [in 1375] . . . [and] Charles VI [in 1407]."[41] Then L'Hôpital outlined a ceremonial plan to implement that precept. In his critical view the traditionally celebrated moments of royal succession could not serve as joyous public celebrations renewing kingship. The moment of Seizure marked the actual instant of succession to the throne, but that moment was dolorous, given the concomitant death of the predecessor king. The Royal Funeral ceremony publicly proclaimed succession to royal office with the heraldic cry *Le roi est mort! Vive le Roi!* (The king is dead! Long live the King!) given at the moment of burial, but the ritual itself was tinged with funereal gloom.

The Coronation ceremony provided confirmation of succession, but it was markedly religious and unsuitable for a public celebration. In contrast, the *Lit de Justice* assembly, celebrating the king's attainment of majority and legislative capacity, constituted a true public celebration of the renewal of kingship in France.[42] Reasoning in this manner, the chancellor effected a transposition of traditional ceremonial symbolism, denigrating the importance of Funeral and Coronation in the succession process and raising the Majority *Lit de Justice* high on the gamut of civic rituals.

The origins of these constitutional notions regarding legal-hereditary succession are now more clear. During the mid-decades of the sixteenth century, a new type of constitutional discourse surfaced in response to critical questions raised by the ascension of a minor king and the attendant shadow of a quasi-legislative interregnum. Fashioned from constitutional concepts advanced by L'Hôpital and Du Tillet, that discourse developed in several phases. First, the older legal maxims from private law, *Le mort saisit le vif* and *Mortuus aperit oculos viventis*, were linked together to explain the process of instantaneous succession in France; then the new French maxim of Public Law, *Le royaume n'est jamais vacant* (derived from the medieval maxim *Dignitas non moritur*), was invented as an analogue to underline the legal nexus of succession to royal office. Second, the Law of Majority (a legislative amendment of Charles V in 1375) was placed in historical context as a legitimate precept of the ancient constitution, and the *Lit de Justice* assembly was designated as the succession ceremony which best demonstrated these precepts of French Public Law. Finally, the *Lit de Justice* assembly of 1563, extolled as French historical tradition, demonstrated this network of constitutional axioms. Through the ritual and discourse of the *Lit de Justice* assembly, the ideology of juristic kingship was articulated again.

Part Two: Historical Overview and Case Studies in the Early Seventeenth Century

A. Historical Event and Antiquarian Legend (1610–1641)

The institutional development of the *Lit de Justice* assembly and the progress of the historical legend about it marched apace in the seventeenth century. The second stage from 1610 to 1641 marked the steady aggrandizement of the *Lit de Justice* and the complete demise of the Royal *Séance* (consult table 1.3). In that time Louis XIII convoked the *Lit de Justice* assembly regularly (twenty times in thirty-one years). He treated an expanding array of constitutional issues there, and he introduced ostentatious ceremonial innovations. At the same time, a grand historical legend recounted the august medieval origins and renaissance prominence of the assembly and publicized the *Lit de Justice* as the central ceremony of French kingship. Finally, this magnificent ritual displayed the king as legislator and articulated maxims of dynastic kingship, that is, precepts which regulated kingship, not as a *dignité* conferred by Public Law, but as a right conferred by Bourbon blood lineage. The events of the early seventeenth century unfolded as follows.

In May of 1610 immediately following the shocking assassination of Henry IV, the eight-year-old Louis XIII sat in an extraordinary Inaugural *Lit de Justice* assembly. The ceremonial ritual conducted there broke all established rules for the comportment of a new king and triggered a reformulation of French constitutional ideology. In effect, Louis XIII was inaugurated as king in a *Lit de Justice* and then displayed full legislative capacity there even though a minor (see Case Study 3). As a result, the earlier tripartite inaugural program (Royal Funeral, Coronation, and Majority *Lit de Justice*), which had supported the system of juristic ideology, was instantly displaced in the ceremonial spectrum. When preceded by this Inaugural *Lit de Justice*, Henry IV's Funeral ceremony (perpetuating the legal notion of an immortal royal *dignité*) became an empty exercise in constitutional symbolism.[43] Likewise, the later Majority *Lit de Justice* of Louis XIII in October 1614, shorn of a constitutional role by the Inaugural *Lit de Justice*, served simply as a gala nameday party.[44] Finally, the Coronation ceremony too suffered a constitutional setback, losing the primary inaugural role to the first *Lit de Justice* of Louis XIII, although it retained a foothold in the ceremonial spectrum by confirming the inaugural orientation of the *Lit de Justice*.[45] The first Inaugural *Lit de Justice* of 1610 marked a constitutional crossroads: there the older legal precepts of juristic kingship were replaced by dynastic maxims that introduced another shade of constitutional ideology soon legitimized in France.

Louis XIII's numerous convocations of *Lits de Justice* elicited a second wave of historical research. From the 1620s through the 1660s avid sleuths wrote numerous manuscript compilations and published treatises about the assembly; and a new cadre of royal officers, the masters of ceremonies, charted a programmatic extension of ceremonial ritual for it. All of the new historians, such as André Duchesne, Louis d'Orléans, and Antoine

Arnaud, stood squarely on the research of Jean du Tillet's *Recueil des roys de France;*[46] and the most ambitious projects, the treatises of Bernard de La Roche-Flavin, *Treze livres des Parlemens de France*, Pierre Dupuy, *Traité de la majorité de nos rois et régences du royaume*, and Théodore and Denys Godefroy, *Le Cérémonial françois*, inflated Du Tillet's fiction of the medieval *Lit de Justice* into a major historical legend (see table 3.1, columns D, E, O, and P). This vigorous new research enterprise produced voluminous results, because the new historians, convinced of the antiquity of the *Lit de Justice* assembly, presumed automatically that Royal *Séances* from the fourteenth through the sixteenth centuries were *Lits de Justice* and thus discovered (or invented) more assemblies than ever existed (consult table 3.1).[47] In addition, following the demise of the Estates General in 1614, the new research led to speculation about functions of the *Lit de Justice* that resembled those of the Estates. Chancellor Pierre (III) Séguier owned a large collection of manuscripts on *Lit de Justice* assemblies. His notes in the margins of one mused about the functional similarities of the two and designated the *Lit de Justice* as a substitute for the Estates.[48] Besides this resurgence of antiquarian legend-making about the *Lit de Justice* and the tendency to equate the assembly with the Estates, the ritual of the sessions in the seventeenth century was programmed with grandeur and precision unknown in earlier times.

Whereas earlier the constitutional nature of the issues posed there assumed paramount importance, now the ceremonial ritual itself gained preeminence as a system of conventions that defined public authority. The meteoric rise of the offices of grand master of ceremonies, master and aid of ceremonies, professional experts working under royal auspices, can be discerned from the records left by Guillaume Pot de Rhodes, François Pot de Rhodes, and Nicolas Saintot. The masters of ceremonies received royal orders for *Lit de Justice* assemblies and dispensed summonses for convocation, drew up seating plans for sessions and regulated ceremony there, deposited accounts of sessions in a new repository and provided monarchs with memoranda on protocol when requested.[49] Since French kings had no official throne room outside the Grand-chambre of the Palais de Justice, the regular appearance of the king with the Parlement of Paris became the most celebrated ceremony in the kingdom. Consequently, Parlement at every turn attempted to enlarge its share of ceremonial grandeur but failed to perceive that the rising dynastic cult of kingship expressed in such ritual would eventually absorb even the *Lit de Justice* assembly itself. In the meantime, the ritual of *Lits de Justice* provided a powerful device for shaping constitutional policy.

In *Lit de Justice* assemblies held after 1610 the dramatic royal alliance of dynastic right and legislative power was evident; and the Parlement of Paris, which actively supported the former but wished to temper the latter, was caught in the juncture. Parlement supported the ideology of dynastic right because it buttressed the court's growing dynastic conception of parlementary office. The replacement of the system of *survivance* with that of the *droit annuel* (*paulette* of 1604) encouraged the hereditary transmission of office and gave the enterprise a dynastic dimension of its own. Whereas sixteenth-century *parlementaires* claimed for the court perpetuity as a corporate body beyond the death of a king, seventeenth-century *parlementaires* claimed perpetuity as a corporate body and as individual family proprietors of offices within that body.[50] The ideology of dynastic kingship thus legitimized the aspirations of great *parlementaire* families and fit the court's notion of the right order of things. Conversely, the association of royal legislative power with the *Lit de Justice* assembly was resisted by Parlement, because that linkage seriously undermined the court's presumed colegislative function in the polity. Yet at this point the *Lit de Justice* assembly, institutionalized as Parisian parlementary procedure, brought enormous prestige to the court. Thus even though the assembly's use as a royal legislative vehicle jarred Parlement's notion of right order, the court issued no disclaimers at first.[51] Louis XIII virtually requisitioned the Grand-chambre of the Parlement of Paris as a royal throne room between 1616 and 1641, impressing upon the *Lit de Justice* assembly innovative ceremonial ritual that supported dynastic right and legislative power, the twin pillars of Bourbon kingship (see Case Study 4). During the reign of Louis XIII, therefore, the ritual of the *Lit de Justice* played a significant role in revising French constitutional ideology from a system of juristic kingship, which emphasized French Public Law and the perpetuity of the royal *dignité*, to a system of dynastic kingship, which focused on lineage and the immortality of a series of Bourbon incumbents.

B. Constitutional Ideology in Ritual and Discourse (1610–1641)

Case Study 3: The Inaugural Lit de Justice *of 1610*
On 15 May 1610 Louis XIII was inaugurated as king of France and demonstrated royal legislative authority even though legally a minor. The inaugural aspects of this *Lit de Justice* assembly introduced to the French constitution new tenets of rulership.[52] The ceremonial ritual stressed inauguration by contravening traditional royal ceremonials. Louis XIII (only eight years old) sat enthroned in the *Lit de Justice* assembly the morn-

ing after Henry IV's death, despite the fact that for at least 250 years French kings had not appeared in public until after the Royal Funeral ceremony of their predecessors (see figure 3.2).[53] The duke of Sully, former minister of Henry IV, commented on the impropriety of holding a *Lit de Justice* for the son prior to the Funeral ceremony of the father, and he attended the assembly only under duress.[54] The bishops (ecclesiastical peers) attending the session also complained by indulging in a short-lived refusal to recognize the assembly as a *Lit de Justice*,[55] an objection directed against the public inaugural of an unconsecrated and uncrowned monarch. Yet despite such disclaimers and a contest with Parlement over conference of the regency, there was harmonious agreement in the *Lit de Justice* assembly to acclaim the young Louis XIII as king on the spot, even lacking precedent for such action. Actively supporting the Inaugural *Lit de Justice*, the *parlementaires* accepted the convening order without deliberations, allowed flagrant deviations from protocol to supply grandeur for the event, insisted that four recalcitrant bishops recognize the session as a *Lit de Justice*, and evoked the historical notion of a medieval *Lit de Justice* to legitimize the undertaking.[56] In addition, the chancellor, first president, and *avocat* all advanced compatible legal-philosophical and historical arguments with dynastic themes particularly suitable for the acclamation of a minor king.

Chancellor Nicolas (II) Brulart de Sillery set the inaugural tone. He noted that the process of instant succession, father to son, had taken place, and he dubbed the *Lit de Justice* as the first official public act of the new king. To eradicate the legal problem of minority, he maintained that the active *will* (*volonté*) of Henry IV had the force of law beyond his death and identified the *Lit de Justice* as the inaugural agency that carried out that will by declaring the queen as regent.[57] The chancellor's argument ingeniously adapted medieval legal precepts to suit the moment. Doctrines of Roman law had claimed that the prince's active *voluntas* inherent in him as a *persona publica* had the power of law,[58] and jurists during previous centuries had agreed that written testaments did not regulate French royal succession because the crown devolved by legal-hereditary means through French Public Law.[59] But Chancellor Sillery's adaptation of these precepts to the cause of dynastic succession failed to preserve the jurists' emphasis on the legal aspects of succession and rooted the active royal will in the undying dynastic line rather than in the immortal royal *dignité*. It was directly to the living child-king Louis XIII enthroned in the *Lit de Justice* assembly that Sillery pointed when he spoke of continuity in the dynastic line, and the first president and *avocat* followed suit.

First President Achille (I) de Harlay employed biogenetic doctrines to

Fig. 3.2. Louis XIII: Inaugural *Lit de Justice* held in the Convent of the Augustinians, Paris, 1610. Bibliothèque Nationale, Paris.

explain the instant succession of a minor king. He signified the uniqueness, or sameness, of Henry IV and Louis XIII as partakers of royal
qualities necessary for kingship, and he described Louis XIII enthroned in
the *Lit de Justice* assembly as "the living image of the deceased" (*l'image vive
du défunt*). Presenting a powerful metaphorical vision of dynastic continuity, Harlay allowed that passing clouds might cast a shadow over the *Sun*
[= Henry IV] in one place, but nevertheless that *Sun* [= Louis XIII]
would shine again in another. The first president typed the *Lit de Justice* as
a ceremony that concomitantly witnessed the demise of Henry IV and the
accession of Louis XIII, serving admirably as an inaugural agency.[60] Harlay's message rested upon legal-philosophical doctrines of Aristotle and
Aquinas, Roman Law and Canon Law, which stressed the biogenetic
affinity of father and son, the oneness of the two in both species and
nature as king. Staples of dynastic legitimism in earlier times, these notions had become familiar in French circles by the fifteenth century, as
shown in Jean de Terre Rouge's explanation of the *unigenitus*, the oneness
of the predecessor and successor insofar as appropriation of the *dignité* is
concerned.[61] But Harlay's reformulation of these ideas obliterated the
legal stress on office in favor of a dynastic focus on blood lineage. It was
the very physical presence of the *rex juvenis* Louis XIII in the *Lit de Justice*
assembly that filled the royal *dignité* immediately by reason of dynastic
right and regardless of minority status.

The speech of the *avocat* Louis Servin completed this trilogy of dynastic themes. Picking up the president's argument, Servin pointed to the *Lit
de Justice* assembly, simultaneously funereal and celebrative, as a unique
French practice that commemorated the deceased Henry IV and acclaimed his first-born successor Louis XIII as king. He introduced a gene-
alogical tree for Louis XIII, which reached back to Louis IX. In the next
few weeks others emphasized that lineage: Queen Marie de Médicis replaced the portrait of Philip VI (a Valois) in the Louvre with that of Louis
IX (a Capetian progenitor of the Bourbons), and the royal party tried to
reschedule the Coronation to coincide with the *fête* of Louis IX.[62] Chancellor Sillery, President Harlay, and the *avocat* Servin artfully employed a
new mode of discourse to define French royal succession as a dynastic
process (based on blood lineage). At odds with the discourse of the 1560s
that defined succession as a legal procedure (characterized by assumption
of the *dignité*), this language shifted discussion of the French Law of Succession from legal to dynastic grounds and provided a rationale that legitimized the novel Inaugural *Lit de Justice* assembly in 1610.

Since Louis XIII's first *Lit de Justice* served as an official inaugural ceremony, it preempted the Royal Funeral and the Majority *Lit de Justice*, and it diluted the constitutional substance of the Coronation. Cast in this shadow, the Coronation held five months later on 17 October 1610 appeared somewhat anachronistic. The effort to salvage its constitutional import is particularly suggestive of the changing nature of kingship in the early seventeenth century. Nicolas Bergier, legist and director of the pre-Coronation *Entrée* to Reims, recorded in detail the elaboration of dynastic themes first observed in the *Lit de Justice* and then reemployed in the *Entrée*. He proffered a new interpretation of the Law of Succession that embraced both the Inaugural *Lit de Justice* and the Coronation ceremony.[63] Bergier's scheme posited two related phases in the ceremonial realization of royal succession: first, the *Lit de Justice* assembly in which the king is declared as king; and second, the Coronation in which that declaration is confirmed. In this scheme the Coronation maintained, theoretically at least, a constitutional function. Furthermore, the whole program devised for the pre-Coronation *Entrée* to Reims spelled out for viewers the new precepts of dynastic kingship already realized in the *Lit de Justice* assembly.

The crowds on hand for the festivities that day saw two related tableaus featuring lessons on dynastic succession. The first tableau recalled the *Lit de Justice* assembly of 15 May in Paris. It showed Louis XIII's entrance into the assembly, and the words *Rege designato* (He is designated king) were inscribed on the arch over the scene. The second tableau depicted Louis XIII's *Entrée* to Reims that same day just preceding his Coronation, and the words *Regno suscepto* (He receives the kingdom) were inscribed on the arch. According to Bergier, the first tableau reminded viewers that the young Louis XIII was designated king of France in the *Lit de Justice* immediately upon the death of his father, and the second tableau reminded them that the Coronation ceremony would confirm that designation by uniting king and royalty (*royauté*). Discussing the iconography of these tableaus, Bergier cautiously qualified the role of both succession ceremonies. The Inaugural *Lit de Justice* did not constitute the king but served as a "demonstrative ceremony" whereby the successor publicly "signifies his capability to succeed to the crown under the ancient laws and constitutions of the kingdom [*royaume*]." Likewise the Coronation did not provide the king of France with any new right because "birth makes him king."[64] To clarify these definitions Bergier drafted the marriage metaphor, which had originally signified the inalienability of the realm (see Case Study 1), into the service of dynastic succession. He stated that the Coronation served as "a kind of sacrament through which the king is made the *husband of the kingdom* [*royaume*], which he marries that day by the ring . . . placed on his finger as a sign of spiritual marriage."[65] For Bergier's scheme, this convoluted marriage metaphor, which substituted the *royaume* for the *chose publique* and never mentioned kingdom *qua* dowry, was extended to encompass the *Lit de Justice* and explained the dual ceremonial facets of succession. "By the first act [the Inaugural *Lit de Justice*] in which he [the successor king] is declared and designated king of France, *he betrothes royalty* which [Public] *Law and Nature* give him, and by the Coronation [the second act] he marries it."[66] Sixteenth-century juristic ideology held that the royal *dignité* devolved upon the hereditary successor by virtue of French Public Law and that the act achieved ceremonial realization in the traditional inaugural program (Royal Funeral, Coronation, and Majority *Lit de Justice*). But this redefinition of the system suggested that royalty was inherited through "[Public] Law and Nature," and that the act received ceremonial confirmation in the new two-stage inauguration (*Lit de Justice* and Coronation).

There is no doubt that Rémois and Parisian cohorts designed an ideological framework for the Coronation *Entrée* program which legitimized the *Lit de Justice* of 15 May as an inaugural ceremony and elucidated new precepts of dynastic succession.[67] A careful reading, furthermore, reveals that they formulated the new ideology by amending that of the 1550s and 1560s to suit the situation in 1610. From the text of Chancellor L'Hôpital's speech on the French Law of Succession given at the Majority *Lit de Justice* in 1563, Nicolas Bergier copied almost verbatim L'Hôpital's two precepts governing French succession, Seizure and Majority. When he explained the precept of Seizure, Bergier first repeated L'Hôpital's words exactly; then he added to the passage an interpolation that skewed the chancellor's original text beyond recognition. Bergier began with L'Hôpital's remarks:

our wise rulers ordained as in immutable law [*loy perpetuelle*] [the precept that] *the kingdom is never vacant* [*le royaume n'est jamais vacant*], because there is continuity from king to king so that *as soon as the king's eyes close* [*in death*] [= *mortuus aperit oculos viventis*] there is another king . . . without awaiting Coronation, unction, consecration, or any other ceremonies.[68]

But Bergier then characterized the successor as the one

who is always recognized as the most near and capable to succeed among males of the royal blood even if he is still in the womb and not yet born and named. . . . As a result there has arisen among us the proverb that *The king of France never dies* [*Le roi de France ne meurt jamais*] to which the emblem of our Louis XIII, *Occasum Gallia nescit* [France never knows the setting (sun)], refers.[69]

As pointed out earlier, Chancellor L'Hôpital characterized the first stage in the French Law of Succession, Seizure, as a procedure subject to French Public Law. He invented a French maxim, *Le royaume n'est jamais vacant*, to explain that legal precept of succession which was based on the continuity of royal office.[70] Conversely, Bergier submerged L'Hôpital's legal definition beneath a principle of dynastic right conferred by "Law and Nature" and enjoyed even by a successor "still in the womb and not yet born and named." He subtly equated the kingdom with royalty and employed Jean Bodin's odd proverb from the late sixteenth century, *Le roi ne meurt jamais*,[71] to define this new view of dynastic succession that was based on the immortality of the Bourbon dynasty. Finally, he deftly allied the older marriage metaphor to that dynastic axiom in a manner which transformed the ring-bestowing rubric of the Coronation from a ritual signifying the inalienability of the realm into one turning over the kingdom to the Bourbon dynasty.[72]

To complete the symbolism of dynastic succession evident in Louis XIII's Inaugural *Lit de Justice*, the *Entrée* program displayed a phoenix (bird of the sun). The second tableau portrayed a young phoenix being reborn from his own ashes and extending his wings to take first flight, and the words *Vivit morte refecta sua* (Death restores his life) were inscribed on the scene. In the same refrain Jacques Dorat presented Louis XIII with the keys to the city of Reims and a poem written for the occasion. Decorated with the sun emblem and the inscription *Occasum Gallia nescit*, the poem likened the symbolism of the instantly reborn phoenix to the meaning of the proverb *Le roi ne meurt jamais*.[73] Following the extraordinary Inaugural *Lit de Justice* assembly of 1610, Bergier took the phoenix metaphor out of its medieval context, allied it with the proverb *Le roi ne meurt jamais*, and thus put forth a new mode of discourse that moved beyond the medieval idea of dynastic continuity to characterize a new cult of Bourbon dynastic blood right. No wonder then that provocative phoenix imagery was associated for some time with Louis XIII.[74] Later the themes of phoenix and sun characterized the accession of Louis XIV,[75] but those themes were derived from the ideology of Bourbon dynastic kingship established at the accession of Louis XIII in 1610. Finally, the amended rendition of another succession ritual, the play upon the "Sleeping King" (related to the Coronation ceremony) also fit the circumstances. When used in 1561 to depict the young Charles IX as "sleeping," that ceremony probably referred specifically to his minority status. Yet when applied in 1610 to Louis XIII, the ritual suggested that the child king had been "sleeping" while Henry IV was alive but awakened to full rulership capacity immediately upon his father's death.[76] Consequently, the ritual of the Sleeping King also promoted the principles of dynastic kingship that had been promulgated in the Inaugural *Lit de Justice* at Paris and propagated for the public at large in the Coronation *Entrée* at Reims.

Following the Inaugural *Lit de Justice* assembly of 1610, the ideological framework that supported the French Law of Succession was revised, and the ceremonial program that implemented succession was revamped to support that revision. The earlier legal-hereditary notion of succession, which declared the royal office as separate from the incumbent and defined succession as a process regulated by French Public Law, gave way to the dynastic idea of the royal office, which conflated office and incumbent, wed the office to the Bourbon dynasty, and made succession a matter of dynastic blood right transferred seminally at conception. Moreover, a new mode of discourse accompanied this dynastic shift in constitutional ideology. Whereas the maxim *Le royaume n'est jamais vacant* characterized legal-hereditary succession in the sixteenth century, the maxim *Le roi ne meurt jamais* in league with phoenix and sun metaphors signaled dynastic succession (that is, corporeal succession within the Bourbon dynasty) in 1610. A perfect maxim for elucidating the theme of the Inaugural *Lit de Justice* (which implemented dynastic succession) and the Coronation (which confirmed it) in 1610, *Le roi ne meurt jamais* along with other dynastic motifs (sun imagery, phoenix lore, biogenetic likenesses, and the convoluted marriage metaphor) moved directly into public discourse as the harbinger of the new ideology of dynastic kingship based on a reinterpretation of French Public Law.

Case Study 4: Lit de Justice *assemblies from 1614 to 1641*

During the next few decades the elaborate ritual of Louis XIII's *Lits de Justice* was inflated (see figure 3.3) stressing two critical elements, dynastic right and legislative power.[77] On the dynastic side the ceremony elevated the king and Bourbon crown-worthy males. The Bourbon blood princes enjoyed precedence over other princes, dukes, and peers during the *Lit de Justice* of 1616 in Paris and that of 1620 in Rouen.[78] They took the title of *Monseigneur* in the latter assembly to distinguish themselves from the dukes called *Monsieur* and received ceremonial pillows matching those of the throne paraphernalia.[79] The princes remained seated with hats on while the king spoke in the assembly of 1620 at Bordeaux.[80] Most importantly, Bourbon blood princes constituted a special group for the purposes of consultation in the *Lit de Justice* of 1621.[81] Clearly the Bourbon princes

Fig. 3.3. Louis XIII: Majority *Lit de Justice* held in the Grand-chambre of the Parlement of Paris, 1614. Bibliothèque Nationale, Paris.

formed a separate and distinct order during the early seventeenth century.[82]

Besides elevating the status of Bourbon crown heirs, Louis XIII accorded special status in the *Lit de Justice* to selected royal officers. The most notable case concerned Cardinal Richelieu, who obtained peer rank in 1627 and sat in that capacity in *Lit de Justice* assemblies from 1629, the same year the presidents of Parlement lost first place (granted some decades before) in the order of consultation.[83] The masters of ceremonies also benefited from special privilege. François Pot de Rhodes removed his sword before entering the Grand-chambre with a summons for a *Lit de Justice* in 1616, but Nicolas Saintot entered freely with a sword and a baton of authority in 1635.[84] The seals-keeper (acting chancellor) exacted deference from the presidents of Parlement in the *Lit de Justice* of 1632, and the resulting conflict caused behavior exceedingly bizarre for a public forum.[85] Finally, an astounding reversal of protocol took place at the *Lit de Justice* of 1632. When Charles de L'Aubespine (marquis of Châteauneuf), seals-keeper, approached Louis XIII to request the order for consultation, the Bourbon princes (Condé and Soissons to the king's left) and the cardinals (Richelieu and La Valette to his left) swiftly joined the king *under the canopy* and presented advice directly as a separate order. The presidents objected vociferously, but the seals-keeper retorted that the king regulated ceremony at will. First President Gui-Michel Le Jay granted that there was nothing left to say, and the presidents refused to opine in that assembly.[86] This extraordinary format for consultation allied Bourbon princes and selected royal advisers (a Royal Council) directly with Louis XIII under the thronal canopy and left Parlement to give advice later indirectly through a royal officer. Moreover, the format was employed in every *Lit de Justice* assembly held during the rest of the reign in 1633, 1634, 1635, and 1641,[87] altering the consultation process significantly. In effect this ritual defined the roles of king and Parlement in governance, giving the Bourbon princes and chosen advisers a deliberative voice (as a Council) in the *Lit de Justice* and restricting Parlement to a consultative voice. During the reign of Louis XIII, therefore, the expanded ritual of the *Lit de Justice* revised constitutional ideology and institutionalized new precepts of governance.

The revision is apparent in the treatises of seventeenth-century historians who adapted the juristic mode of discourse on Public Law (developed by Du Tillet, L'Hôpital, and others) to suit the new context. From Pierre Dupuy's rationale one can see at first hand the same shift from juristic to dynastic ideology that accompanied the ritual of the *Lit de Justice* (see table 3.1, column O). Dupuy no longer treated the king's relation to the kingdom (*royaume*, or *chose publique*) primarily in terms of what was constitutional (that is, legal). Rather, he spoke of the king's association with royalty (*royauté*, or dynasty) mainly in terms of what was constitutional (that is, "fundamental" and natural).[88] In sixteenth-century discourse the Public Law of the kingdom (*Loy de France, Loy perpetuelle*) was on the docket; in seventeenth-century discourse the Fundamental Law (*Loy fondamentale*) of royalty filled that bill.

A reading of the *Lit de Justice* assembly from fictions and facts, ritual and discourse, between 1527 and 1641 suggests that constitutional ideologies—juristic and dynastic—were articulated in that forum. The archival research of historians produced a fiction, then a legend, about the pristine medieval origins of the *Lit de Justice* assembly held in the Grand-chambre of the Parlement of Paris. In turn, the provocative legend underwrote numerous *Lits de Justice* in the seventeenth century. The ceremonial rituals performed in these sessions, controlled by the crown, manipulated by Parlement, framed and reframed constitutional precepts. The crown employed ritual to vest sovereign authority in the monarch, separate legislative (royal) and judicial (parlementary) functions, and provide a consultative, not deliberative, body of orders, or Estates, which included the Parlement of Paris. Parlement bent ritual to vest sovereign authority in the monarch but insinuate colegislative capacity; assume superiority (as the seat of the *Lit de Justice*) over rival councils and courts, and confirm its corporate continuity, as well as the hereditary tenure of individual office-holders. Overshadowing all contests, however, was the formidable stature of the *Lit de Justice* and the ritual bond that it forged between crown and Parlement: hence, kings promoted the grandeur of the assembly in the Grand-chambre, and the *parlementaires* traded legislative prerogative to maintain the prestigious forum in their quarters.

The discourses associated with such sessions revealed and shaped constitutional ideologies. In the sixteenth century the juristic maxim described a monarchy in which the royal *dignité* was conferred upon kings by the Public Law of the kindgom, or *chose publique*. In the early seventeenth century the dynastic maxim, *The king never dies*, described a monarchy in which royalty was conferred upon a series of corporeal incumbents by dynastic right and Fundamental Law.

These discourses also shaped constitutional ideologies by countenancing different modes of perception. The sixteenth-century historical method for comprehending the French past, nominalist and philological in conception, offered a new means for apprehending reality. Conversely, the later appeal to nature and tradition in time immemorial, more idealist and rhetorical in orientation, became the guide to the French past and set a different standard for the apprehension of truth. All the while, the fortunes of the *Lit de Justice* assembly flourished on the vine of history, withered at the root of tradition. In the end, the long reign of Louis XIV witnessed another shift of constitutional ideology from dynastic to absolutist kingship;[89] and the Sun King abandoned both the *lit de justice* (throne paraphernalia) and the *Lit de Justice* (assembly) for the gilded splendor of Versailles, which epitomized absolutism as a system of cultural hegemony.

Notes

Abbreviations

A. N.   Archives Nationales
B. N.   Bibliothèque Nationale
B. Maz.   Bibliothèque Mazarine
B. V. P.   Bibliothèque de la Ville de Paris
B. I. F.   Bibliothèque de l'Institut de France

This article is a revised version of a paper presented at the symposium on "Symbolism, Ritual, and Political Power," Shelby Cullom Davis Center for Historical Studies, Princeton University, 14 March 1981. Excerpts of this article, and all of table 3.1, were printed in Sarah Hanley, *The* Lit de Justice *of the Kings of France: Constitutional Ideology in Legend, Ritual, and Discourse.* Copyright © 1983 by Princeton University Press. Reprinted by permission of Princeton University Press.

1. See the dictionaries of institutions: Adolph Chéruel, *Dictionnaire historique des institutions, moeurs et coûtumes de la France* (Paris, 1974), 2:670–73; Marcel Marion, *Dictionnaire des institutions de la France aux XVIIe et XVIIIe siècles* (Paris, 1923), pp. 336–38; Gaston Zeller, *Les institutions de la France au XVIe siècle* (Paris, 1948), pp. 156–60; and Roger Doucet, *Les institutions de la France au XVIe siècle* (Paris, 1948), 1:186. The same view appears in monographs: Charles Desmaze, *Le Parlement de Paris* (Paris, 1853); J. J. M. Blondel, *Mémoires du Parlement de Paris* (Paris, 1856 [?]), quoting passages verbatim from Louis-Adrien Le Paige (see n. 2); Ernest D. Glasson, *Le Parlement de Paris, son rôle politique depuis le règne de Charles VII jusqu'à la révolution*, vols. 1, 2 (Paris, 1901); Edouard Maugis, *Histoire du Parlement de Paris*, vols. 1–3 (Paris, 1913–16); J. H. Shennan, *The Parlement of Paris* (Ithaca, 1968), following Glasson and Maugis.

2. Louis-Adrien Le Paige, *Réflexions d'un citoyen sur les Lits de Justice par L-A Le Paige* (n.p., n.d. [c. 1787]), pp. 5–12, first published as *Lettre sur les Lits de Justice, 18 Août 1756* (n.p., n.d.) [brackets added].

3. Scholars root the origins of the assembly in medieval times, usually the fourteenth century. For some examples (in addition to n. 1), see Ennemond Fayard, *Aperçu historique sur le Parlement de Paris* (Paris, 1876–78); Felix Aubert, *Le Parlement de Paris de Philippe le Bel à Charles VII, 1314–1422* (Paris, 1886), esp. pp. 196–97 citing the Royal *Séance* of Charles V in 1369 as the first *Lit de Justice*. Particularly influential in propagating the fiction of a medieval *Lit de Justice* in modern times is Maugis, *Histoire du Parlement*, 1:22, 120, 524, and 628. Other works include Roger Doucet, *Etude sur le gouvernement de François Ier dans ses rapports avec le Parlement de Paris* (Paris, 1921–26), and Robert J. Knecht, *Francis I and Absolute Monarchy* (London Historical Society, No. 72, 1969), and *Francis I* (Cambridge, 1982).

4. For a full study of the *Lit de Justice*, see Sarah Hanley, *The* Lit de Justice *of the Kings of France: Constitutional Ideology in Legend, Ritual, and Discourse* (Princeton, 1983).

5. Ibid., gives the complete table 3.1 (to 1713) with a discussion of the sources.

6. Consult Hanley, "The *Lit de Justice* and the Fundamental Law," *The Sixteenth Century Journal*, vol. 7, no. 1 (Apr. 1976): 3–14; and "L'Idéologie constitutionelle en France: Le Lit de Justice," *Annales: Economies, Sociétés, Civilisations*, no. 1 (Jan.-Feb. 1982): 32–63.

7. Zeller, *Institutions de la France*, p. 100.

8. In addition to n. 6 above, consult Ralph E. Giesey, *The Royal Funeral Ceremony in Renaissance France* (Geneva, 1960), and "The Presidents of Parlement at the Royal Funeral," *The Sixteenth Century Journal*, vol. 7, no. 1 (Apr. 1976): 25–34; Richard A. Jackson, *Vive le Roi! A History of the French Coronation from Charles V to Charles X* (Chapel Hill, 1984); and "The Sleeping King," *Bibliothèque d'Humanisme et Renaissance*, 31 (Sept. 1969): 527–51; Lawrence M. Bryant, *The French Royal Entry Ceremony: Politics, Society, and Art in Renaissance Paris* (Ann Arbor, University Microfilms, 1978), and "*Parlementaire* Political Theory in the Parisian Royal Entry Ceremony," *The Sixteenth Century Journal*, vol. 7, no. 1 (Apr. 1976): 15–24.

9. Historians of cultural systems should note the importance of symbolism in ritualized forms of authority; see Clifford Geertz, "Thick Description: Toward an Interpretive Theory of Culture," and "Ideology as a Cultural System," in *The Interpretation of Cultures* (New York, 1973), pp. 3–30 and 193–233; Geertz, *Negara: The Theatre State in Nineteenth-Century Bali* (Princeton, 1980); and Geertz, *Local Knowledge: Further Essays in Interpretive Anthropology* (New York, 1983).

10. For the critical alliance of contextual and lexical elements, consult J. G. A. Pocock, "Languages and Their Implications: The Transformation of the Study of Political Thought," in *Politics, Language and Time* (New York, 1973), pp. 3–41; *The Machiavellian Moment: Florentine Political Thought and the Atlantic*

Republican Tradition (Princeton, 1975). For discussion of varying modes of discourse and political thought as a history of ideologies, see Quentin Skinner, "Conventions and the Understanding of Speech Acts," *The Philosophical Quarterly*, 20 (1970): 118–38, and *The Foundations of Modern Political Thought*, vols. 1, 2 (Cambridge, 1978).

11. Organized into two conceptual units, this essay allows readers to approach the *Lit de Justice* through the historical overview or through the ceremony itself. One unit, parts one (A) and two (A), offers a diachronic view, tracing the historical and legendary life of the *Lit de Justice* from 1527 to 1641; the other, parts one (B) and two (B), offers a synchronic view, recounting individual *Lit de Justice* assemblies in 1537, 1563, 1610, and (summary) 1614–1641.

12. For the first two assemblies in 1527, see Hanley, *The* Lit de Justice *of the Kings of France*, chap. 2; for the third of 1537, see Case Study 1 below and ibid., chap. 3.

13. Jean du Tillet, *Recueil des roys de France, leurs couronne et maison* (Paris, 1607), is the most complete edition. It was published posthumously as *Les Mémoires et les recherches* (1577, 1578), then in the expanded version cited above (1580, 1586, 1587, 1588, 1602, 1607, 1618). The edition of 1607 contains three different sections separately paginated. Two are cited here as follows: (1) *Recueil des roys de France, leurs couronne et maison* (same title as the whole work), pp. 1–456, hereafter referred to as *Recueil des roys;* and (2) *Recueil des rangs des grands de France*, pp. 1–130, hereafter referred to as *Recueil des grands* (consult table 3.1, column D). For the importance of this treatise in French historiography, see Donald R. Kelley, *Foundations of Modern Historical Scholarship* (New York, 1970), pp. 215–38, and André Lemaire, *Les Lois fondamentales de la monarchie française* (Paris, 1907), pp. 82–91. The identification of Du Tillet as an "antiquarian" refers to the scholarly method followed by early modern historians, a compilation of sources with little analysis.

14. Du Tillet, *Recueil des roys de France* (preface), fols. A ii^v–a iii^r, with an example of faulty chronicle lore, *Recueil des roys*, p. 365.

15. For a reconstruction of that typology, see Hanley, *The* Lit de Justice *of the Kings of France*, table 2.

16. For the historical and philological explanation, see ibid., chap. 1. The parlementary clerks Jean Willequin and Nicolas de Baye recorded the events of 1387, 1392, 1396, 1406, and two of 1413, using the phrase *lit de justice* in a manner which misled Du Tillet (consult table 3.1, columns B and D). Discovery of the fourteenth-century ushers' accounts, A. N. KK 336, revealed the proper provenance of that phrase.

17. A. N. X1a 1565, fols. 205^r–207^r (2 July 1549).

18. A. N. X1a 1565, fols. 207^v–210^r (2 July 1549).

19. Three royal commissions allowed the clerk access to archives and repositories normally closed: the first from Francis I, A. N. X1a 1548, fol. 271^v (25 February 1541); the second from Henry II, Théodore and Denys Godefroy, *Le Cérémonial françois* (Paris, 1649), vol. 1, fol. E iv^r (delivered 22 December

1548); and the third from Francis II, B. N. ms. fr. n. a. 20256, fol. 55ᵛ (mistakenly dated 12 May 1562, actually issued in 1559 or 1560).

20. See the documents gathered by Pierre Dupuy, *Traité de la majorité de nos rois et des régences du royaume* (Paris, 1655), pp. 407–9 [Registers of Parlement].

21. See Hanley, *The* Lit de Justice *of the Kings of France*, chap. 8, for this contest.

22. Historians have accused the Valois, particularly Henry III, of using the *Lit de Justice* as an absolutist weapon to force registration of financial edicts in Parlement; see, for example, William F. Church, *Constitutional Thought in Sixteenth Century France* (New York, 1969), pp. 150–55; and Maugis, *Histoire du Parlement*, 1:602–31. Yet the fact is that neither Henry II nor Henry III ever convoked a *Lit de Justice*, although they made use of the Royal *Séance* in that manner; see Hanley, *The* Lit de Justice *of the Kings of France*, chap. 9.

23. A. N. X1a 1640, fols. 451ᵛ–452ʳ (18 September 1573) where a decision regarding the Law of Succession allowed the future Henry III to accept the Polish throne without forfeiting succession to the crown of France.

24. A. N. X1a 1749, fols. 470ᵛ–471ᵛ (21 May 1597), where Henry IV attempted quite unsuccessfully to draft the *Lit de Justice* as a vehicle for forced registration of edicts.

25. The original record made by Du Tillet in the civil registers of Parlement disappeared in the mid-sixteenth century. An abbreviated version survives in Du Tillet, *Recueil des grands*, pp. 93–95 (15 January 1537), and a fuller version in papers of Barnabé Brisson (*avocat* in 1575, president of Parlement in 1580), reprinted in Godefroy, *Cérémonial françois*, 2:501–3 [Brisson]. Finally, there is another account written by a pleadings clerk, Pierre Le Maistre, now in the records of the Chambre des Comptes, A. N. P 2306, fols. 353ʳ–382ᵛ (15 January 1537), extracts in Godefroy, *Cérémonial françois*, 2:503–17 [Le Maistre].

26. Ibid.

27. Ibid.

28. Ibid.

29. For Cappel's speech, A. N. P 2306, fols. 356ᵛ–379ᵛ [Le Maistre]; and in Godefroy, *Cérémonial françois*, 2:505–11 [Le Maistre].

30. Ibid. [italics and brackets added].

31. De Selve's speech provides a very early example of the marriage metaphor in a constitutional nexus; for other examples, see Hanley, *The* Lit de Justice *of the Kings of France*, chaps. 2 and 3.

32. Cappel's notion that the Coronation oath legalized the fictive marriage between king and kingdom received implicit expression in Henry II's Coronation order (1547) and explicit statement in Henry IV's rubrics (1597); see Ernst H. Kantorowicz, *The King's Two Bodies: A Study in Medieval Political Theology* (Princeton, 1957), pp. 221–22.

33. Ibid.

34. Dupuy, *Traité de la majorité*, pp. 356–97, cites "*L'Histoire de Normandie*" (= [Jean Nagerel], *Description du pays et duché de Normandie . . . Extraict de sa*

cronique de Normandie . . . , Rouen, 1580). The anonymous engraving (figure 3.1) is a valuable early example of the king enthroned in a *Lit de Justice* assembly, but it contains errors. For instance, the queen sits at the left, rather than right, of Charles IX; and the fifteenth-century painting, *Le retable du Parlement*, which was hung in the Grand-chambre of the Palais de Justice following Louis XII's renovation at the turn of the sixteenth century, is shown here in the Parlement of Rouen. For details on the iconography of *Lit de Justice* assemblies in this and other figures, see Hanley, *The* Lit de Justice *of the Kings of France*, figs. 1–16.

35. Michel de L'Hôpital, *Oeuvres complètes de Michel de L'Hospital, Chancelier de France* (Paris, 1824–25), 2:9–18.

36. Ibid., 2:17–18.

37. Dupuy, *Traité de la majorité*, pp. 362–65 [Cron. de Norm.]. [Italics and brackets added.]

38. The idea of "simple succession," or legal-hereditary succession, was discussed by Jean de Terre Rouge, *Contra rebelles suorum regnum* (Lyons, 1526) in the fifteenth century; see Giesey, *The Juristic Basis of Dynastic Right to the French Throne*, Transactions of the American Philosophical Society, 51:5 (Philadelphia, 1951), pp. 12–17.

39. The jurist Baldus de Ubaldis (c. 1327–1400) quoted the proverb *Mortuus aperit oculos viventis* to show that one born unfree could become a freedman on the death of his master (*Codex* 7, 15, 3, n. 2, fol. 12). In the early sixteenth century the French jurist André Tiraqueau (d. 1558) quoted that proverb to explain the famous maxim of French private law on inheritance, *Le mort saisit le vif*, calling for immediate seizure, or possession, of property by the rightful heir, but Tiraqueau denied that the concept could apply to the assumption of a public office (as the crown); (Tiraquella, *De jure primogenitorum*, q. 40, n. 31 [*Tractatus varii*, Frankfurt, 1574, 4:70, and 5:73]). On the continuity of office derived from *Dignitas non moritur*, consult Kantorowicz, *King's Two Bodies*, pp. 393–94, nn. 267, 268.

40. Herbert H. Rowen, *The King's State: Proprietary Dynasticism in Early Modern France* (New Brunswick, 1980), chap. 2.

41. Dupuy, *Traité de la majorité*, pp. 362–65 [Cron. de Norm.]. L'Hôpital recounted the historical thesis on the Law of Majority spelled out in Du Tillet's tracts, *Pour la majorité du roy très chrestien contre les escrits des rebelles* (Paris, 1560), and *Pour l'entière majorité du roy tres chrestien contre le légitime conseil malicieusement inventé par les rebelles* (Paris, 1560). [Bracketed dates added.]

42. Dupuy, *Traité de la majorité*, pp. 362–65 [Cron. de Norm.].

43. The rules of the funeral ritual required that red-robed presidents of Parlement surround the royal effigy, symbolizing the perpetuity of the royal *dignité* and the continuity of royal justice, while the new king refrained from public appearance until the removal of that symbolic effigy following the burial of his predecessor at Saint Denis; consult Giesey, *Royal Funeral Ceremony*, pp. 122–23, 188–91, and fig. 14.

104 Sarah Hanley

44. Majority *Lit de Justice* assemblies were held also for Louis XIV in 1643 and Louis XV in 1723; see Hanley, *The* Lit de Justice *of the Kings of France,* chap. 8.
45. See Case Study 3.
46. Duchesne, *Les antiquitez et recherches . . . des roys de France* and *Les antiquitez et recherches . . . des huict Parlemens* (Paris, 1609), followed Du Tillet's division of royal and parlementary topics; d'Orléans, *Les ouvertures des Parlements faictes par les roys de France, tenant leur lict de justice* (Lyon, 1620), cited Du Tillet; and Arnauld, *La justice aux pieds du roy pour les Parlemens de France* (n.p., 1608), built the legend.
47. Consult table 3.1 for the important works that underwrote the legend.
48. B. N. ms. fr. 18411, fols. 146^r–154^r. At the same time, trials of peers were removed from the assembly and treated in separate ad hoc sessions; see Hanley, *The* Lit de Justice *of the Kings of France,* chap. 11.
49. Ibid.
50. Ibid., chap. 12.
51. Ibid., chap. 13. In the reign of Louis XIV, Parlement traded legislative prerogative to maintain the Inaugural *Lit de Justice* of 1643 in the Grand-chambre. Moreover, even when that king, still a minor, convoked three more *Lits de Justice* between Inaugural and Majority assemblies in 1645 and 1648 (an unprecedented action that signaled the shift from dynastic to absolutist kingship), the *parlementaires'* angry denunciations were not against the *Lit de Justice* itself but were against departures from tradition told as by them through the legend of the *Lit de Justice.*
52. A. N. X1a 1829, fols. 226^v–233^v (15 May 1610), contained in Dupuy, *Traité de la majorité,* pp. 460–74.
53. The anonymous drawing (fig. 3.2) provides a reasonably accurate scene; see Hanley, *The* Lit de Justice *of the Kings of France,* chap. 10, for details. Two more Inaugural *Lits de Justice* were held for Louis XIV in 1643 and Louis XV in 1715; ibid., chaps. 13, 14.
54. Maximilien de Béthune, Duc de Sully, *Mémoires du Sully, principal ministre de Henri-le-Grand* (new ed., Paris, 1814), 5:xxviii, 139–40.
55. Dupuy, *Traité de la majorité,* pp. 460–74 [Reg. Parl.].
56. Ibid.
57. Ibid.
58. See Kantorowicz, *King's Two Bodies,* pp. 93–97 and 418–19, n. 349, on the part played by the concept of a public *voluntas* in the movement from liturgical to law-centered kingship.
59. See the work of Jean de Terre Rouge (n. 38 above).
60. Dupuy, *Traité de la majorité,* pp. 460–74 [Reg. Parl.].
61. On biogenetic likenesses used to substantiate the undying nature of the *dignité* through dynastic continuity earlier, see Kantorowicz, *King's Two Bodies,* pp. 328–36, 391–401.
62. Dupuy, *Traité de la majorité,* pp. 460–74 [Reg. Parl.]; consult Godefroy, *Céré-*

monial françois, 2:273, for the portrait replacement; see n. 67 below for the Coronation schedule.

63. Nicolas Bergier [and P. de La Salle], *Le bouquet royal, ou le parterre des riches inventions qui ont servy à l'Entrée du roy Louis le Juste en sa ville de Reims* (Reims, 1637). Bergier composed the narration of the pre-Coronation *Entrée* (fols. 1ʳ–71ᵛ), La Salle the Coronation (fols. 72ʳ–88ᵛ), and Jacques Dorat the poems (fols. 89ʳ–100ᵛ). La Salle published the treatise after Bergier's death.

64. Ibid., fols. 53ᵛ–57ʳ.

65. Ibid. [italics added].

66. Ibid. [bracketed words added].

67. The planning began just eleven days after the *Lit de Justice* when royal letters from Paris arrived at Reims on 26 May 1610. After a series of delays, the Coronation was scheduled for 17 October; for details see Hanley, *The* Lit de Justice *of the Kings of France*, chap. 11.

68. Bergier, *Bouquet royal*, fols. 54ᵛ–55ᵛ. [Italics and bracketed words added.]

69. Ibid.

70. See Case Study 2, n. 37, for L'Hôpital's rendition.

71. It has been suggested that the adage of Jean Bodin, *Le roi ne meurt jamais*, was commonly used in the sixteenth century although not published until 1576; Giesey, *Royal Funeral Ceremony*, pp. 177–83, and Kantorowicz, *King's Two Bodies*, pp. 409–10. But that adage was peculiar to Bodin's treatise and not part of the constitutional discourse of the 1560s. L'Hôpital's expression *Le royaume n'est jamais vacant* supplied the first French analogue for *Le mort saisit le vif*, capturing much more precisely the sense of the progenitor, *Dignitas non moritur*, than did Bodin's formulation which lent itself to dynastic theorizing; Hanley, *The* Lit de Justice *of the Kings of France*, chap. 7.

72. See Case Study 1.

73. Bergier, *Bouquet royal*, fol. 58ʳ; and the poem, ibid., fol. 89ᵛ: "Le lis françois d'immortelle semence / Ne recognoit l'accident du cercueil . . . / Voulant qu'ainsi que l'oiseau du soleil [phoenix], / La mort de l'une donne à l'autre naissance . . . / Puis que *les rois en la France ne* meurent." [Italics and bracketed words added.]

74. For these allusions, see Hanley, *The* Lit de Justice *of the Kings of France*, chap. 11 and fig. 9.

75. The examples for Louis XIV are discussed in Giesey, *Royal Funeral Ceremony*, pp. 191–92, fig. 18; and Kantorowicz, *King's Two Bodies*, pp. 413–14, fig. 24.

76. For this ritual, see Jackson, "Sleeping King," *Bibliothèque d'Humanisme et Renaissance*, 31:527–51.

77. For figure 3.3, B. N., Départment des Estampes. On the Majority of 1614, see Hanley, *The* Lit de Justice *of the Kings of France*, chap. 7.

78. A. N. X1a 1878, fols. 149ʳ–356ʳ (7 September 1616); and Godefroy, *Cérémonial françois*, 2:609–13 (11 July 1620).

79. Godefroy, *Cérémonial françois*, 2:609–13 (11 July 1620).

80. Ibid., 2:613–18 [Pontac, clerk of court] (28 September 1620).

81. A. N. X1a 1918, fols. 8ᵛ–15ʳ (3 April 1621).
82. B. Maz. 2745, fol. 164ᵛ, a comment made later by master of ceremonies, Michel Ancel Desgranges.
83. A. N. X1a 2009, fols. 199ᵛ–204ᵛ (15 January 1629).
84. A. N. X1a 1878, fols. 145ᵛ–149ʳ (6 September 1616) for Rhodes; and Godefroy, *Cérémonial françois*, 2:632 [Saintot] (19 December 1635), for Saintot.
85. Hanley, *The* Lit de Justice *of the Kings of France*, chap. 12, recounts the incidents.
86. A. N. X1a 2055, fols 385ʳ–392ᵛ (12 August 1632).
87. A. N. X1a 2064, fols. 161ʳ–168ʳ (12 April 1633); A. N. X1a 2074, fols. 301ʳ–311ʳ (18 January 1634); Godefroy, *Cérémonial françois*, 2:632–34 [Saintot] (20 December 1635); and A. N. X1a 8387 [unnumbered folios] (21 February 1641). In working notes Godefroy remarked on this innovative procedure; B. I. F., Collection Godefroy 395.
88. Dupuy, *Traité de la majorité*, pp. 1–13. The linguistic shift is reflected also in the comments of Charles Loyseau and Antoine Loisel; see Hanley, *The* Lit de Justice *of the Kings of France*, chaps. 7, 11.
89. See ibid.

PART THREE

The Limits of Symbolic Power: Spain, c. 1157–1643

4

TEOFILO F. RUIZ

Unsacred Monarchy: The Kings of Castile in the Late Middle Ages

In the year of Our Lord 1332, Alfonso XI (1312–50), by the grace of God king of Castile, León, Galicia, Seville, Córdoba, Murcia, Jaén, the Algarve, and lord of Molina, came to the monastery of Las Huelgas in Burgos to be anointed with holy oil and crowned. While preparations for the ceremonies were completed, the king traveled along the pilgrimage road to Santiago de Compostela. There, on the main altar of the cathedral, he was knighted by the mechanical arm of a statue of St. James, the Apostle and Patron of Spain. A few days afterward upon his return to Burgos, Alfonso XI was anointed on the right shoulder. Once the ritual unction had concluded, the king ascended alone to the altar, took the royal diadem and placed it on his head.[1]

The chronicler's description of these events and of the festivities that followed remind us of similar accounts in other parts of the medieval West. The act of self-coronation and the manner in which Alfonso XI was knighted and anointed might seem a bit peculiar to those acquainted with the rituals of monarchy in other parts of Europe,[2] but the symbols and rites associated with royal authority and sacrality—crown, holy oil, and knighting—were common in other medieval kingdoms. Yet, what makes the anointing and crowning of Alfonso XI so interesting—and a point of departure for a discussion of medieval royal rituals in Castile—was less its familiarity than its peculiar place in Castilian history.[3] For almost two centuries before 1332 no Castilian king had been anointed, and none was anointed afterward. Moreover, the surviving documentary evidence records only one formal crowning of a Castilian king after Alfonso VII's death in 1157, and only another king crowned himself. After Alfonso XI's self-coronation we know of only two more kings who followed his example. In short, from 1135 on, the Castilian and Spanish rulers consciously rejected the traditional emblems of power and authority in use elsewhere in the medieval West and in the early modern period.[4] The Castilian kings did not consider their office sacred, even though they believed that as kings their responsibilities were of the highest order and were entrusted to them by God. Never did the kings of Castile and later of Spain claim seriously to have the power to heal the sick. Nor did their birth, crowning, dying, and burial enjoy any of the elaborate rituals associated with royalty in England and France. The kings of Castile in the late Middle Ages had their rituals and symbols of authority to mark their ascension to the throne and their exercise of political rule, but these differed from those of England, France, and other western medieval kingdoms. The question is why?

In the following pages I would like to describe the symbols of kingship and power that the kings of Castile in fact employed, and to suggest why the evolution of ceremonial in Castile deviated from the experiences of England, France, and, to a lesser extent, the Holy Roman Empire. To do so, we must follow a circuitous road. We begin by examining the Visigothic-Asturian precedents, and then proceed to describe the evolution of rituals after 1135 within the context of Castilian political and institutional history. We should then show how the Castilian kings sought to legitimize their rule, what gave them the right to be kings, and what symbols of authority they chose as representative of their power.[5] The first two tasks are not difficult, inasmuch as it is a story which can be read in the chronicles, and which has already been described, although not in any systematic fashion, by previous historians.[6] Finally, I wish to explain why Castile and thus Spain evolved as it did—and to suggest how events in the medieval period not only explain the peculiarities of Castile, but may help us understand modern Spanish politics.

Visigothic, Asturian, and Navarrese Precedents

By ceasing to be anointed or, in most instances, even crowned, the kings of Castile and León broke with what they believed, and later medieval chronicles maintained, had been a rich and long tradition.[7] For centuries before 1135, most of the Visigothic kings of Spain and, after the mid-eighth century, most of the rulers of Asturias and León were anointed and crowned. Following an ancient Germanic tradition, the Visigothic kings of Toulouse and, later, those of Toledo were also raised upon the shield. They wore no distinctive clothing; nor did they have special emblems of their authority apart from the sword and banner. These early Visigothic kings were elected and acclaimed by the assembly of all free men, although they were generally selected from the members of the ancient family of the Balthi. After Leovigild (568–86) subdued most of the peninsula, he adopted the ceremonial and symbols of the Byzantine court. From his reign on, the Visigothic kings adopted the title Flavius, and the throne, crown, scepter, and purple mantle, the regal symbols of the Late Empire.[8] As the rulers of Visigothic Spain sought to consolidate their rule and turn the realm into their hereditary possession, they were hindered in their efforts by their heretical beliefs and the influence of the Catholic Church. After the conversion of Recared (587), however, the Church was willing to cooperate with the monarchy. The sacral elements of unction, ecclesiastical coronation, and the royal oath to the people and popular oath to the king were added to the imperial symbols introduced by Leovigild half a century before.[9]

Unlike in Frankland, where the hereditary principle became established fairly early and where the monarchs established a theocratic kingship,[10] the sacral elements of Visigothic kingship and the hereditary principle were always tempered by assassination, the survival into post-Visigothic time of the elective principle, and by the law. Dynastic violence and regicide were common among the Visigoths, and the ordinances of the Visigothic church councils, as well as St. Isidore, had stated that any free nobleman of Gothic blood and good character could be king.[11] Theoretically, kingship was the birthright of any Goth and a well-earned reward for deeds of arms. Moreover, a king who acted unjustly and selfishly was considered a tyrant and hence undeserving of royal power.[12] The level of dynastic violence was so high that more than five centuries later the *Primera crónica general* invoked the Visigothic example to explain the fratricidal battles of the Castilian and Leonese kings.[13]

Although the Visigothic church councils, St. Isidore, and other Church fathers supported the theory that all power, including political power, came from God and, although the Visigothic kings attempted to use these sacral trappings to strengthen the hereditary principle, both custom and law restricted the dynastic and theocratic pretensions of the Spanish rulers in the early medieval period. The canons of the Church councils, the *Lex visigothorum*, also stated the duties, conditions, and limitations placed upon the monarch.[14] Thus the idea that kings should be elected survived into the post-Visigothic period always as a dangerous alternative to political stability and dynastic continuity.

When Visigothic Spain fell to the Muslim invaders in 711, the northern mountain region of Asturias and Cantabria remained free from Muslim domination. Slowly, through the eighth, ninth, and tenth centuries, the Christians moved out of these well-protected enclaves into the plain. Most Spanish historians have maintained that the kings of Asturias, León, and Galicia had adopted, as early as the reign of Alfonso II (791–842), the Visigothic rituals of royal anointment and crowning. These sacral ceremonies were accompanied by the acclamation or election of the king by the magnates and the clergy and the elevation or raising of the king if not on a shield, then on a chair. The chronicles and iconography of a later period point to the use of ceremonies and liturgical tokens that emphasized the sacred character of the king and that were similar to the ceremonies of royal ordination prevalent in the kingdoms of northern Europe. Recently, however, Peter A. Linehan has argued for the absence of anointing and sacral ceremonial in the Asturian period. Later chronicles and some present-day historians, above all Don Claudio Sánchez Albornoz, had either fabricated or been misled into believing in the continuity of sacred kingship from Visigothic Spain to the Asturian and Leonese period. I find Linehan's arguments most convincing, although there remain unanswerable questions. What were the aims of late twelfth- and thirteenth-century chroniclers in inventing such ceremonies? Did they believe that they had truly taken place?[15] Whether or not the Asturian kings were ritually anointed, contemporary and later chronicles emphasized the role of the Asturian kings and later the Castilian monarchs as military leaders or, to use a word employed often by the late chroniclers—and put to such forbidding use by Franco—*caudillos*. Indeed, the real test and glory of a king resided in his prowess as a fighter and in his ability to retain and to augment the territory of the kingdom.[16] Within this context one must note that although medieval kings in northern Europe also stressed their roles as military leaders, they often chose to emphasize their sacred functions over the martial aspects of their rule. In the north, unlike Castile or other Iberian kingdoms, there was no sustained struggle (seven centuries) against a well-defined enemy.

In Asturias, León, and later in Castile the position and authority of the king was also qualitatively different from that of rulers north of the Pyrenees. Inasmuch as feudal and vassalic ties may never have developed to the extent that they did in France, England, and Germany, political authority was not as extensively fragmented. Moreover, a combination of factors—the Muslim example, the revival of Visigothic ideology, a reaction to Carolingian influence—led the kings of Asturias and León to lay claim to the imperial dignity and, with the title, exemption from the political relationships that existed in the rest of the western medieval world. The Asturian and Leonese kings and their successors, the kings of Castile, thought themselves exempt from imperial and papal authority in political and sometimes even ecclesiastical issues. The land was theirs because they had conquered it with their swords: not unlike other places in Europe, the kings and their subjects thought of their land as a unique place. Spain, as Isidore of Seville wrote, and as rephrased by the thirteenth-century *Primera crónica general*, was a unique, plentiful land. Nowhere, the *crónica* claimed, had there been as many saints and martyrs: Rome kept the body of St. Paul, but it was Spain, the best place in the whole world, that had kept St. Paul's words.[17]

The Asturian and Leonese kings, it was believed, were solemnly anointed on the head and crowned. The city of León became associated with the imperial claims of the revival of Visigothic rituals and a royal pantheon, blessed with the body of St. Pelayo, served as a reminder of the power and ambitions of the Asturian dynasty.[18] The regal symbols of the Late Empire and the Visigothic period and the title of Flavius were used, although some of the royal tokens—such as the sword and the standard—did not yet play the important role they acquired in the thirteenth and fourteenth centuries. The kings were still acclaimed and elected, even if in a symbolic manner; they were raised upon a shield or chair. After almost three centuries, their rule had become an established tradition by the late tenth and early eleventh centuries, but their time of glory was coming to an end.

Through victories on the battlefield and dynastic marriages, Sancho III of Navarre (1004–1035) became the master of the peninsula by 1030. In 1034 he traveled to the city of León to be crowned and to take for himself the imperial title and the ancient primacy of the Leonese realm. Nevertheless, in spite of the attention Sancho paid to ancient forms, the Navarrese were the vanguard of northern influences and of new ideas. Sancho's children and grandchildren, as rulers of Castile and Aragón, promoted the work of Cluny and the final opening of the road to Compostela to pilgrims from beyond the Pyrenees and, thus, to new social, economic, and political concepts. Moreover, in Navarre the kings were neither anointed nor crowned but raised on a shield at the cry of "Real, real, real." This Navarrese inheritance further reinforced the martial character of Iberian kingship. The *Primera crónica general* traced the origins of the family to an obscure northern knight who wandered into Navarre and "fought so well against the Moors, that the people of the region elected him king because he was a good warrior and defended them well."[19] Clearly, the chronicle once again chose to emphasize military ability over bloodline or saintly origins. In the Iberian kingdom there was not a saintly founder of the dynasty, or a saintly blood connection to sanctify the royal family. There was no Edward the Confessor, Charlemagne, or St. Louis. Ferdinand III, the only royal saint, was not canonized until the early modern period; by then other Spanish saints canonized during those years, St. Ignatius, St. Theresa, and St. John of the Cross, obscured the figure of the medieval king.

The Late Middle Ages: Politics and Rituals

The reigns of Alfonso VI and of his grandson, Alfonso VII (1126–57), are landmarks in the history of Castile. Alfonso VI's conquest of Toledo in 1085, his opening of the realm to the Roman liturgy and the influence of Cluny, his claiming of the imperial title, and his family connections with France and Burgundy, altered the institutional and political development of the realm. Alfonso VII also laid claim to the imperial title, but his pretension of hegemony in the peninsula was tempered by new political realities—a peninsula divided among five kingdoms and the end, at least for that period, of any dream of political unity. In the south, the advances of the reconquest were once again checked, this time, by the invasion of the Almohads. The rule of Alfonso VII's grandson, Alfonso VIII (after the brief reign in Castile of Sancho III), was marked by a long and violent minority. Once the new king reached age, however, he proved to be capable of restoring order and defending the integrity of the realm. Moreover, in 1212 Alfonso VIII won a signal victory at Las Navas de Tolosa, which irrevokably changed the balance of power in the peninsula in favor of the Christians. After one more minority (that of Henry I) and further nobiliary unrest, Ferdinand III, Alfonso VIII's grandson, continued his grandfather's work. The successful campaigns of this king in Andalusia, highlighted by the conquests of Córdoba (1236) and Seville (1248), brought most of this rich and populous region under Castilian rule. Furthermore, under his rule León, which had been an independent kingdom for almost a century, was now united to Castile forever. The mid-thirteenth century, which seemed to promise a golden age, witnessed the point of farthest advance for the Christian armies, but it also marked the beginning of a series of long-lasting economic, social, and institutional crises. These structural dislocations plagued Castile for most of the next hundred years and set new patterns of development for the kingdom.

The reigns of Alfonso X, Sancho IV, Ferdinand IV, and Alfonso XI were often disrupted by civil wars, nobiliary unrest, and turbulent minorities. Only after Alfonso XI came to age in 1325 did Castile return to some semblance of order. In the 1340s Alfonso XI, well in command of the realm, initiated important institutional reforms, aimed at strengthening royal power by taming the nobility and controlling the financial resources of the cities. He also renewed the march of the Reconquest, which for all practical purposes had come to a stop in the 1250s. His untimely demise from the ravages of the Black Death at the siege of Algeciras in 1350, and the subsequent dynastic conflicts that led to the rise of the bastard-royal branch of the Trastámaras, opened a new period in the life of Castile.

From the ascent of Henry II in 1365, after murdering his half-brother and rightful king Peter I, to the beginnings of Isabella's rule in 1474, the rule of the Trastámaras encompassed a period of great political, economic, and social upheaval. Castile became entangled in the Hundred Years War and the power of the high nobility became a threat to the stability of the realm. Frequent minorities, civil wars, economic stagnation, a galloping inflation, and social unrest, manifested in the violent pogroms of 1391, are some of the elements that made this period generally unstable. In short, from the reign of Alfonso VII to that of Isabella I, Castile was seldom stable enough to allow for normal institutional development.

Few of the kings and queens who ruled Castile and León after the death of Alfonso VII, from Sancho III (1157–58) to Isabella the Catholic (1474–1504), enjoyed enough time as rulers to develop coherent policies. Alfonso VIII and Alfonso XI's long reigns included long and troubled minorities. Those kings who did have the time—Alfonso X (1252–1284) and Juan II (1407–59)—were failures.[20] Of these kings, only Alfonso XI was anointed (on the shoulder), as far as we know; Alfonso X crowned himself; Sancho IV (1284–95) was crowned; while Alfonso XI, Henry II (1369–79), and Juan I (1379–90) also crowned themselves. Clearly by the twelfth century the kings of Castile had abandoned a policy of royal theocracy, and the rites and symbols that accompanied such policy had been downgraded or substituted by more secular ceremonies and emblems.

Although solemn coronations did not occur regularly, the kings of Castile in the late Middle Ages had crowns. We know that Sancho IV chose to be buried with the crown of his great-grandfather, but there is no evidence that any other king did so. In the thirteenth and fourteenth centuries two kings bequeathed crowns to their descendants. Moreover, manuscript illuminations, sculptures, and lead seals show the Castilian rulers wearing the royal diadem, though I believe that in most cases it was an artistic device to identify the king.[21]

With the demise of sacred monarchy, new symbols of royal authority emerged. Instead of the rituals found elsewhere or, at times, even together with them, the Castilian monarchy repeatedly used a series of secular ceremonies during the late Middle Ages and into the early modern period. Although most of these formal acts had a distinctive popular character, they were clearly associated with the claims to kingship and political power. Some of these symbols and secular ceremonial dated back to tribal Germanic customs and even earlier precedents, but they remained alive in Castile without too many attempts at disguising them under a Christian veneer. Many of them were unique to Castile or to the Iberian kingdoms and quite different from the royal symbols of England and France. Among them we find the following: (1) the bestowing of regal attributes to those who were not of the blood royal, (2) emphasis on the martial abilities of Castilians as compared to that of foreigners (above all, the French), (3) the role of heredity in the succession to the throne, (4) succession by election, (5) knighting, (6) royal arms, (7) raising of the standards of Castile to a traditional cry, (8) exchange of oaths between people and monarch, (9) a royal horse that could be ridden only by the king, (10) kissing of the king's hand.

One can already identify a few of these practices in the reigns of Alfonso VI and Alfonso VII, and before the Castilian monarchs discarded anointment, coronation, and the ideological trappings of sacral kingship. Before Alfonso VI could claim the kingdom of Castile, he had to swear on the Bible his innocence of his brother's death to the Castilian nobility gathered at the church of Santa Gadea in Burgos. The dramatic ceremony, in which Ruy Díaz de Vivar, the Cid, speaking for the nobility of Castile, pressed the king again and again to swear his innocence, captured the imagination of contemporaries and of later chronicles, and serves as fair evidence of the contractual nature of the Castilian monarchy. Only after he swore his innocence did Alfonso receive the oath of fidelity and homage from the magnates and from the Cid himself. Only then could he be crowned. There is no indication that he was ever anointed. Instead, the

TABLE 4.1

The Kings of Castile in the Late Middle Ages

Name	Year of Birth	Year Became King	Age	Year of Death	Age	Length of Reign	Minority Time	Illegitimate (I) Contested (C)	Relation to Previous King
Sancho III	1134?	1157	23	1158	24	Less than one year	No		son
Alfonso VIII	1156?	1158	2	1214	58?	56 yrs.	Yes	(C)	son
Henry I	1203	1214	11	1217	14	3 yrs.	Yes	(C)	son
Berenguela	1180?	1217	37	1246	66	A few days	No	(C)	eldest sister son of B
Ferdinand III	1200?	1217	17	1252	52	35 yrs.	No	(I) (C) for Leon	nephew of H
Alfonso X	1221	1252	31	1284	63	32 yrs.	No	(C) by his son	son
Sancho IV	1258	1284	26	1295	38	11 yrs.	No	(C) by nephews	second-son
Ferdinand IV	1285?	1295	10	1312	27	17 yrs.	Yes	(I) uncanonical marriage (C)	son
Alfonso XI	1311	1312	1	1350	38	38 yrs.	5 yrs. Yes	(C)	son
Peter I	1333/4	1350	16	1369	35	16 yrs.	14 yrs. No	(C)	son
Henry II	1333?	1369	36	1379	46	10 yrs.	No	(I)	half-brother
Juan I	1358	1379	21	1390	32	11 yrs.	No	(C)	son
Henry III	1379	1390	11	1406	27	16 yrs.	Yes		son
Juan II	1405	1406	1½	1454	49	48 yrs.	3 yrs. Yes		son
Henry IV	1425	1454	29	1474	49	20 yrs.	14 yrs. No	(C)	son
Isabella I	1451	1474	23	1504	53	30 yrs.	No	(C)	half-sister

117

ceremonies of investiture with the sword and the exchange of oaths played a more important role. Great attention is paid to the Cid. Inasmuch as Ruy Díaz de Vivar was a thorn in the side of Alfonso VI, it is surprising, regardless of the influence of the *Poem of the Cid* on later writers, to see the regal attributes employed to describe someone who was at best a freelance adventurer. The Cid's heroic deeds of arms are praised to excess by royal chroniclers. After his death in 1099, his body, anointed, embalmed, and dressed in purple, sat uncorrupted in the church of the monastery of San Pedro de Cardeña for ten years. His horse could not be ridden again. Miracles and conversions of Jews took place around his body. These are indeed some of the symbols of royalty: the horse, which would have no other rider; the deeds of arms, which served as means of identifying the rulers of Castile and León rather than unction and crowning. Alfonso VI, the chronicle tells us, marveled at the greatness of the warrior who had increased by his victories over Christians and Moors the size of the kingdom.[22]

Although Alfonso VI sat on the imperial throne in Toledo as emperor of the three religions and heir to Visigothic glory, he chose to be buried at Sahagún. In doing so he broke (as did many Castilian kings) with the practice established by his father and grandfather of burial in the church of St. Isidore in León.[23] Alfonso VI's grandson, Alfonso VII, was raised on the shield as king of Galicia and crowned at Compostela while still a child. In 1135 Alfonso VII traveled to León and, after a solemn meeting of the *curia regis*, he was, according to the *Primera crónica general* (written more than a century later), anointed and crowned, though the contemporary chronicle of Alfonso VII makes no mention of the anointing. The *Primera crónica* describes how his head and body were consecrated with holy oil, and how, after the ceremony had concluded, surrounded by vassal kings from al-Andalús, Aragón, and Navarre, Alfonso was proclaimed "emperor of all the Spains" *(imperator totius Hispaniae)*. One must emphasize the association between León, the imperial title, and the ritual ceremonies of unction and coronation. In coming to the city of León, Alfonso VII was asserting the continuity with three hundred years of Asturian history. In the same fashion he went to Toledo to be crowned once again and finally to be buried there. He thus joined the Visigothic and Asturian heritages under one crown.[24]

Later chronicles compared Alfonso VII, the mighty emperor, to Louis VII, king of France. According to Castilian sources, Louis came across the Pyrenees on the pretense of making a pilgrimage to Compostela, but in reality to learn whether or not his wife, Alfonso VII's daughter, was legitimate. The emperor's court at Toledo, crowded with vassal kings and great lords, where precious metals, jewels, and exotic foreign imports were found in abundance, bedazzled the French king. He returned to Paris assured of his wife's honor and carrying a rare and precious stone, which he donated some time after to the abbey of St. Denis.[25] Here, the chronicles revealed an air of national pride not unlike that found in later royal wills and proclamations. They have, of course, all the medieval trappings of religion and devotion, but there is also a hard, practical outlook, a sense of the uniqueness and superiority of the Castilian-Leonese enterprise, of resolves forged in battle. Furthermore, the chronicles do not limit their unfavorable comparisons of Castilians and Frenchmen to Alfonso VII and Louis VII. The martial superiority of the Castilians and their secular efforts to reconquer their land are themes often found in the writings of the period. Discussing Spanish "nationalism" in general and the works of Vicentius Hispanicus in particular, Gaines Post writes: "His glorification of Spanish virtues appears as early as 1210–15. 'With deeds like a Spaniard,' he says, 'not with words like a Frenchman. . . .' Rejecting Innocent III's praise of the kingdom of the French, Vicentius declares 'that Spain, not France (the French Church), is greater than other ecclesiastical provinces, for when Charles with all the northerners *(Francigenae)* wished to invade Spain, the Spanish blocked their passage, overcame them in battle and killed twelve peers.'"[26] The chronicle of Sancho IV accuses the French of being subtle, deceitful, and always willing to appeal to and bend the law for their own benefit, the implication being that what the French did not have the courage to earn in battle, they sought in litigation. Similar sentiments are found elsewhere in the Castilian chronicles of the late Middle Ages.[27]

In Castile royal succession took place immediately after the reigning monarch's death, but it was closely tied to the acclamation of the new king by the magnates, the prelates, and the people or the acceptance by the Cortes. Here the two claims, consanguinity and primogeniture on the one hand, and the elective principle on the other, met in the single process of making a king. As Schramm has rightly pointed out, the hereditary and elective principles are not exclusive. Such was the case in Castile, whereas in France and England the prestige of specific blood lines had made the election of kings by the magnates and the people a relic of a distant past.[28]

At the death of Alfonso VIII (1158–1214) and after his burial at the monastery of Las Huelgas of Burgos, the archbishop of Toledo, other bishops present at the funeral, and some of the high nobility of Castile took the eleven-year-old Infante Henry, "heir to king Alfonso and to

whom was due the kingdom by right and lineage, and with the clergy
singing *Te Deum laudamus*, they raised him king."[29] In 1252, according to a
later addition to the chronicle of Lucas de Tuy, after the death and burial
at Seville of Ferdinand III (1217–52), his son, Alfonso the first-born, told
"the prelates and knights present there, 'I am now the king,' and those
who were there answered: 'we know certainly that of your father you are
the primogenitus and thus it is for you to receive the government of the
realm.'" Once the funeral ceremonies had concluded, all came into the
church and gave Alfonso the royal horse. In front of the altar of the
Blessed Virgin, the magnates raised the king to the horse, calling him with
one voice, the Lord King Alfonso. The new monarch changed his mourning clothes into festive royal garments and was led through the streets of
Seville at the sound of trumpets and cries of "your king, give him reverence and honor. Obey him for he is our king and prince of all the Spaniards." They sat Alfonso on "his father's chair," and he promised to
respect the privileges and charters granted by previous kings and to make
no demands that would contravene the customs of the realm. In his biography of Alfonso X, Antonio Ballesteros offers a somewhat different account. "The prince Alfonso," he writes, "was proclaimed king as it has
been done during the period of the ancient elective principle; the magnates
raised him upon the shield." Citing a charter of 1253, Ballesteros maintains that since no one could crown the king, Alfonso X took the crown
from the altar and placed it on his head with both hands. Later in the day a
mechanical statue of St. James knighted him.[30]

These two lengthy accounts contain elements of interest. In both
cases, Henry I and Alfonxo X undoubtedly had the right to be kings by
law and because of primogeniture. The majority of the prelates and great
men accepted this without great opposition. In the case of Alfonso X it
was not so clear, however, that he could inherit both kingdoms. There
was, after all, a long-standing precedent for the separation of Castile
and León. Eventually Alfonso X's brother, the Infante Henry, rebeled
against his exclusion from the kingdoms, and the king was forced to grant
the high nobility large holdings in Andalusia to secure their support.[31]
The hereditary principle was also reinforced by the common practice
among Castilian kings of demanding recognition of their first-born, male
or female, shortly after birth. This was done at two levels, one by the
approval of the Cortes, to gain the support of the Castilian cities in case of
a minority, the other by an oath taken by the princes of the blood royal
and the *ricos hombres*, all of them potential pretenders to the crown.

Unlike England or France, where kingship was vested in one family blessed with thaumaturgical and sacred attributes, the legal and practical requirements to be king in Castile, as set in both the *Fuero juzgo* and the *Siete partidas*, made access to kingship less restrictive than in England or France. The legal codes reveal obvious contradictions. Castilian jurists could not help but be influenced by the theories of royal power, which had been for a long time part of the Christian heritage and which were favored in other medieval kingdoms. Thus, according to the legal codes the king is the head of the realm as God is the head of the Celestial Court. Moreover, kings are vicars of Christ: each is emperor in his realm *(imperator in regno suo)*. As the saints have explained, the king holds the place of God on earth, to enforce justice, to give each person his or her due. The monarch is the heart and soul of the people, put there to protect, guard, and increase the realm.[32]

Yet if we look closer at both the *Fuero juzgo* and the *Partidas*, we find alternative states. Both state that a king is king because he rules. Emperors and kings came into existence because of a social contract. Long ago, differences of opinions and discord had prevailed among the people, a Hobbesian state of nature. The people agreed, therefore, to have a king and later emperors (king preceded emperors) to make things right, to crush the proud and the troublemakers. The old Visigothic law, still in force in most parts of Castile and León until late in the thirteenth century as the *Fuero juzgo*, stated that the king ought to be elected either in Rome or in the place where the last king died, with the advice of the bishops, the great men of the realm, and the people. According to the *Partidas*, the throne could be gained in the following four ways: (1) by inheritance, (2) by agreement (election) of all the people of the realm if there is no heir, (3) by marriage, (4) by grant of the pope or the emperor.[33] The legal codes of medieval Castile also state that the king is king as long as he behaves in a manner befitting his status and the welfare of the realm, as long as he rules according to law and tradition. If the ruler disregards the good customs and abuses his people, he can be challenged and indeed deposed. The codes also state explicitly that the monarch is not above the law but subject to it. These two last points are, of course, commonplace elsewhere in medieval western Europe and found in most medieval legal and political treatises.[34] We must return, however, to the point raised above, that access to the throne in Castile was not as restricted as it was elsewhere.

In Castile royal succession was not always clear; the first-born did not always follow his father to the throne. Unfortunately for Castile there were more troubled than untroubled successions, for many of the kings of Castile had dubious claims to the crown. Their rule was therefore legitimized not only by an appeal to inheritance, even if spurious, but above all by election and acclamation of the nobility and people. When the young king Henry I died in an accident in 1217, the magnates and prelates "gave" the kingdom to his older sister Berenguela, because "she was Alfonso VIII's first-born and all her brothers were dead." The *Primera crónica general* invoked a privilege of Alfonso VIII, kept at the cathedral of Burgos as authority for Berenguela's election as queen. Such care was needed, since it was not clear if her sister Blanca, Louis VIII's wife and mother of St. Louis, had equal rights to the throne. Most probably, the Castilian nobility found the idea of a French prince, the future Louis VIII, ruling Castile unacceptable and the hereditary principle was subverted. Mariana, who believed that to be the case, describes the acclamation of Berenguela under an elm tree in Nájera, accompanied by the cries of "Castilla, Castilla, real for the queen."[35] Days later the citizens of Valladolid, gathered in the public market of the city, acclaimed and recognized Berenguela heir by nature and right to the throne of Castile. Immediately the queen resigned the throne in favor of her son Ferdinand. In a ceremony of distinctly popular flavor, the prince was carried from the open market to the church of Our Lady. There he took the oath as king and received the homage of the magnates (who kissed his hand in obeisance), prelates, and people, as well as their oath of fidelity. Two years later, on 26 November 1219, Ferdinand completed the rituals and ceremonies of becoming king of Castile by keeping vigil through the night over his sword and armor at the main altar of the monastery of Las Huelgas. In the morning, after being knighted by the mechanical arm of St. James, Ferdinand took the sword from the altar and girded it around his waist.[36]

After his father Alfonso IX of León's (1188–1230) death, Ferdinand rushed to León where, through a show of force and the prudent negotiations of his mother and stepmother, he was proclaimed king of León in a ceremony not unlike that of Valladolid. He was neither crowned nor anointed as he joined the two kingdoms, which would never be parted again. This did not imply, however, that heredity and bloodline could be ignored completely. Ferdinand became king because he also had rights to the throne on the basis of heredity. Yet when others appear to contest the throne with better claims, election and military pressure preceded the right of heredity. The chronicle carefully emphasizes, by using the words *lindo* and *lindamente*, the legitimacy of Berenguela and her son and, thus, their right to rule. In fact they had none. Ferdinand was born two years after Pope Innocent III had branded the marriage of Alfonso IX and Berenguela incestuous, and no attempt to legitimize his birth is known to have occurred. Ferdinand was a bastard, and his claims to the thrones of Castile and León were not as valid as those possessed by others. Force of arms and election or acclamation by the magnates and people granted the legitimacy that blood and the right of succession did not.[37] Others could rule in Castile with equally weak or even weaker claims to kingship. Sancho IV, his son Ferdinand IV, the bastard Henry II and, last but certainly not least, Isabella the Catholic, all of them with dubious rights of succession, assumed the throne with ceremonies and rituals that did not differ from those described above.[38]

If bloodline, primogeniture, and election played an important role in the making of the king, what other important rituals and symbols were used in Castile and early modern Spain? The exchange of oaths constituted the binding legal agreement between a king and his people. This ceremony, which remains to this day an important part of the English coronation rites and one of the reasons for the loyalty of the Spanish army to its present king, had specific connotations in medieval Castile. In this context, the king's duties seem far more numerous than his rights.[39] The king, by his oath, entered into a contract with his subjects, and they in turn, bound themselves to him. For the king's part, the agreement involved the exercise of justice, and the protection of the laws and customs of the realm, but, in the thirteenth and fourteenth centuries, it was also a commitment to fight the Moors and recover the lands once held by the Visigoths. Kings who advanced the Reconquest were praised; those who did not were condemned. Unfortunately, we do not have the precise text of the royal oath, but one can gather most of its contents from the chronicles and, above all, from the proceedings of the meetings of the Cortes. When the new monarch came to the Cortes to make his financial requests, he was presented with an elaborate list of demands by the procurators of the Castilian and Leonese cities represented in the Cortes. These petitions, dealing with tax collections, policies toward the religious minorities, municipal rights, monetary policy, control of aristocratic violence, and war, became a contract between the monarch and the urban oligarchy and repeated reign after reign through the next centuries.[40]

Implicit also in the royal oath, in the *cuadernos* of the Cortes, and in the *Partidas* was the duty of the ruler to approach, in the words of Gimeno Casalduero, "the ideal image of the king." The monarch should be a tireless warrior, pious, articulate, a good father, a faithful husband, moderate in his eating and drinking, continent, a good hunter, a scholar. Yet he must also choose his mistresses from good families, be handsome, and dress in silk, gold, and precious jewels and still remain modest. These are the impossible injunctions pressed on the kings of Castile by the law and emphasized in royal writings, as for example, Sancho IV's written admonitions to his son. There is, of course, nothing remarkable in this "mirror of princes" literature. Similar ideals are found in other medieval kingdoms. There are, however, some differences in the emphasis placed in Castile on the Reconquest and the latitude in sexual matters, that is, the choice of concubines from good families, and of having bastards only from noble women.[41] It goes without saying that with the exception of Alfonso VIII and, to a lesser extent, Ferdinand III and Isabella the Catholic, all the Castilian rulers between 1157 and 1504, as their northern counterparts did, fell far short of the ideal. The people, the magnates, the prelates, and municipal councils proved as fickle to their oaths as their kings. Rebellion, conspiracies, wanton nobiliary violence, and frequent urban resistance to royal encroachment were the answers to the errors of the Castilian monarchy.[42]

Another rite associated with kingship was the ceremony of knighting and the self-girding of the sword. On this matter the Castilian kings were insistent. No one could knight them; no one could bear the royal arms except the king. The knighting and the royal arms were, in a sense, magical symbols of their promise as warriors, of their right to be kings. When the time came to be knighted, the Infante Don Sancho, the second-born, refused to be invested by his brother and heir to the throne, Ferdinand de la Cerda, even though his younger brothers had been knighted by him already. Sancho was old enough and ambitious enough to be king, as he did become eventually over the rightful claims of his nephew, Alfonso de la Cerda, and the objections of his father. To receive knighthood from someone implied obligations and service to the person who granted it, which Sancho might not have been willing to accept.[43] The tradition was already so clearly set in the thirteenth century that no exceptions were made for minors. In 1295 Sancho's son, Ferdinand IV (1295–1312), aged nine, was acclaimed king of Castile and León with the traditional cries and elevation. He took the oath to keep the *fueros* (charters), and his hand was kissed by the regents and magnates. With Ferdinand already a king, Don Nuño González de Lara, first among the *ricos hombres* of the realm, put the royal arms around his neck and walked with the young monarch through the streets of Toledo. We should compare this Castilian attitude with Edward's (the future Edward I of England) ready acceptance of knighthood at the hands of Alfonso X at Las Huelgas of Burgos.[44] Edward must not have thought that receiving knighthood from Alfonso X, or having him handle his sword, placed him under any obligation.

Linked to this knightly tradition we find other ceremonies and tokens of royalty, such as the royal horse, the lifting of the *pendones* (standards) of Castile to the cry of "Castilla . . . real for the king" and the *besamanos* or kissing of the king's hand. With the exception of the last ritual, all these ceremonies are linked to the Visigothic tradition. They are martial and secular rites which, while they had diminished in importance elsewhere, still played an important role in medieval Castile and early modern Spain.

On several occasions I have referred above to the royal horse, as for example, those used in the self-coronations of Alfonso X and Alfonso XI. The chronicles do not specify what they mean by the term *cavallo real*, but clearly the king's horse was set apart from other horses. In the seventeenth century if the king of Spain rode a horse, no one else could ride it afterward. The tradition must probably date back to the medieval period and, as with all the others, was associated with the role of the Castilian kings as leaders of the Reconquest.[45]

The raising of the banners of Castile to a traditional acclamation is rooted in Visigothic practice, but it can also be traced back to early medieval Navarre. As the chronicles attest, the raising of the *pendones* of Castile gained in importance through the years. The devotion given to the banner flown at Las Navas de Tolosa and kept at Las Huelgas of Burgos serves as an indication of the importance of these symbols. After Isabella took the oath to the people and kingdom and was acclaimed, she embraced the standard of the realm and offered it to God. The sources of the period stress the fact that the standards were never raised for Juana la Beltraneja, the rightful heir to the throne.[46] In the sixteenth and seventeenth centuries the ceremonial raising of the standards and the ritual cries in the Plaza Mayor of Madrid and elsewhere in the city marked the ascent of the Habsburgs to the throne of Castile and other Iberian kingdoms. The descriptions of these rituals closely parallel the medieval accounts.[47]

If all these rites had a strong martial flavor and were in Castile and later in Spain associated with the glorification of deeds of arms, honor, and courage, the *besamanos* belongs in a somewhat different category. The kiss was a sign of feudal homage and also of the essential equality between two warriors, but the Castilian *besamanos*, while retaining some of its feudal connotations, was far removed from the kiss of peace or the traditional kiss of French feudal custom. As Américo Castro has pointed out, in Castile the kissing of the king's hand and, sometimes, his feet imitated Muslim custom. The ceremonial kissing of the hand, so prominent in the descriptions of enthronement of medieval Castilian kings and early modern Spanish rulers, was an act of submission performed by the great lords of the realm, and even lowly royal officials. Such was the case of the three men commissioned by Sancho IV to undertake an investigation in Ávila, who in their report symbolically stated, "we kiss your hand as natural lord in whose mercy we are." This established a bond of loyalty, which, I should note, was broken again and again.[48]

Unlike Aragon, England, Germany, or France, where quite early a recognizable shrine was associated with the ruling dynasty either as a place of coronation or royal pantheon—Westminster, St. Denis, Reims, Aächen, Zaragoza—Castile never had a specific site around which a tradition crystallized. Lacking a real capital until the sixteenth century, the peripatetic Asturian, Leonese, and Castilian kings were crowned, became kings, and were buried in Oviedo, León, Santiago, Sahagún, Nájera, Burgos, Valladolid, Segovia, Toledo, Seville, and Granada. Their choices of burial places and sites for their enthronement show an obvious association with the Reconquest and the moving frontier. As the Castilians advanced southward, so did the center of power. Most often the kings were buried in the most important city that they had captured. Ferdinand III, for example, was buried in Seville, Alfonso requested to be buried in Murcia, the Catholic kings in Granada. In the late thirteenth and early fourteenth centuries, whenever there were no victories, the kings were laid to rest in Burgos, Toledo, Valladolid, or whatever city was close by. After 1157 only Alfonso VIII and Sancho IV attempted to establish royal pantheons in Las Huelgas of Burgos and Toledo, but their enterprises did not succeed, and no pantheon existed until the building of the Escorial.[49]

Neither did the kings of Castile and León attempt to establish elaborate genealogies by forgery or otherwise. They paid some attention to bloodline and family connections, but in the end such ties had little importance. When the pope asked Sancho IV to reject his wife, María de Molina, and to wed a princess of France, he refused in spite of all the clear political advantages. "Other kings of my house," he said, "had married within similar degree of consanguinity without [ecclesiastical] dispensation, and from the union were born many good kings, adventurous, conquerors against the enemies of the faith who increased [the size] and made their kingdoms better."[50]

There was no tradition of royal names. The kings named their first male child after their fathers or selected other names apparently in arbitrary fashion. Thus Alfonso VIII named his first son Henry, after his father-in-law Henry II of England. Alfonso XI named his first legitimate child Peter, and his first bastard son Henry. Their fathers had been named Sancho and Ferdinand, respectively. Moreover, in their charters and proclamations the Castilian kings seldom referred back beyond their grandfather or at the most great-grandfather. There was no need to appeal to ancient tradition. There was no Charlemagne or Arthur in their past.[51]

Religion, Politics, and Warfare: The Making of Unsacred Monarchy

At first glance it would appear that weak and troubled kings (such as most Castilian rulers were between 1157 and the advent of Isabella I in 1474) would have benefited by adopting an ideology of sacral kingship, by surrounding their rule with all the religious and magical panoply of *rex et sacerdos*, by claiming to belong to a sacred race, to have thaumaturgical powers. This was not difficult to accomplish, and the kings of Castile had what they believed was a rich tradition in the Visigothic past to which they could appeal. If this had been the case, the kings of Castile might have been spared the continuous challenges to constituted authority that so often plagued them and the realm. Convenient as the adoption of sacral kingship would have been, it was, however, unacceptable to the kingdom and to the kings themselves.

The easiest explanation for this rejection or failure to maintain a sacral kingship is one familiar to students of Castilian and Spanish history, the practical character of Castilian religiosity in the Middle Ages. Paradoxically in a reign and a country that have become so identified with exalted religiosity and fanaticism, medieval Castile and, later on, Spain have always shown an ambivalent and, at times, quite practical approach to institutionalized religion. Furthermore, the Castilian clergy was certainly notorious for its misbehavior on sexual matters and its lack of regard for Church discipline or obedience to Rome.[52] Castilian kings often accepted the authority of the Church only if it suited their own political ends or did not interfere with their private lives. Spaniards in general and Castilians in particular had, and still have, a rather personal and arbitrary view of religion. Writing about Philip II, John Elliott puts this idea across very well: "He [Philip II] considered religion too serious a matter to be left to the Pope." The tendency toward mysticism, the fierce nationalism and independence of both Church and monarchy, and the well-known arrogance of Castilians toward foreigners were deterrents in the institutionalization of sacred rites that depended to such large extent on the doctrines of a church with its center elsewhere, influenced and dominated by non-Castilians. As the Infante Don Juan Manuel wrote in the early fourteenth century, "he was certain of one thing only: the pope had less power in Castile than anywhere else." That suited the Castilians just fine.[53]

Sánchez Albornoz and others have pointed out the pragmatic nature of the Castilians. One could say that in that respect earlier than in the rest of

Europe, Castilians had a more down-to-earth, practical outlook toward the uses of power and authority. The boundaries between the religious and the secular in the Middle Ages are vague, and one cannot speak of secular attitudes. The Castilians remained religious in spite of their practicality, but perhaps with a different understanding of the ideal relations between the spiritual and the temporal than that of their northern counterparts. When the Cid left Castile for the lands of the Moors, he did so, above all, "to earn his bread." This dichotomy between the spiritual and the practical is a topic in Spanish literature and the other obvious theme of *Don Quixote*. Nevertheless, there are more Sancho Panzas in Spain than Don Quixotes. Nor was there in Castile a mystification of power or history. Castile never had a revival of Celtic lore in the twelfth century nor a Geoffrey of Monmouth to tell the story. There were no fairies, trolls, or witches. If at all, they were imported or confined to remote and backward Galicia or the Basque region. Without myths, the monarchy used and still uses temporal symbols, and they were strengthened through the centuries, while paradoxically in such a Catholic country the royal sacral elements tended to disappear.[54]

In *Cantiga* 321 Alfonso X tells the story of a young girl from Córdoba who was sick for three years with a throat tumor. After the mother tried unsuccessfully to find a doctor to cure her daughter, a man advised her to take the ailing child to the king the next day, "because all Christian kings have the power to heal this sickness by laying of their hands." When the king heard this story, he told them that the advice was "not worth a very bad fig. When you say that I have such power, you are talking nonsense." Instead the king counseled the woman to wash an image of the Virgin Mary with pure water and afterward "drink that water from a chalice . . . for five days, a day for each letter of the name Maria. . . . And so it was that the girl was restored to full health." In the story Alfonso ridiculed the thaumaturgical claims of English and French kings and offered, as an alternative, what Américo Castro has described as Jewish-Muslim magic. The point is, of course, that Alfonso said that kings do not have the power to heal. Someone like Alfonso X, with his well-known interest in science and the occult, would rather trust the magical lore of the East (which for him was rational and scientific) than the hands of a king.[55]

Practicality and the peculiarities of Castilian religiosity, however, do not fully explain the differences that existed between northern medieval kingdoms and Castile. Other explanations can be offered. They are, of course, tentative answers to a question which may not have a single or set of satisfactory answers. Some of them have been implied in previous pages: (a) the institutional example and influence of Islamic political practices, (b) a change in the balance of power between Christians and Moors in favor of the former after 1157, (c) the martial nature, the personal character of kingship and mentality of the Castilian monarchy and people.

The influence of Islam also modified Germanic and Christian concepts of power and authority. For centuries before the Christians gained the upper-hand in the peninsula, Castilian princes and lords had traveled to al-Andalús, had lived in the courts of Muslim rulers as hostages, guests or exiles. After 1085, and above all, 1212, Muslim princes often accompanied the peripatetic Castilian kings, confirmed their charters, were, at times, enemies, often allies. Alfonso X, for example, sought Muslim help against his son Sancho; Alfonso XI often dressed in Muslim garments. In the caliphate of Córdoba and in the kingdoms of *taifas* afterward, religion was subordinated to the ruler. After Almanzor (d. 1002) political power in Muslim Spain was almost always gained because of personal valor, through assassination and intrigue, maintained by personal ability and violence against the continuous conspiracies of the ruler's own family.

Institutional developments in the caliphate of Córdoba and the kingdoms of the *taifas* thus served as models for the kings of Asturias, León, and Castile. There was a cultural, economic, institutional, and scientific interdependence between al-Andalús and the Christian north; and in the schools of the south the kings of Castile, and more importantly their subjects, learned more than astronomy, magic, and chess. Furthermore, Jamous's recent research on aspects of North African society shows that to this day violence is both ritualized and legalized as a means to political power in the Riff. *Baraka* or the charismatic qualities of the leader, is best revealed in his military prowess and in the continuous struggle against internal and external enemies. As Geertz describes aspects of political rule in present Muslim society, "the strong man aspects of his [the Sultan] role inevitably clashed with and usually dominated the holy man aspects." Clearly, there is a strong relationship between the traditional concept of authority and power in medieval and present Islamic societies and those mental attitudes which in Castile led to the development of unsacred monarchy.[56] There is a further point. If the preparations and fighting of a crusade shaped and transformed the reigns of some English and French kings,[57] how would a struggle but also a symbiotic relation of seven hundred years shape a nation and its rulers?

At a more obvious level, one should note the clear connection between a change in the Christian-Muslim balance of power in the peninsula during the reign of Alfonso VII and his successors' apparent failure to use the rites of anointment and coronation. Alfonso VIII's victory at Las Navas de Tolosa (1212) was the final turning point in a five-century conflict. After the early thirteenth century the issue of mastery over al-Andalús was decided once and for all in favor of the Christians. There was no longer any need to invest the figure of the king with sacred trappings, as had been done when the Christian kings were merely puppets of the proud caliphs of Córdoba. Relations with other Christian kingdoms beyond the Pyrenees were never as important as political ties and conflicts in the peninsula, and by 1212 the power of the kings of Castile had been proven and sanctified in the battlefield. Yet the frontier remained open, beckoning the rulers of Castile to one more expedition in the south, one more victory, almost as if those campaigns were the symbolic and necessary equivalent of unction and coronation. It is not a coincidence, after all, that as soon as the last outpost of Muslim power in Spain, Granada, surrendered to the Catholic kings in 1492, other frontiers were opened: one across the Ocean Sea, in the taming, raping, and conversion of new worlds; the other in central Europe in wasteful and ephemeral battles for empire and religion; and finally an inner frontier engaged in battle against crypto-Jews, heretics, purity of blood, and the mystical search for God.

Finally, the law (both Visigothic *Fuero juzgo* and the Roman inspired *Partidas*) opposed the idea of sacral kingship, even if these codes admitted that God chose the king. To a large extent the kings and the kingdom defined their legitimacy in terms of a warrior tradition. There is enough evidence in the previous pages to see that the ruler was, above all, lord of the armies. He was king because he carried on and directed the war against the Moors, because he led the realm in the centuries-old struggle to recover the land from the enemy. This, in spite of the *divinal* or divine aspects emphasized so much by Castro and others, was no racial or religious war. It was not the glorious Reconquest of Spanish historians. Of course, there were strong religious elements, but it was in many respects the response to the dynamics of a frontier society and territorial expansion.[58] When the kings of Spain claimed special rights over the Church in the *Partidas*, they did so because: (1) they conquered the land from the Moors, turned mosques into churches, and drove out the name of Mohammed and brought in the name of Christ; (2) founded churches where there had never been any; (3) gave these churches large gifts.[59] One can read in this a sense of kings and people engaged in the building up of a nation and an ideal, developing over centuries of battle and conflict. In Castile, although kings were to a certain extent special—how could it be otherwise as they held political power and were leaders of the Reconquest?—they made no sacred claims. Castile was a place where a good number of princes of the blood royal, royal bastards, and powerful magnates could and did assert their rights to be king. These princes, bastards, and magnates, as well as most of the Castilian kings in the thirteenth and fourteenth centuries, had a deep belief in their own individual worth. Unlike France or England, the institutional traditions that, through several centuries, had slowly subordinated the king's human personality to the needs of the realm and the strengthening of royal institutions were not as developed in Castile. Those who ruled and those who wanted to rule had, more often than not, one body instead of two. They often placed their own political ambitions, their pursuit of pleasures and revenge, over the welfare of the realm and the survival of royal institutions. We can see that in the wills of Alfonso X, Henry II, Henry III, and Juan I which are, above all, personal statements. In them the kings, as they contemplated their deaths, sought to please their mistresses, concubines, and bastards while they also attempted to placate God. There is little regard for the needs of the kingdom. In one case, Alfonso X's first will, the king sought to punish his undutiful son Sancho by bequeathing the kingdom to his grandsons and in their absence to the king of France. The idea of Philip IV or Edward I willing their kingdoms to the ruler of Castile is absurd. Above all, Alfonso X's poetry, the *Cantigas of Santa Maria*, bespeaks his personal fear of death, his zeal for life, the unbearable pain of his sickness, his passion, his faith. These are not the words of a king in his majesty but the words of a troubled, weak, and interesting human being. There were, of course, other medieval rulers who entertained similar ideas but never with such intensity or through such long periods of time.[60]

Visigothic law opened kingship to anyone of Gothic blood and good character. In thirteenth-, fourteenth-, and fifteenth-century Castile this was almost true. Between the reigns of Alfonso VIII and Henry IV, every ruler had to contend with a rival king or with nobiliary unrest, and in the case of Ferdinand IV and Alfonso XI's minorities, with several kings. Of these pretenders, Sancho IV, Henry II, and Isabella succeeded in becoming rulers, proving that it was not a futile effort after all. In France and England, magnates and princes of the blood rebelled against the king, but they did not claim the crown until the king's death or removal.

This challenge to the authority of kings came about partly owing to the individual sense of self-worth, a social perception in Castile that a noble-man, a warrior, was the equal of a king. In his *King's Touch* Marc Bloch mentions the tradition that lions were afraid of kings. There are three instances in Castilian and Spanish history and literature showing a lion afraid of a man. In all three cases, the characters are rebels or individuals outside the system. They are heroes or fictional characters with the cour-age and dignity that kings should have: the Cid, the Infante Enrique (Alfonso X's brother), and Don Quixote.[61] Or as Sancho put it in an entirely different context: "I am an Old Christian, and to become an earl that is sufficient." With some poetic license a Castilian noble could have said, Since I am a noble and a warrior, I could be king. In fact, poor *hidalgos* from the ends and dregs of Spain, Extremadura, did conquer worlds and untold wealth by the effort of their swords. Nobility, as Fer-nando Mexía, a fifteenth-century writer, emphasized, came before kings, and in parts of Old Castile almost everyone was a noble.[62]

Conclusion

Here at the end of the story, we must return to our initial account of Alfonso XI's anointment and self-coronation and, in doing so, complete the circle. The discontinuity of those events between prior and subse-quent time is significant and raises questions as to the role of sacral sym-bols in Castile. Clearly these symbols neither shaped royal policies nor were fundamental in shaping the mentality of Castilians. These symbols of holy oil and coronation, so important elsewhere and so often mentioned in the models of anthropologists and historians of rituals, could be sum-moned from obscurity, used for one occasion, for a specific purpose and, soon afterward, forgotten, put aside. With far greater consistency, the rulers of Castile, in spite of the law and the tokens of royalty, expressed their power in the crudest and ultimate manifestation of individual power: in personal acts of violence. The chronicler Lucas de Tuy describes these kings as ferocious, taking arms against brothers and fathers. In the thir-teenth and fourteenth centuries such was the case of Sancho IV and the fifteen-year-old Alfonso XI, who marked their assumption of power by killing with their own hands rebellious nobles, or Henry II, who killed his own half-brother and king.[63]

Juan de Mariana, a Jesuit and a keen observer of sixteenth-century political life, put it best. After a long discussion on the legal advantages and disadvantages of hereditary or elective kingship, Mariana added that all these legal arguments "were worth little, for it was the custom of men to carry the title of kingship in the point of their lances and in their weapons. The strongest is the one who captures the jewel [the crown]. And he wins it from his opponent without regard for the laws which are silent in the face of the clamor [noise] of arms, of trumpets and drums. And there is no one who, being able to become king by the strength of his hands, will venture his business to the opinion and judgments of jurists."[64]

This exercise of sheer power does not explain all—otherwise the martial rites and ceremonies developed over centuries and identified with the monarchy would not have been necessary. Yet when all the laws were read, and all the banners had been raised, and all the traditional cries given, the Castilian rulers often acted as if power came, as Mariana wrote and Mao rephrased it, from the barrel of a gun. Alas! as we come to the end of this, by far, too long journey, let us remember that Franco's only claim to legitimacy was to be the *caudillo*, the old medieval leader of hosts, by the grace of God, victorious against the Red infidels of the twentieth century, a caretaker, a tenancy held not by law or sacred rites but by the "sanctity" of the force of arms. Unfortunate Castile! Unfortunate Spain!

Notes

This article first appeared in French as "Une royauté sans sacre: La Monarchie castillane du Bas Moyen Age," *Annales E.S.C.*, 3 (May-June 1984); 429–53. The idea for this article came from Professor John H. Elliott's presentation to the Davis Center in 1981. I would like to acknowledge the many suggestions, invaluable ideas and bibliographical leads which I was fortunate to receive from those attending the Davis Center Seminar and, above all, from Professors Elizabeth A. R. Brown, Joseph R. Strayer, John H. Elliott, Charles Radding, and Javier Gil Pujol. A shorter version of this article was presented at the Centre de Recherches Historiques of the Ecole des Hautes Etudes en Sciences Sociales. I would like to thank Professors Jacques Le Goff, Jean-Claude Schmitt, Jacques Revel, and others for their gracious hospitality, valuable comments, and encouragement. Professor Le Goff's seminar on the rites and ceremonies of the French monarchy sharpened for me the distinctions between the French and Castilian models of kingship. Last but certainly not least, I owe an immense debt of gratitude to Peter A. Linehan of Cambridge University for his careful reading of this article and intelligent comments. In truth this has been a collective enterprise, though for the opinions and mistakes, I am solely to blame.

1. There are no suitable monographs on the reign of Alfonso XI. Salvador de Moxó wrote a series of articles on the early fourteenth century in preparation for a book on Alfonso XI and an edition of the royal documents. Moxó's death in 1980 has left the work incomplete. See Salvador de Moxó, "La sociedad política castellana en la época de Alfonso XI," *Cuadernos de historia*, 6 (1975): 187–326 and bibliographical references therein. The best source for the reign of Alfonso XI, besides the thousands of unpublished documents in the Archivo histórico nacional, is the *Crónica de Alfonso XI* in *Crónicas de los reyes de Castilla*, ed. Cayetano Rosell (Biblioteca de autores españoles, 66, Madrid, 1953) where the ceremony is described in detail on pp. 235–37. This volume of the *Crónicas* includes those of Alfonso X, Sancho IV, Ferdinand IV, Alfonso XI, and Peter I (hereafter cited as the chronicle of each individual king). See also *Poema de Alfonso onceno rey de Castilla y de León* in *Poetas castellanos anteriores al siglo XV*, ed. T. A. Sánchez, P. J. Pidal, and F. Janer (Biblioteca de autores españoles, 57, Madrid, 1966), p. 489 (hereafter cited as *Poema de Alfonso XI*). The ceremonial itself, which Claudio Sánchez Albornoz has studied and edited, was composed by a Portuguese bishop. See Claudio Sánchez Albornoz, "Un ceremonial inédito de coronación de los reyes de Castilla," in *Estudios sobre las instituciones medievales españolas* (Mexico, 1965), pp. 739–63 (hereafter cited as *Estudios*). The ceremonial (p. 762) calls for the king to be crowned with a bishop's miter and, above that, the royal diadem. Alfonso XI did not follow this injunction. Included in the text is also an ideal description of the conduct of kings. See below.

    The king is anointed on the shoulder, because as Christ carried the cross and with it the weight of the world, the king carries on his shoulders the burden of his people. See Partida 1, 4.3 in *Los códigos españoles concordados y anotados*, ed. M. Rivadeneyra, 12 vols. (Madrid, 1847–51), 2:39 (hereafter *Códigos*). The *Partidas* make a distinction between the old law (when kings were anointed on the head with holy oil) and the new law (when they are consecrated only on the shoulder). Mariana adds that the queen was not anointed because of her "honesty" and "because she was pregnant." Juan de Mariana, *Historia general de España*, ed. Francisco Oliva, 7 vols. (Barcelona, 1839), 4:7.

    On the king by the "grace of God," Américo Castro points to the widespread use in Spain of formulas taken from the Arabs and employed by the Mozarabs, "que Deus defenda, que Dios mantenga" and their association with the official naming of the king. To this very day in Spain and, above all, in Latin America "con el favor de Dios," by God's favor or grace, is a common epistolary or speech formula, especially among the old. See Américo Castro, *La realidad histórica de España*, 2d. ed. (Mexico, 1962), p. 234.

2. T. F. Ruiz, "The Transformation of the Castilian Municipalities: The Case of Burgos, 1248–1350," *Past & Present*, 77 (1977): 18–20. For the practice of self-coronation Alfonso XI only had to look across the border to Aragón where the practice had been in use since the late thirteenth century, or to the history of Castile itself. There was in addition the example of Frederick II. See Bonifacio Palacios Martín, *La coronación de los reyes de Aragón, 1204–1410: Aportación al estudio*

de las estructuras medievales (Valencia, 1975), pp. 81ff.; Ernst Kantorowicz, *Kaiser Friedrich der Zweite*, 2 vols. (Berlin, 1928–31), 1:183. Note that Jaume I (1213–76) also insisted upon taking the sword himself. For similar emphasis on the taking of the sword see Hartmut Hoffman, "Französische Fürstenweihen des Hochmittelalters," *Deutsches Archiv* (Cologne, 1962), pp. 104–5. Also Percy E. Schramm, *Las insignias de la realeza en la Edad Media española*, trans. L. Vázquez de Parga (Madrid, 1960), pp. 92–93. Ballesteros maintains that Alfonso X crowned himself. Antonio Ballesteros y Beretta, *Alfonso X, el sabio* (Barcelona, 1963), p. 54. There is a notice of an even earlier self-crowning, that of Sancho II (1065–72) in *Primera crónica general: Estoria de España que mando componer Alfonso el sabio y se continuaba bajo Sancho IV en 1289*, ed. Ramón Menéndez Pidal (Nueva biblioteca de autores espanoles, 5, Madrid, 1906), p. 505 (hereafter cited as *Primera crónica general*). See also Carlrichard Brühl, "Fränkischer Krönungsbrauch und das Problem der 'Festkrönungen,'" *Historische Zeitschrift*, 194 (1962): 265–326; "Kronen und Krönungsbrauch im Frühen und Hohen Mittelalter," *Historische Zeitschrift*, 234 (1982): 1–31; also his "Les auto-couronnements d'empereurs et de rois (XIIIe-XIXe S.). Remarques sur la fonction sacramentelle de la royauté au Moyen Age et à l'Epoque Moderne," Académie des Inscriptions & Belles-Lettres. *Comptes rendus des séances de l'année 1984*, January-March (Paris, 1984), pp. 102–18.

3. That Alfonso XI broke with an established tradition of unsacred monarchy is not too difficult to explain. These explanations can be here summarized by pointing to the problems of his minority, prevailing conditions in Castile, and to his personality. The king was deeply influenced by northern examples, and loved chivalrous acts and distinctive ceremonies.

4. For the ordination of Visigothic and Asturian kings see C. Sánchez Albornoz, "La sucesión al trono en los reinos de León y Castilla," in *Estudios*, pp. 639–704; "La '*ordinatio Principis*' en la España goda y postvisigoda," in *Estudios*, pp. 705–37; J. M. Ramos y Loscertales, "La sucesión del rey Alfonso VI," *Anuario de historia del derecho español*, 13 (1941): 36–79. For the tokens of the Asturian, Leonese, and Castilian kingship see Schramm, *Las insignias*, pp. 26–27, 32, 61–63. Schramm limits his discussion to crowns, throne, scepter, etc., a different category from the symbols discussed in this paper.

5. On this point see Clifford Geertz, *The Interpretation of Cultures: Selected Essays* (New York, 1973), pp. 6–7, 29, 362–63: "To commit oneself . . . to an interpretative approach to the study of it [culture] is to commit oneself to a view of ethnographic assertion as, to borrow W. B. Gallie's by now famous phrase, 'essentially contestable.'" See also Edward Evans-Pritchard, *The Divine Kingship of the Shilluk of the Nilotic Sudan* (Cambridge, Eng., 1948); Reinhard Bendix, *Kings or People: Power and the Mandate to Rule* (Berkeley and Los Angeles, 1978). See also the old but still wonderful mine of information in James G. Frazer, *The Golden Bough: A Study in Magic and Religion*, 1-vol. abridged ed. (New York, 1927), pp. 1–10, 83–92, 146–58 et passim. It is not my intention, however, to approach this inquiry with an anthropological or strictly interdisciplinary meth-

odology. Rather, my task here is the modest one of describing the rituals and symbols of Castilian kingship and to advance a tentative explanation for its uniqueness. It might be proper for historians to take to heart Felix Gilbert's review of Richard C. Trexler, *Public Life in Renaissance Florence* in *The New York Review of Books* (21 Jan. 1982), pp. 62–64.

6. A great deal has been done elsewhere. See for example Percy E. Schramm, *A History of the English Coronation*, trans. Leopold C. Wickham (Oxford, Eng., 1937); *Kaiser, Könige und Päpste*, 4 vols. in 5 (Stuttgart, 1970); *Der König von Frankreich*, 2 vols. (Weimar, 1939); Ernst H. Kantorowicz, *The King's Two Bodies: A Study in Mediaeval Political Theology* (Princeton, 1957); *Laudes Regiae: A Study in Liturgical Acclamations and Medieval Ruler Worship* (Berkeley and Los Angeles, 1946); Joseph R. Strayer, "France: The Holy Land, the Chosen People and the Most Christian King," in *Medieval Statecraft and the Perspectives of History: Essays by Joseph R. Strayer*, ed. J. F. Benton and T. N. Bisson (Princeton, 1971), pp. 300–14; also "Defense of the Realm and Royal Power in France," in *Medieval Statecraft*, pp. 291–99; *The Reign of Philip the Fair* (Princeton, 1980), pp. 380–423; Andrew W. Lewis, *Royal Succession in Capetian France: Studies in Familial Order and the State* (Cambridge, Mass., 1981), pp. 118–31. For Castile see nn. 1, 2, 4, and 58. For a good short summary of the rituals and symbols of the medieval Spanish kingdoms see Luis García de Valdeavellano, *Curso de historia de las instituciones españolas* (Madrid, 1968), pp. 186–94, 411–30; Schramm, *Kaiser, Könige*, vol. 4, pt. 1, pp. 316–419, and above all, 319–48. Also Pedro Longás Bartibas, "La coronación litúrgica del rey en la Edad Media," *Anuario de Historia del Derecho Español*, 23 (1953): 371–81 (mostly an edition of a relevant document); Rafael Gibert, *Historia general del derecho español* (Granada, 1968); Manuel Colmeiro, *Reyes cristianos desde Alfonso VI hasta Alfonso XI* (Madrid, 1893).

7. Possibly in imitation of Visigothic rituals, the Frankish kings introduced into Frankland the practice of anointing of the monarch with holy oil, and soon afterward this practice spread to the rest of western Europe. This opinion by Bloch is disputed by others. See n. 2 and Marc Bloch, *The Royal Touch: Sacred Monarchy and Scrofula in England and France*, trans. F. E. Anderson (London, 1973), pp. 37, 262–63.

8. García de Valdeavellano, *Curso de historia*, p. 193; Alfonso García Gallo, *Manual de historia del derecho español*, 3d ed., 2 vols. (Madrid, 1967), 1:532–43. Vol. 2 contains long excerpts of primary sources providing evidence for García Gallo's contentions. Margaret Deanesly, *A History of Early Medieval Europe 476–911*, 2d ed. (London, 1969), p. 99.

9. Deanesly, *History*, p. 102; Bloch, *Royal Touch*, pp. 262–63; García Gallo, *Manual*, 1:544.

10. Kantorowicz, *The King's Two Bodies*, pp. 71, 81 et passim; Walter Ullmann, *A History of Political Thought: The Middle Ages* (Baltimore, 1968), pp. 53–99.

11. *Fuero juzgo*, 1:1.8; "Cuando el rey muere, nadie debe tomar el reino, ni hacerse rey, ni ningun religioso, ni otro hombre extraño, si no hombre del linaje de los

godos, e hijodalgo . . . y noble et digno de costumbre." in *Códigos*, 1:100; García Gallo, *Manual*, 1:540.

12. *Fuero juzgo*, 1. Introducción: "Onde los antigos dicen tal proverbio; Rey seras, si fueres derecho, et si non fecieres derecho, no seras rey." *Códigos*, 1:97; García Gallo, *Manual*, 1:540; Aloysius K. Ziegler, *Church and State in Visigothic Spain* (Washington, D.C., 1930), pp. 55–88.

13. *Primera crónica general*, p. 495: "because the kings of Spain came from the strong blood of the Goths, and many times the Gothic kings killed each other, brother killing brother . . . "

14. *Fuero juzgo*, 1:1; 1:1.2, 3. in *Códigos*, 1:97–98; García Gallo, *Manual*, 1:540. Quoting St. Isidore: "El Poder no existe para provecho de alguno o daño de los demas . . . todo Poder viene de Dios y solo se usa rectamente cuando se ejerce para el bien y la *utilitas populi* 'provecho del pueblo y en defensa de la Iglesia.' " Also García Gallo, *Manual*, 1:627, and 2:F734.12, F811.71.5, F646–49.50.

15. Mariana, *Historia*, 2:148ff.; Sánchez Albornoz, "La '*ordinatio Principis*,' " pp. 720–27 (p. 721): "Como ilustración del '*Officium in ordinatione regis*' del Antifonario de León, se representa al rey postrado ante los obispos y al metropolitano vertiendo sobre su cabeza el óleo santo por la punta de un cuerno litúrgico, que recuerda al que fue empleado segun la Biblia por Samuel para ungir a David." Also Schramm, *Las insignias de la realeza*, pp. 22–27.

16. Castro, *La realidad histórica*, p. 85: quoting the bishop Don Alonso de Cartagena in 1434. "Los reyes de España—entre los quales el principal e primero e mayor, el rey de Castilla e de León—nunca fueron subjectos al Emperador, ca esta singularidad tienen los reyes de España que *nunca fueron subjetos al Imperio Romano* (el Sacro Romano Imperio) *nin a otro alguno mas ganaron et alçaron los regnos de los dientes de los enemigos*" (emphasis mine). The kings of Spain were never subjects of the Holy Roman Empire (or of anyone else), but they gained and raised the kingdom from the teeth of the enemy. The same feelings had been expressed before by Alvarus Pelagius. See Joaquín Gimeno Casalduero, *La imagen del monarca en la Castilla del siglo XIV* (Madrid, n.d.), p. 24; *Primera crónica general*, pp. 356, 382, 475 et passim. See also nn. 26 and 27.

17. On the imperial question see Cayetano J. Socarrás, *Alfonso X of Castile: A Study on Imperialistic Frustration* (Barcelona, 1979), pp. 9–63 (a summary of the bibliography on the subject). Also *Primera crónica general*, pp. 310–12, 356 and below nn. 26 and 27. According to the chronicles and legends, the Spaniards defeated Charlemagne at Roncesvalles (the feat of the legendary Bernardo del Carpio), and by their efforts opened the road to Compostela. Legend and epic poems have given this glory to Charlemagne, but epic and legends, the chronicler maintains, lack the veracity of history.

18. On medieval royal tombs in Castile see Heath Dillard, "Medieval Convent Tombs: Dynastic Burial at Iberian Nunneries," paper given at Kalamazoo, Mich., May 1981. Professor Dillard has kindly given me a copy of her yet unpublished paper.

19. García Gallo, *Manual*, 1:635, 2:F823.1; *Primera crónica general*, pp. 467–68.
20. For the history of Asturias and Castile, which serves as background to the devel-
     opment of rituals of kingship, see Luis García de Valdeavellano, *Historia de Es-
     paña*, vol. 1 (Madrid, 1952); Joseph O'Callaghan, *A History of Medieval Spain*
     (Ithaca, N.Y., 1975); Angus MacKay, *Spain in the Middle Ages: From Frontier to
     Empire, 1000–1500* (London, 1977); and the polemical Claudio Sánchez Al-
     bornoz, *España: Un enigma histórico*, 2 vols. (Buenos Aires, 1956). Also MacKay,
     Spain, pp. 15–35. How confusing some aspects of Castilian medieval history can
     be is best expressed in a paragraph from Christopher Brooke, *Europe in the Cen-
     tral Middle Ages, 962–1154* (New York, 1966), p. 380. After attempting to make
     sense of Iberian affairs in the mid-twelfth century, Brooke writes, "Thus the
     mid-1150s saw three kingdoms firmly established in Christian Spain, with an
     Alfonso growing old in Castile, an Alfonso in the prime of life in Portugal, and a
     small Alfonso growing up to be heir of Aragón, all dedicated to spread moderate
     confusion among Muslims of their own day, and extreme confusion among his-
     torians until the end of the world." On the general crisis of the early fourteenth
     century Julio Valdeón Baruque, *Los conflictos sociales en el reino de Castilla en los siglos
     XIV y XV*, 2d ed. (Madrid, 1976), pp. 54–65; "Aspectos de la crisis castellana en
     la primera mitad del siglo XIV," *Hispania*, 111 (1969): 5–24; Salustiano Moreta
     Velayos, *Malhechores-feudales: Violencia, antagonismos y alianzas de clases en Castilla,
     siglos XIII y XIV* (Madrid, 1975), pp. 70ff.; T. F. Ruiz, "Expansion et chan-
     gement: la conquête de Séville et la société castillane (1248–1350)," *Annales
     E.S.C.*, vol. 34, no. 3 (1979): 548–65. Also in Ruiz, *Sociedad y poder real en Castilla*
     (Barcelona, 1981), ch. 1; Antonio Ubieto Arteta, *Ciclos económicos en la Edad Media
     española* (Valencia, 1969); Ramon Menéndez Pidal, *La España del Cid*, 7th ed., 2
     vols. (Madrid, 1969); MacKay, *Spain in the Middle Ages*, pp. 20–29; García de
     Valdeavellano, *Historia de España*, pp. 768–97, 858. Also Julio Valdeón Baruque,
     Enrique II de Castilla; la guerra civil y la consolidación del regimen (1336–1371) (Valla-
     dolid, 1966); Luis Suarez Fernández, *Nobleza y monarquia: Puntos de vista sobre la
     historia castellana del siglo XV*, 2d ed. (Valladolid, 1959); César González Minguez,
     Fernando IV de Castilla (1295–1312). La guerra civil y el predomino de la nobleza
     (Vitoria, 1976).
21. Schramm, *Las insignias*, pp. 36–38, 56–57. For sculptures and miniatures see
     José Guerrero Lovillo, *Las Cantigas, estudio arqueológico de sus miniaturas* (Madrid,
     1949); *Miniatura gótica castellana (siglos XIII y XIV)* (Madrid, 1956); Rafael Cómez
     Ramos, *Las empresas artísticas de Alfonso X, el sabio* (Sevilla, 1979); *Crónica de Enrique
     III* in *Crónicas de los reyes de Castilla*, ed. C. Rosell (Biblioteca de autores españoles,
     68, Madrid, 1877), p. 193. This volume of the *Crónicas* includes those of Henry
     II, Juan I, Henry III, and Juan II, and will be cited hereafter as the chronicle of
     each individual king. See also Françoise Dumas, "Le thrône des rois de France et
     son rayonnement," *La monnaie, miroir des rois* (Paris, 1978), pp. 231–50; R. H.
     Bautier, "Echanges d'influences dans les chancelleries souveraines du Moyen
     Age, d'après les types des sceaux de majesté," *Comptes rendús de l'Académie des
     Inscriptions et Belles-Lettres* (Paris, 1968), fn. 3, pp. 207–8. Bautier notes that al-

though there is a seal from the reign of Alfonso VII, showing the king in his majesty, the seals of the Castilian kings of the thirteenth and fourteenth centuries were equestrian seals.

22. *Primera crónica general*, pp. 560–643. This account is revealing at different levels. The heirs of Navarre and Aragón, by kissing Alfonso VI's hand in the name of the Cid, acknowledge themselves vassals of both the Cid and Alfonso. Miracles are reported, including the conversion of a Jew who comes to Cardeña to mock the body of the Cid. Yet on the same page the miraculous is explained and made rational. Alfonso VI is amazed at seeing the Cid, dead for many days, still uncorrupted and riding his horse, but when the attendants explain to him that the Cid did not eat for the last seven days of life and was embalmed immediately after his death the king was no longer amazed. "He had heard that in the land of Egypt they did that to their *kings*." Ibid., p. 640. See below for the lion's fear of el Cid.

23. *Primera crónica general*, pp. 539, 645; Dillard, "Medieval Convents," p. 10; Mariana, *Historia*, 2:310, 406.

24. For the reign of Alfonso VII see García de Valdeavellano, *Historia de España*, pp. 875–924; Mariana, *Historia*, 2:446–69; *Primera crónica general*, pp. 653–54, 663. Neither Linehan nor Bruhl believe that Alfonso VII was anointed. Again, we are faced with the distortion of the past by later chronicles. Was it a mistake or conscious distortion?

25. *Primera crónica general*, p. 657; Lucas de Tuy, *Crónica de España*, ed. Julio Puyol (Madrid, 1926), p. 339. Lucas de Tuy attributes a quote to Louis VII: "I swear that there is no similar glory [that of Alfonso VII's court] as this in the whole world."

26. See Castro, *La realidad histórica*, pp. 92–96; Gaines Post, *Studies in Medieval Legal Thought: Public Law and the State, 1100–1322* (Princeton, 1964), pp. 482–90; *Primera crónica general*, pp. 310–12, 356. See also Peter Linehan, *The Spanish Church and the Papacy in the Thirteenth Century* (Cambridge, Eng., 1971), pp. 102–6.

27. Lucas de Tuy, *Crónica*, pp. 3–11; José A. Maravall, *El concepto de España en la Edad Media*, 2d ed. (Madrid, 1964), pp. 23, 280 et passim; *Crónica de Sancho IV*, pp. 3, 72. See also Sancho's attitude toward the pope and the papal messengers in *Crónica de Alfonso X*, p. 65. Alfonso X in his first will paid the French a left-handed compliment by commenting on what good businessmen the French were but neither good warriors nor as courageous as the Spaniards. *Memorial histórico español*, 47 vols. (Madrid, 1851–1915), 2:110–22; Schramm, *Kaiser, Könige*, vol. 4, pt. 1, 378–88. See table 4.1. Although there is certainly a religious and mystical aspect to this hard-nosed chauvinism, I find at the heart of it very little of a religious crusade in the sense in which crusades were understood in the north. Anyone who has lived in Spain or dealt with Spaniards for a while will recognize today, even if it is probably a defensive mechanism, that individual and national pride which already existed in the medieval past.

28. Schramm, *A History of the English Coronation*, pp. 1, 141; Lewis, *Royal Succession*, pp. 76–77.

29. *Primera crónica general*, p. 709.
30. Lucas de Tuy, *Crónica*, pp. 449–50. This part of the vernacular chronicle is a later addition. See the introduction by Puyol, pp. xviiff. See also Joseph O'Callaghan, "The *Cantigas de Santa María* as an Historical Source: Two Examples," paper given at a symposium on the *Cantigas* held in New York (November 1981) and forthcoming in the proceedings of the symposium. I would like to thank Professor O'Callaghan for providing me with a copy of his paper. See also Ballesteros, *Alfonso X*, p. 54, who quotes a privilege of Alfonso X of 6 December 1253: "E por mi que fu hy Rey e recebi hy cabelleria." Schramm incorrectly traces self-coronation to Aragón.
31. Ruiz, *Sociedad y poder real*, p. 36; Ballesteros, *Alfonso X*, p. 54; *Crónica de Alfonso X*, p. 7.
32. *Fuero real de Castilla*, 2:2, in *Códigos*, 1:350; *Partida*, 2:1.5, 6 in *Códigos*, 2:317–25.
33. *Fuero juzgo*, 1:1.7, 8, 9 in *Códigos*, 2:319, 326–68. See also Gimeno Casalduero, *La imagen*, pp. 26–37. See also Wilhelm Berges, *Die Fürstenspiegel des hohen und späten Mittelalters* (Leipzig, 1938), pp. 86–88, 93–101.
34. *Fuero juzgo*, 1:1 in *Códigos*, 1:97; 2:1.2, p. 107; "Que el rey e los pueblos deven seer sometidos de las leyes," *Fuero viejo de Castilla*, ley ccxxviii in *Códigos*, 1:337; *Fuero real*, tit 2 in *Códigos* 1:351 instructs how to obtain redress from the evil actions of kings, including "going public." *Partida*, 1:1.16, in *Códigos* 2:16; *Partida*, 2:1.10 in *Códigos*, 2, 329.
35. *Primera crónica general*, p. 713; Mariana, *Historia*, 3:127–28 claims that the succession was not legal and that Doña Blanca was the rightful heir. Commenting on the troubled succession of Henry III, Mariana, *Historia*, 4:350–53, describes how the king's will in favor of his young son, the Infante Don Juan, was challenged. He goes on to show the many instances in thirteenth- and fourteenth-century Castilian history in which the rightful heir did not succeed to the throne. "Seria forzoso confesar," Mariana added, "que los Reyes pasados no tuvieron justo titulo." The throne of Castile was offered to the Infante Fernando (Henry III's brother), who did not accept it. *Crónica de Enrique III*, p. 262. See also, for Isabella I, John H. Elliott, *Imperial Spain 1469–1716* (Harmondsworth, 1975), pp. 22–23.
36. *Primera crónica general*, pp. 713–18; Lucas de Tuy, *Crónica*, p. 417; Rodrigo Ximénez de Rada, *Opera* (reimpression, facsimile of ed. of 1793. Valencia, 1968), pp. 192–96. The Portuguese kings also girded their swords themselves.
37. Ballesteros, *Alfonso X*, pp. 10–50; *Primera crónica general*, pp. 722–23. It is remarkable to see how early the Capetians established dynastic succession and the uniqueness of a bloodline when compared with Castile. See Lewis, *Royal Succession*, pp. 19–20, 35–36, 76, 107–16; Schramm, *A History of the English Coronation*, p. 106.
38. See *Crónica de Sancho IV*, p. 69; *Crónica de Fernando IV*, p. 93; *Crónica de Alfonso XI*, p. 173; *Crónica de Enrique II*, p. 1; *Crónica de Juan* I, 65; *Crónica de Enrique III*, p. 161; *Crónica de Juan II*, pp. 261–62; Fernando del Pulgar, *Crónica de los Reyes Católicos*, 2 vols. (Madrid, 1943), 1:65–66.

39. García Gallo, *Manual*, 1:628.
40. See Ferdinand III's advice to his son Alfonso: "Sir, I leave you all the lands on this side of the sea which the Moors won from King Roderick of Spain. All this now lies within your power, one part of it conquered and the other laid under tribute. If you should manage to hold it all in the way in which I leave it to you, then you are as good a king as I; and if you should lose any of it, you are not as good as I." Quoted in MacKay, *Spain*, p. 59. According to the *Crónica de Alfonso X*, p. 53, after the death of the Infante de la Cerda, heir to the crown, the magnates requested from Alfonso X that he name Sancho as his successor because "he defended the land and defeated the Moors." See also *Poema de Alfonso XI*, p. 481. For the oath see Mariana, *Historia*, 4:11, describing how Alfonso XI took an oath to the Basques under the famous and ancient tree of Guernica. For the oath of Charles I see Schramm, *Las insignias*, p. 74. For the relations between king and Cortes in the thirteenth and fourteenth centuries see T. F. Ruiz, "Oligarchy and Royal Power: The Castilian Cortes and the Castilian Crisis, 1248–1350," in *Parliaments, Estates & Representation*, vol. 2, no. 2 (1982): 95–101. On contracts in general see H. Hopfl and M. P. Thompson, "The History of Contracts as a Motif in Political Thought," *American Historical Review*, 84 (1979): 929–44; also Ralph E. Giesey, *If Not, Not. The Oath and the Legendary Laws of Sobrarbe* (Princeton, 1968), pp. 158–226. On the emphasis of military symbols and ideal warriors see a different approach in Frances Yates, *Astraea: The Imperial Theme in the Sixteenth Century* (London, 1975), pp. 21–23 and the motif of Hercules in the symbols of the Spanish monarchy of the early modern period in Jonathan Brown and John H. Elliott, *A Palace for a King* (New Haven, 1980), pp. 156ff.
41. *Partida*, 2:4.1–5 in *Códigos*, 2:334–48; *Castigos é documentos del Rey don Sancho*, ed. Pascual de Gayangos (Biblioteca de autores españoles, 51, Madrid, 1952), pp. 79–228; Gimeno Casalduero, *La imagen*, pp. 46–52. On the "mirror of princes" literature in general, see Wilhelm Berges, *Die Fürstenspiegel des hohen und späten Mittelalters*, pp. 86–101. On the sexual mores see Linehan, *The Spanish Church*.
42. See nn. 6 and 36 and Elliott, *Imperial Spain*, pp. 86, 93, 151–56.
43. *Crónica de Alfonso X*, p. 13. This was the same Alfonso de la Cerda who girded Alfonso XI's spurs. See also n. 2.
44. For the knighting of Prince Edward see Ballesteros, *Alfonso X*, p. 101. For Ferdinand IV see *Crónica de Fernando IV*, p. 93.
45. Professor John H. Elliott was kind enough to direct me to this source. "Voyage d'Antoine de Brunel en Espagne," *Revue hispanique*, 30 (1914): 213: "Il est vray que, pour le respect qu'on rend au roy et à ceux qui l'approchent, on a quantité de petites coustumes toutes extraordinaries, et entr'autres on à celle que personne ne monte jamais un cheval quand le roy s'en est servy. L'on raconte qu'après la prise de Barcelonne en la cavalcade que sa Majesté fit à l'Atocha, le duc de Medina de las Torres luy envoya presenter son beau cheval, qui est si fameux à Madrid; mais le roy le renvoya, devant: seria lastima, c'est à dire que seroit dommage qu'il le montast, puisque par là il deviendroit inutile à tout le

monde, et ne seroit monté que de quelques escuyers." See also references to the *cavallo real* in Lucas de Tuy, *Crónica*, p. 450; and Frazer, *Bough*, pp. 174, 459, 639–40 et passim.

46. Schramm, *Las insignias*, p. 67; García de Valdeavellano, *Curso de historia*, p. 193. The proclamation of Isabella as queen of Castile and the description of the ceremonies are found in the minutes of the council of Segovia. The *acta* have been edited and published by M. Grau, *Estudios segovianos*, 1 (1949): 24–36; Luis Suárez Fernández notes that the *pendones* were not raised for the Beltraneja, *Historia de España*, ed. R. Menédez Pidal (Madrid, 1969), vol. 17, pt. 1, pp. 85–87. One should note the similarities with Louis VII of France receiving the standard of St. Denis. See Robert Fawtier, *The Capetian Kings of France: Monarchy and Nation 987–1328*, trans. L. Butler and R. J. Adam (New York, 1965), p. 80. To this very day small towns in Castile and León, such as that of my ancestors in the province of Burgos, keep their banners in the local church, to be paraded in the patron saint's procession. See J. W. and R. L. Fernández, "El escenario de la romería asturiana," *Expresiones actuales de la cultura del pueblo* (Madrid, 1976). Ruth Behar is at work on a study of the *romería* of the Virgin del Camino, forthcoming in *Archivos leoneses*. For the inheritance of the throne by bastards see Charles T. Wood, "Queens, Queans, and Kingship: An Inquiry into Theories of Royal Legitmacy in Late Medieval England and France," in *Order and Innovation in the Middle Ages*, ed. W. C. Jordan, et al. (Princeton, 1976), pp. 387–400.

47. I also owe this note to Professor Elliott. Antonio de León Pinelo, *Anales de Madrid* (Biblioteca de estudios madrileños, 9, Madrid, 1971), pp. 168, 235. The Plaza Mayor also served as a bull ring and as the showcase for great Inquisition trials. It was also one of the scenes of the popular uprising against the Napoleonic armies. It is as if in one place, the Plaza Mayor, the central themes of Castilian and Spanish history—martial monarchy, bullfighting, Inquisition, and popular violence—met within the serene and formal majesty of the square.

48. García de Valdeavellano, *Curso de historia*, p. 384; Marc Bloch, *Feudal Society*, trans. L. A. Manyon, 2 vols. (Chicago, 1966), pp. 162, 180, and for Castile, 182; Schramm, *A History of the English Coronation*, p. 20. Some examples from the chronicles can be seen in *Crónica de Fernando IV*, pp. 96, 117; Castro, *La realidad histórica*, pp. 234–35. For the kissing of feet as a sign of submission see the *Dictatus Papae*, item no. 9, in Brian Tierney, *The Crisis of Church and State 1050–1300* (Englewood Cliffs, N.J., 1964); Linehan, *The Spanish Church*, p. 240; Angel Barrios García, *Documentación medieval de la catedral de Ávila* (Salamanca, 1981), p. 145.

49. Schramm, *A History of the English Coronation*, p. 38; Jofré de Loaysa, *Crónica de los reyes de Castilla: Fernando III, Alfonso X, Sancho IV, Fernando IV (1248–1305)* (Murcia, 1961), p. 141. For the rearranging of tombs as means of advancing dynastic claims and royal funerals see Elizabeth A. R. Brown, "The Ceremony of Royal Succession in Capetian France: The Double Funeral of Louis X," *Traditio*, 34 (1978): 227–71; "Philippe le Bel and the Remains of Saint Louis," *Gazette des Beaux-Arts* (May 1980): 175–82; "The Ceremonial of Royal Succession in

Capetian France: The Funeral of Philip V," *Speculum*, 55 (1980): 266–93; "Death and the Human Body in the Later Middle Ages: The Legislation of Boniface VIII on the Division of the Corpse," *Viator*, 12 (1981): 221–70. Only Alfonso X, a great admirer of Louis IX of France, requested in his will that his body be divided, in imitation, he said, of his German grandfather, but probably because Louis's example was close at hand. All the other Castilian kings avoided the French royal custom of division of the corpse.

50. *Crónica de Sancho IV*, pp. 72–73. See also Gimeno Casalduero, *La imagen*, pp. 93–116, for Henry II's bizarre propaganda against his half-brother, accusing Peter I of being illegitimate, which, of course, made him a bastard as Henry was, and their common father, Alfonso XI, a cuckold.

51. Socarras, *Alfonso X*, p. 79. Nobility in Spain was established when three successive generations were exempted from taxes. See Ruiz, *Sociedad y poder real*, p. 46.

52. Linehan, *The Spanish Church*, pp. 29–30.

53. Ibid., pp. 102–6, 186, 240: "Alvarus Pelagius 'forced to admit that even he was accustomed to kiss the King's hand,—as the vile Spanish prelates' did." For the quote by Don Juan Manuel, p. 224. John H. Elliott, *Imperial Spain, 1469–1716* (London, 1963), p. 230.

54. Claudio Sánchez Albornoz, *España*, 1:316–17. For the attitude toward myths and witches, a thoroughly rational one, see Julio Caro Baroja, *Inquisición, brujería y criptojudaísmo*, 3d ed. (Barcelona, 1974), pp. 183–282; *The World of the Witches*, trans. O. N. V. Glendinning (Chicago, 1973), pp. 180–89. Think of the attitude toward religion in the Spanish picaresque novels or the debunking of St. James in *Don Quixote*. Also Berges, *Die Fürstenspiegel*, p. 89, and n. 53.

55. *Cantigas de Santa María*, ed. Walter Mettmann, 4 vols. (Coimbra, 1959–72), 3:175–77; O'Callaghan, "The *Cantigas*," p. 2; Evelyn Proctor, *Alfonso X of Castile, Patron of Literature and Learning* (Cambridge, Eng., 1951), pp. 24–45; John Esten Keller, *Alfonso X: El Sabio* (New York, 1967), pp. 64–95; Castro, *La realidad histórica*, p. 371; Bloch, *The Royal Touch*, pp. 85–89.

56. García Gallo, *Manual*, 1:561ff.; García de Valdeavellano, *Curso de historia*, pp. 629–76. For the interaction of Islamic and Christian cultures see Thomas F. Glick, *Islamic and Christian Spain in the Early Middle Ages: Comparative Perspective on Social and Cultural Formation* (Princeton, 1979). See also R.P.A. Dozy, *Histoire des musulmans d'Espagne*, ed. E. Leví-Provençal, 3 vols. (Leyde, 1932); E. Leví-Provençal, *L'Espagne musulmane au Xéme siècle: Institutions et vie sociale* (Paris, 1932), pp. 41–114; Raymond Jamous, *Honneur et baraka: Les structures sociales traditionneles dans le Rif* (Cambridge, Eng., 1981), pp. 221–28; Clifford Geertz, *Islam Observed: Religious Development in Morocco and Indonesia* (New Haven, 1969), pp. 44, 53.

57. See William C. Jordan, *Louis XI and the Challenge of the Crusade* (Princeton, 1979); Lewis, *Royal Succession*, p. 125.

58. Quoting Alonso de Cartagena, Castro describes the wars of the *hispano-cristianos* as *divinales*. See Castro, *La realidad histórica*, p. 140. See also p. 246: "El modelo para la estructuración colectiva no fue ni el visigodo, ni el francés, ni el inglés en

los cuales la dimensión política predominaba sobre la religiosa. La base de la nación fue la circumstancia de haber nacido la persona dentro de la casta religiosa a la que pertenecía cada uno de los tres grupos creyentes." Castro contradicts himself on pp. 38–39. He published in parallel columns the epitaph of Ferdinand III, written in Latin, Castilian, Arabic, and Hebrew. Only the Latin version, a clerical production, refers to religious matters: "qui civitatem Hispalensem que capud est et metropolis tocius Hispanie de manibus eripuit paganorum et cultui restituit christiano." The other three versions address Ferdinand's human qualities and his deeds of arms. Sánchez Albornoz, "La *'ordinatio Principis,'* " p. 737, explains the decline in the influence of the Church. To a certain extent he is correct, but it is perhaps more accurate to speak of the peculiar relationship between Church and king in Castile and later in Spain due to the martial tradition, the frontier, and the Muslim influence. On the Castilian church see the excellent work by Peter Linehan, *The Spanish Church and the Papacy in the Thirteenth Century* (Cambridge, Eng., 1971). For the later relations between Church and king see Elliott, *Imperial Spain*, pp. 99–110. Schramm, *A History of the English Coronation*, p. 96, advances a one-line explanation, "the relation of the king to the Estates. . ." for the peculiarities of the Castilian ordination of kings. See also A. Barbero and M. Vigil, *Sobre las orígenes sociales de la Reconquista* (Barcelona, 1974). See also n. 53.

59. *Partida*, 1:5.18 in *Códigos*, p. 82; Castro, *La realidad histórica*, p. 85.

60. See *Memorial histórico español*, 2:110–34. For other wills see *Crónica de Enrique II*, pp. 39–44; *Crónica de Enrique III*, pp. 186–94. Compare with the will of Philip IV of France. See Elizabeth A. R. Brown, "Royal Salvation and Needs of State in Late Capetian France," in *Order and Innovation*, pp. 363–83. For the sense of individuality in Alfonso X's *Cantigas* see Marisel Precillas, "The Image of Death in the *Cantigas* of Santa María," forthcoming, *Proceedings of International Symposium on the Cantigas of Santa María*.

61. Bloch, *The Royal Touch*, p. 142; *Crónica de Alfonso X*, p. 7; *Poema del Cid* (Biblioteca de autores españoles, 57), p. 25; *Don Quixote*, 2: ch. 17. Dumas, "Le throne," p. 247, seal no 41.

62. Fernando Mexía, *Nobiliario perfetamente copulado* (Seville, 1492), f. 164; Mariana, *Historia*, 4:70.

63. Lucas de Tuy, *Crónica*, p. 363: "Ciertamente, los reyes de España se dize aver seydo de tanta ferocidad, que aun en la hedad non cumplida tomaron armas, quier contra hermano, quier contra padre si fuesse bivo, y aparejan contender por sus fuerças que el derecho real solo se lo tenga." Jofré de Loaysa, *Crónica*, p. 121; *Crónica de Sancho IV*, p. 74 (Juan Martínez de Negrita spoke in defense of his lord, and Sancho IV beat him to death with a stick). *Crónica de Fernando IV*, p. 169; *Crónica de Alfonso XI*, p. 202; *Poema de Alfonso XI*, p. 484; *Crónica de Pedro I*, p. 592.

64. Mariana, *Historia*, 4:390.

5

J. H. ELLIOTT

Power and Propaganda in the Spain of Philip IV

Although power and ideology march together through the centuries, there are ambiguities in their relationship that still need to be explored. Where early modern Europe is concerned, the possibilities for exploration are considerable, and the prospects look promising for some redirection of a historical debate that is at present in disarray. Nineteenth- and early twentieth-century historiography tended to emphasize, and often indeed to exaggerate, the effectiveness of state building in the early modern period. More recent historical writing, by contrast, has moved sharply in the opposite direction. It has been less impressed by the effectiveness of monarchical power in early modern Europe than by its limitations. It has paid more attention to participation than coercion, more attention to resistance than to the exercise of power, more attention to survival than to innovation. In so doing, it has tended to cast doubt on what was previously taken for granted: the *transforming* power of the state.[1]

More recent fashions in research, however, have introduced a new and not yet fully integrated element into this post–Second World War picture of the early modern state as a leviathan *manqué*. Contemporary fascination with the problems and possibilities of image making and ideological control has done much to inspire these fashions, and has helped to stimulate historical inquiry into attempts by those in authority to manipulate public opinion by means of ritual, ceremonial, and propaganda, whether in written, pictorial, or spoken form.

Contemporary interest in the deployment of images and symbols by those in power has undoubtedly added an important new dimension to our knowledge and understanding of early modern Europe. This dimension can be especially valuable for the seventeenth century, a time when new instruments and techniques of visual representation made it possible for authority to resort extensively to those illusionistic tricks that are essential to the process of image building. It was a century, too, that possessed an unusually acute awareness of the complex relationship of image and reality. The word *reputation* figured prominently in the vocabulary of seventeenth-century statesmen, and the Spanish political theorist Saavedra Fajardo was only expressing a commonplace of the times when he wrote in his *Idea of a Political-Christian Prince* (1640): "if the crown is not firmly planted on this central column of reputation, it will fall to the ground."[2] Reputation was the other person's perception of oneself, and if it had to be grounded on at least a minimal basis of reality, it could still be enhanced by ingenious sleights of hand.

As an age captivated by the art of the theater, the seventeenth century displayed an almost obsessive concern with appearance. If the world is perceived in terms of the theater, the enhancement or transformation of appearance becomes an essential component of the statesman's art. The application of the arts of the theater to political life, and especially to the projection of kingship, is one of the principal characteristics of seventeenth-century monarchies; and it would be valuable to have more systematic research into the ways in which the symbols of monarchy were manipulated to enhance the power and majesty of seventeenth-century kings. But at least two *caveats* should be borne in mind when this research is undertaken.

If the leviathan of the seventeenth-century state proves on closer inspection to be a beast skilled in the arts of illusion, these skills would make it less of a leviathan *manqué* than has recently been assumed. While this may indeed prove to be the conclusion, it is not a conclusion that should be embraced without some awareness of the problems inherent in the study of propaganda and image making. There is some danger of our being more impressed by the workings of a propaganda machine than were those at whom it was directed, simply because of the quantity of evidence left behind for later generations. The example of the Spain of Olivares suggests that the new propaganda resources of the seventeenth-century state were perfectly capable of being counterproductive, and of damaging the very cause they were intended to promote.

Even if we reach the plausible conclusion that ritual, ceremonial, and propaganda were capable, if deftly used, of enhancing monarchical authority, there remains another danger: that an excessive concentration on them is liable to distract attention from other and possibly more potent weapons in the armory of seventeenth-century monarchs and statesmen. The exercise of power is, after all, something more than the manipulation of images. While capitalizing, then, on our sharpened awareness of the significance of symbolism and the creation of images, it would be unwise to assume that this is enough. The effectiveness of those images in any given historical situation still needs to be tested, and then set alongside that of other and perhaps more formidable devices by which rulers elicited the obedience and assent of the ruled.

The complex nature of the relationship between power and ideology can be illustrated from the history of the Spain of Philip IV during the twenty-two years of government of his favorite and principal minister, the count-duke of Olivares (1621–43). Many features of the Spanish situation were, as always, unique; but the way in which the Olivares regime attempted to extend the range of its power by resorting to ceremonial, propaganda, and image making is characteristic enough of seventeenth-century monarchies to suggest something of the nature of contemporary governments and the difficulties that they faced.

On coming to power in 1621 Olivares made it his principal objective to restore Spain, and especially Castile, to the greatness that it had enjoyed under Charles V and Philip II. In his view the achievements of Spain's sixteenth-century monarchs had been undermined by the ineptitude and corruption of the regime preceding his own, that of the duke of Lerma, the favorite and first minister of Philip III (1598–1621). He planned also to give Spain and its empire an effective system of military and naval defense against its numerous actual or potential enemies, and especially the Dutch, who had shown in their short period of independence how intelligent economic organization could enhance the military capabilities of a second- or third-rate European power.

He aimed, therefore, both to restore and to modernize, and in so doing committed himself to a program that may from the start have been flawed by internal contradictions.[3] A particular set of values and assumptions had made Castile what it was, and Olivares shared the common belief that the departure from these values and assumptions had set in motion the process of decline. Yet even while he sought to revive Castile's ancient virtues, he was also well aware that a society with a traditional value system needed to adapt in order to meet the challenge of hard economic times. Traditionally, for instance, Castilians despised the values of the marketplace, but it was Olivares's intention to "turn Spaniards into merchants."[4]

What were the values and assumptions on which Spain's historical greatness had been predicated—the ideological underpinnings, as it were, of the Spanish Monarchy and empire? The first of them was the sense of global mission, conceived both in religious and dynastic terms. Tradition- ally, it was the Holy Roman Empire, now governed by the junior branch of the House of Austria, which had universalist claims. But in practice it was the *Monarquía Española*, the Spanish Monarchy, which was at once truly global and imperial in character, and which could claim with good reason to be the dominant world power.

It was clear to the men who governed sixteenth-century Spain that only God's special favor could have endowed their king with so many dominions, and given him an empire of unprecedented size, on which the sun never set. Therefore the justification of Habsburg rule and Spanish domination must be the furtherance of God's cause. In consequence, Habsburg Spain had a mission: to preserve, defend, and extend the faith, acting—in close concert with the Austrian branch of the family—as the right arm of the Church. If this mission were effectively sustained, a properly ordered world would enjoy the innumerable blessings of a *pax hispanica*.

This sense of Christian providentialism—of the defense of the Catho- lic cause against the forces of infidels and heretics—gave Habsburg Spain its raison d'être. It found expression in a large body of apologetic literature in the sixteenth and seventeenth centuries, of which Fray Juan de Salazar's *Política Española* of 1619 provided a particularly strident example. "The principal foundation of this high edifice," he wrote, "the hinges and axles on which this great machine turns, lies not in the rules of the impious Machiavelli, which atheists call 'reason of state'. . . but in religion and the service and honor of God."[5]

This sense of global mission was complemented by a close identifica- tion of throne and altar: the ruler of Spain was the standard-bearer of God's cause. Nowhere was the historic mission of the dynasty more effec- tively expressed than in Titian's great portrait of Charles V at Mühlberg (1548) (fig. 5.1).[6] Here Charles is represented as the *miles christianus*, an image that his descendants would seek to make their own. They took for granted the existence of a special relationship between God and them- selves. God conferred victories upon a king who served Him well; and conversely, as Philip IV became agonizingly aware, defeat was provoked by royal sinfulness.

While the sacred character of Spanish kingship was taken as axiomatic, it did not assume many of the forms associated with divine kingship in other parts of Europe. The king of Spain, for example, possessed no heal-

Fig. 5.1. Titian, *Charles V at Mühlberg*. Prado Museum, Madrid.

ing powers, and Spaniards in need of healing would travel to Paris, not Madrid, for a cure.[7] Moreover, there had been no coronation ceremony in Castile since 1379: the heir to the throne would receive homage as a prince, and the only ceremonies on his accession were the raising of banners and the official proclamation of his style and titles. This seems to suggest a confidence about the divinely ordained nature of Spanish king-

Fig. 5.2. Vasari, *Apotheosis of Duke Cosimo*. Palazzo Vecchio, Florence.

ship, operating through a legitimate line of descent, which precluded the need felt elsewhere to reinforce the image of kingship with the visible symbols of royalty. Indeed, at the end of the sixteenth century the kings of Spain apparently had no official throne, no scepter, no crown.[8]

It is perhaps not surprising, then, that Spanish royal portraiture of the sixteenth and seventeenth centuries fails to develop an elaborate symbolic language, in sharp contrast to the practice followed at the courts of lesser European rulers. Vasari's apotheosis of Grand Duke Cosimo I of Tuscany (fig. 5.2) would have seemed out of place in the more restrained world of

Fig. 5.3. Sánchez Coello, *Philip II.* Prado Museum, Madrid (left).
Fig. 5.4. Velázquez, *Philip IV.* Prado Museum, Madrid (right).

the Spanish court. It is as if a form of "Avis principle" operates in the world of political imagery and propaganda: those who are only second try harder. Where, as in Habsburg Spain, the supremacy of the king is taken for granted, political imagery can be studiously understated, and there is no need to deck out the ruler with elaborate allegorical trappings (figs. 5.3, 5.4). This form of understatement may well represent the ultimate in political sophistication.

By papal concession, however, the kings of Spain proudly bore the title of Catholic Kings, and they made a point of emphasizing their supremely Catholic character, more Catholic in their own eyes than of their rival, *le roi très Chrétien.* Their public appearances were largely connected with religious occasions, such as attendance at mass or at *autos de fe*, and participation in religious processions. In consequence, the association between the king and the faith was automatically made by his subjects. In the festivities to celebrate the inauguration of the palace of the Buen Retiro in December 1633, Philip IV, to be shielded from the elements, was seated on a balcony adorned with red velvet and gold damask hangings and protected by glass panels. To one observer he looked like a holy relic in a reliquary.[9]

The special relationship between God and the king was also emphasized in the official style of court architecture inspired by the Escorial, part palace, part church, part monastery (fig. 5.5). Even Philip IV's pleasure palace of the Buen Retiro, built on the outskirts of Madrid in the 1630s, adjoined the royal church and convent of San Jerónimo, and its spacious gardens were dotted with hermitage chapels. The very name of Retiro was a play on the idea of retreat, which included that of religious retreat. Calderón's allegorical drama, *El Nuevo Palacio del Buen Retiro*, presented at court in 1634, took place simultaneously on two planes, the celestial and the earthly. God was equated with the king; the church with the queen; and New Jerusalem with the new palace of the Buen Retiro. Judaism, forbidden entry into the palace, was forced to watch the enactment of the Eucharist, which was followed by the emergence of the king bearing the cross aloft, after his temporary *retiro* into the bread.[10]

This constant allusion to the sacred ties that bound God and king would seem to have had a dual purpose. To the world at large it helped to define the position of the king of Spain as the most Catholic of kings; but within Spain itself it also provided an important element of political and social cohesion. Church and king were the two common elements in the disparate and fragmented Spanish Monarchy; and religious uniformity, enforced by king, Church, and inquisition, was the guarantee of continuing political order and stability. It also guaranteed the continuation of a hierarchical social order which mirrored that of the universe. The sermon, therefore, had an important part to play in maintaining the political and social status quo,[11] and the same role was also fulfilled by the theater. Theater was supposed to be exemplary, or, in the words of Tirso de Molina, himself a friar, "to teach by giving pleasure" (*enseñar deleitando*).[12] It is not surprising, therefore, to find that a central theme of seventeenth-century drama is that of the moral, social, or political order undermined by sin or ignorance, with a dénouement that results in the restoration of the status quo. More unqualified expressions of the divine right of kings are to be found in the work of seventeenth-century Spanish dramatists

Fig. 5.5. The Escorial. Patrimonio Nacional, Madrid.

than in that of contemporaneous political theorists. "What the king orders is never unjust," proclaims Ruiz de Alarcón.[13]

Along with the universalism of a global mission, and the recurring identification of king and altar, the Spanish Monarchy traditionally rested on a third central principle: the combination of constitutional pluralism with unitary kingship. The Monarchy was in effect a supranational community, made up of a complex of kingdoms and provinces, which differed in their laws, customs, and languages, and were united only in their adherence to a common faith and their allegiance to a common king. Jealously guarding their semiautonomous status, the different constituent parts acknowledged only the overlordship of an almost permanently absentee monarch. The king of all was also, in a seventeenth-century phrase, the king of each;[14] and the fact that he was king of each was more important to the individual kingdoms and provinces than that he was also king of all.

The Spanish Monarchy, established in Madrid in 1561, was in consequence a centrifugal structure, which the king sought to hold together by a carefully organized institutional system of viceroys and councils. In such a structure the role of the king, and the image he presents to his various peoples, must be of prime importance, since in his own person he embodies unity. To retain their allegiance and reinforce their loyalty there were various guises in which he could present himself to the subjects of his different realms. Both Charles V and Philip II were presented as the champions of militant orthodoxy, although Charles V was the more convincing of the two in the role of warrior king. Philip II, on the other hand, developed with great skill the image of the concerned ruler in an age of bureaucratic government, creating a new model of the king as bureaucrat toiling over his papers. He also projected himself as the supreme upholder of law and the defender of justice, a royal Solomon, whose palace of the Escorial was itself conceived as the Temple of Jerusalem.[15] It is no accident, then, that the king repeatedly appears at the climactic moment of seventeenth-century Spanish plays as the *deus ex machina* who, with Solomonic equity, redresses grievances, gives to each his deserts, and restores the political and social order jeopardized by oppressive landlords or evil councilors.

The image of a supremely just king, remote but—when necessary—available, provides the indispensable safety valve in societies subject to social and financial exploitation and administrative abuse. When rebels shouted "long live the king and down with bad government!" as they did in Catalonia and Spanish Italy in the 1640s, the safety mechanism was working as it was supposed to work. Philip II was well aware of the political advantages to be gained from fulfilling his God-given duty to sustain justice and uphold the law. But the consequence of acting as the custodian of law in a constitutionally diversified monarchy was to condemn it to a high degree of political immobility. The laws of each kingdom were sacrosanct; the king had sworn to maintain them. It was therefore difficult, if not impossible, to change the political structure, even where this worked against the crown's best interests, because the laws could not be changed. The sixteenth-century Spanish crown had found an ingenious formula for the conservation of empire, but the price of conservation was abstention from tampering with the status quo.

These three governing principles of the Spanish Monarchy helped to determine both the shape of the program on which Olivares embarked after the accession of Philip IV in 1621, and the constraints under which he had to operate. The Monarchy had arrived at a critical juncture in 1621, not least because of the growing incompatibility of two of these three principles: an activist foreign policy conceived in terms of a global mission to defend the faith, and a passive domestic policy dominated by the desire to avoid disturbing the status quo in the various territories owing allegiance to the king.

The activist foreign policy, pursued over many decades, although with some recent slackening, had proved enormously expensive in terms of manpower and money; and such was the constitutional structure of the Monarchy that the burden of sustaining this foreign policy had fallen with particular intensity on the heartland of the Monarchy, Castile, which was deficient in legal and institutional defenses against financial exactions by the crown. Royal fiscalism had done irreparable damage to the Castilian economy, and the damage had been compounded by twenty years of mismanagement under the rule of Philip III's favorite, the duke of Lerma, whose corrupt administration had devalued the authority of the crown and played into the hands of sectional interests in Castilian society.

Olivares came to power in 1621 committed to an activist foreign policy, which seemed to him all the more necessary because of the simultaneous resumption of war with the Dutch and the threat posed by the outbreak of war in Germany to what were perceived as the vital interests of the House of Austria. But he came to the conclusion that the condition of Castile and of the Spanish Monarchy as a whole made it impossible to sustain this activist foreign policy without radical reform at home—a reform both of institutions and of mental attitudes. In the 1620s and 1630s, therefore, a new and unprecedented political activism overtook Madrid's domestic policy as the count-duke attempted to restore Spain's international standing—its "reputation"—along with the political and economic base needed to sustain it.

His activist program dictated the character of the Olivares regime and gave a new, if temporary, dynamism to the power of the state in seventeenth-century Spain. This more aggressive deployment of state power coincided with a similar movement in the France of Richelieu and, to a lesser degree, in the England of Charles I. Insofar as it was a general European movement, it seems to have been both a response to the renewal of warfare in the difficult economic climate of the 1620s and 1630s, and a reflection of new assumptions about the character and purpose of the state.

The critical problem confronting Olivares, as also Richelieu, was how to maximize power. Greater international power could only come from the more effective mobilization of economic and social resources to meet the demands of war; but war—or at least victorious war—was in turn one of the most effective devices for enhancing the domestic power of the state.

In setting about his task of maximizing power, Olivares lacked two important elements on which at least some of his contemporaries were able to build. One was the idea of nationality. The supranational character of the Spanish Monarchy meant that national loyalties could not be used to animate the structure as a whole. Different regions had their own sense of identity, and Castile in particular had developed its own brand of messianic nationalism, although this was faltering by the early seventeenth century and clearly had no validity beyond Castile itself. Any reactivation of Castilian nationalism was likely, indeed, to be counterproductive, setting up shock waves of local nationalism in other parts of the Monarchy. But what alternative, if any, existed? How was it possible to generate a sense of loyalty to a supranational bureaucratic organism?

Richelieu was able to make much of the state, both as a concept and a word. But where and what was the state in a worldwide monarchy of disparate provinces? Not surprisingly, although Olivares speaks of "reason of state" or "matters of state," he does not appear to have possessed Richelieu's high conception of the state as an abstract entity. He refers instead to the "crown," the "monarchy," or to the "royal authority," operating within the framework of an organic relationship between king and people. Where Richelieu, then, sought to elevate the power of the state,

Olivares sought to enhance the power and authority of the king, although the difference may have been more semantic than real. In Olivares's opinion the balance of power, both at home and abroad, had been tilting against the king of Spain, and this had to be redressed before it was too late. The king was therefore at the center of his plans for the revival of Spain. His mission was to elevate his royal master to new heights of authority.

His first task was to enhance Philip's majesty, transforming a rather petulant and self-willed adolescent into *Felipe el Grande*—Philip the Great— a king supreme in the skills of government, and in the arts of peace and war. With an eye both to international and domestic opinion, Olivares set out to groom Philip for his stellar role. Where government was concerned, the model was to be that untiring civil servant, the king's grandfather, Philip II. The image of a working king was needed to efface the image of a *roi fainéant* governed by a favorite—an image that had survived the nominal reign of Philip III and the actual reign of the duke of Lerma, and looked set for a repeat appearance with Philip IV and the count-duke of Olivares. The count-duke eschewed the name of favorite—*privado* or *valido*—preferring to be known as the king's "faithful minister." But if the old image were to be banished, he must persuade the king to work. In the opening years of the reign this proved an uphill task, since Philip preferred the pleasures of the chase to the tedium of the study. But in a mood of remorse following a serious illness in 1627 he at last began to settle down to his state papers, and was soon putting in long hours at his desk, to the delight of Olivares. If he never quite became another Philip II, he turned himself under Olivares's prompting into a conscientious monarch, and the two men seem to have established a genuine working partnership.

Where the arts of peace were concerned, Philip proved an admirable pupil. Again with Olivares's encouragement, he set out to repair the deficiencies of an inadequate education, and embarked on an impressive reading program in the best ancient and modern authors.[16] He showed an early taste for music and the theater, and became, like so many of his family, a great connoisseur and picture collector, adding some two thousand paintings to the royal collections over the course of his reign. He therefore moved instinctively to fill the part envisaged for him by Olivares as a prince of patrons. He was to be the *rey planeta*—the Planet King, after the sun, the fourth of the planets—and although it was left to his future nephew and son-in-law, Louis XIV of France, to develop systematically the conceit of the sun, Philip shone as the central luminary in a brilliant court.

The old palace of the Alcázar, however, was not an ideal setting for the court of the Planet King, but this deficiency was remedied in the 1630s with the construction of the Buen Retiro. Closely following the traditional style of Spanish royal architecture, the exterior of the new palace lacked grandeur by seventeenth-century standards. But the principal rooms were lavishly furnished and hung with paintings, some of which constituted thematic series, although no general attempt was made to achieve a tightly woven symbolism, except in the principal hall of the palace, the famous Hall of Realms. The palace courtyards were used for tournaments and jousts. The extensive gardens were carefully laid out with different forms of royal recreation in mind; and the island set in the great artificial lake was used for the mounting of elaborate plays by Calderón and other court dramatists, staged by the brilliant Italian scenographer Cosimo Lotti. With the completion in 1640 of a special court theater, the Coliseo, it was possible to stage complex *comedias de tramoyas*—machine plays—capable of producing the most spectacular scenic effects.

The court of Philip IV therefore became, as Olivares had planned, a great center of patronage and a showcase for the arts. The cultural patronage of Philip's court was perhaps unsystematic by later standards, but if it did not add up to a formal program or convey a coherent set of values, it nurtured some men of genius, among them Lope de Vega, Calderón, and Velázquez, and helped project the image of a country inferior to none in the arts of peace as well as war.

The arts of war were not, as Philip IV had wistfully hoped, to be embodied in his person. His ambition to lead his armies into battle was consistently thwarted by Olivares, and he was forced to find his compensation on the hunting field. But no effort was spared to present to the world the image of a victorious king, and it was in the Hall of Realms of the Buen Retiro that the military greatness of Philip IV and the power of Spain were given visible expression. The decoration of the hall was planned and executed between 1633 and 1635, and was clearly intended to dispel the impression, created by the palace as a whole, that the king was concerned only with frivolity and pleasure in times of war and hardship. In an iconographical program in which the desires of the king and Olivares were clearly paramount, some of the major themes of the reign were splendidly rehearsed.[17]

The ceiling of the hall, with its twenty-four coats of arms of the different realms, emphasized the multiplicity and the close mutual relationship of the many kingdoms owing allegiance to Philip IV. The two end walls were devoted to the immediate past, present, and future of the dynasty, with equestrian portraits by Velázquez of Philip III and Philip IV and their queens, and the young Baltasar Carlos, the heir to the throne (figs. 5.6, 5.7). Along the two side walls ran ten scenes by Zurbarán of the life of Hercules, the conqueror of discord, the model of princely virtues, and the founding father of the dynasty. Placed between the windows of these same walls were the most striking feature of the room—a series of twelve great battle paintings by different Spanish artists. Five of these paintings, including Velázquez's masterpiece, *The Surrender of Breda* (fig. 5.8), depicted victories won by Spain in 1625, which had passed into official mythology as the *annus mirabilis* of the reign of Philip IV. Another four commemorated the victories of 1633, the very year the paintings were commissioned, with the obvious intention of representing it as a second *annus mirabilis*. The common format of these paintings, with a victorious general prominently placed against a scene of victory or surrender, remained squarely within the Spanish iconographical tradition of narrative and literal representation, almost ostentatiously eschewing the allegorical approach that characterized, for example, Rubens's splendid cycle of the life of Marie de' Médici.

The central message of this program was plain for all to read. It presented Philip IV, baton in hand, as the worthy upholder of his dynasty's mission, holding in check the forces of heresy, discord, and rebellion. He was a king who had been—and still was—victorious in his wars, but at the same time (as Velázquez's *Surrender of Breda* brilliantly testified) magnanimous in the moment of triumph. Here indeed was *Felipe el Grande*, the greatest monarch in the world.

If one objective of the count-duke was to emphasize the majesty of Philip as supreme among the princes of the world both in peace and war, another was to make sure that he became the true master of his own dominions. He had inherited a diversified and fragmented Monarchy, and Olivares's intention was to give it unity. "The most important piece of business in your Monarchy," he told Philip in a famous state paper of 1624, "is to make yourself king of Spain: by which I mean that Your Majesty should not be content with being king of Portugal, of Aragon, of Valencia, and count of Barcelona, but should secretly work and plàn to reduce these kingdoms of which Spain is composed to the style and laws of Castile."[18] If this were achieved—if the laws were made uniform, the internal customs barriers removed, the king able to deploy his ministers wherever he wanted—then Philip would indeed be in reality what he already was in name, the most powerful monarch in Christendom.

Fig. 5.6. Velázquez, *Philip IV on Horseback*. Prado Museum, Madrid.

Fig. 5.7. Velázquez, *Baltasar Carlos on Horseback*. Prado Museum, Madrid.

Fig. 5.8. Velázquez, *The Surrender of Breda.* Prado Museum, Madrid.

This insistence on unity conceived as uniformity, which runs right through Olivares's twenty-two years of power, directly contravened that fundamental principle of the Spanish Monarchy, its respect for constitutional diversity. It was, then, a radical and dangerous enterprise on which Olivares was embarked, and one that was bound to bring him into conflict with provincial rights and liberties. While aware of the difficulties he was also a man in a hurry, desperately anxious to mobilize all the resources of the Monarchy in order to ward off the assaults of its enemies. To preach the need for unity to peoples who prided themselves on the retention of their distinctiveness was to fly in the face of prudent tradition, but in his early years of government Olivares believed that the advantages of his proposals would speak for themselves. As the first step toward the achievement of unity he proposed a scheme for military cooperation between the different kingdoms, a Union of Arms, which was laid before the Cortes of Aragon, Valencia, and Catalonia in 1626, introduced by carefully drafted broadsheets outlining the benefits to be expected from closer union.[19]

The notable lack of enthusiasm in the Crown of Aragon for this novel idea compelled the Olivares regime, increasingly short of men and money for its wars, to resort to cruder forms of pressure to achieve its ends. As in early Stuart England, the doctrine of necessity and *salus populi* became the principle theoretical justification of the regime: the needs of self-defense were held to override all lesser laws. In a Spanish version of that great drama which was being played out all over western Europe, the resort of the crown to its prerogative power was countered by the contractualist arguments of peoples determined to retain their ancient laws and liberties. The ensuing revolts of Catalonia and Portugal in 1640 not only led to the downfall of Olivares himself, but discredited with the taint of failure his program for a closer unification of the Spanish Monarchy.

The steady opposition of the peripheral provinces of the Iberian Peninsula to the Union of Arms underlines the more general problem of obedience which faced Olivares at every turn as he tried to mobilize the Monarchy for war. Recalcitrant generals, undisciplined aristocrats, and self-interested ministers all stood in the way of that smooth execution of orders which he regarded as essential for any well-governed monarchy. It was no good proclaiming the greatness of Philip if the king was not obeyed.

The enforcement of obedience therefore became as high a priority as the enhancement of majesty and the imposition of unity, and indeed constituted an integral component of the Olivares program. The regime developed its coercive machinery, including a special *Junta de Obediencia* to deal with cases of resistance to the execution of royal orders. But repression by itself was at best a partial response to a problem that confronted the ruler of every early-modern state. In the face of apparently endemic disobedience, princes and statesmen strove to inculcate social discipline, no doubt raising their expectations of conformity in the same degree as they raised the level of their demands on their peoples. In the early seventeenth century a convenient doctrine of social discipline lay to hand in the neo-Stoic writings of Justus Lipsius.[20] Neo-Stoicism, with its insistence on the Roman virtues of *auctoritas, temperantia, constantia,* and *disciplina,* was an eminently appropriate ideology for the aspiring absolutist state; and it is no accident that it should have been embraced by Olivares, for the influence of Lipsius was strong in Spain, and not least in the learned circles of early seventeenth-century Seville, where he spent his most formative years.[21]

Philip and Olivares were quick to see the possibilities of the royal court, with its formal procedures and rules of etiquette, as an instrument for instilling the discipline that they found so defective in the Spanish aristocracy. Philip himself revised and emended the elaborate *etiquetas* which governed palace ceremonial, and developed to perfection that impassive *gravitas* which served at once to distance himself from his subjects and to instruct them in the proper rules of comportment. Unruly nobles were banished from court, and the palace became, in the words of a contemporary, "a school of silence, punctiliousness, and reverence."[22]

Yet human nature remained obstinately intractable, and as Olivares despaired of disciplining the nobles of his own generation, his thoughts turned increasingly toward the education of their children. His aim was to create a genuine service nobility, which would place itself unhesitatingly at the disposal of the king, serving him with absolute loyalty in government, diplomacy, and war. His first attempt in this direction was the foundation of *Estudios Reales* at court under royal patronage, and in 1629 the Jesuit-run Colegio Imperial opened its doors to aspiring nobles with much pomp and fanfare. Its curriculum included classical languages, history, natural philosophy, the military arts, "politics and economics, including those of Aristotle, adjusting reason of state to conscience, religion, and the Catholic Faith."[23] But the new foundation, which came under immediate attack from the universities and the religious orders, was a failure, and from the early 1630s Olivares was casting around for some alternative. His next scheme was for the establishment in the peninsula of noble academies, but enthusiasm was muted, there was no money to found them, and the proposal never left the drawing board.[24]

The extreme difficulty experienced by Olivares in securing compliance with his wishes—in itself hardly unusual in early seventeenth-century states—provides some indication of the degree of opposition, whether covert or open, to his government. The scale and character of this opposition have yet to be determined, but some of the principal centers can at least be identified. Within the court there was fierce hostility to Olivares and his men—his *hechuras* or "creatures" in seventeenth-century parlance—among the grandees and titled nobility. The count-duke, too, came up against the stolid resistance of the bureaucracy, which resented his slighting of the councils and his resort to ad hoc committees, or juntas, of his own hand-picked men. He was also faced with a constitutionalist opposition, not only in the Crown of Aragon, but also in Castile, where the Cortes in the last years of Philip III and the first of Philip IV were showing surprising signs of life.[25] If this opposition spoke primarily on behalf of the urban elites, it also reflected, however imperfectly, the growing popular hostility to the regime as its fiscal demands became more insistent and extreme.

While the various elements of opposition were strikingly unsuccessful in making common cause, they did succeed in their various ways in harassing the regime and driving it increasingly on to the defensive. Much of the aristocratic opposition inevitably took the form of palace intrigue, especially in the 1620s, when the residence in the palace of the king's two younger brothers created alternative centers of loyalty. To judge from the plays commissioned from Tirso de Molina by members of the Pimentel family, there may have been a theater of opposition,[26] but more serious for the regime was the posting of pasquinades and the circulation of clandestine pamphlets. This covert opposition literature, circulating either in manuscript or in clandestine imprints, repeated certain standard themes: the disastrous consequences for Spain of the count-duke's economic and foreign policies; the arbitrary character of his government, and his usurpation of the powers of the king.

Opposition came to a head in 1629 at a time of widespread discontent over the consequences of the count-duke's involvement of Spain in the War of the Mantuan Succession, and in the summer of that year serious attempts were made to detach Philip from his favorite. An anonymous manifesto on behalf of the nobility bluntly told Philip that "Your Majesty is not a king, you are a person whom the count seeks to conserve in order to make use of the office of king—a mere ceremonial ruler."[27]

Faced with the evidence of its unpopularity, the administration made increasing use of its machinery of repression. Already in 1627 it had introduced a new and more stringent censorship law, prohibiting the printing without formal license by the Council of Castile of "letters and relations, apologies and panegyrics, gazettes and newssheets, sermons, discourses, and papers on affairs of state and government";[28] but this did not prevent the clandestine printing in Castile of seditious literature, and it did not apply to publications in the Crown of Aragon, which was outside the Council of Castile's jurisdiction. The spoken as well as the written word was subjected to surveillance. Preachers critical of the regime were banished from court, and attempts made to control the contents of sermons.[29] Olivares, like any seventeenth-century statesman, had his network of spies and informers feeding him with information and misinformation alike. Evidence is scarce, but it is unlikely that the arrest of Andrés de Mendoza in 1626 for "writing discourses"[30] was a mere isolated incident.

But the government did not restrict itself to repressive measures. It also sought, where possible, to seize the offensive, mobilizing court preachers, playwrights, and artists on its behalf. There was no equivalent in Spain to the *Gazette* founded in France in 1631 by Théophraste Renaudot with Richelieu's blessing,[31] but there was an unending stream of *avisos* and *relaciones* conveying officially inspired or authorized information. The theater, too, was brought into service. Francisco de Quevedo's *Cómo ha de ser el privado* (1629) is an attempt to show Olivares, under the transparent anagrammatic disguise of the Marquis of Valisero, as the selfless minister, a new Spanish Seneca, totally devoted to his master's service.[32] This was how Olivares was seen by himself and his friends, and this was how he wanted to be seen by the rest of the world.

Quevedo, who wielded the sharpest pen in Spain, was also drafted to respond to the anonymous manifesto of 1629 and other contemporaneous attacks on the regime, along with two other writers in the Olivares circle, the Count of La Roca and Antonio Hurtado de Mendoza.[33] All three in their countermanifestoes presented fundamentally similar defenses of the regime, admitting to occasional and inevitable setbacks, but dwelling on its successes, and particularly the victories of 1625, as evidence of the wise management of affairs by the count-duke himself. But these were essentially *pièces d'occasion*, and Olivares often expatiated on the need for a proper history of the reign. He eventually found his historian in the wraithlike person of the Bolognese Marquis Virgilio Malvezzi, a man after his own heart, who settled in Madrid in 1636 and became the house historian of the regime.

Court writers, then, in singing the praises of the king, were also expected to sing the praises of his minister. It was, after all, in Olivares's interest to associate himself and his policies as closely as possible with those of his master. It was for this reason that the decoration of the Hall of Realms was not confined to the glorification of the king. It also glorified the minister as his right-hand man. Although this was implicit in all the battle paintings—especially the cluster of victories of 1625 that had been singled out by Quevedo and his colleagues as proof of Olivares's wise counsel and prudent stewardship of the king's affairs—it was explicitly spelled out in the most unusual of the twelve paintings, Juan Bautista Maino's *Recapture of Bahía* (fig. 5.9).[34]

Just as Velázquez's *Surrender of Breda* drew its inspiration from a play especially commissioned for court performance when news of the surren-

Fig. 5.9. Maino, *The Recapture of Bahía*. Prado Museum, Madrid.

der first reached Madrid (Calderón's *El sitio de Bredá*), so Maino's *Recapture of Bahía* borrowed some of its ideas from a play by Lope de Vega, *El Brasil restituido*. But Maino skillfully turned to account the raw material provided by Lope de Vega to make certain statements about the count-duke and his policies. Since Bahía was recaptured from the Dutch by a joint Spanish-Portuguese naval expedition, it was traditionally selected by the regime's defenders as a classic example of the Union of Arms in action. By showing the returning Portuguese inhabitants of Bahía tending a wounded Castilian soldier, Maino provided further evidence of that close co-operation between the peoples of the Monarchy which in the past had all too often been impeded by what Olivares called "the separation of hearts."

But if Maino's painting may be taken as a visual expression of the universal benefits of Olivares's policy for a Union of Arms, it also made a statement—possibly without parallel in seventeenth-century works of art—about the special relationship of king and minister. In Lope de Vega's play, the commander of the expeditionary force, Don Fadrique de Toledo, at one point repairs to his tent and addresses a portrait of the king, asking if he should offer clemency to the Dutch (a proposal to which Philip graciously nods his assent). The play culminates in the crowning of Don Fadrique with laurels by the figure of Brazil. Maino appropriates these two subjects—the king's portrait and the crowning with laurels—but strikingly reworks them (fig. 5.10). In his version of the surrender of the garrison, the defeated Dutch are forced to kneel as Don Fadrique de Toledo points to a tapestry in which it is not he but the king who is crowned with a wreath of laurels, while the figures of Heresy, Discord, and Treachery lie crushed beneath his feet. Two figures place the laurels on Philip's brow. One is Minerva, the goddess of war. The other is the count-duke of Olivares.

At this point, then, the king's favorite and first minister makes his own dramatic personal entry into the Hall of Realms. There was no doubting the significance of his presence, as the architect of Philip's victories and his right-hand man. Here was a striking affirmation both of the king's continuing confidence in Olivares, and of the closeness of their relationship as they worked together for the salvation of Spain. If the Hall of Realms set out to magnify the king, it was also intended to vindicate resoundingly the record of his minister.

But how many were willing and able to read the message? As far as the Hall of Realms was concerned, this was essentially designed for court purposes, and the audience for its message was inevitably restricted. There is no indication of any attempt to reproduce the battle paintings for a wider public, partly perhaps because Spain lacked a native school of engravers. On the other hand, the government was able to reach the provincial public in other ways, notably through newsletters and broadsheets; and victories were celebrated with Te Deums in the cathedrals of Spain.

In Madrid itself, and more specifically at court, there was a hard core of opposition that was unlikely under any circumstances to be swayed by the propaganda of the regime. On the other hand, there is also likely to have been a large body of the uncommitted, generally unenthusiastic about the Olivares regime but susceptible to appeals to their patriotism, especially in the spring of 1635, which saw not only the unveiling of the battle paintings in the Hall of Realms but also the outbreak of war with France. But again, although the decoration of the hall clearly had a didac-

Fig. 5.10. Maino, *The Recapture of Bahía*, detail.

tic purpose, how many people were actually given the opportunity to fall under its spell?

At this point, the inadequacies of an approach to the seventeenth century couched exclusively in terms of *propaganda* begin to appear. Although the Hall of Realms, like Malvezzi's history, was designed to influence contemporary opinion, its creators obviously had in mind a much larger audience than could possibly have seen it in the 1630s. Its appeal was not only to contemporaries but also to future generations, symbolized by the young heir to the throne, Baltasar Carlos, whose spirited portrait hung on its walls. It was an appeal, in fact, to posterity.

The Olivares regime, in commissioning these works, and in mobilizing poets and painters and artists, was engaged in a gigantic exercise in self-projection. It was making, in what it hoped would be a permanent form, a statement about the way in which it saw itself, and the way in which it wanted to be seen by future ages. In making its statement it was bidding for fame, and claiming for itself a glory that would outlast time.

This being so, it is natural to wonder whether the most receptive contemporary audience for these celebratory statements may not have been the men of the regime that commissioned them. In fact, may not the perpetrators have been the first to fall for their own propaganda? This at least is what the evidence of the 1630s seems to suggest. Olivares and his men dominated the court and the government; but they were a small, inward-looking coterie, increasingly isolated from the outside world. Like Charles I and his circle, they had developed through the world of the arts and of the theater their own elaborate illusion of power.[35] But because of their growing isolation, their own image of themselves and their accomplishments diverged at more and more points from the reality. This in turn provided splendid opportunities for Olivares's critics, who seized on the Buen Retiro as a symbol of the government's failings, and mocked Malvezzi as a mendacious hack. Olivares, they claimed, had taken Philip captive, and had closed his eyes to what was happening beyond the confines of his court.

As soon as this began to happen, it is clear that the attempt to mobilize artists, writers, and intellectuals in the service of the regime had backfired disastrously. When Olivares fell in 1643 he fell because his regime had lost the last shreds of credibility. It had proclaimed unity, and yet—with the revolts of Catalonia and Portugal—the Spanish peninsula had been hopelessly fragmented; it had endlessly trumpeted Spain's triumph over its enemies, and yet it had visibly been defeated; it had insisted on the greatness of *Felipe el Grande*, and yet, as a satirical poem unkindly remarked, "the king is great as a hole is great."[36]

The fiasco of the Olivares regime was a warning that the next generation took to heart. As a result of the count-duke's failure, activism by the central government was discredited, and it would come back only in the eighteenth century with the Bourbons, whose program for the revival and modernization of Spain bore striking similarities to that of Olivares. The transformation of society by the state—especially in Spain—was to prove a long and slow process, and the habit of obedience was not easily instilled. In the seventeenth century there were important forces working in this direction: the desire for order, which looked for satisfaction to the king; Lipsian doctrines of social discipline; the overwhelming need to concentrate power in an age when warfare made heavy demands on society. But the political careers both of Olivares and Richelieu illustrate the extreme difficulties that faced the early seventeenth-century statesman in his attempt to enhance the authority of the crown and maximize the power of the state. The two men were using similar techniques, and the greater success of Richelieu may indicate not so much a greater skill in exploiting the apparatus of power, as the fact that the shortest road to absolutism at home lay through victory abroad.

The seventeenth-century leviathan possessed greater capacity than its predecessors for projecting a favorable image of itself to the world; and Louis XIV—who may have appropriated more from the Spanish tradition than has so far been allowed—would in due course develop that capacity to the full. But if the repertoire of illusionistic devices had grown, so too had the dangers involved in its use. The fate of Olivares showed how easily a gulf could open between rhetoric and reality; and if his regime came close to developing modern forms of propaganda, it paid a no less modern price when it fell into a pit of its own digging, known today as the credibility gap.

Notes

This essay is in substance the text of a talk given at the Shelby Cullom Davis Center in October 1980. It draws extensively on my own research, published and unpublished, into the Spain of Philip IV and Olivares, and especially Jonathan Brown and J. H. Elliott, *A Palace for a King: The Buen Retiro and the Court of Philip IV* (New Haven and London, 1980), which provides further evidence and substantiation for many of the points briefly discussed here. Footnoting has been deliberately kept light, and the essay is intended primarily as a contribution to discussion on the theme of power and ideology, rather than as a close survey of Olivares's program and policies, which I have examined elsewhere.

1. These points are admirably made by Gerhard Oestreich in his important article, "Strukturprobleme des europaischen Absolutismus," reprinted in his *Geist und Gestalt des frühmodernen Staats* (Berlin, 1969), pp. 179–97. An English version of this and other selected writings by Oestreich may be found in his *Neostoicism and the Early Modern State* (Cambridge, 1982).

2. Diego Saavedra Fajardo, *Empresas políticas: Idea de un príncipe político-cristiano*, ed. Quintín Aldea Vaquero (Madrid, 1976), 1:310 (*empresa* 31).

3. See J. H. Elliott, "Self-perception and decline in early seventeenth-century Spain," *Past and Present*, no. 74 (1977): 41–61.

4. John H. Elliott and José F. de la Peña, *Memoriales y cartas del Conde Duque de Olivares*, 2 vols. (Madrid, 1978–80), 1:98 (*Gran Memorial*, 1624).

5. Ed. Miguel Herrero García (Madrid, 1945), pp. 53–54 ("proposición tercera").

6. See Erwin Panofsky, *Problems in Titian, Mostly Iconographic* (New York, 1969), pp. 84–87.

7. Marc Bloch, *Les rois thaumaturges* (Paris, 1961), p. 155.

8. For the discontinuation of the coronation ceremony, and the disappearance of the regalia, see Percy Ernst Schramm, *Herrschaftszeichen und Staatssymbolik*, vol. 3 (Stuttgart, 1956), pp. 1025–31. Schramm does not, however, explore the possible reasons for the developments in the Spanish kingdoms.

9. See Brown and Elliott, *A Palace for a King*, p. 68.

10. Ibid., p. 230.

11. José Antonio Maravall, *La cultura del barroco* (2d ed., Madrid, 1980), pp. 299–300. The sermon in Spain deserves far more attention than it has so far received, but see Hilary Dansey Smith, *Preaching in the Spanish Golden Age* (Oxford, 1978).

12. Charles Vincent Aubrun, *La comédie espagnole, 1600–1680* (Paris, 1966), p. 131.

13. See José Antonio Maravall, *Teatro y literatura en la sociedad barroca* (Madrid, 1972), pp. 124–27, for this and other examples.

14. See J. H. Elliott, *The Revolt of the Catalans* (Cambridge, 1963), p. 8.

15. See René Taylor, "Architecture and Magic. Considerations of the *Idea* of the Escorial," in *Essays in the History of Architecture presented to Rudolf Wittkower*, ed. D. Fraser, H. Hibbard, and M. J. Levine (London, 1967), pp. 81–109. For the impact of this idea on Charles I of England, by way of the Spanish Jesuit Villalpando, see Roy Strong, *Britannia Triumphans: Inigo Jones, Rubens and Whitehall Palace* (London, 1980), pp. 59–63.

16. Brown and Elliott, *A Palace*, pp. 41–42.

17. For an iconographical examination of the Hall of Realms, see Brown and Elliott, *A Palace*, ch. 6.

18. Elliott and de la Peña, *Memoriales y cartas*, 1:96.

19. Ibid., documents 9 and 10.

20. See Oestreich, *Neostoicism and the Early Modern State* for this theme of social discipline.

21. Elliott and de la Peña, *Memoriales y cartas*, 1:xlvi–lii.

22. Alonso Carrillo, *Origen de la dignidad de grande* (Madrid, 1657), p. 12.
23. José Simón-Diaz, *Historia del Colegio Imperial de Madrid* (Madrid, 1952), 1:67–68.
24. See Elliott and de la Peña, *Memoriales y cartas*, 2: document 12.
25. See especially Jean Vilar, "Formes et tendances de l'opposition sous Olivares," *Mélanges de la Casa de Velázquez*, 7 (1971): 263–94; and Charles Jago, "Habsburg Absolutism and the Cortes of Castile," *The American Historical Review*, 86 (1981): 307–26.
26. See Ruth Lee Kennedy, *Studies in Tirso, I: The Dramatist and His Competitors, 1620–1626* (Chapel Hill, 1974), pp. 211–14.
27. Brown and Elliott, *A Palace*, pp. 51–52.
28. Elliott and de la Peña, *Memoriales y cartas*, 2:184.
29. Maravall, *La cultura del barroco*, p. 158.
30. Ibid., p. 160, n. 70.
31. See Howard M. Solomon, *Public Welfare, Science, and Propaganda in Seventeenth-Century France* (Princeton, 1972).
32. For this play, and Quevedo's relationship to Olivares, see my essay on "Quevedo and the Count-Duke of Olivares," in *Quevedo in Perspective*, ed. James Iffland (Newark, Del., 1982), pp. 227–50.
33. Brown and Elliott, *A Palace*, pp. 162 and 164.
34. For a detailed analysis of this painting, see Brown and Elliott, *A Palace*, pp. 184–90.
35. See Stephen Orgel, *The Illusion of Power* (Berkeley and Los Angeles, 1975).
36. "Memorial a S. M. el rey don Felipe Cuarto," in Teófanes Egido, *Sátiras políticas de la España Moderna* (Madrid, 1973), p. 115.

PART FOUR

Rites of Power Since the Age of Revolution: France, Britain, and Russia

6

MAURICE AGULHON

Politics, Images, and Symbols in Post-Revolutionary France

For several decades, the study of political history—often stigmatized as "traditional"—has been giving way to work in sociocultural history, work that is touted as something new. From this shift in interest has come a revived curiosity about all aspects of material culture—everyday life, *mentalités*, "popular culture," the "decor" of life, and so on. Without this revival, imagery would not have become a "serious" historical category: beyond study of the work of art (high art as well as popular art), the object itself, something beloved by ethnographers, had to become worthy of historical interest; cultural history had to learn to present itself as a kind of retrospective ethnology in order to escape the contemptuous label of "little" history.

But this new interest in ethnology and imagery can be redirected toward the study of politics; indeed, it may improve our understanding of political history by encouraging us to look less hastily or less carelessly at visual elements we usually take for granted. Political power does not consist simply of men who establish and operate certain institutions, who claim certain ideas and perform certain actions. It also uses an entire system of signs and emblems—a system in which the principal signs are the most visible ones and in which those who seek or wield power try to gain recognition and, if possible, acclamation. At the simplest level, these emblems are supposed to have three basic functions: to distinguish a particular political power from foreign powers or from a regime previously overthrown; to translate clearly the principles upheld by that power (for instance, the hammer and sickle: the union of workers and farmers); finally, if possible, to make a good impression on the spectator, to appeal to him and win his sympathies.

But enough abstractions! Historians have their own responsibilities, quite distinct from devising a theory of signs—responsibilities that should precede such theorizing. How then are we to treat historically the political imagery of a given time and place (in this case, France, from the Revolution to the present)?[1]

First, we need a *survey* of the relevant distinctive signs. As far as France is concerned, such a survey is especially complicated because of the numerous changes in political regimes that have taken place since the Revolution, particularly between 1789 and 1870.

Next, we must study the effective *role* of imagery as a historical factor. Is there really any historical importance to imagery apart from the anecdotal or the picturesque (present, almost by definition, in everything visual)? The matter deserves discussion. As everyone knows, in democratic countries with an old established culture, like France, all citizens are expected to be literate: ballots consist only of words—the official headings of the political parties and the names of the candidates, or, in case of a referendum, the issue being voted on and the words "yes" and "no." But in other countries, where illiteracy persists, ballots include colored, drawn signs as well, which are assumed to be more readily understood by the voters. We might deduce from this that the role of imagery was at its height in archaic times, and that it has declined with the onset of modernization. Similarly, the sculpted facades of gothic churches—"catechisms in stone" for illiterate believers—are commonly said to contrast with the sobriety of reformed churches, where the faithful use Scripture, the Book. Does political imagery reflect this kind of contrast, this progression? And if so, can changes in imagery be considered final and definitive, or subject to change?

Beyond these global reflections, it is possible to conceive a historical study of individual emblems, the history of the initial choice of an emblem, and then the more complicated but perhaps more useful history of how the emblem was received—of its popularity or its failure, and of the presumed reasons for these reactions. Sticking to emblems that have lasted, images that have succeeded in becoming popular, we might ask if they attained their emotional charge and their multiple meanings in a way that permits us to call the emblematic image a symbol.[2] Is there, in fact, a visual *symbolic system* in politics? Such are some further problems that historians might want to deal with, if not completely resolve.

To discuss this entire agenda, needless to say, would require a lengthy book. Let us content ourselves, in these few pages, with a few reminders, some fresh information, and a few provisional and personal reflections, based on continuing work in progress.

Survey

First, a modern state has a *flag*, the primary visual symbol, the one we think of immediately. Second, the state is *personified*, either by the presiding head of state (a hereditary monarch or an elected president) or by an allegorical figure, the embodiment of the Nation, usually represented in the form of a woman. This personified State appears in two main series of images: on the one hand, on the official effigies on currency (later, postage stamps) and decorative medals; and, on the other, in large memorials, like statues in public squares. Third, each political power traditionally possesses a set of *visual symbols of different kinds*, nonanthropomorphic symbols like coats of arms, official seals (provided these do not depict the sovereign), and illustrations used on official or unofficial stationery headings. Finally, it is possible to construct a fourth category of the symbols of power[3]—*historical notables*. Every regime has its own Pantheon (in the literal as well as the figurative sense) and places statues of the appropriate notables in public squares.

The Flag

In France, the history of the flag is the most familiar.[4] The first symbolic act of the Revolution was the invention of the tricolor (white for the king, blue and red for the city of Paris), which has been the flag of France ever since, except during the counterrevolutionary period of the Restoration (1814–30).

In the mid-nineteenth century, the tricolor, representing the France inspired by the events of 1789, could be regarded as having links to a certain political philosophy. Thus, the flag itself was challenged—from the extreme Right by the upholders of the white flag (that is, those who favored a return to the traditional monarchy) and, from the extreme Left, by the upholders of the red flag (the champions of a social, popular, anti-"bourgeois" republic). The former faction, however, after its apparent victory in 1873 (to which we will return), abandoned its own emblem: from the end of the nineteenth century on, the extreme Right rallied to the tricolor, accepting the idea that the flag no longer necessarily represented the ideals of 1789, modernity, or the republic—which would have been bad—but simply represented France—a good thing. It would take much longer for the revolutionary extreme Left and the workers' movement to accept this shift in interpretation—to see France, and not the "bourgeois"

republic, in the three colors. Already implicit among socialists at the beginning of the twentieth century, the shift was ratified by the Communists when they accepted it in 1934: the tricolor and the red flag could,
they proclaimed, be brandished at the same time, since the proletarian
belonged to a national community as well as to an international class.[5]
More recently, the Communists have promised that a socialist (indeed,
communist) France could be represented by "the colors of France." The
red flag, although a complement to the tricolor, is no longer its competi-
tor; the tricolor has evolved from an ideological-political symbol into a
simple territorial symbol. Thus, at present, the tricolor's only direct competitors are strictly territorial—the European flag on a supranational level,
the flags of a few ancient provinces with separatist tendencies (notably
Brittany and Corsica) on the infranational level. Such is the present situation. These flags are linked to territorial entities; thus, when a particular
municipality agrees to fly the regional and European flags alongside the
national emblem, it announces that the town belongs to three concentric
sets of loyalties, all capable of being reconciled. Some less optimistic observers might interpret this differently, as an expression of potential conflicts. But no matter. It is clear how the significance of the flag has
changed over the last century.

Personification of the State

The history of the personification of the state is much less well known,
and it was for that reason we decided to shed light on at least one of its
aspects in our studies of the feminine allegory of the republic.[6] Under the
monarchy, the king's statue sat in the public square and his profile appeared on the coin of the realm. In 1792, the First Republic replaced the
king-state effigy with the goddess Liberty, represented by a woman with a
Phrygian cap, in accordance with classical iconology. Thus was born the
impersonal personification, so to speak (allegorical, abstract, permanent),
of the republican state as an eternal woman, clearly opposed to the monarchical state, which was officially represented by a succession of men. It all
might have happened differently, since at the same time, the American
republic was starting to give its elected presidents a featured role in official
representation. (The French First Republic was anything but presiden-
tial.)

From the start, in August-September 1792, the Republic understood
the dangers that great men, the Mirabeaus and the Lafayettes, could pose

to the Revolution, and it thus presented itself as being vigilantly collegi-
ate. Thereafter, as the history of our republics unfolded with the unhappy
experience of Robespierre in the Year II and the Bonapartes in the Year
VIII and in 1851, republican France developed a hardened suspicion of
living great men and—to limit ourselves to iconography—to a fidelity to
the feminine ideal of the state.

In 1940, the Vichy counterrevoulation involuntarily provided evidence *a contrario* to this thesis. The "National" Revolution of 1940, which
abolished the Republic and its main institutions, also suppressed the feminine image and replaced it, on postage stamps, with a picture of the
head of state (Marshal Pétain)—something that had not been seen since
Napoleon III.

The matter of personification is complicated by the fact that the picture of the King (in France as elsewhere) never precluded the existence of
an iconography of the Nation itself—Britannia, Germania, Francia (or
Gallia). Painters, sculptors, and engravers always knew how to represent
France before 1792—with a woman, of course,[7] because in our Western
culture, all things with feminine names recall an image of the correspondent sex. This practice was not lost after 1792 because iconography and art
have their specific traditions; under such conditions, we can easily understand why it was inevitable that in the nineteenth century, the recent
creation of the image of the Republic would be sullied by the old image of
France-Nation. We might say here that if a woman wore a helmet or was
encircled by ornaments, she represented France, and if she wore a Phrygian cap she represented the republic—but this would be too simple: there
have been representations of the First Republic, and later of moderate
republics, without the red cap. The context, more than the specific iconographic attributes, can tell us more exactly whether a particular feminine
allegory stood for France (in contrast to foreign countries) or the Republic
(the antithesis and antagonist of monarchist reaction). It is important to
remember the special importance of feminine allegory to French history.
The contrast with Britain is, in this instance, illuminating. British iconography includes Britannia (a familiar stereotype: rigid stature, a spear or a
trident, a shield, a lion beside her, the ocean at her feet) as well as the
monarch's portrait. When France is a republic, it is, in effect, a single
image, one that must convey the sense of both Britannia and of Victoria or
Edward: France the woman is, at the same time, the emblem of the State
and the emblem of the Nation.

There are more complexities still. The Republic has been overthrown
three times (in the Year VIII, in 1851–52, and in 1940) and has been threat-

ened on several other occasions. For decades in the nineteenth century, the
Republic was therefore the ideal and the flag of an opposition—an ideal and
flag that were all the more passionately held because the struggle was difficult
and its constituency was a popular one. In the ranks of the opposition from
1800 to 1848 and even more from 1851 to 1870 (and even from 1875 to 1880),
the idea of Liberty, Justice, and Love of the People began to be associated with
the image of the militant Republic and its red cap. It was this image that was
known, in some regions, as "Marianne."[8] With the advent of the Third Republic, this militancy naturally tended toward a kind of triumphalism, although, as we have shown elsewhere, it was tempered by a certain
opportunistic caution.

After the decade 1870–80, when official France stabilized as the
French republic, a feminine image emerged, which projected three distinct but convergent themes: the tradition of Gallia (several centuries old),
the conventional feminine form of the nonmonarchical state, and the more
appealing head of "Marianne," the last avatar of the Goddess Liberty.
This image was widely disseminated, through all of the media already
mentioned, not without some variations, the details of which would be
interesting to follow—but which we will not take up here. It is important
to note just how widespread the image became. The Third Republic was a
period not only of republicanization but also of acculturation.[9] In books,
in newspapers, in town halls (with their busts of Marianne), in the
schools, in the army, the picture of the state affected more and more
people. Moreover, the figure also appeared in public squares, either as
homages to the republic itself or in the form of France which always
appeared on monuments to the war dead and revolutionary dead of 1870–
71, or as allegorical accompaniments to statues of patriotic and republican
notables. Citizens became truly familiar with the multifaceted image of
France, an image at once eternal and modern.

Other Attributes

On the other hand, the Third Republic was rather sober as far as other
emblematic attributes were concerned. It is with these emblems—which,
admittedly, we know less well—that each regime devised its own particular images; consequently, it was these images that varied most after 1789.
We shall limit our remarks about them to a few insufficient notes.

A whole series of images, often derived from earlier iconography (either humanist or "statist"), sprang from the French Revolution.[10] It is in

this way that the central image of the republic, the woman with her Liberty cap, could be linked with Minerva and her martial display (helmet, spear, sword), with the symbols of light (either the sun, a torch, or a flare), with symbols of well-regulated authority (the Tables of Law, the fasces of the Roman lictors), or, finally, with symbols of power (Hercules with his bludgeon, the lion). All of these symbols are open to a humanist (or, if you prefer, a left-wing) interpretation; thus all, except perhaps Hercules[11] (whose career was short, unless we want to think that he reappeared at the end of the nineteenth century in working class iconography, in the form of the blacksmith with his hammer), were able to enjoy long careers as semi-official emblems of the republic. The Second Empire tried to distinguish itself by replacing all or part of the earlier bric-a-brac with the emblem of the eagle, borrowed from the Roman Empire. Banished in 1814 and 1815, the eagle returned with the Empire, only to be banished again in 1870. In the nineteenth century, history was supposed to be advancing toward Liberty; the end of the two imperial dictatorships led to their absolute rejection.

The Restoration monarchy restored itself with the white flag and the fleur-de-lis (iris) of the ancient French coat of arms. Obviously, these emblems did not survive the Revolution of 1830—another violent rejection. But one cannot reduce the Restoration's contribution to the history of French symbolism to the iris, the white flag, and a few newly erected royal statues. This regime was also that of "the union of the throne and the altar": in large measure, it confused its expressions of political revenge with expressions of revenge by the Catholic Church. This confusion lasted (indeed, it grew stronger, if that is possible) after 1830. For more than three-quarters of a century after the July Revolution, the most vigorous counterrevolutionary groups confused royalist legitimacy with militant, Catholic intransigency, and they borrowed their symbols from the latter, not the former. Around 1900, as we have noted, the white flag was rarely carried, and the iris was merely a decorative motif, more old-fashioned than provocative. It was the churches, the crosses, the Blessed Virgins and (to anticipate a bit) the Joan of Arcs which constituted the true antagonistic response to republican monuments and statuary.

The July Monarchy, which brought back the tricolor and the crossed irises of the national coat of arms, also had two images of its own, destined for very different fates. Officially, the open book (representing the Charter of 1814, violated by Charles X and restored, with a few revisions, by the July Monarchy) replaced the fleur-de-lis. Never very popular, forgotten today, this image of the Charter became obsolete after 1848; nevertheless, the idea it represented converged with that of the Table of Laws—an idea of respect for the law and the Constitution, in accordance with liberal ethics.

Along with the return of the tricolor, the great success of 1830 was the emblem of the rooster, the Gallic rooster, a symbol of courage and pride—a patriotic symbol as well, since it bore the Latin homology: *gallus*, rooster; *gallus*, Gallic. The rooster was popular enough to survive 1848; indeed, it was as much a republican symbol as an Orléanist symbol—which led to its being eclipsed by the eagle under Napoleon III and allowed its revival after 1870.

The Third Republic, like the Second, had only to draw upon the panoply of emblems from the Great Revolution. Officially, however, the Third Republic was extremely sober, with no other "arms" on its coats than the initials R. F., standing for République Française.[12] It was in a semiofficial manner, suited to their own personal beliefs and tastes, that architects of the period added one or another of the emblems we have mentioned—the flame or the sun, the Book of Law or a collection of weapons, the Gallic rooster or the quiet, forceful lion—to the R. F. abbreviation, the tricolor and the feminine image of republican France (now with or without a Phrygian cap).

The emblems on the memorials from the First World War, which still await exhaustive and systematic study, give us an idea of the relative popularity of these national symbols.[13] The biggest monuments in the important cities consisted of varied and complex groups of structures; at the other end of the scale, the little monuments, in poor *communes*, were often reduced to simple steles or pyramids; between these extremes, there was a distinct kind of relatively simple monument, with a single figure. This figure was either a woman (who could be interpreted, according to her attributes, to mean homeland, town, region, republic, or even a mourning woman of the common people), a soldier, or a rooster (never a lion, despite the prestigious example of Bartholdi's Lion of Belfort in Paris: it seems that, from this time on, the lion was perceived as uniquely British). These ways of representing France have scarcely changed since the First World War.

The Second World War brought with it, from 1940 to 1944, the explicitly counterrevolutionary interlude of the Vichy regime. Vichy did not alter the tricolor—definitive proof that the tricolor had evolved from an ideological symbol into a territorial one. The regime did try to remove or reduce the feminine allegorical representation of the state—apparently because such a representation mixed up the idea of France with the idea of the republic—and it consequently revived the monarchical tradition of representing the state with a picture of its leader (Pétain). Finally, it chose an official object-emblem from the traditional collection, the hatchet. The emblem itself had some resemblance to the Roman fasces—but the Vichy regime distinguished itself by adopting the double hatchet of the Franks, an emblem that evoked a national past, a past that was supposed to be respectable because it was so distant in time.[14]

The Resistance protested in two ways against the short-lived resurgence of ancient, Traditional France. The domestic Resistance—largely civilian, leaning toward the Left—tended to revive and exalt the customary symbols of France and the republic—the woman with a Phrygian cap (Marianne), the Gallic rooster, and so on. On the contrary, the overseas Resistance (the "Free France" of General De Gaulle) invented its own emblem, the Cross of Lorraine. For a while, it was believed—in London, in Algiers, and even in "Free France"—that the Cross of Lorraine would become yet another state symbol, enriching the national collection. It did become so, to a certain extent, in the official Second World War memorials (in Paris, and at Mont Valérien, for instance)—that is to say, in specific historical memorials. Could it be used elsewhere, as a substitute for republican symbols that were considered old-fashioned? Even if he had tried, De Gaulle could not have done it.[15] Indeed, De Gaulle's withdrawal from power in 1969 led to the relegation of the Cross of Lorraine to the rank of a party symbol—a minor role, used only because of its association with a specific, historically dated Resistance. Things have hardly changed since then.

Historical Notables

Finally, a political power expresses itself with the historical characters it chooses to honor. The old French monarchy erected statues of kings and saints almost exclusively.[16] The idea of bestowing this honor on other "great men"—on servants of the state or on national heroes—came only with the Enlightenment. It was expressed under Louis XVI and was integrated into the secularism and didacticism of the French Revolution. We have explained elsewhere why the major waves of "statumania" came following the events of 1830 and 1880; after each major democratic turning point, there was a push further to the Left and further down the social scale to find notables to be honored by statues. This phenomenon was also encouraged by the growth of the public purse, by the spread of towns, and by the embellishment of public places and crossroads. Statumania then, ultimately, became a fashion, deriving from the competition between different towns as well as competition between political parties.

Yet politics did not disappear altogether. If statumania had, indeed, become a fashion by the end of the nineteenth century, it did not entirely lose its role as an affirmation of political power—which, by this time, had become republican. With the great actors of the Revolution and the liberal struggles of the nineteenth century, with the great political figures who died either prematurely (Gambetta) or dramatically (Sadi Carnot), with the paragons of scientific progress and social utility (Pasteur), a regime and an ideology began to take shape. As we shall see, ideology would be at work again after 1940, when the antirepublican Vichy reaction undertook to purge the People—considered too numerous and too far to the Left to be honored—and did so without hiding the fact that the ostensible purpose for this enterprise (saving rare metals in a time of shortage) was not the only one.

Because the Third Republic was liberal, it tolerated public oppositional statuary. The favorite figure, here, was Joan of Arc, a figure whose extraordinary success cannot be understood merely in a political context. In just a very few years, after about 1890, this heroine (not yet canonized by the Church) became by far the French historical figure most often represented in statues. The significance was obvious enough. Joan of Arc embodied, at the same time, the values of Christian inspiration and loyalty to the monarchy defended by the Right against the secular Republic, as well as patriotic values—not the least of all that was at stake. The cult of Joan of Arc denied absolutely official republican discourse, a discourse which tended to assume that French patriotism arose suddenly in 1789 and tended to compromise the Right by reminding it of memories of the treason of the *Chouans*, of the *émigrés*, even going to the limits of the ultramontanes.

Whether the elevation of Joan of Arc was a cheap trick, to offset the Third Republic's female personification (Revolution, Republic, "Marianne") is by no means obvious, and it is not, in any case, demonstrable—but the idea cannot be set aside. At all events, Joan of Arc remained highly representative of that antirepublican ensemble of symbols in which the signs of the Roman Catholic Church and those of military history were juxtaposed and sometimes blended together.

It was only after the First World War when the Republic—momentarily pushed rightward by nationalist pressures—officially promoted Joan of Arc to the rank of national heroine. This did not prevent Joan of Arc from remaining (especially in Paris) an indicator and symbol of the organized extreme Right, which retained its autonomous sympathies and symbolism. Nevertheless, this period also marked the beginning of a decline in the great popularity of political statuary, a decline caused by a complex series of factors, by no means all of them political.

But even so, no tendency is unique and straightforward, without its reversals. This survey, rapid as it has been, only leads us to another problem: Did all of this symbolism have any historical importance? Have emblems been central or marginal to politics or to state affairs? Or are they merely *folklorique* (with all of the deprecatory connotations the term conveys in modern French)?

Role

Flags unfurled atop omnipresent public buildings; painted or engraved pictures in an outpouring of books and newspapers; monuments and statues that look like the inevitable accompaniments of urban modernization—all this, presented to a more politicized, better educated populace, might prompt us to conclude that symbolism became increasingly important after 1789. Is it that simple? Without question, political symbols had a greater presence. But did people attach much importance to this widespread imagery? In all likelihood, they attached less.

In abstract terms, one could suggest the following: If a particular power is successful, the importance it attaches to a certain system of signs may lead to the diffusion of that system. But this diffusion brings with it vulgarization, familiarity, and addiction, which serve, in turn, to lessen the symbols' influence and practical importance. Let us examine the matter in more concrete terms.

From the Revolution to 1914

As we have said, there is a primary assumption that, in effect, symbolic language is most strongly linked to the mental habits of traditional societies, and must necessarily be weaker when politics are self-consciously modern, rational, and secular, conducted by equally enlightened rulers and citizens.

In the distant past, when political powers evolved slowly, a particular set of signs could be used for a long time; their symbolic authority, supported by the prevailing religion, easily partook of the sacred; both familiar and sacred signs became objects of perception common to the cultured elite and common folk.

In principle (and I take care to say in principle) the liberal epoch in the West (after 1776 in the United States, after 1789 in France, after 1732 in Great Britain, etc.) has given rise to precisely the opposite set of symbolic circumstances. In recent regimes, especially those of post-revolutionary France—secularized, sometimes contested regimes, based not on consensus but mostly on liberal political ideals—signs no longer refer to a universal religious culture but instead often refer to a sophisticated humanistic culture, one possessed by the elite but one that the common people have had to acquire (for what did an average French man or woman know about the conventional vocabulary of painted or carved allegory?).

The visual symbols of power of the modern period are less studied, probably because they are presumed to be less important. In historical studies there is a category of "serious" work—which can be useful, at least as a warning. A study of the solar imagery and myth of the Sun King, Louis XIV, sounds serious; a study of the female imagery of the French Republic brings condescending smiles. Is there a grain of truth in this distinction?[17]

From this viewpoint, the history of the French Revolution is still on the serious side. In effect, the revolutionaries of 1789 could not do exactly as they wished; they had to contend with the force of circumstances, which in history is often the force of habit. They could abolish the monarchy and execute the king, and exercise power through a changing collective of citizens. But the king was not only a person and a state functionary, he was also a symbol—as on money, for example. After the Revolution, would it be necessary to mint coins with the pictures of successive secretaries? Impossible. Or should coins be minted without an image? Hard to imagine. So the sign of the new system was used, the allegorical head of Liberty.

The image of the king also appeared in public statuary in the large cities; after 1789, it was only natural to overturn them. But were the pedestals to be left empty? Or, so to speak, were the beautiful "royal squares" to be stripped naked by removing the pedestals? No one could bear to do so, and statues of the French Republic replaced the statues of the fallen kings.

Thus, those who adhered to the Revolution expected a change of content inside of unchanging formal structures. Because revolutions do not accomplish miracles as far as mass *mentalités* are concerned, Parisian popular psychology was the same in 1790 as it had been in 1788. New opinions are taken up much more easily and quickly than original mentalities and cultures; revolutions create new mixtures in people's hearts and minds, in which antiquated attitudes are mingled with new ideas. I clarified this point in *The Republic in the Village*, although a dozen years earlier, Albert Soboul discussed the matter—with little comment at the time—in his great work on the Parisian sans-culottes,[18] where, for example, he sheds light on the survival of Catholic religiosity among the pious devotees of "the Sacred Heart of Marat." One of the reasons such importance continued to be attached to political symbolism in the nineteenth century was, thus, that the masses were not as modernized as they should have been.

The Revolution of 1789 began, then, with a tremendously symbolic act, the storming of the Bastille, on July 14, 1789. Everything has been said about the role—more symbolic than "real"—that the seizing of this fortress-jail had for the patriots: the Bastille housed almost no prisoners; its garrison was ridiculously weak. A symbol of the strength of the state in the heart of Paris, it was captured and then razed. The stones that remained after the demolition were recut in the shape of little fortresses and put on sale by "Patriot" Pulloy, as treasured keepsakes. The vacant lot left after the demolition was immediately designated as a place for a commemorative monument. The project was completed after the Revolution of 1830, that decisive revival of the movement of 1789, and it was the famous July Column, topped by the Genius of Liberty (usually called the Genius of the Bastille), that became the center of popular Parisian worship for nearly a century. The memory of the Bastille was so strong (signifying, among other things, that no fortress of power should threaten Paris) that during the 1840s even the republicans, despite their bellicose nationalism, again fought against plans to fortify Paris, even for military purposes. The memory remained so strong that the word persisted in everyday political language to signify any abuse of power which has to be removed ("there are still Bastilles to be taken" was a common phrase heard in France not long ago).[19] The memory remained so strong that the great law of 1880 established July 14 as the national holiday of France, as it remains today. Thus when Americans, each Fourth of July, celebrate the memory of an act of pure politics, the signing of a well-thought-out document, the French associate July 14 with an act of combat, and with a great symbolic accomplishment.

Symbols, symbols, symbols: everything about the Bastille is a symbol, a ghost that appears on the threshold of contemporary French history. The half-century of French history after 1789, the most agitated and complicated possible, was a period in which, without question, symbols still figured prominently in struggles for political power.

The replacement of the signs of the state was complete, as we have seen. The day after the taking of the Bastille, the tricolor was invented, to signify, with this total invention in the emblematic realm, the break in continuity.

We know that the tricolor of 1789 was abolished in April 1814 and replaced by the white flag; on his return from Elba in March 1815, Napoleon restored the tricolor, under which he was beaten at Waterloo; the Second Restoration, in June 1815, reestablished the white flag, and the July Revolution of 1830 finally returned the tricolor. These struggles over the flag (and, more generally, over colors, for under the Restoration a clandestine underground circulated cockades and other three-colored objects) were imbued with considerable passion. They were not simply a kind of epiphenomenon of political battles, a mere sanctioning of results, but also actively contributed to shaping the outcome of these events. The obscure militants who, on July 28, 1830, went to raise the tricolor on the towers of Notre-Dame and over the Hôtel-de-Ville while the outcome of the struggle was as yet uncertain, contributed to throwing the people into battle with a redoubled ardor (the sight was said to have produced *un effet electrique*). This was because the tricolor, linked above all to the ideology of Liberty, was also linked to powerful feelings of national pride, whereas the white flag was linked, at once, to the counterrevolution and to the memory of the national humiliation of 1815. In any case, the flag was a political chip, and perhaps was itself a political actor, of the greatest importance.

The same was true for statues, which were still rare and were almost always reserved exclusively for the sovereign. Napoleon had removed, little by little, the statues of the Republic and had begun to model for sculptors himself (notably in Paris, for the column in the Place Vendôme). The Restoration quickly and violently overturned Napoleon's statue in the Place Vendôme and systematically restored the statues of the kings dating back before 1792; the large inscription on the statue of Henri IV on the Pont Neuf still serves as a reminder to passersby of this solemnity and importance. The Restoration also undertook the construction of memorials to Louis XVI and to the other victims of the Revolution.[20] July 1830 could do nothing less than stop this enterprise and put Napoleon back atop the Vendôme Column.

It was with the July Monarchy, however, that the fever began to break. The government of Louis Philippe wanted to appear wise and liberal, and in essence it was so. Liberal institutions became part of everyday life. Memories of civil war grew faint; the level of general culture increased; in short, France calmed down and became civilized.

One aspect of these developments was that visual political symbolism slowly became more and more commonplace and less and less passionate. The tricolor was retained after 1830; the chances of restoring the white flag dwindled with time. In 1848, the red flag threatened to replace the tricolor: Now that we've changed regimes, demonstrators urged, let's change the flag! Since the people are in power, let us carry the people's flag! The important point here, though, is that the Second Republic's Provisional Government easily maintained the tricolor and held at bay those who clamored for the red flag; above all, we should recall the remarks of Lamartine, spokesman for the new republican order: the red flag is a party insignia, which represents a new (and disastrous) system, while the tricolor is not a party insignia but the emblem of France.

And statuary? Louis Philippe's reign was critical, even decisive, in the history of this little-studied topic.[21] Eighteen thirty halted the ostentatious reactionary demonstrations of the kind that would have raised statues in the image of Louis XVI—a project which the brothers of the "Roi Martyr" had not managed to complete during their fifteen years in power! But the restoration of statues of Louis XIV continued without abatement almost everywhere in France. Paris, above all, provided the definitive symbolic geography.[22] The regime celebrated itself and celebrated the France of the Revolution by erecting the July Column on the site of the Bastille. At the same time, it balanced this Jacobinism by encouraging the Napoleonic cult—by restoring Napoleon to the top of the Vendôme Column, by completing the Arc de Triomphe, and, finally, by rescuing Napoleon's corpse from St. Helena and placing it in the chapel at Invalides. Between a virtually republican eastern Paris and a western Paris devoted to evocations of the military and Bonaparte, the central city was neutralized. The square that had originally carried the name of Louis XV and contained his statue, and was later called Place de la Revolution with the statue of Liberty, took the name Place de la Concorde, with its centerpiece the obelisk of Luxor, a timely present from France's Egyptian protégé Mehemet Ali.

But even more profound than these spectacular Parisian signs were the developments in the countryside. Here we see most clearly the first great surge of the French national statumania, with its obvious democratic connotations; statues appeared of illustrious men other than saints, princes, and great soldiers. To have a statue erected in one's honor was no longer so exceptional. Suddenly, all political parties went to work, protected by the flexible tolerance of those in power. It became natural to see statues erected in the same year (if not in the same towns or the same neighborhoods) to marshals of the Empire and constables of the old monarchy, great holy orators and free-thought heroes.

Who can fail to see that this banalization, or better, this eclecticism, this pluralism, changed what it meant to commission a statue? From this point on, the erection of a statue would no longer constitute a victor's celebration over the ruined statues of the vanquished; rather, it would serve to consecrate one reputation after another, side by side. The honor of a public memorial, once capable of becoming a partisan challenge, could now aspire to become part of a common culture.

This was, we hasten to add, only an aspiration, a tendency and a hope—for social and political conflict continued: not everyone was a liberal. Moreover, there were counterrevolutionary flareups, the most famous being the Coup d'Etat of December 2, 1851, followed by seven or eight years of an authoritarian Empire. But this only delayed the general thrust of development characteristic of the century.

Nothing better emphasized the general drift toward appeasement in the symbolic struggle—and thus to the general decline of the importance of symbols in political competition—than the two surprises of *1871*.

Let us explain what we mean by these two surprises. Many things happened in 1871, the *année terrible*, and we assume that most of them are familiar. Two, in particular, concern us.

First was the Paris Commune. To express their hatred for Bonaparte and militarism, the Communards decided to demolish the Vendôme Column—which they proceeded to do. Enormous scandal! We should not forget that the conservative majority (*Versaillais*) were eager to accuse the Communards of having committed every sort of crime and vice, and they were only too happy to turn the destruction of the Vendôme Column into one more indictment. It was one thing to oppose the Bonaparte family (which had few defenders in 1871), but quite another thing to destroy one of the most famous monuments in Paris! This was no longer politics, but vandalism, barbarism. . . . In this new language, Napoleon and his column were no longer political symbols; they had become works of art, and as such they were supposed to be preserved. People did not yet talk of an artistic "patrimony"—but the idea already existed.[23]

Somewhat later, at the other political extreme, another matter arose. Victorious in its struggle with the Communards, the Versailles Assembly, with its royalist and conservative majority, appeared to have a free hand to restore the counterrevolutionary monarchy and, indeed, came within an inch of doing so. But the restoration proved impossible, because the expected king, to be called Henri V, the earl of Chambord (grandson of Charles X, who had been overthrown in 1830), refused to reign under the tricolor and insisted that he be coronated under the white flag. Astonishment and despair gripped the earl's partisans, who could not understand how a regime could be associated with a flag—so deeply rooted was the relatively recent idea that the tricolor was the flag of France and not the flag of a party. The head of state at the time, Marshal de MacMahon, no doubt would have gone along with the return of the king, were it not for the question concerning the flag. But for this old military man, whose whole career had been in service to the tricolor (he had entered the army under Louis Philippe and served under the Second Republic, the Second Empire, and, finally, the Third Republic), it was unthinkable to give up the tricolor—it would have been a betrayal of his soldierly honor, as he put it, or a disavowal of an entire part of his culture, as we might put it.

Between the marshal and the pretender—both men of the same political camp—the misunderstanding centered on the essential shift in the flag's significance: from a symbol of ideological adherence between 1789 and 1830 to a sign of national-territorial adherence since then.

We have already seen the relevance of this shift to the history of the flag itself, and for the history of right-wing ideology. But it is also important to the global history of French politics. The problem here is to determine the developmental tendencies and to establish a chronology. As we have said, there were surprises in 1871—the Communards who executed Napoleon in effigy, like Chambord, who sacrificed his cause to his fidelity to a flag, *treated political symbols just as they had been treated in 1830. Now, however, forty years after the July Days, this behavior came to be seen as anachronistic. The era of detached symbolic politics had arrived.*

This era coincides precisely with the Third Republic, to which we now return. The historical evolution consciously extended by this regime— the reason we have to recall it so extensively—amounted to the winning of a reasonable Liberty, one which tended to eliminate naïvetés, violence, and, if possible, conflict.

The tricolor, perceived more and more as a symbol of national belonging and patriotism, ceased to be a political chip. Despite occasional passionate outbursts, the monuments—especially the statues of great men, those motionless visual messages—tended to inspire less zeal. At first there were, in effect, many tendencies. Above all, the number of monuments weakened their impact by making them a commonplace. Statuary passed quickly from the politico-civic category to that of folklore—and, consequently, to derision.

It might have happened differently. After all, even in 1914, political, social, and ideological tensions, though less spectacular than in 1830 or in 1871, were nevertheless strong. They could have given rise again to some important historical representations, if all the actors of history had contributed. But this did not occur. The major fact in this connection is that the republican camp was not united by a desire for a politics of symbolic expression.

For many men of the last century, part of the logic of liberalism, rationalism, and secularism involved the elimination or reduction of figurative symbols, the "rattles" of power, in favor of a simple politics, with a language of reason and common sense—a relegation of the sacred and the mystical to private life, well hidden. Such, in France, was more or less the view of Jules Ferry. But this was not the only possible logic. Other republicans, equally cultivated and thoughtful, pointed out that even with the abolition of the monarchy, the counterrevolution remained a threat, because of the influence of the Roman Catholic Church with its impressive system of rites, mysteries, symbols, and representations. This prompted the idea to fight the conservatives, in a sense, on their own ground[24]—to fight religion with religion, symbols with symbols—to solemnize, for example, civic burials or secular baptisms in order to confute the pomp of the Roman church, to construct a splendid town hall with inscriptions and allegories carved on its facade, in defiance of the old religious buildings, to build a statue to the Republic in the fountain square [*place de la fontaine*], in order to counteract the statue of the Blessed Virgin that, under the Second Empire, was ordinarily placed at the entrance to the village, and so on.

This phenomenon of republican religiosity—or counterreligiosity—was, however, very rare in France. As my current study of imagery and republican symbolism will show,[25] the "republicanization of scenery" was not a systematic, general enterprise of those in power (who were, in most cases, moderate republicans) but the products of local influences of those radical republicans who favored a combative secularism (the counter-religion thesis) and were supported by popular enthusiasm for quaint cultural expressions.

The moderate republicans' very moderation no doubt explains, at least partly, their lack of symbolic enthusiasm: an unprovocative Republic that proclaims little can more easily rally the Right to its "bourgeois" principles. And, in effect, something like that took place.

Still, the "low profile" of the republicans' expressions conformed more closely to the logic of republican ideology than the expressions of the extreme Left, visible here and there. It was natural for the champions of the past to have their churches, rituals, and rites, but a contradiction for the supporters of a rationalist future to oppose church against church, rite against rite, idol against idol. Scorn for the old cults is best expressed by refusing to copy them, and by getting people used to a deritualized, devisualized, austere, transparent, and cold politics.

Such may have been a growing tendency during the nineteenth century. But prior to 1914 there were no symbolic struggles in France of a similar intensity to those raised by the Revolution. The French had become accustomed to republican language and decor. The outburst was to come from elsewhere.

The First World War and Its Consequences

The First World War was accompanied by an intense display of patriotic propaganda with, naturally, the tricolor and the feminine figure of France as the principal visual elements. Above all, the war left behind a legacy of multiple transformations, one of which affected the symbolic field in a most lasting and concrete way.

It was a gloomy legacy, since the war was won only with an immense loss of human life, so much so that the mourner's wailing was louder than the cry of triumph, and that the Cult of the Dead became the prevalent expression of patriotism.

The topographical consequences are familiar. Ever since the burial of the coffin of the unknown soldier under the vault of the Arc de Triomphe—symbolic of all of the war's victims—this memorial has been the most animated of all those in Paris.[26] Periodically honored and visited by official processions, it outranks all other tombs (even Invalides and the Pantheon) because of the continuation of these visits, and it dominates other memorials (the Lion of Belfort, the statue of the Republic, the July Column) because of the sacred quality imparted by the presence of the dead. Similarly, in the provinces, every town and every village erected in the 1920s a commemorative monument dedicated to the dead of that particular locality. This was some sort of new step toward the standardization of French districts (probably the final step): for ten centuries, every town had had its own church; for less than a century, each had had its own town hall and its own schoolhouse; after the 1920s, each had "its monument." It goes without saying that these are dedicated to "the Dead": the universality of the military mobilization of 1914 led, for the first time in French history, to an absolute ubiquity of sacrifice and of commemoration. The omnipresence of the monuments to the dead of "14–18" had the effect, not of cancelling the civic monumental effusions of the nineteenth century (statues, monuments to 1871 or earlier wars, allegories of the Republic, and so on), but of relegating them to a place of secondary importance (which, speaking in terms of numbers, they were), making them particular, minor monuments with little impact.

The memorial to the dead of 1914–18 thus became by far the principal pillar of visual symbolism in France. Here, the imagery of the twentieth century had arrived. It consisted of more or less traditional elements; its main images were, as we have already noted, the soldier, the Gallic rooster, and the woman-fatherland. The ways in which these different themes were divided and combined remains to be studied completely. Let us add only that for most spectators, the strongest impression came, not from the chosen symbol, but from the length of the list of names engraved on the memorials' funeral plaques.

These familiar dead are themselves celebrated. The date of the celebration has been fixed on November 11, in memory of the armistice of November 11, 1918. It is, of course, the most universal of all French celebrations, since everywhere there are the war dead and memorials. It enjoys a ubiquity that the national and republican July 14 never completely obtained, because the latter came from above and lacked real local support. At the least, November 11 was a second French national holiday, begun immediately after the Great War.

Attached, one might say, to the material symbols, the war memorials, November 11 strongly reminds us of the moral (ideological) consequences of the war.[27] The national cult that flourished between the wars in effect prolonged, at the same time, the lessons of the Republic and those of the conservative clerical Right. But the war *weakened*, on the one hand, the unanimity that was being reinforced on the other: if French nationalism seemed to consolidate with the political convergence of the heirs of Gambetta and MacMahon, it was also jeopardized, because left-wing republicans remained terrified by the devastation wrought by the war. The intellectual havoc of intense nationalism, which turned into chauvinism, "brainwashing," and all the lying stupidity unsupported by enlightened and critical spirits—and even more the physical and human destruction—led progressives to think that war and national absolutism (which accompanied and was itself, perhaps, the cause of war) were henceforth the major evils to be fought.

Since then, the ideological field has continued to disintegrate and rebuild itself. The Right has ceased to define itself principally in terms of hostility to the Republic and defense of the Church above the State and

Society; the Left (on the contrary) no longer defines itself simply in terms of its attachment to the Republic and to secularism.

Henceforth, the Right identified itself, above all, in terms of its intransigent nationalism, while the Left did so in terms of its ability to keep a critical distance from such national absolutism. Of course, there were numerous variations of these basic themes, especially on the Left: there was, for example, a tremendous difference between the Bolshevik internationalism of the 1920s and the timid ideas of supranationality favored by confident radicals, in the spirit of Woodrow Wilson and the League of Nations. But even these factions had at least one thing in common: both were more or less open to pacifism and humanitarianism, values which the Right (whose constituents willingly called themselves *les Nationaux*) deemed potentially anti-French.

All this certainly requires further development and much more nuance; it is enough, here, to take account of these developments in order to help untangle the following problem: where are we to locate symbolic struggles, and of what importance were they?

In the aftermath of the struggles of the period 1870–1914, it would be easy to conclude, extending the line of evolution we drew earlier, that the confrontation between republican symbolism and its royalist-clerical opposite progressively diminished in both real importance and emotional impact. New statues were no longer erected to the Republic and the republican figure slipped into the realm of folklore; if there was a struggle, it consisted more of condescending smiles than of indignant sarcasm.

The Vichy regime—considered scandalous because of its acceptance of defeat and, even more, because of its collaboration with the Nazis—created, with its specifically antirepublican reaction, a sort of second scandal, which, with its anachronisms and old-fashioned character, was not altogether void of silliness. Of course, this reaction led to something of a counterreaction and a revival of fidelity to republican imagery and symbolism. But the revival hardly outlived Vichy. By repeating MacMahon, Pétain had prompted the Resistance to repeat, for a time, Gambetta; once Pétain had been eliminated, the neo-Gambettist outburst did not last. Vichy was, all in all, the exception that proved the rule.

We must admit that today we are in a time when the symbolic aspects are of reduced importance in struggles for political power. Let us illustrate what we mean with a final example, the case of the postage stamp.

For several decades the common postage stamp featured the head of a woman wearing a Phrygian cap, with the words, "République Française." Toward the end of President Giscard d'Estaing's term (1974–81) a new stamp appeared, with the inscription "France" (no mention of the Republic), and a woman with no cap.[28] The simultaneous suppression of the word "République" and of the Phrygian cap was a case of sheer symbolic aggression. Thus, one of the first actions taken by the government formed by President Mitterand (elected May 10, 1981) was to reintroduce the word *République* and the woman with a red cap on the postage stamp.[29]

All, then, is well; however, the important thing to note is that this postage-stamp war held the interest of only a small number of French citizens, who, for the most part, found it amusing. The vast majority of the population remained profoundly indifferent. This symbolic skirmish had little to do with Giscard d'Estaing's loss in 1981. Perhaps other symbols were important—but these were of a nonvisual nature.

Yet if, instead of extending the line of symbolic battles from *before* 1914 to the present, we considered above all those that have occurred *since* 1914–18, we gain a very different impression about the vitality of symbolism, even figurative symbolism.

The various ideologies that challenge the Nation, its cults, and "its" dead, either in the name of proletarian internationalism, anarchy, and strict pacifism, or in the name of regional autonomy, do not conduct their fights dispassionately. This new kind of challenge, this "anti-politics," this "ultra-Left"—the terms matter little—based on traditional left-wing critical formulations but with an unexpected radicalism; its supporters hardly disdain symbolic expression. Have we not seen, for example, the militants of one of the provincial separatist movements blow up a section of the wall at Versailles, in order to damage, in effigy, a French power they deemed guilty of exploiting the conquered provinces in order to glut its own luxury? Such an event, of course, was charged with a passion a thousand times greater than that seen during the postage-stamp conflict.

It is much to early to survey the new symbolic antagonisms that mark our maturing twentieth century. But it is not too early to suggest that the role of figurative affirmations (and disputes) may yet be an important and "serious" component of political struggles.

If this is so, we might then conclude that this role is not destined to be reduced with the supposed advances of our rational civilization. Rather, the role of symbols is, perhaps, linked to the degree of importance, much more variable and fluctuating, of the conflicts that pervade real politics. In this connection, it is essential to determine which are, at any given time, the conflicts that matter. But this point leads us to some general reflections.

Problems

The history of political imagery is, thus, worth pursuing, not only because, as we could argue, there is nothing that is not worth studying, but because the history of symbolism is not necessarily situated on the fringe of "great" history. Indeed, the history of symbolism has sometimes been a central element of "great" history; at times, it may be of less importance, and may then return to occupy a central place.

The intensity of attachment to images and signs is not necessarily an index of lack of education or of arcaism, and even less of a certain national temperament: it seems, rather, to be inseparable from the combativeness displayed in those conflicts that arise in a given society at a given time. In other words, there is always an active historical symbolism, but it is important to place this symbolism in its specific context.

A British reviewer of *Marianne into Battle* pointed out that its stories about symbols were typically French, because France is represented by a woman (Marianne) and because it is very feminine to attach importance to symbols. In the virile world of John Bull, things were different.[30] Let us pass over the entertaining but inexact theme of the sex of nations, and the facile chatter linking symbolism and feminine psychology. The assertion remains that French history has been richer in symbolic struggles than has British history (referring, of course, to the nineteenth century). This is certainly true, but with reference to *politics*. At the time when the French, in effect, fought over flags and busts, the ever-present, even ostentatious, British symbolism of power (the display of the royal family, the solemnity of Parliament, the venerable longevity of the old heraldic lion) was held more or less above the fray. In this sense, British symbolism was less of a presence in political struggles. On the other hand, symbolic struggles—visible conflicts—were much more evident in *social struggles* in Britain. In these conflicts it was the British model that opposed distinct categories and cultures,[31] while France, which certainly did not tend toward uniformities in these matters, provided at least a variety of gradations, transitions, and continuities. In one country as in the other, however, the major conflict (here social, there ideological) expressed itself in the highest degree and by every possible means—including figurative means.

The history of political emblems is cluttered with studies of the origins of symbolism, a subject which in time attracts legends, fascinates the curious, and provides numerous opportunities for erudite quarrels. When was the red flag first flown?[32] Why the Gallic rooster?[33] Who created Marianne?[34] The Cross of Lorraine?[35] The rose in the fist?[36] These are simple questions, for which there are factual answers. In themselves, though, these questions are insufficient. To matter historically, it is not enough that a color or an emblem be chosen; it must be accepted by the public, perceived, received—in short, it must be successful. How can such success be explained? Why did the popular revolution identify itself with red rather than with the green of July 14, 1789,[37] or the black of November 1831?[38] Was there any connection to the brightness and warmth of the optic red? Or with the red of blood? The red of wine? The red discovered by erudites and the red analyzed by students of collective psychology—are they united by something more than coincidence? Did the Cross of Lorraine owe part of its success to the infusion of Lorraine into French patriotism (Joan of Arc) or even French folklore (the song, "On passant par la Lorraine . . . ")? Does the ready association of the rose with socialism owe something to the old habit (itself slightly ironic) of taking pink as the natural color of an attenuated form of social transformation—the more advanced being the (communist) red?

If these links are merely coincidences, then History is truly a fanciful goddess. But if they are more than coincidences, if they are kinds of causal relationships, how do they function? Now, if the search for origins requires techniques touched by erudition, on the contrary, trying to establish why an invention won spiritual acceptance, was received with favor, and maintained in a durable way, leads to speculation about *collective mentalities*.[39] But what methods of verification are open to us here?

One could imagine conducting a public opinion poll, in order to find out if the man on the street really identifies the Socialist party with the rose, and if he does so with the official party emblem in mind, or some older political symbolism. But it is hard to imagine a questionnaire clever enough to test (without shocking the respondent) the correlations between sanguinity, taste in wine, and revolutionary aspirations! And even if it were possible to conduct such inquiries today, one could not project them into the past because, by definition, the objects of history, people, are dead and thus they are mute.

What we commonly refer to as the history of collective mentalities, or sometimes as sociocultural history or the history of cultures, would often like to see itself as a sociology or anthropology of the past. This is a legitimate ambition. The problem is that if sociology, ethnology, and psychoanalysis supply historians with suggestions and concepts, they do not easily supply us with methods, since their own methodology is based on surveys done on the spot.

The most important of all the political images we have encountered is, without question, the image of a woman (or, more properly, in the original, a goddess). The effigy of Liberty became the emblem of the First Republic, then the symbol of the republican idea, and then tended increasingly to be taken for France, as contemporary France stabilized as the French Republic. France and the Republic (and here we slight the distinction between the two, so important in other contexts) are both perceived mainly as a woman. It is easy to see the original reasons for this: the Convention, in making its choice of emblems, took advantage of the established allegorical conventions, a choice that was all the more necessary given that, at that very moment, the French were getting rid of monarchs. But it is less clear why the association lasted, and what connection (beyond coincidence) this success may have had with the feminine nature of the image—in other words with sexuality.

To what extent is psychoanalysis helpful here? Can the concept of the murder of the father and desire of the mother help us understand the people who guillotined Louis XVI and then "fell in love" with Marianne? Yes—provided that the psychology of an entire people is analogous to that of an individual. But this is precisely what has never been demonstrated. There is a certain act of faith involved when one reaches the border of symbolic speculation, at least in its most directly psychoanalytic versions. For it is decidedly a question of symbolism if one admits that an emblem becomes a symbol as soon as it assumes multiple meanings, at different levels of consciousness, or even unconsciousness.

Perhaps those images that have stood the test of time are those which, in this sense, are the most symbolic. Quite a few thinkers would readily agree. If, in spite of everything, some symbolism subsists—if it does not completely vanish, if it can be reborn, if it changes or transforms itself, these scholars claim, it is because "the symbol, the myth, the image, are part of the substance of spiritual life; they can be hidden, mutilated, and degraded, but they can never be eliminated"[40]—or in other words because symbolic thought is as essential as discursive thought. In this sense, given all that we have said about the allegorical tradition, the effigy of Liberty, the Republic, the absence of kings, the "ideas" of France, the sarcasm directed at Marianne, which then turned into adoration, a sort of Mariology—we shall always confront the hypothesis that the deepest "truth" associated with Marianne involved a resurgence of the eternal symbol of Mother Earth. Others, imbued with rationalist standards, will not easily accept the idea of a multifaceted symbol, an idea hardly compatible with the principle of noncontradiction. In any case, the discovery of "profound" reality has not negated the study of common realities any more than psychoanalysis has rendered anatomy and physiology useless.

Each intellectual tendency nourishes a kind of historical literature, in which another tendency in turn points out the first tendency's deficiencies. There are some very down-to-earth historians who accumulate important data about images, but who refuse to engage in symbolic speculations, which they disdain as unverifiable pipe dreams. Others, starting out with the cultural prestige that goes with studies of symbolism, hastily pick out a few examples from masses of information, and then proceed to psychoanalyze France with a few strokes of the pen. The latter group is dazzling and fashionable, but the former group is more useful. Historians should try to reunite the two approaches.

Notes

1. We return here to the substance of a presentation delivered in March 1982 to the seminar on political power and ideology at the Shelby Cullom Davis Center for Historical Studies, Princeton University. The present article takes into account several observations made at that time during the discussion.

2. There is a vast literature concerning the notion of the symbol in general, and we admit experiencing difficulty mastering it. The article "Symbolism and Iconography" in the *Encyclopaedia Britannica* (Macropoedia vol. 17, 15th ed.) was useful. As major works, we looked at Mircea Eliade, *Images et symboles— Essai sur le symbolisme magico-religieux* (Paris, 1952); Carl G. Jung, *Man and his Symbols* (New York, 1964); Erwin Panofsky, *Meaning in the Visual Arts* (New York, 1955). More general and more simple, but also useful, were two works in the collection *Que sais-je?* (Paris), *Signes, symboles et mythes* by Luc Benoist (1975), and *La symbolique* by Olivier Beigbeder (1957).

3. On the particular problem of the symbolics of political power, the fundamental work appears to have been written by Percy Ernst Schramm, *Herrschaftszeichen und Staatssymbolik*, 3 vols. (Stuttgart, 1954–56), summarized in French by Philippe Braunstein in *Le débat* (July 1981). See also Luc de Heusch, *Le pouvoir et le sacré* (Bruxelles, 1962); and J. P. Gourevitch, *L'imagerie politique* (Paris, 1980).

4. Arthur Maury, *Emblèmes et drapeaux de la France* (Paris, [1904]).

5. Georges Lefranc, *Histoire du front populaire* (Paris, 1963).

6. Cf. our *Marianne au combat: Imagerie et symbolique républicaine en France de 1789 à 1880* (Paris, 1979); English translation, *Marianne into Battle* (New York, 1981). This will be followed by *Marianne au pouvoir: Imagerie et symboles républicains en France de 1880 à nos jours*.

7. The representation of monarchistic France is the subject of work in progress by M. Jean Lecuir, assistant professor at the University of Paris X, Nanterre.

8. About this term, as well as about other assertions made quickly here, one should refer to the volume mentioned above, n. 6.

9. On this point, see Eugen Weber, *Peasants into Frenchmen* (Stanford, 1976).

10. Jules Renouvier, *Histoire de l'art pendant la Révolution considéré principalement dans les estampes* (Paris, 1863).

11. On Hercules, symbol of the people in the Year II, see Lynn Hunt, "Hercules and the Radical Image in the French Revolution," *Representations*, 1 (1983): 95–117.

12. Maury, *Emblèmes et drapeaux*, p. 243.

13. One can find the basis for a study of this subject in Antoine Prost's *Les anciens combattants dans la société française*, 3 vols. (Paris, 1979).

14. We ignore the circumstances and the precise reasons for the choice of the hatchet instead of other more or less traditional emblems. One might think of the relationship with the fasces of Mussolini's Italy. One might also notice that a republican fasce, close to the hatchet, was on the facade of the Vichy town hall. Might this be the direct origin?

15. There was something to this: in 1958, the official medal honoring De Gaulle's election had on its reverse side the emblem of the Cross of Lorraine, whereas all other presidents, from Jules Grévy (1879) to René Coty (1959) had chosen a feminine republican effigy as their emblem. De Gaulle's successors abandoned the Cross of Lorraine, but re-adopted the feminine emblem.

16. M. Agulhon, "La statuomanie et l'histoire" in *Ethnologie française*, nos. 2–3 (1978): 3–4, 145–72.

17. Mircea Eliade, the author of *Images et symboles*, already mentioned, from whom we borrowed the initial postulate in this paragraph, did not consider it beneath him to think about the myth of "Marianne" in a seminar about national images which took place in September 1949 at the Centre Culturel International de Royaumont (France). It seems that his reflections were not published, but see the summation by G. Gadoffre in "French national images and the problem of national stereotypes" in *International Social-Science Bulletin* (UNESCO), vol. III, no. 3 (1951): 579–87. We should have known about this article while writing *Marianne au combat*; we learned about it only after the book appeared. It does not duplicate our research because it is (prematurely?) synthetic, and our work is absolutely analytic.

18. *La république au village: Les populations du var de la révolution à la Seconde République* (Paris, 1970; re-ed. 1979; English translation, Cambridge University Press and Maison des sciences de l'homme, 1982); Albert Soboul, *Les sans-culottes parisiens en l'An II: Mouvement populaire et gouvernement révolutionnaire* (Paris, 1958, English translation, *The Parisian Sans-Culottes* [Oxford, 1964]).

19. This word has tended to fall away from common use, replaced by another locution inspired by the present era: One "decolonizes" this or that. In the same way, in France, to evoke a mass murder, the sinister but recent expression *génocide* has dethroned the old locution with historical reference to "St. Barthélémy."

20. J. M. Darnis, *Les monuments expiatoires du supplice de Louis XVI* . . . (Paris, 1981).

21. See our book already mentioned above, n. 6.

22. M. Agulhon, "Géographie politique des monuments de Paris," forthcoming in *Les lieux de la mémoire*, anthology edited by Pierre Nora.

23. This was much talked about in France in 1980, consecrated as "Year of Patrimony"; the word became fashionable.

24. This problem deserves considerable study. Until then, one may find certain basics in the work edited by J. M. Mayeur, *Libre pensée et religion laique en France* (Strasbourg, 1980).

25. *Marianne au pouvoir.* See, for now, my communication to the *Société d'histoire moderne:* "La place des symboles dans l'histoire d'après l'exemple de la République francaise," Bulletin of the Société, supplement to the *Revue d'histoire moderne et contemporaine*, no. 3, 1980.

26. Even though there are dead buried under the July Column, this has been forgotten today. The heroes of July as Dead, as objects of an extreme left-wing cult, were supplanted by the Dead of the Commune of 1871, honored at the back of the Père-Lachaise cemetery. Cf. our article mentioned above, n. 22.

27. About these, one recalls the classic René Rémond, *Les Droites en France de 1815 à nos jours* (Paris, 1981).

28. The head of one of the Sabine women in David's painting *The Rape of the Sabine Women.*

29. The head of Liberty from Delacroix's painting *La liberté guidant le peuple.*

30. *Journal of the Franco-British Council* (1981).

31. The study of "working-class culture" occupies a much bigger place in British historiography than in French historiography.

32. Maurice Dommanget, *Histoire du drapeau rouge des origines à la guerre de 1939* (Paris, 1966).

33. A. Maury, *Emblèmes et drapeaux*, and Vallet de Viriville, "Les emblèmes de la monarchie . . . ," in *Le courier français*, July-August 1845.

34. M. Agulhon, *Marianne au combat.*

35. Charles de Gaulle, *Mémoires de guerre*, vol. 1, *L'appel* (Paris, 1954), pp. 73 and 79. De Gaulle was imprecise about this choice except that its extension to all armed elements of Free France was "an idea voiced by d'Argenlieu" (Thierry d'Argenlieu, a naval officer from a noble family, then entered a religious order, mobilized again for the war 1939–40, one of the first naval officers to support De Gaulle after June 1940). The Cross of Lorraine does not seem to have been an official emblem; the British-French agreement (De Gaulle-Churchill) of August 7, 1940, the real charter of Free France, does not mention it. It is true that it would not have been logical. De Gaulle, who grandly pretended to be the real France, could not display a modified national flag for fear of abandoning to Vichy the advantage of having the only one with authentic colors. The Cross of Lorraine remained, then, simply a kind of combat pennant—which did not prevent it from being popular.

36. Personal survey with M. Jacques Guyard, a historian, currently a socialist deputy of the Essonne. The emblem was chosen by the Parisian Federation of the Socialist party around 1969, inspired by a poster of the Italian May '68 movement; in the background, an echo of the formula attributed to Karl Marx: "There will be bread and also roses for all."

37. The leaf of a chestnut tree given by the patriot-orator Camille Desmoulins as a sign of recognition to the demonstrators who went to capture the Bastille—connotation: hope.

38. A revolt by Lyon silk workers to obtain better pay ("To live by working or to die by fighting")—connotation: death, despair.

39. At least in countries and periods of relative freedom—for, in some cases, lack of sufficient freedom has prevented spontaneous symbolism. The thesis attended by Tchakhotine, not without merit, in the famous *Viol des foules par la propagande politique* (Paris, 1939), is that a symbol which is completely invented and which has neither substratum nor prior relationships can be *imposed* on the crowd's reception by a fairly clever and intense propaganda. He gives two examples, one of which he detests, the Nazi Swastika, and one of which he admires, the three arrows of the German Social-Democratic party, then a sign of international socialism.

40. M. Eliade, *Images et symboles*, p. 12.

7

DAVID CANNADINE

Splendor out of Court: Royal Spectacle and Pageantry in Modern Britain, c. 1820– 1977

Despite the continued centrality of the monarchy in British political, social, and cultural life, the changing nature of its public image during the last two hundred years has received remarkably little attention from historians. The "theater of power" of Tudor and Stuart courts—the manner by which royal and republican prestige was enhanced by elaborate ceremonial—has been extensively investigated, not only for Britain but for Europe as a whole.[1] For the late nineteenth and early twentieth centuries, a second efflorescence of "invented" ritual and tradition in Wilhelmine Germany and the French Third Republic has been the subject of a number of studies, which throw out suggestive hints as far as contemporary British ceremonial is concerned.[2] And, in interwar Europe, the elaborate rituals of the new fascist and communist regimes have recently begun to attract extensive scholarly attention.[3] Yet, English royal ritual has been almost entirely ignored for the period since the late seventeenth century. By setting such modern royal ceremonial, pageantry, and display in the context of its times, this essay hopes to uncover the changes that have taken place—in both the nature and the meaning of such spectacles— between the coronation of George IV and the silver jubilee of Elizabeth II.

Viewed in this light, there are ten aspects of the context that need to be investigated: the political power of the monarch; the personal character and standing of the monarch; the nature of the economic and social structure of the country over which he ruled; the type, extent, and attitude of the media; the prevailing state of technology and fashion; the self-image of the nation over which the monarch ruled; the condition of the capital city in which most royal ceremonials took place; the attitude of those responsible for liturgy, music, and organization; the nature of the ceremonial as actually performed; and finally, the extent of commercial exploitation.

Set in this descriptive context, four distinct phases in the development of the ceremonial image of the British monarchy emerge. The first period, lasting from the 1820s and before to the 1870s, is a period of ineptly managed, uninventive ritual, performed in what was preponderantly a localized, diversified, preindustrial society. The second, beginning in 1877, when Victoria was made Empress of India, and extending until the outbreak of the First World War was, in Britain as in much of Europe, the heyday of "invented tradition," a time when old ceremonials were staged with an expertise and appeal that had been lacking, and when new pageants were self-consciously invented to accentuate this development. From 1918 until Queen Elizabeth's coronation in 1953, Britain's former rivals in royal display—Germany, Austria, and Russia—dispensed with their monarchies, leaving Britain alone in the field. Finally, since 1953, the decline of Britain as a great power, combined with the massive impact of television, suggests that the "meaning" of royal ceremonial has once again changed profoundly. Each of these successive phases will now be examined in turn.

I

The period from the 1820s to the 1870s saw the British monarchy at its most significant in terms of real, effective political power. In 1807, for example, George III dissolved a Parliament less than one year old to increase the strength of a ministry hostile to Catholic Emancipation. Four years later, when the Prince of Wales assumed the regency, it was generally supposed that had he so wished, he could have removed the Tory administration and put in the Whigs in their place.[4] Thereafter, he remained an exasperating and important figure in the political firmament, a constant irritant to Canning, Liverpool, and Wellington alike. And his successor, William IV, was even more energetic. Nor was Victoria, in her early years as queen, exactly quiescent. In 1839, by refusing to accept Ladies of the Bedchamber who were agreeable to Peel, she succeeded in artificially prolonging the life of Melbourne's government. In 1851, she effectively sacked Palmerston from the Foreign Office and, after Albert's death, remained "a shrewd, persistent and opinionated adviser and critic of her governments."[5]

Renewed royal unpopularity accompanied continuing royal power. The lives, loves, and morals of George III's children were such as to make them, arguably, the most unloved royal generation in English history. In particular, George IV's extravagance and womanizing brought the monarchy to a low ebb, the nadir of which was reached in 1821 when his marriage to Queen Caroline became both public politics and public scandal. "There never was an individual more regretted by his fellow creatures than this deceased king," noted the *Times* in its damning editorial on his death.[6] In the same way, William IV's short honeymoon of popularity vanished as a result of his hostility to the Whig reforming government, so that the *Spectator* could castigate him for his "feebleness of purpose and littleness of mind, his ignorance and his prejudices."[7] Nor, initially, did Victoria fare any better. Her partiality for her first prime minister earned her the soubriquets "Mrs. Melbourne" and "Queen of the Whigs," and Albert's Germanic intensity was generally frowned upon—"a Prince who has breathed from childhood the air of courts tainted by the imaginative servility of Goethe."[8] The new Prince of Wales, ensnared successively in the Mordaunt Scandal and the Aylesford Case, damningly described by Bagehot as an "unemployed youth," was hardly able to add any luster to this dowdy and unpopular crown.

In short, the monarchy was neither impartial and above politics nor Olympian and above society, but was actively part of both. And, because both politics and society were quintessentially London-based, metropolitan activities, the ceremonial appeal of the monarchy was only further circumscribed. Between the age of Wilkes and the age of Chamberlain, the national influence of London was relatively restricted, as provincial England reasserted itself. Local loyalties and rivalries remained strong; the county community was still a cohesive and realistic unit.[9] Furthermore, the uneven development of the economy and slow adoption of steam power meant that while Britain may have been the "workshop of the world," the workshops were small and relatively few. Engels's Manchester, with its massive mills and segregated suburbs, was the exception rather than the rule. In 1851, agriculture remained the largest employer of labor. "The England of the rectory and the modest mansion house and the farm house" was preponderant. "Country towns, both large and small, . . . were still the norm, so far as urbanization in the mid-nineteenth century was concerned."[10] In such a localized, differentiated, face-to-face world there was little scope for a ceremoniously enhanced monarch, Olympian, aloof and detached, the father figure of the nation and focus of all loyalties.

The condition and attitude of the press further impeded such a development. While the great royal ceremonies were fully reported in provincial as well as metropolitan newspapers, the press remained hostile to the monarchy. In the early decades of the nineteenth century, the attacks in the London papers of Gillray, Rowlandson, and the Cruikshanks made the monarchy "without doubt the most regular topic and target for the cartoonists."[11] From the 1850s to the 1870s, Victoria was constantly the object of criticism in newspaper editorials. The provincial press, Liberal, intellectual, rational, middle-class, opposed to display as much as to emotion, was in general no more favorable to the monarchy than its metropolitan counterparts.[12] In addition, the lack of pictures in an age that had no cheap illustrated press made even the greatest of royal ceremonial something of a mystery to all except the most literate and wealthy. Under these circumstances, great royal ceremonies were not shared, corporate events, but remote, inaccessible group rites, performed for the benefit of the few rather than the edification of the many.

The prevailing state of transport technology served further to contain the monarchy within society rather than elevate it above. There was nothing particularly anachronistic, romantic, or splendid about the way in which English royalty traveled. Victorian England was, as Professor Thompson reminds us, a horse-drawn society, in which there were 120,000 privately owned large carriages and 250,000 light two-wheelers by 1870.[13] Indeed, the carriages that members of the royal family drove today were in widespread use tomorrow. The phaeton, for example, was introduced by George IV, the wagonette by the prince consort, and the Victoria by the Prince of Wales.[14] As a result, the monarchy's carriages were no more grand than those of lesser mortals. At William IV's coronation, the most outstanding coach was that of Prince Esterhazy. And at Victoria's coronation seven years later, the carriage of Marchall Soult, the French ambassador, rather than that of the queen herself, was regarded as the most splendid.[15]

This lack of concern about successful foreign rivalry in trivial matters was the reverse side of supreme confidence in international competition in important affairs, as the defeat of Napoleon left Britain without a rival in Continental Europe. Palmerston's "Don Pacifico" speech embodied this self-confidence perfectly, combining as it did a panegyric on Britain's unique social and constitutional stability with a strident and popular assertion of its unchallenged role as policeman of the world.[16] The early and mid-Victorians saw themselves as the leaders of progress and pioneers of civilization; they prided themselves on the limited nature of their government, their lack of interest in formal empire, their hatred of show, extravagance, ceremonial, and ostentation.[17] The certainty of power and the assured confidence of success meant that there was no need to show off. Little Belgium might spend more than Great Britain on its metropolitan law courts: but the reality of power and religion of parsimony meant that the English regarded such petty one-upmanship with disdain or indifference.[18]

This attitude goes far in explaining why London was ill-suited to be the setting for grand royal ceremonial, and why the English positively made a virtue of it. Even the most ardent champion of the "infernal wen" conceded that it could not rival the careful planning of L'Enfant's Washington, the venerable ruins of Rome, the magnificence of Haussmann's Paris, the grand schemes for the reconstruction of Vienna instituted by Francis Joseph in 1854, or the splendid constellation of five squares constructed in St. Petersburg during the first half of the nineteenth century.[19] Mid-Victorian London, as Donald Olsen has argued, was "a statement against absolutism," a proud expression of the energies and values of a free people.[20] Grandeur in the style of Paris or St. Petersburg spelled despotism: how else could enough power be wielded or funds mobilized to make it possible to complete such mammoth schemes? London, by contrast, might be slovenly, but at least its people were not enslaved. As one contemporary explained, "The public buildings are few, and for the most part mean. . . . But what of all this? How impressively do you feel that you are in the metropolis of a free people?"[21]

Such love of freedom and economy and hatred of ostentation was the kiss of death for grand royal ceremonial, and the ineptitude with which the musical arrangements were made only further darkened the picture. The first seventy years of the nineteenth century were among the bleakest in England's musical history: no major work by any English composer has survived; still less the relatively trivial ephemera of ceremonial music.[22] The national anthem was far from being the venerated patriotic hymn it was later to become: it was not even sung at Victoria's coronation; new choral arrangements were relatively infrequent; and during the reign of George IV,[23] alternative versions criticizing the king and praising his queen proliferated. Successive Masters of the King's Musick were men of no distinction, whose duties were limited to conducting the royal orchestra, and Sir George Smart, organist of the Chapel Royal, to whom the musical arrangements for all great royal ceremonies from the funeral of George IV to the coronation of Victoria were entrusted, was singularly inept. This lack of inspiration and leadership at the top was also reflected in the sad state of English cathedral choirs, especially those of the Abbey and St. Paul's. Rehearsals were unknown; surplices were not worn; choirs did not process; absenteeism, indiscipline, and irreverent behavior were endemic; services were long and badly planned.[24]

Part of the problem derived from a lack of interest in ritual on the part of the clergy, who were either indifferent or hostile. The combination of poverty of means and absence of taste made the first three quarters of the nineteenth century a low point in ecclesiastical ritual and ecclesiological concern.[25] At Westminster Abbey, Wren's incomparable altarpiece was removed at the time of George IV's coronation and was replaced by an undignified, mock-Gothic structure. Thereafter, the choir was remodeled, and the stalls were placed so close together, with accommodation for some of the congregation between, that choral singing of any merit was impossible—even if the choir had been competent. James Turle, organist from 1831 to 1882, was unable to bring any discipline to the choir, and the organ he played was old and inaudible. In 1847–48, Dean Buckland again reorganized the choir, and placed most of the congregation in the transepts, where they could neither hear nor see the clergy. When, finally, the congregation was restored to the nave, they were obliged to sing the hymns "from large posters placed on the columns." With good cause, Jebb castigated the "coldness, meagreness and irreverence in the performance of the divine offices." Even as late as the time of Dean Stanley (1870–91), the administration of the Abbey was marked by "ignorance of finance and incapacity for business."[26]

2

It is in this context that the inept performance and limited popularity of royal ritual and ceremonial during the first three-quarters of the nineteenth century needs to be set. In 1817, at the funeral of Princess Charlotte, the daughter of the prince regent, the undertakers were drunk. When the duke of York died, ten years later, the chapel at Windsor was so damp that most of the mourners caught cold, Canning contracted rheumatic fever, and the bishop of London died.[27] George IV's coronation, although conceived in the grandest manner possible, in a desperate and unsuccessful attempt to win some popularity, was so overblown that grandeur merged into farce. It was necessary to employ prizefighters in Westminster Hall to keep the peace between the distinguished but belligerent guests. George himself, although sumptuously clad, "looked too large for effect, indeed he was more like an elephant than a man." And the pathetic, unsuccessful attempt made by Queen Caroline to gain access to the Abbey marred the whole proceedings.[28]

George IV's flirtation with grandeur was so unsuccessful that it was not repeated for the next half century. At George's own funeral at Windsor, William IV talked constantly and walked out early. "We never saw so motley, so rude, so ill-managed a body of persons," noted the *Times* in its description of the mourners.[29] William, for his part, loathed ceremonial and ostentation, and tried to dispense with his coronation altogether. Eventually, he allowed it to proceed, but it was so truncated that it became mockingly known as the "Half-Crownation." His funeral was equally squalid—"a wretched mockery," Greville described it. The ceremony was long and tedious, and mourners loitered, laughed, gossiped, and sniggered within sight of the coffin.[30] Nor was Victoria's coronation any more impressive. It was completely unrehearsed; the clergy lost their place in the order of the service; the choir was pitifully inadequate; the archbishop of Canterbury put the ring on a finger that was too big for it; and two of the trainbearers talked throughout the entire ceremony.[31] Albert's funeral was almost a private affair at Windsor, as was the wedding of the Prince of Wales. In London, where Alexandra was greeted, commentators noted "the poor taste of the decorations, the absence of outriders, and the extraordinary shabbiness of the royal equipages." *Punch*, in turn, protested that the wedding should take place at Windsor—"an obscure Berkshire village, noted only for an old castle with no sanitary arrangements." Once again, the planning and organization were woefully inadequate. Palmerston had to travel back from Windsor third class on the special train, and Disraeli was obliged to sit on his wife's lap.[32]

But the nadir of royal grandeur and ceremonial presence was reached in those two decades following Albert's death, when the queen's reclusive widowhood and the public scandals involving the Prince of Wales "provided the matter for inumerable denunciations."[33] Between 1861 and 1886, the queen, now known in the popular press as "Mrs. Brown," opened Parliament only six times. Even the *Times* felt "regret" at her continued absence at Windsor, Balmoral, and Osborne.[34] In 1864 a notice was pinned to the rails of Buckingham Palace in the manner of an advertisement: "These commanding premises to be let or sold, in consequence of the late occupant's declining business."[35] Walter Bagehot, although in favor of a grand and splendid monarchy, constantly stressed that such was not, in fact, the case. "To be invisible," he noted "is to be forgotten. . . . To be a symbol, and an effective symbol, you must be vividly and often seen." Or, as he put it even more stridently, "From causes which it is not difficult to define, the Queen has done almost as much to injure the popularity of the monarchy by her long retirement from public life as the most unworthy of her predecessors did by his profligacy and frivolity."[36]

This picture of ineptly managed ceremonial, with only limited appeal, is corroborated by the restricted scale of commercial exploitation which these pageants stimulated during this first period. Commemorative pottery, for example, had been a recognized genre since the 1780s. But the monarchy was much less often depicted than other contemporary figures. Frederick the Great was far more popular than George II, and Nelson and Wellington were more frequently commemorated than George III. During the reign of George IV, more pottery was produced in support of Queen Caroline than in favor of the king himself. The coronations of William IV and Victoria received little attention, and between 1861 and 1886, despite numerous royal marriages, there was virtually no royal commemorative pottery produced at all. The private production of medals for sale tells a similar story. Once again, more medals were issued in support of Queen Caroline than in commemoration of the coronation of her husband, and the coronations of William and Victoria were scarcely noticed.[37] Until the 1870s the royal family was so unpopular, and the appeal of its ceremonial was so limited, that it was not deemed worthy of large-scale commercial exploitation.

3

Between the late 1870s and 1914, however, there was a fundamental change in the public image of the British monarchy, as its ceremonial, hitherto inept, private and of limited appeal, became splendid, public and popular. To some extent, this was facilitated by the gradual retirement of the monarchs from party politics. Victoria, however obstinate and obstructive she had been at the beginning of her reign, wielded much less effective power by the end. The growing size and importance of the electorate, combined with increased party consciousness, meant that assertions of the royal prerogative of the kind that had precipitated the Bedchamber crisis were much less in evidence. Once the electorate had spoken in 1880, for example, the queen empress could no more keep Disraeli in than Gladstone out.[38] Edward VII came to the throne old and inexperienced, had little taste for desk work, spent three months of the year abroad and, apart from occasional interference in matters of foreign policy and the award of honors and decorations, played only on a minimal role in political life.[39] As the real power of the monarchy waned, its chances of becoming once more a center of grand ceremonial improved.

At the same time, power was exchanged for popularity. Victoria's longevity, probity, sense of duty, and unrivaled position as matriarch of Europe and mother figure of Empire came to outweigh, and then eclipse, the earlier, hostile attitude toward her. At her death, she was no longer "Mrs. Guelph," the "Queen of the Whigs," but the "most excellent of sovereigns," who "bequeathed a name eternally to be revered."[40] Nor was time any less generous to Edward VII. His extravagant life; the zest and style with which he traveled; his notable racing successes; and the incomparable beauty, charm, and appeal of his consort: all these advantages were his during the brief years of his reign. As one rhymster put it at his death:

> Greatest sorrow England ever had
> When death took away our dear old Dad.[41]

This change in the position of the monarch, placing both Victoria and Edward above politics as patriarchal figures for the whole of the nation, was rendered increasingly urgent by economic and social developments during the last quarter of the nineteenth century. Once more, London reasserted its national dominance, as provincial identity and loyalties markedly weakened.[42] It was at the end, rather than the beginning, of the nineteenth century, that Britain became a preponderantly urban, industrial, mass society, with class loyalties and class conflicts set in a genuinely national framework for the first time. The new unionism, the controversies surrounding Taff Vale and the Osborne Judgment, and the growing, unprecedented industrial unrest in the years immediately before the First World War, all betokened a harsher social and economic climate.[43] Moreover, as was stressed at the time of Edward's coronation, the "antique character of many of the material circumstances of life at the date when Queen Victoria was crowned" contrasted markedly with the dramatic, disorienting developments that had taken place in the subsequent sixty years—a widening franchise, the railway, the steamship, the telegraph, electricity, the tram.[44] In such an age of change, crisis, and dislocation, the "preservation of anachronism," the deliberate, ceremonial presentation of an impotent but venerated monarch as a unifying symbol of permanence and national community became both possible and necessary.

Of particular importance in promoting this new picture of the monarch as head of the nation were developments in the media from the 1880s. With the advent of the yellow press, news became increasingly nationalized and sensationalized, as the old, rational, intellectual, middle-class, provincial Liberal press was gradually superseded by the great national dailies, London-based, increasingly Conservative, strident, vulgar and working-class in their appeal.[45] In 1896 Harmsworth launched the *Daily Mail*, which sold for one-half penny, and achieved a daily circulation of 700,000 within four years. The *Mirror*, the *Sketch*, and the *Daily Express* soon followed. At the same time, the savage cartoons and editorials of the earlier period disappeared almost entirely. Edward VII's liaisons were discreetly ignored, and cartoonists such as Partridge and Carruthers Gould depicted great occasions in the lives and deaths of monarchs in a restrained and respectful way.[46] A third major change concerned the development of new techniques in photography and printing, which meant that illustrations were no longer confined to expensive, middle-class weeklies. By the end of the nineteenth century, the great royal ceremonies were described with unprecedented immediacy and vividness in a sentimental, emotional, admiring way, which appealed to a broader cross-section of the public than ever before.[47]

If the press was one major agent in exalting the monarchy to venerated Olympus, then changes in transport technology produced a similar effect, by rendering the monarchs' coaches increasingly anachronistic, fairy-tale, and splendid. From the 1870s, the carriage trade received a severe check in its hitherto spectacular growth rate.[48] The invention of the pneumatic bicycle tire by Dunlop in 1888 led to the cycling boom of the next decade. By 1898 there were more than one thousand miles of tramways in English cities, and by 1914 that figure had trebled.[49] For town dwellers in particular (who were by now the majority of the population), the horse ceased to be part of their way of life as it had previously been. Under these circumstances, the royal carriages, previously commonplace, became endowed with a romantic splendor that had never been attainable before. While coachmakers like Mulliner were obliged to turn to motor cars because of the decline in demand for their more traditional products, Edward VII actually commissioned a new state landau in which he drove back from the Abbey after his coronation. Described "in its build, proportions and adornment as probably the most graceful and regal vehicle ever built," it was emphatic proof of the monarchy's new and unique capacity to call in the old world to redress the balance of the new.[50]

Internationally, the same trends were in evidence, as the novelty of a mass society at home was reflected in the newness of formal empire abroad. And, once more, the originality of the development was concealed and rendered acceptable by associating it with the oldest national institution, the monarchy. During the first three-quarters of the nineteenth century, no royal ceremonial occasion could plausibly have been called an imperial event. But from 1877, when Disraeli made Victoria Empress of India, and 1897, when Joseph Chamberlain brought the colonial premiers and troops to parade in the diamond jubilee procession, every great royal occasion was also an *imperial* occasion.[51] As Bodley noted, during the final decades of Victoria's reign, her crown became "the emblem of the British race, to encourage its expansion over the face of the globe."[52] Even Edward's illness at the time of his coronation worked to imperial advantage: while the European delegations departed, those from the Empire remained, making the coronation—when it finally happened—"a family festival for the British Empire."[53]

Whether these royal ceremonials, in part reflecting a novel consciousness of formal imperial possession, were an expression of national self-confidence or of doubt is not altogether clear. It remains widely believed that Victoria's jubilees and Edward's coronation mark the high noon of Empire, confidence, and splendor.[54] Yet, following the mood of Kipling's "Recessional," there are good reasons to regard them in a very different light—as an assertion of show and grandeur, bombast and bravado, at a time when real power was already on the wane.[55] Certainly, during this period, Britain was increasingly challenged by new, rival world powers, economically, colonially, and politically. The unification of Italy and Germany, the recovery of the United States from the traumas of the Civil War, the scramble for Africa, the tariffs adopted by the Continental powers, the decision by Britain to abandon "Splendid Isolation" and seek alliance and support in Europe, the Boer War, and the crises of Fashoda, Agadier, and Morocco, all betokened a world of fear, tension, and rivalry that had not existed in the balmy days of Palmerston.

This growing international competitiveness was mirrored in the large-scale rebuilding of capital cities, as the great powers bolstered their self-esteem in the most visible, ostentatious manner. In Rome, the Master Plan of 1883 sought to create a capital city worthy of a new nation, with grand avenues and boulevards on the Parisian model. The completion of the massive Victor Emmanuel Monument in 1911 was a further emphatic assertion of national grandeur and pride.[56] In Vienna, that clutch of grand buildings facing the Ringstrasse, most of which were constructed in the 1870s and 1880s, specifically intended to reflect "the greatness of Empire."[57] In Berlin, German unification was expressed visually in "magnificent spacious streets, tree-planted squares, monuments and decorations," including the Column of Victory, the Reichstag, the Siegesalle, and the Cathedral, all buildings conceived in a spirit of chauvinistic ostentation, "the silent sentinels of national glory."[58] In Paris, the Eiffel Tower, constructed for the Exhibition of 1889, was designed to *"frapper le monde,"* to stand as "a triumphal arch as striking as those which earlier generations have raised to honour conquerors."[59]

In this environment of extreme international competition, the smugness and pride with which Londoners of a previous generation had venerated their shabby capital city was no longer tenable. The establishment of the London County Council in 1888 finally provided London with a single administrative authority, beholden neither to royal despotism nor state power, visibly embodied in the construction of a grand County Hall begun in 1908.[60] The War Office in Whitehall, the government buildings at the corner of Parliament Square, the Methodist Central Hall, and Westminster Cathedral all added to the feeling of grandeur and magnificence.[61] In London, as in other great capital cities, monumental, commemorative statues proliferated. But the most significant, coherent piece of rebuilding was the widening of the Mall, the building of Admiralty Arch, the refacing of Buckingham Palace, and the construction of the Victoria Monument in front. This grand, monumental, imperial ensemble, which gave London its only triumphal, ceremonial way, was accomplished between 1906 and 1913 under the auspices of the Queen Victoria Memorial Committee, whose chairman was Lord Esher.[62] In London as in Rome or Paris, the element of international competition was strongly present. As Balfour explained when setting up the committee, its aim was to produce a grand, stately, monumental ensemble, "of the kind which other nations have shown examples, which we may well imitate and can easily surpass."[63]

Such developments, in London as elsewhere, provided the setting for ceremonial that was itself a further aspect of international rivalry. The *parvenu* monarchies of Germany and Italy not only sought to rival the more venerable dynasties of Europe in their court ritual, yachts, and trains; they also self-consciously competed in grand public displays of royal pageantry.[64] Thus in Austria the six hundredth anniversary of the Habsburg monarchy, the millenium of the Kingdom of Hungary, the golden and diamond jubilees of Francis Joseph and the emperor's eightieth birthday were all celebrated with unprecedented pomp and grandeur.[65] Italy retaliated with an extravagant funeral for Victor Emmanuel II in 1878, and the unveiling of his monument in 1911, which was also the jubilee of Italian Unification.[66] In Russia, the funeral accorded to Alexander III in 1894 was without precedent in splendor and magnificence, and the tercentenary celebration of the Romanov dynasty in 1913 were conceived on the grandest possible scale. In Germany, the funeral of Kaiser Wilhelm I and the Silver Jubilee of his grandson were similarly magnificent.[67] Even republican regimes joined in. In France, Bastille Day was invented in 1880, and was repeated annually thereafter. The funeral of Victor Hugo in 1885 and the centennial of the Revolution four years later were further pageants in the grand manner.[68]

The same sense of competition existed in Britain. An English reporter in Moscow and St. Petersburg, covering the funeral of Alexander III for the *Times*, recalled that "rarely or never, perhaps, in all history, had a more gorgeous open-air pageant been seen. It was only rivalled, though not, perhaps, outshone, by Victoria's jubilee procession to Westminster Abbey."[69] Likewise, when King Edward VII visited Germany in 1909, the Kaiser was determined to dazzle the English king with a display of ceremonial grandeur. Despite the occasional hitch, he succeeded. "The Emperor," the Controller of the Household later confided to his diary, "was delighted with the visit of King Edward, and said: 'The English cannot come up to us in this sort of thing', meaning the splendour of the procession, the royal apartments in the Castle, the Banquet, the Court Ball and so forth."[70]

In such competitive circumstances, it was perhaps fortunate—if largely accidental—that the English musical renaissance coincided with this upsurge of interest in ritual and ceremony, instigated by Parry, promoted by the entrepreneurial zeal of Stanford, and presided over by the genius of Elgar, the first English composer of international renown since Purcell.[71] Such an efflorescence made it possible for the great royal occasions to be presented, not as embarrassing indictments of the dearth of music in England, but as festivals of native talent. Accordingly, the coronations of Edward VII and George V were adorned with specially commissioned works by Stanford, Parry, Elgar, German, and Sullivan.[72] At the same time, the improvement in the standards of choirs and orchestras meant that they were also well performed. In this development, the key figures were Sir George Stainer, organist at St. Paul's from 1872 to 1888, and Sir Frederick Bridge, his opposite number at Westminster Abbey from 1882 to 1918. Under their firm, efficient guidance, choirs became expertly drilled and trained, processed and behaved in a dignified manner, and were dressed in surplices.[73] As a result, the standard of performance at the early twentieth-century coronations was incomparably better than those that had gone before. Finally, Sir Walter Parratt was Master of the King's Musick from 1893 to 1924, which meant that the overall organization was also improved: during his tenure in the post, it ceased to be a sinecure, as he became the supreme authority in arranging the music of great royal events.[74]

During the same period, the attitude of the established Church toward ritual and ceremony also changed markedly. Unconsciously echoing Bagehot, Samuel Wilberforce had noted as early as 1865 that "there is, I believe, in the English mind a great move towards a higher ritual," and in ensuing decades his prediction was borne out. Bishops began to wear purple cassocks and carry pastoral staffs.[75] Vestments, surplices, incense, and altar candles became increasingly common in cathedrals and city churches. In 1887 and again in 1897 the officiating clergy at Victoria's jubilee services dressed in copes and colored stoles, a novel and picturesque innovation. And, as with the secular side of royal ritual, the motive was in part a wish to appeal to the working classes. As E. W. Benson, archbishop of Canterbury, noted after the golden jubilee, "days afterwards, everyone feels that the socialist movement has had a check."[76] Significantly, the biographies and reminiscences of late Victorian and Edwardian prelates contain full accounts of elaborate preparations for the great royal ceremonials—something conspicuously lacking in similar books by and about their predecessors. In particular, Randall Davidson became an unrivaled ecclesiastical authority on royal ritual, participating in Victoria's golden jubilee as dean of Windsor, in her diamond jubilee and Edward's coronation as bishop of Winchester, and in that of George V as archbishop of Canterbury.[77] At the same time, Westminster Abbey itself was transformed into a more colorful and dignified setting for great ceremonial. The organ was rebuilt in 1884 and 1894; the choir was remodeled and lit with electricity; the choristers were provided with red cassocks in 1897; and Lord Rosebery presented a new cross for the High Altar in 1899.[78]

4

It is in this significantly changed context, both domestic and international, that the more elaborate and more appealing royal ritual of this second phase must be set. From the 1870s onward, in England as in other western countries, the position of the head of state was ceremonially enhanced. A venerated monarch, conveyed in a splendid state coach along triumphal thoroughfares, was no longer, as his predecessors had been, just the head of society, but was now seen to be the head of the nation as well.[79] In England, as elsewhere in Europe, the unprecedented developments in industry and in social relationships, and the massive expansion of the yellow press, made it both necessary and possible to present the monarch, in all the splendor of his ritual, in this essentially new way, as a symbol of consensus and continuity to which all might defer.[80] As international relations became increasingly tense, this further induced the "invention of tradition," as national rivalry was both expressed and sublimated in ceremonial competition. Only in one major regard did the English experience differ from that of other western nations: in Russia, Germany, Italy, and Austria, this flourishing of ceremonial was centered on a head of state who still exercised real power. But in England, while the ceremonial shadow of power was cast over the monarch, the substance increasingly lay elsewhere.

In retrospect, these developments in context and circumstance seem helpful to explain the changes in the performance and "meaning" of ritual. At the time, such change was perhaps not as deliberate as this might imply: only slowly, as one ceremony followed another, did a coherent pattern and structure of symbols and meanings emerge. In 1887, after fifty years on the throne, the widow of Windsor was persuaded—although only with the greatest reluctance—to participate in a grand state pageant in London. It was, indeed, a risk, for her recent unpopularity made it impossible to predict what sort of reception she would receive. Victoria's refusal to wear the crown and robes of state only seemed to support such forebodings. Nevertheless, the resulting golden jubilee, with its procession and service of thanksgiving in the Abbey, was a great success: "Pageantry such as this generation never saw. . . . The grandest state ceremony of this generation."[81] The diamond jubilee, planned with more confidence and certainty ten years later, was even more splendid. As the queen herself noted, with delighted surprise, "No one, ever, I believe, has met with such an ovation as was given to me passing through these six miles of streets. . . . . The crowds were quite indescribable, and their enthusiasm truly marvellous and deeply touching."[82] Thereafter came Victoria's funeral, the coronation and funeral of Edward VII, the coronation and durbar of George V, and the investiture of his son as Prince of Wales at Carnarvon Castle.

Insofar as the success of these pageants depended on improved performance, three people in particular were of major significance. The first was Reginald Brett, Viscount Esher, the *éminence grise* in British governing circles at the turn of the century, friend of Victoria, Edward VII, and George V, secretary of the Office of Works from 1895 to 1902, and deputy constable and lieutenant governor of Windsor Castle from 1901 to 1928. He was responsible, not only for the redecoration of the royal palaces and the sorting of the royal archives after Victoria's death, but also for much of the planning of every great state pageant from the diamond jubilee of Victoria to the funeral of Edward VII.[83] In theory, responsibility for such occasions lay with the duke of Norfolk as Hereditary Earl Marshal, the Master of the Horse, the Lord Steward, and the Lord Chamberlain. But Esher's charm, tact, historical sense, flair for organization, and love of ceremonial ensured that the lion's share of the work was done by him.

Esher's interest in royal ceremonial was matched by that of Edward VII himself. For while his mother had been a reluctant participant in public ceremonial who loathed splendid costume and public appearances, Edward was eager to "show himself to his subjects, clothed in his attributes of sovereignty."[84] He had been a constant critic of his mother's mournful gloom, and had also bitterly resented the way in which his nephew, the Kaiser, had outshone him in splendor. So it was entirely characteristic that one of his earliest acts as king was to revive the state opening of Parliament as a full-dress ceremonial occasion, with a procession in the state coach through the streets of London, and with the king, clad in his full regalia, personally reading the speech from the throne—something that Victoria had not done in forty years.[85] Ironically, it was Edward's funeral, in which the ubiquitous Esher once more had a hand, that was " the grandest state pageant in which he was to take part." Of especial significance was the lying-in-state at Westminster Hall—"an innovation which proved extremely popular." One quarter of a million people filed past the coffin: never before had so many ordinary people, personally, individually, paid their last respects to a British monarch. This novel precedent, combined with the long procession through the streets of London, with the coffin placed on a gun carriage pulled by naval ratings, followed by the more private interment at Windsor, was emulated at the funerals of both George V and VI.[86]

If Esher provided the expertise and organizing flair, and Edward himself supplied the enthusiasm and support, it was Elgar whose compositions raised ceremonial music from mere trivial ephemera to works of art. His "Imperial March" of 1897 was the smash hit of the diamond jubilee; it successfully established him as the nation's unofficial musical laureate. Five years later, he composed the "Coronation Ode" to commemorate the accession of Edward VII, which included, at the king's request, the choral setting of the broad and soaring melody of "Pomp and Circumstance Number One" which has since gone around the world as "Land of Hope and Glory." Then, for the accession of George V, came the "Coronation March," and the masque "The Crown of India" for the Delhi durbar. Such works, which reflected Elgar's genuine love of color, pageantry, precision, and splendor, provided the ideal martial musical background to the great royal ceremonies.[87]

Assisted by the strong personal contribution of these three men, the public image of the British monarchy was fundamentally transformed in the years before the First World War, as old ceremonial was successfully adapted in response to the changed domestic and international situation, and new ceremonial was invented and added. Such changes are well reflected in the unprecedented manner in which these royal occasions were commercially exploited. Although no precise figures are available, it is clear that the massive outpouring of royal commemorative pottery dates from this time, as manufacturers cashed in on the appeal of royal ceremonial to a mass market that had never existed.[88] Likewise, new, consumer-oriented firms such as Rowntree, Cadbury, and Oxo exploited royal events to help their advertising campaigns, and local authorities began to distribute beakers, mugs, and other gifts in commemoration. In the same way, there were more private commemorative medals produced for sale for Victoria's golden jubilee than for the previous four great events combined, and the coronation of Edward VIII was another medal-maker's paradise. In addition, in 1887 commemorative medals in the manner of campaign medals, to be worn on the left breast, were first issued, another novelty that was emulated at all subsequent coronations and jubilees in this period.[89] In mugs and medals, as in music and magnificence, the last quarter of the nineteenth century and the first decade of the twentieth were a golden age of "invented traditions," as the appeal of the monarchy to the mass of the people in an industrialized society was broadened in a manner unattainable only half a century before.

During the third period, from 1914 to 1953, the context once again shifted profoundly, so that the ceremonial of the British monarchy ceased to be merely one aspect of widespread competitive inventiveness and became instead a unique expression of continuity in a period of unprecedented change. The late Victorian and Edwardian formula of a ceremonially grand but politically impartial monarchy was repeated in an even more strictly constitutional manner. For the limited power that Edward VII wielded was further eroded during the reigns of his three successors. Although, for example, George V was obliged to play some part in the constitutional crisis that he inherited on his accession, in the choice of a Conservative prime minister in 1923, and in the formation of the national government in 1931, and although his private preferences were for the Conservatives, he maintained, in his public, constitutional duties, scrupulous rectitude and impartiality.[90] The abdication of Edward VIII was further proof that it was Parliament that made and unmade kings, and George VI was his father's son, not only in terms of his preference for the Conservatives, but also in terms of his public impartiality. Even his rights to be consulted, to warn, and to encourage were relatively attenuated. In 1940, he would have preferred Halifax as prime minister, and in 1945 he was sorry to see Churchill depart. But on neither occasion did he have any power to influence events.[91]

From impotence to aloofness to veneration to grandeur the line ran unbroken, reinforced by the high reputation of the monarchs as individuals. In particular, George V, by allying the private probity of his grandmother with the public grandeur of his father, created a synthesis that both his long-serving successors have emulated.[92] On the one hand, like his father, he was assiduous in attention to public ritual and ceremonial, and obsessed with matters such as the correct dress and manner of wearing decorations.[93] But at the same time, his private life combined the unpretentiousness of the country gentleman with the respectability of the middle class. Perhaps accidentally, but certainly with great success, George V contrived to be both grand and domestic, a father figure to the whole empire, yet also in his own right the head of a family with which all could identify. (Significantly, Edward VIII overrode both elements of the Georgian synthesis, caring not at all for ceremony, and living an eventful and indiscreet private life.)[94] George VI, by contrast, deliberately took that name to emphasize the return to the style of his father. Once again,

the monarch assiduously carried out public, ceremonial duties, while at
the same time enjoying a domestic life that was the very antithesis of his
elder brother's.[95] Like his father's, his qualities were "courage, endurance,
kindliness, devotion": he was the man who conquered his stammer and
resolutely refused to leave London during the Second World War.[96]

Under these circumstances, the monarchy appeared, particularly on
grand, ceremonial occasions, as the embodiment of consensus, stability,
and community. During the years 1914 to 1953 Britain experienced a
series of internal changes that far surpassed those of the preceding period
in magnitude. Between 1910 and 1928 Britain moved from being a nation
with one of the narrowest electoral franchises in Europe to full adult suffrage, with what was feared as "a war-worn and hungry proletariat endowed with a huge preponderance of voting power."[97] The Liberal party
was eclipsed by Labour as the second party in the state and, especially
after the Second World War, the demise of the great aristocratic families
left the Crown increasingly isolated in London society. The General Strike
and the Great Depression brought with them animosity and distress on an
unprecedented scale, as did the two world wars. Accordingly, a politically
neutral and personally admirable monarchy was presented, with great
success, as "the rallying-point of stability in a distracted age," the most
effective aspect of which was its restrained, anachronistic, ceremonial
grandeur.[98]

In part, this was greatly facilitated by the sustained obsequiousness of
the media, which continued to report the great ceremonies of state in an
awed and hushed manner. From Partridge to Shepherd and Illingworth,
royal cartoons were restricted to tableaux, congratulating members of the
royal family on successful imperial tours, hailing the House of Windsor,
or mourning the death of a sovereign. Significantly, when Low tried to
publish a cartoon in 1936 that was critical of the monarchy at the time
of the abdication, no newspaper in London would accept it.[99] Editors
and reporters, like cartoonists, remained deferential, as the gentleman's
agreement among the press lords at the time of the abdication eloquently
illustrated. In the same way, newspaper photographs, like newsreel
films, were carefully edited. After the coronation of George VI, the Earl
Marshal and the archbishop of Canterbury were empowered to edit
"anything which may be considered unsuitable for the public at large
to see."

But the most important development during this period was the advent of the British Broadcasting Corporation (B.B.C.), which was of profound significance in conveying the dual image of the monarchy so

successfully built up by George V. On the one hand, the Christmas broadcasts, instituted in 1932 and immediately adopted as "traditional," enhanced the image of the monarch as the father figure of his people, speaking to his subjects in the comfort and privacy of their homes.[100] At the same time, the B.B.C.'s first director general, Sir John Reith, himself a romantic devotee of pageantry and the monarchy, quickly recognized the medium's power to convey a sense of participation in ceremonial, which had never been possible before.[101] From the time of the duke of York's wedding in 1923, "audible pageants" became a permanent feature of the B.B.C.'s programs, as each great state occasion was broadcast live on the radio, with special microphones positioned so that the listener could hear the sound of bells, horses, carriages, and cheering. Indeed, this technical development made possible the successful presentation of state pageants as national, family events in which everyone could take part. If the evidence of Mass Observation is any guide, they did: record audiences were a constant feature of the outside broadcasts of great royal occasions.[102]

The combination of the novelty of the media and the anachronism of the ceremonial made royal ritual both comforting and popular in an age of change. By now, the monarchs' mode of conveyance, already unusual and grand in the preceding period, had become fairy-tale. At the coronation of George VI, for example, even the majority of peers attending arrived in cars; Henry Channon, whose eye for color and romance was unerring, counted only three in coaches.[103] By then, the horse-drawn society of the mid-nineteenth century was so long forgotten that the scavengers who cleared up the horse droppings after the main procession had passed by received some of the loudest cheers of the day.[104] In the world of the airplane, the tank, and the atomic bomb, the anachronistic grandeur of horse carriages, swords, and plumed hats was further enhanced. By the time of Elizabeth's coronation, even the royal household possessed insufficient coaches to accommodate all the visiting royalty and heads of state, and it proved necessary to borrow seven extra carriages from a film company.[105]

The advanced organization involved in acquiring these extra carriages was evidence that the tradition of administrative expertise initiated by Esher was fully maintained. The sixteenth duke of Norfolk, Hereditary Earl Marshal, although only twenty-nine at the time of the coronation of George VI, soon acquired a reputation for punctuality, showmanship, and theatrical flair that rivaled Esher's. By 1969, when he produced his last great pageant, the investiture of the Prince of Wales, his experience of royal ritual spanned forty years. At the 1937 coronation, he was prepared to pay a colleague £1 for every minute that the actual crowning was too late or too early, and he lost only £5.[106] For that ceremony, Norfolk was assisted by the archbishop of Canterbury, Cosmo Gordon Lang, himself described by Hensley Henson as "a born actor," and by his biographer as displaying great "attention to the minutest details of an occasion which called for all the drama and pageantry which, with him, were so strong an impression of religious feeling." Like Norfolk, the archbishop thought in "the language of the theatre," and it was these representatives of church and state who dominated the three committees and superintended the eight rehearsals in preparation for the coronation.[107] Moreover, by this time, largely as a result of the efforts of Dean Ryle and the sacrist Jocelyn Perkins, Westminster Abbey itself was a more fitting setting for ceremonial. The choir was improved and the stalls gilded; the bells were restored in the towers; and processions with banners and copes were revived. The "development of stateliness and colour in the services of the Abbey" meant that the additional demands of the great royal ceremonials could be met with unprecedented ease, experience, and expertise.[108]

Likewise, as far as music was concerned, the innovations of the previous period were consolidated and further extended. In 1924, on the death of Parratt, Elgar himself was made Master of the King's Musick, the first composer of distinction to occupy the position for over a century, and emphatic recognition of the importance of his music in royal ritual.[109] Thereafter, the post has continued to be filled by composers of merit, and the incumbent has retained control of the musical arrangements of royal ceremonies. By the time Elgar was appointed, his creative passion was spent, and no more great works or popular music came from his pen. But other composers assumed his mantle, and continued the recently established tradition that each great royal occasion was also to be a festival of contemporary British music.[110] Bax, Bliss, Holst, Bantock, Walton, and Vaughan Williams all wrote music to command for the coronations of George VI and Elizabeth II. Walton's two coronation marches, "Crown Imperial" (1937) and "Orb and Sceptre" (1953), rivaled Elgar himself, not only in their melodic richness and colorful orchestration, but also in that they have both become regular, established concert-hall pieces.[111]

These developments in the domestic context of royal ritual were accompanied by even greater changes in the international sphere. In the previous period, British ceremony, however much improved on the mid- and early Victorian era, was of a piece with other nations' grand pageants. But in this third phase it ceased to be one instance of competitive inventiveness and became instead unique by default. During the reign of George V, the majority of great royal dynasties were replaced by republican regimes. In 1910, the German emperor, eight kings, and five crown princes attended the funeral of Edward VII as representatives of their respective nations. During the next quarter of a century, "the world witnessed the disappearance of five emperors, eight kings and eighteen minor dynasties—one of the most spectacular political landslides in history."[112] At the end of the Second World War, the Italian and Yugoslavian dynasties were vanquished, and the Japanese emperor was discredited. In this spectacularly changed international context, the ritual of the British monarchy could be presented as the unique embodiment of a long and continuing tradition in a way that had not been possible before.

What was true of constitutions was true of capital cities as well. For while the rebuilding of London had largely been completed before the First World War, the capitals of other new, or newly assertive powers were constantly being reconstructed as further expressions of national greatness. In Italy, for example, it was Mussolini's wish that Rome "must appear marvelous to all the peoples of the world—vast, orderly, powerful, as in the time of the Empire of Augustus," and the 1931 Master Plan had as its first objective the creation of a splendid monumental capital, including the making of the Piazza Venezia, and the great, monumental access roads, such as the Via dell'Imperio, which led to the Coliseum.[113] In Germany, too, the massive, monumental, megalomanic buildings of the Third Reich, the fruits of collaboration between Hitler and Albert Speer, embodied a similar view. The House of German Art, the Berlin Chancellery, and the buildings and parade grounds of Nuremberg, to say nothing of the later and unrealized schemes for triumphal ways and arches in Berlin, all reflected Hitler's abiding belief that a civilization was judged by the great buildings it left behind.[114] Nor was such innovative neoclassicism confined to fascist powers. In Moscow, the making of Red Square as a ceremonial center may be seen as part of a similar expression, as was the massive (and unrealized) plan for the Palace of the Soviets in stupendous, neoclassical style.[115] And in Washington, the completion of the Lincoln Memorial, the building of the Jefferson Memorial and Arlington Bridge, as well as a clutch of administrative offices on Constitution Avenue, showed the force of the same influence on the other side of the Atlantic.[116]

But, in buildings as in constitutional arrangements, London was once more the exception. While other countries completed or rebuilt the theatres in which the ruling elite performed its pageants, in London the stage remained largely unaltered after the Buckingham Palace–Admiralty Arch *ensemble* was inaugurated. In the interwar years, only County Hall was added to the great public buildings, and that had been begun before 1914. Even the Cenotaph, for all its symbolic connotations, was a relatively insignificant addition to London's architectural heritage. These buildings, which had been novel in 1910, became, compared with the rush of construction in other capitals, venerable within two decades. Instead of smugly accepting chaos, as in the first phase, or belatedly seeking to catch up and compete, as in the second, Londoners now viewed their city as the most stable capital architecturally—a physical stability that aptly expressed the comparative stability of its politics.

These contrasts were exactly reflected in the ceremonial itself. In Italy, as in Russia, the new political order brought with it strident, emotional, technologically sophisticated forms of ritual, the very antithesis of those prevalent in England. In Germany, in particular, the use of tanks, planes, and searchlights implied a commitment to technology and an impatience with anachronism at odds with state coaches and ceremonial swords. Instead of lining the streets, cheering but orderly, as was the case with Londoners, one quarter of a million Germans participated annually in the Nuremberg rallies, where they listened with "delirious rapture" to the "unbridled emotionalism" of Hitler's oratory. The semiliturgical chanting and intercession between speaker and audience; the manner in which the words seemed to erupt through the body of the Führer; the state of almost sexual exhaustion in which he was left after his speeches: all this contrasted strongly with the "unassailable dignity" of George V and his Queen.[117]

In these diverse and disorienting national and international circumstances, the appeal of Empire, and the ceremonial association of the Crown with it, only increased—partly as a distraction from internal problems, and partly as an expression of the comforting belief that, in a newly competitive world of great power politics, Britain and her Empire remained at the forefront. The Irish treaty, the independence of Egypt, the end of the raj in India, and the departure of Ireland and India may have implied that it was already on the wane. But the outstandingly successful tours of the Prince of Wales and the duke of York to the Dominions and India only cemented the bonds between crown and empire the more closely, so that each royal ceremonial remained an imperial, as well as a domestic occasion.[118] As George VI himself put it in his coronation broadcast: "I felt this morning that the whole Empire was in very truth gathered within the walls of Westminster Abbey."[119] And the coronation of his daughter was seen in the same broad, ample perspective, as in Elizabeth's own words: "I am sure that this, my Coronation, is not a symbol of a power and a splendour that are gone, but a declaration of our hopes in the future."[120]

6

Under these circumstances, the "meaning" of royal ceremonial was further developed and extended. Assuredly, the political power and personal appeal of the monarch, the attitude of the media, the condition of London, and the state of technology, all of which had changed profoundly during the previous period, remained unaltered. As before, the monarch was the father of his people, and the patriarch of empire, and the royal pageantry was as splendid and successful as in the days of Esher. Yet, paradoxically, it is such very real elements of *continuity* which both disguised and explain *changes* in "meaning." For the very fact of continuity, at a time of internal unrest and international revolution, imparted to royal spectacle in England those attributes of uniqueness, tradition, and continuity which, in the previous period, they had so conspicuously lacked. It was not so much despite, as because of, the continuity in style and circumstance that the "meaning" of royal ritual altered once more.

Moreover the impression of continuity and stability was further enhanced by innovation, as new ceremonials were invented. One such series of innovations was centered on queens consort. During the period from the 1870s to the 1910s no spouse of a monarch had died: Albert predeceased Victoria, and Alexandra outlived Edward. In this third phase, however, the role of the queen consort and queen dowager became important, and this was reflected in royal ritual. At her death in 1925, Queen Alexandra was accorded a state funeral that owed more to the precedent of her late husband than to Prince Albert.[121] Again, there was a lying in state (this time in Westminster Abbey), followed by the procession through the streets of London and then the private interment at Windsor. In the case of Queen Mary in 1953, the ceremonial resembled that of the monarchs themselves even more closely, for she actually lay in state in Westminster Hall.

The two public funerals of dowager queens were not the only new royal occasions invented during this period. Because of the age of Victoria and Edward, there were few weddings of the monarch's children during the second period, the last being in 1885 when Princess Beatrice married Prince Louis of Battenberg. But with two relatively young kings on the throne between 1910 and 1953, the potential for ceremonial that derived more from the rites of passage of the earlier stages of the family life cycle was enhanced. In 1922, Princess Mary married Viscount Lascelles, and George V took the occasion to transfer royal marriages back from the privacy of Windsor or the Chapel Royal to the streets of London, by staging the ceremony in the Abbey, with a full procession beforehand.[122] As the duke of York explained, the result was a great public success: "it is now no longer Mary's wedding, but (this from the papers) it is the 'Abbey Wedding' or the 'Royal Wedding' or the 'National Wedding,' or even the 'People's Wedding.'"[123] This was followed in 1923 by the marriage of the duke of York, the first time a prince of the royal house had been wed in the Abbey for five hundred years. In 1934 the duke of Kent was also married there, and in 1947 so was Princess Elizabeth. But significantly, the wedding of the duke of Gloucester, which took place in 1935, was staged in the relative seclusion of the Chapel Royal at Buckingham Palace, for fear that, in a jubilee year, there might be too much royal ceremonial, and that its scarcity value might be eroded.[124]

But the novelty of Abbey weddings for royal children and state funerals for dowager queens was far surpassed by the silver jubilee of George V, for which, again, there was no exact precedent, the twenty-fifth anniversary of Victoria's accession having fallen at exactly the time of Albert's death and her seclusion. Once more, the innovation was a great success, arousing widespread feelings of enthusiasm and support. In Lord Salisbury's opinion, the occasion represented "an astonishing testimony to the deeply founded stability and solidarity of this country and empire under Your Majesty's authority."[125] And Ramsay Macdonald, who described the service on jubilee day as "glowing with emotion," was even more moved by a reception for the Dominion prime ministers: "Here the Empire was a great family, the gathering of a family reunion, the King a paternal head. We all went away feeling that we had taken part in something very much like a Holy Communion."[126] The idea of the monarchy as secular religion could not be more explicitly articulated.

The remainder of the pageants of this period were of the type already established in the preceding phase of development. George V's funeral was an act of thanksgiving for the king who had survived the war and weathered the peace.[127] George VI's coronation was an extravagant, imperial reaffirmation of the stability of monarchy after the interruption of the abdication. His funeral further expressed national appreciation for a man who had not wished to be king, but had triumphed over war and a stammer by a strong sense of duty. The records of Mass Observation record widespread grief, shock, and sympathy, so much so, indeed, that it does seem likely that Richard Dimbleby's famous radio commentary describing the lying-in-state at Westminster Hall did in fact embody the feelings of the majority of his audience: the contrast between his proud, loyal, reverential, popular broadcast, and the savage *Times* editorial on the occasion of the death of George IV, well illustrates the extent to which popular attitudes toward royal ceremony and royal occasions had altered.[128]

The last great ceremony in this sequence, successfully conflating monarchy and empire, stressing stability in an age of change, and celebrating the continuity of Britain as a great power was the coronation of Elizabeth II in 1953. It was still avowedly an *imperial* occasion, with the queen's dress containing embroidered emblems of the dominions, with regiments of Commonwealth and colonial troops marching in procession, with the prime ministers of the dominions and India present in the Abbey, and an assortment of heads of state from various exotic protectorates.[129] At the time, it seemed as though the threats and challenges of the war and austerity period had been surmounted: the Empire was still largely intact; the problem of Indian independence and republican status within the Commonwealth had been triumphantly resolved; Churchill was back at Ten Downing Street; Britain had once more asserted her place as a great power; there was a new Elizabethan age around the corner. According to the *Delhi Express*, "the second Elizabethan era begins on a note of spiritual buoyancy which Britain has never experienced before. At no time in British history has she enjoyed the moral prestige which the Commonwealth, including Britain, now commands." In this euphoric context, it is not surprising that the archbishop of Canterbury should feel that Britain was close to the Kingdom of Heaven on coronation day, or that Elizabeth herself should make her ringing declaration of faith in the future.[130]

The appeal of this sequence of ceremonies is well gauged by the high level of commercial exploitation and commemoration. Once more, at jubilees and coronations, commemorative pottery proliferated. Birmingham Corporation offered local children a choice between a Bible, *Elizabeth Our Queen* by Richard Dimbleby, a spoon and fork, two commemorative mugs, a tin of chocolate, propelling pencils, a pen knife, or a dish with a portrait of the queen.[131] Commemorative medals in the manner of campaign badges were once more awarded, and collectors' medals were again privately produced. But these were in smaller numbers than before, largely because two new modes of commemoration were appearing. The first was the planting, throughout the Empire, of trees, an innovation particularly noteworthy at the coronations of George VI and Elizabeth II.[132] The second, dating from the time of George V's Silver Jubilee, was the issuing by the Post Office of specially designed commemorative stamps. Previously, the issuing of royal commemoratives had been limited to the Empire, and in England only such secular festivals as the Empire Exhibition at Wembley had received notice. But from 1953, every royal jubilee, coronation, major wedding, and wedding anniversary (but not, significantly, births or funerals) has been the subject of a special issue.[133] Once more, it was an innovation; but well within "traditional" molds.

7

By definition, the period since the coronation in 1953 is too recent for detailed or satisfactory historical analysis. While it seems clear that the "meaning" of royal ritual has entered a new phase, in which many of the presuppositions of the previous period have ceased to be valid, it is not as yet entirely clear how, positively, it might be described. But, in the interest of completeness, here are some observations consistent with the analysis employed thus far. To begin with, the political power of the monarch remains limited, or at least is exercised so discreetly that it seems not to matter. In a recent poll, 86 percent of those asked felt that the queen "was a figurehead, signing laws and doing what the government directs her to do."[134] At the same time, the queen has carried on those traditions of "extreme conscientiousness and dutifulness" which have characterized the British monarchy since the reign of her grandfather, and remained loyal to the Georgian synthesis of private probity and public grandeur. Above all, in a period when large parts of London have been rebuilt, men have been put on the moon, and the Concorde has brought New York within commuting distance, the romantic glamour of anachronistic ceremony has become all the more appealing.

Of greater significance has been the way in which royal ceremony has been an antidote to, or legitimation of, social change domestically, in a manner closely reminiscent of the previous period. As the lengthening perspective makes clear, the effect of the Second World War was in many ways far greater, socially and economically, than the first. The aristocracy has virtually vanished as part of government. There has been a decline in public conformity to Christian ethics. Problems of race, color, violence, crime, and drug addiction have proliferated. Opinion, and legislation, has changed markedly on issues such as the death penalty, abortion, premarital sex, and homosexuality. Wealth and income have been redistributed, not drastically, but certainly more than ever before this century. So, in an egalitarian, sexually permissive, and multiracial society, the monarchy remains true to that public, ceremonial role identified by Harold Nicolson when describing the silver jubilee of George V: "a guarantee of stability, security, continuity—the preservation of tradition values."[135]

Moreover, royal spectacle has also acquired a new meaning in an international context, as Britain's world position has declined profoundly. The fond, euphoric hopes of the coronation—that there was a new Elizabethan age ahead—have proved vain. Since then, the slide into impotence has only accelerated, with the breakup of the Colonial Empire, the disappearance of the last generation of imperial statesmen like Smuts and Menzies, the fiasco of Suez, the problems of Biafra and Northern Ireland, recurrent economic crises, and the entry of Britain into the Common Market. Indeed, the state funeral of Sir Winston Churchill in 1965, poised exactly halfway between Elizabeth's coronation and silver jubilee, was not only the last rite of the great man himself, but was also self-consciously recognized at the time as being the requiem for Britain as a great power.[136]

So, "as the power of Britain waned . . . , pride grew in the Royal family as something which was uniquely ours and which no country could match."[137] Just as, in previous periods of international change, the ritual of monarchy was of importance in legitimating the novelty of formal empire and in giving an impression of stability at a time of international bewilderment, so in the postwar world it has provided a comfortable palliative to the loss of world-power status. When watching a great royal occasion, impeccably planned, faultlessly executed, and with a commentary stressing (however mistakenly) the historic continuity with those former days of Britain's greatness, it is almost possible to believe that they have not entirely vanished. And, since 1953, this attitude has become more widespread, as evidence of decline has proved inescapable. In the words of D. C. Cooper, "while people can see the gloved hand waving from the golden coach, they feel assured that all is well with the nation, whatever its true state." The "tendency to elevate royalty as national prestige declines," to stress as never before the grandeur and uniqueness of its ceremonial in particular, has been particularly marked in postwar Britain.[138]

As such, it has been greatly facilitated by the impact of television, which has made the royal pageants accessible in a vivid and immediate manner that neither radio nor newsreels could achieve. Here, as in other ways, the coronation of Elizabeth was a bridge between an older world and a new phase of development. For while the tone of Richard Dimbleby's commentary placed it in a world that had more in common with 1935 (or even 1897) than 1977, the fact that it was a television commentary, and that more people *watched* the ceremony on television than *listened* to it on radio, made it clear that a new way of reporting the great occasions of state had been perfected.[139] Largely as a result of television, Elizabeth was, indeed, the first British sovereign truly to be crowned, as the rubric requires, "in the sight of the people." Hence the comment of Shils and Young, who regarded the whole occasion as an "act of national communion."[140]

But, as with the press or radio, the medium of television also contained a message. Significantly, while television has cut politicians down to size, so that the grand manner in Parliament or Whitehall is now no longer effective, it has continued to adopt the same reverential attitude toward the monarchy that radio pioneered in the days of Reith. On the one hand, such programs as the film *Royal Family* have successfully perpetuated the picture of the queen and her family as quintessentially middle-class.[141] On the other, the coverage of the great state ceremonials has enhanced the picture of grandeur and fairy-tale splendor that Reith and B.B.C. Radio did so much to promote. Of special significance in this regard were the commentaries of Richard Dimbleby, who covered every major royal occasion for B.B.C. between the coronation and his death in 1965. His eloquent, emotional commentaries, lit up by profound devotion to the monarchy and a romantic feeling for history and tradition, described royal ritual in the most fulsome, obsequious terms. By explaining the ceremonial and expressing a sense of history in the manner he did, Dimbleby's commentaries were of the greatest significance in presenting the ritual of monarchy as a festival of freedom and celebration of continuity in a worried and distracted age. As his biographer notes, in the 1950s and early 1960s, Richard Dimbleby, by his commentaries, "did more than any other individual to secure the position of the monarch in the affections of the British people."[142]

Despite the initial misgivings about the live broadcast of the coronation, it proved to be so successful that all subsequent royal ceremonial occasions have been primarily television spectaculars. Indeed, this element has brooked so large that it has even influenced the nature of the ceremonials themselves. At the Prince of Wales's investiture at Carnarvon, for instance, the canopy above the dais was deliberately made transparent so that the television cameras might see through it.[143] As for the ceremonies themselves, they have again had more in common with the monarchies of George V and VI than with Victoria or Edward: they have been the rites of passage of a relatively young family, rather than the jubilees, funerals, and coronations of venerable monarchs. The weddings of Princess Margaret (1960), the duke of Kent (1961), Princess Alexandra (1963), and Princess Anne (1973), the investiture of the Prince of Wales (1969), and the Queen's silver jubilee (1977), as well as the state opening of Parliament since 1958 have all been essays in television ritual.

It is in this "traditional" but changed context that the silver jubilee of 1977 may most usefully be set. At one level, that of public reaction, the occasion may be seen as part of a tradition harking back to the silver jubilee of George V and the more venerable celebrations of Victoria: a popular piece of well-planned pageantry which the public enjoyed. At another level, however, the grand, unrivaled pomp and circumstance of the occasion was seen as a perfect tonic to Britain's declining self-esteem: "We were all sharing a rich piece of history. . . . Somebody said that Britain may have lost out on a number of things, but we can still show the world a clean pair of heels when it comes to ceremonial. Yesterday's pageantry was a superb example. . . . It proves there is something to be said for doing things the old-fashioned way."[144] But, at the same time, the experts also recognized that the diminished scale of the ceremonial placed the event emphatically in a new, postimperial age: "Only a few members of the Royal Family would accompany the queen on her drive to St Paul's; there would only be a handful of troops from overseas to supplement the anyway modest British contingent; no foreign potentates . . . would lend exotic glamour to the proceedings."[145] In different ways, then, the jubilee ceremonial was an expression of national and imperial decline, an attempt to persuade, by pomp and circumstance, that no such decline had taken place, or to argue that, even if it had, it really did not matter.

Notes

This essay is an abridged version of a longer study, "The Context, Performance and Meaning of Ritual: The British Monarchy and the 'Invention of Tradition,' c. 1820–1977," published in E. J. Hobsbawm and T. Ranger, eds., *The Invention of Tradition* (Cambridge, 1982), to which readers are referred for more extended argument and documentation.

1. R. E. Giesey, *The Royal Funeral Ceremony in Renaissance France* (Geneva, 1960); R. Strong, *Splendour at Court: Renaissance Spectacle and Illusion* (London, 1973); S. Anglo, *Spectacle, Pageantry and Early Tudor Policy* (Oxford, 1969); D. M. Bergeron, *English Civic Pageantry, 1558–1642* (London, 1971); F. A. Yates, *The Valois Tapestries* (London, 1959); E. Muir, "Images of Power: Art and Pageantry in Renaissance Venice," *American Historical Review*, 89 (1979): 16–52; G. Reedy, "Mystical Politics: The Imagery of Charles II's Coronation," in P. J. Korshin, ed., *Studies in Culture and Revolution: Aspects of English Intellectual History, 1640–1800* (London, 1972), pp. 21–42; C. Geertz, "Centers, Kings and Charisma: Reflections on the Symbolics of Power," in J. Ben-David and T. N. Clark, eds., *Culture and Its Creators: Essays in Honor of E. Shils* (Chicago/London, 1977), esp. pp. 153–57.

2. G. L. Mosse, "Caesarism, Circuses and Monuments," *Journal of Contemporary History*, 6 (1971): 167–82; C. Rearick, "Festivals and Politics: The Michelet Centennial of 1898," in W. Laqueur and G. L. Mosse, eds., *Historians in Politics* (London, 1974), pp. 59–78; Laqueur and Mosse, "Festivals in Modern France: The Experience of the Third Republic," *Journal of Contemporary History*, 12 (1977): 435–60; R. Samson, "La fête de Jeanne d'Arc en 1894: controverse et célébration," *Revue d'histoire moderne et contemporaire*, 20 (1973): 444–63; M. Agulhon, "Esquisse pour une archeologie de la Republique: l'Allegorie civique féminine," *Annales: Economies, Sociétiés, Civilisations*, 28 (1973): 5–34: E. J. Hobsbawm, "Inventing Traditions in Nineteenth-Century Europe," Past and Present Conference Paper, 1977, pp. 1–25.

3. G. L. Mosse, "Mass Politics and the Political Liturgy of Nationalism," in E. Kamenka, ed., *Nationalism: The Nature and Evolution of an Ideal* (London, 1976), pp. 39–54; H. T. Barden, *The Nuremberg Party Rallies, 1929–39* (London, 1967).

4. C. Hibbert, *George IV* (Harmondsworth, 1976), pp. 379–83, 675–86, 694.

5. D. Beales, *From Castlereagh to Gladstone, 1815–1885* (London, 1971), pp. 111, 163, 166; J. Ridley, *Palmerston* (London, 1972), pp. 529–40; K. Martin, *The Crown and the Establishment* (London, 1962), p. 52.

6. Hibbert, *George IV*, pp. 782–83.

7. Martin, *Crown and Establishment*, p. 27.

8. R. Fulford, *The Prince Consort* (London, 1966), pp. 156–59.

9. A. Briggs, *Victorian Cities* (Harmondsworth, 1968), pp. 312, 357–59; H. Pelling, *A History of British Trade Unionism* (Harmondsworth, 1963), pp. 14–15.

10. W. L. Burn, *The Age of Equipoise: A Study of the Mid-Victorian Generation* (London, 1968), p. 7; Briggs, *Victorian Cities*, p. 32; W. A. Armstrong, *Stability and Change in an English County Town: A Social Study of York, 1801–1851* (Cambridge, 1974), pp. 10–11; P. Mathias, *The First Industrial Nation: An Economic History of Britain, 1700–1914* (London, 1969), pp. 259–73.

11. M. Wynn Jones, *A Cartoon History of the Monarchy* (London, 1978), pp. 40–45, 68–77; M. Walker, *Daily Sketches: A Cartoon History of British Twentieth-Century Politics* (London, 1978), p. 23.

12. A. J. Lee, *The Origins of the Popular Press, 1855–1914* (London, 1976), pp. 38, 45, 74, 120–21.
13. F. M. L. Thompson, *Victorian England: The Horse-Drawn Society* (London, 1970), p. 16.
14. Sir W. Gilbey, *Modern Carriages* (London, 1905), pp. 46–53, 63–64; G. A. Thrupp, *The History of Coaches* (London, 1877), pp. 87–90.
15. Thrupp, *Coaches*, pp. 89–90; P. Ziegler, *King William IV* (London, 1971), p. 193.
16. Burn, *Age of Equipoise*, p. 103; Ridley, *Palmerston*, pp. 523–24; A. Briggs, *Victorian People* (Harmondsworth, 1965), pp. 10–11, 24, 51.
17. R. Robinson and J. Gallagher, *Africa and the Victorians: The Official Mind of Imperialism* (London, 1961), pp. 1–4.
18. Sir J. Summerson, *Victorian Architecture in England: Four Studies in Evaluation* (New York, 1971), p. 115.
19. E. J. Hobsbawm, *The Age of Capital, 1848–1875* (1977), pp. 326, 328, 329, 334, 337; E. N. Bacon, *Design of Cities* (rev. ed., London, 1978), pp. 196–99, 220–23; J. W. Reps, *Monumental Washington: The Planning and Development of the Capital Center* (Princeton, 1967), pp. 5, 20, 21; A. Sutcliffe, *The Autumn of Central Paris: The Defeat of Town Planning, 1850–1970* (London, 1970), ch. 2; D. H. Pinkney, *Napoleon III and the Rebuilding of Paris* (Princeton, 1958); P. Abercrombie, "Vienna," *Town Planning Review*, 1 (1910–11): 221, 226–27; G. R. Marek, *The Eagles Die* (London, 1975), pp. 171–72; I. A. Egorov, *The Architectural Planning of St. Petersburg* (Athens, Ohio, 1969), pp. 104–5, 182, 192; J. H. Bater, *St. Petersburg: Industrialisation and Change* (London, 1976), pp. 17–40.
20. D. Olsen. *The Growth of Victorian London* (London, 1976), pp. 51–53, 61, 329.
21. Quoted in ibid., pp. 55–56.
22. M. Kennedy, *The Works of Ralph Vaughan Williams* (London, 1964), p. 1.
23. P. A. Scholes, *"God Save the Queen": The History and Romance of the World's First National Anthem* (London, 1954), pp. 147–48, 165, 203–4, 209.
24. B. Rainbow, *The Choral Revival in the Anglican Church (1839–72)* (London, 1970), ch. 13; Sir F. Bridge, *A Westminster Pilgrim* (London, 1919), pp. 72–75, 196–201.
25. W. O. Chadwick, *The Victorian Church*, pt. 2 (2d ed., London, 1972), pp. 366–74.
26. J. Perkins, *Westminster Abbey: Its Worship and Ornaments*, 3 vols. (London, 1938–52), vol. 1, pp. 89–94, 106–9, 144, 153–63; vol. 2, p. 16; vol. 3, pp. 141, 149, 152, 155, 160, 163–64; R. E. Prothero, *The Life and Correspondence of Arthur Penrhyn Stanley, D.D., Late Dean of Westminster*, 2 vols. (London, 1893), vol. 2, pp. 282–83.
27. C. Hibbert, *The Court at Windsor: A Domestic History* (London, 1964), pp. 171–72.
28. J. Perkins, *The Coronation Book* (London, 1902), pp. 97, 115, 175, 258; Hibbert, *George IV*, pp. 597–604. It is important to stress that there is much about George IV's public style that anticipates subsequent developments: grandeur

in London (Regent's Street), royal visits (to Scotland and Ireland), and an expensive coronation. My point is that, despite all this, without the appropriate concatenation of contextual circumstance (as was to occur later), it simply did not work.

29. Hibbert, *George IV*, pp. 777–79.
30. Ziegler, *William IV*, pp. 152–53, 291.
31. E. Longford, *Victoria, R.I.* (London, 1966), pp. 99–104.
32. Ibid., p. 395; G. Battiscombe, *Queen Alexandra* (London, 1972), pp. 45–46.
33. P. Ziegler, *Crown and People* (London, 1970), p. 21.
34. *The Times*, 9 November 1871.
35. Longford, *Victoria, R.I.*, p. 401.
36. W. Bagehot, "The Monarchy and the People," *The Economist*, 22 July 1871; Bagehot, "The Income of the Prince of Wales," *The Economist*, 10 October 1874.
37. J. and J. May, *Commemorative Pottery, 1780–1900* (London, 1972), pp. 22, 40–45, 51, 58–59, 73; D. Rodgers, *Coronation Souvenirs and Commemoratives* (London, 1975), pp. 25–30, 31–33, 36; J. Edmundson, *Collecting Modern Commemorative Medals* (London, 1972), pp. 39–42.
38. Longford, *Victoria R.I.*, pp. 537–38.
39. P. Magnus, *King Edward VII* (Harmondsworth, 1967), pp. 342, 348, 373–77.
40. R. Davey, *The Pageant of London*, 2 vols. (London, 1906), vol. 2, p. 623.
41. Magnus, *Edward VII*, p. 526; Martin, *Crown and Establishment*, p. 68; Ziegler, *Crown and People*, p. 28.
42. Briggs, *Victorian Cities*, pp. 312–13, 327, 330, 356–59.
43. Chamberlain, "The Growth of Support for the Labour Party," pp. 481, 485; Palling, *History of British Trade Unions*, p. 89; J. Lovell, *British Trade Unions, 1875–1933* (London, 1977), pp. 9, 21–23, 30–33, 41–46.
44. J. E. C. Bodley, *The Coronation of Edward the Seventh: A Chapter in European and Imperial History* (London, 1903), pp. 203–6.
45. Briggs, *Victorian Cities*, pp. 356–8.
46. Walker, *Daily Sketches*, pp. 7–8, 13; Wynn Jones, *Cartoon History of the Monarchy*, pp. 130, 138–9; Lee, *The Origins of the Popular Press*, pp. 120–30, 190–6; H. Herd, *The March of Journalism* (London, 1952), pp. 233–40.
47. Symon, *The Press and Its Story*, pp. 235–39.
48. Thompson, *Victorian England*, pp. 16–18.
49. P. S. Bagwell, *The Transport Revolution from 1770* (London, 1974), pp. 150, 155.
50. Gilbey, *Modern Carriages*, pp. 36–38; M. Watney, *The Elegant Carriage* (London, 1961), p. 81.
51. J. L. Garvin and Julian Amery, *The Life of Joseph Chamberlain*, 6 vols. (London, 1932–69), vol. 3, pp. 185–95.
52. Bodley, *Coronation of Edward the Seventh*, p. 19.
53. J. Perkins, *The Coronation Book* (London, 1911), p. 329; Ziegler, *Crown and People*, pp. 56, 66; P. E. Schramm, *A History of the English Coronation* (Oxford, 1937), p. 104.

54. For two recent works which take this view, see: J. Morris, *Pax Britannica: The Climax of an Empire* (London, 1968); C. Chapman and P. Raben, *Debratt's Queen Victoria's Jubilees, 1887 and 1897* (London, 1977).

55. S. Hynes, *Edwardian Turn of Mind* (Princeton, 1968), pp. 19–20.

56. S. Kostof, "The Drafting of a Master Plan (or *Roma Capitale:* An Exordium)," *Journal of the Society of Architectural Historians*, 35 (1976): 8; A. Robertson, *Victor Emmanuel III: King of Italy* (London, 1925), pp. 104–6; R. C. Fried, *Planning the Eternal City: Roman Politics and Planning Since World War II* (London, 1973), pp. 19–29; C. Meeds, *Italian Architecture, 1750–1914* (New Haven, 1966), pp. 189ff. For one specific episode, see: E. Schroeter, "Rome's First National State Architecture: The *Palazzo della Finanze*," in H. A. Millom and L. Nochlin, eds., *Art and Architecture in the Service of Politics* (Cambridge, Mass., 1978), pp. 128–49.

57. Marek, *The Eagles Die*, pp. 173–77.

58. P. Abercrombie, "Berlin: Its Growth and Present-Day Function—II—The Nineteenth Century," *Town Planning Review*, 4 (1914): 308, 311; D. J. Hill, *Impressions of the Kaiser* (London, 1919), pp. 59–62; Prince von Bülow, *Memoirs, 1897–1903* (London, 1931), p. 543.

59. M. Trachtenberg, *The Statue of Liberty* (Harmondsworth, 1977), p. 129.

60. Briggs, *Victorian Cities*, pp. 325, 332–33.

61. A. Service, *Edwardian Architecture: A Handbook to Building Design in Britain, 1890–1914* (London, 1977), ch. 10; M. H. Port, "Imperial Victorian," *Geographical Magazine*, 49 (1977): 553–62.

62. G. Stamp, *London, 1900* (London, 1978), p. 305.

63. E. and N. Darby, "The Nation's Monument to Queen Victoria," *Country Life*, 164 (1978): 1647.

64. For court ritual in late nineteenth-century Europe, see: Baron von Margutti, *The Emperor Francis Joseph and His Times* (London, 1921), pp. 166–85; Princess Fugger, *The Glory of the Habsburgs* (London, 1932), pp. 100–140; A. Topham, *Memories of the Kaiser's Court* (London, 1914), pp. 85–86, 123, 184–202; Hill, *Impressions of the Kaiser*, ch. 3; Count R. Zedlitz-Trütschler, *Twelve Years at the Imperial German Court* (London, 1924), pp. 46–60, 70–71, 95, 117, 165; N. Buchanan, *Recollections of the Imperial Russian Court* (London, 1913), p. 143.

65. K. Tschulppik, *The Reign of the Emperor Francis Joseph, 1848–1916* (London, 1930), pp. 272, 354, 400.

66. G. S. Godkin, *Life of Victor Emmanuel II, First King of Italy*, 2 vols. (London, 1879), vol. 2, pp. 233–44; Robertson, *Victor Emmanuel III*, pp. 103–6.

67. C. Lowe, *Alexander III of Russia* (London, 1895), pp. 65–76, 289–303; R. K. Massie, *Nicholas and Alexandra* (London, 1968), pp. 42–45, 224–27; Vassili, *Behind the Veil*, pp. 199–203; B. Tuchman, *The Proud Tower: A Portrait of the World Before the War, 1890–1914* (New York, 1978), p. 403.

68. Moses, "Caesarism, Circuses and Monuments," p. 172; Rearick, "Festivals in Modern France," pp. 447–48.

69. Lowe, *Alexander III*, pp. 66–67.

70. Zedlitz-Trützschler, *Twelve Years at the Imperial German Court*, p. 257.

71. F. Howes, *The English Musical Renaissance* (London, 1966), chs. 7–9; Kennedy, *Ralph Vaughan Williams*, ch. 1.

72. For full accounts of the music at these two coronations, see *Musical Times:* 43 (1902): 387–88, 577–84; 52 (1911): 433–37. See also: Sir A. C. Mackenzie, *A Musician's Narrative* (London, 1927), p. 155; C. L. Graves, *Hubert Parry: His Life and Work*, 2 vols. (London, 1926), vol. 2, pp. 28–31, 56–57; W. H. Scott, *Edward German: An Intimate Biography* (London, 1932), pp. 152–54; P. M. Young, *Sir Arthur Sullivan* (London, 1971), pp. 248, 261; H. P. Greene, *Charles Villiers Stanford* (London, 1935), pp. 223–24.

73. Chadwick, *Victorian Church*, pp. 385–87; Rainbow, *Choral Revival in the Anglican Church*, pp. 286–89; W. Sinclair, *Memorials of St. Paul's Cathedral* (London, 1909), pp. 411–12; Bridge, *Westminster Pilgrim*, pp. 65–77, 172–78, 182–86, 222–34.

74. Sir D. Tovey and G. Parratt, *Walter Parratt: Master of the Music* (London, 1941), pp. 90–91, 96–102, 119.

75. Chadwick, *Victorian Church*, p. 311.

76. A. C. Benson, *The Life of Edward White Benson, Sometime Archbishop of Canterbury* (London, 1899), p. 133.

77. G. K. A. Bell, *Randall Davidson: Archbishop of Canterbury* (3d ed., London, 1952), pp. 118–19, 307–11, 351–57, 367–72, 608–11, 1300–1404.

78. Perkins, *Westminster Abbey: Its Worship and Ornaments*, vol. 1, pp. 112, 187, 189; vol. 2, pp. 16–17, 111; vol. 3, pp. 163, 179.

79. See the letter from Professor Norman Cohn to Professor Terence Ranger quoted in T. Ranger, "The Invention of Tradition in Colonial Africa" (Past and Present Conference Paper, 1977), p. 85, note 31.

80. Hobsbawm, "Inventing Traditions," p. 15.

81. *Illustrated London News*, 25 June 1887; Longford, *Victoria R.I.*, p. 626.

82. Ziegler, *Crown and People*, p. 23; Longford, *Victoria R.I.*, pp. 685–91.

83. P. Fraser, *Lord Esher: A Political Biography* (London, 1973), pp. 68–71, 80–83.

84. Bodley, *The Coronation of King Edward the Seventh*, p. 205.

85. Sir S. Lee, *King Edward the Seventh*, 2 vols. (London, 1925–27), vol. 2, pp. 21–23.

86. Ibid., p. 720.

87. T. Parratt, *Elgar* (London, 1971), pp. 7, 18, 65; P. M. Young, *Elgar, O.M.: A Study of a Musician* (London, 1955), pp. 79, 97, 222, 288.

88. May, *Commemorative Pottery*, pp. 73–74; D. Seekers, *Popular Staffordshire Pottery* (London, 1977), pp. 30–31.

89. Official medals were also produced by the Royal Mint—a further innovation—in 1887, 1897, 1902, and 1911. See Rodgers, *Coronation Souvenirs*, pp. 38–41; Edmundson, *Collecting Modern Commemorative Medals*, pp. 54–61; H. N. Cole, *Coronation and Commemoration Medals, 1887–1953* (Aldershot, 1953), p. 5.

90. H. Nicolson, *King George the Fifth: His Life and Reign* (London, 1967), pp.

98–101, 218, 486–90, 597–601; E. Longford, *The Royal House of Windsor* (London, 1976), pp. 65, 91; R. Rhodes James, ed., *Memoirs of a Conservative: J.C.C. Davidson's Memoirs and Papers, 1810–37* (London, 1969), pp. 177–78.

91. Sir J. Wheeler-Bennett, *King George VI: His Life and Reign* (London, 1965), pp. 636–37, 649–50; Longford, *House of Windsor*, p. 91.

92. J. A. Thompson and A. Mejia, Jr., *The Modern British Monarchy* (New York, 1971), p. 38.

93. Longford, *House of Windsor*, p. 63.

94. Thompson and Mejia, *Modern British Monarchy*, pp. 73, 79.

95. For the iconography of the royal family in the twentieth century, see: R. Strong, "The Royal Image," in Montgomery-Massingberd, ed., *Burke's Guide to the British Monarchy*, p. 112.

96. Ziegler, *Crown and People*, pp. 76–77.

97. Wheeler-Bennett, *King George VI*, p. 160.

98. Longford, *House of Windsor*, p. 91.

99. Walker, *Daily Sketches*, pp. 13, 23, 126–27; Wynn Jones, *Cartoon History of the Monarchy*, pp. 132, 157–64, 174–79.

100. Ziegler, *Crown and People*, p. 31; Nicolson, *George the Fifth*, pp. 670–71.

101. A. Boyle, *Only the Wind Will Listen: Reith of the B.B.C.* (London, 1972), pp. 18, 161, 281.

102. J. C. W. Reith, *Into the Wind* (London, 1949), pp. 94, 168–69, 221, 238–41, 279–82; A. Briggs, *The History of Broadcasting in the United Kingdom*, 4 vols. so far (Oxford and London, 1961–79), vol. 1, *The Birth of Broadcasting*, pp. 290–91; vol. 2, *The Golden Age of Wireless*, pp. 11, 81, 100–101, 112–13, 157, 266, 272, 396, 505.

103. R. Rhodes James, ed., *"Chips": The Diaries of Sir Henry Channon* (London, 1967), p. 123.

104. R. Jennings and C. Madge, *May the Twelfth* (London, 1937), pp. 112, 120.

105. H. McCansland, *The English Carriage* (London, 1945), p. 85; C. Frost, *Coronation: June 2 1953* (London, 1978), pp. 57–58.

106. Frost, *Coronation*, p. 39.

107. H. Henson, *Retrospect of an Unimportant Life*, 3 vols. (London, 1942–50), vol. 2, pp. 380–85; J. G. Lockhart, *Cosmo Gordon Lang* (London, 1949), pp. 408–23.

108. Perkins, *Westminster Abbey: Its Worship and Ornaments*, vol. 1, pp. 113–17, 193–94; vol. 2, p. 207; vol. 3, pp. 180–87; M. H. Fitzgerald, *A Memoir of Herbert E. Ryle* (London, 1928), pp. 290–92, 307–10; L. E. Tanner, *Recollections of a Westminster Antiquary* (London, 1969), pp. 65–68, 114–52.

109. For the work of one particular incumbent, see: H. C. Coles, *Halford Davies: A Biography* (London, 1942), pp. 157–61.

110. For the music performed at the coronations of George VI and Elizabeth II, see: *Musical Times*, 78 (1937): 329, 497; 94 (1953): 305–6.

111. I. Holst, *The Music of Gustav Holst* (2d ed., London, 1968), pp. 46, 162; C.

Scott-Sutherland, *Arnold Bax* (London, 1973), pp. 118–21; S. Pakenham, *Ralph Vaughan Williams: A Discovery of His Music* (London, 1957), pp. 118, 164–65; F. Howes, *The Music of William Walton* (2d ed., London, 1974), pp. 119–21.

112. Nicolson, *King George the Fifth*, p. 154.

113. Fried, *Planning the Eternal City*, pp. 31–33; E. R. Tannenbaum, *Fascism in Italy: Society and Culture, 1922–1945* (London, 1973), p. 314; S. Kostof, "The Emperor and the Duce: The Planning of *Piazzale Augusto Imperators* in Rome," in Millon and Nochlin, eds., *Art and Architecture in the Service of Politics*, pp. 270–325.

114. A. Speer, *Inside the Third Reich* (New York, 1970), chs. 5, 6, 10, 11; B. M. Lane, *Architecture and Politics in Germany, 1918–1945* (Cambridge, Mass., 1968), pp. 185–95; Barden, *Nuremberg Party Rallies*, ch. 6.

115. M. F. Parkins, *City Planning in Soviet Russia* (Chicago, 1953), pp. 33–43; A. Kopp, *Town and Revolution: Soviet Architecture and City Planning, 1917–1935* (London, 1970), pp. 219–26; J. E. Bowlt, "Russian Sculpture and Lenin's Plan of Monumental Propaganda," in Millon and Nochlin, eds., *Art and Architecture in the Service of Politics*, pp. 182–93.

116. Reps, *Monumental Washington*, pp. 167, 170–74; Craig, *The Federal Presence*, pp. 309–27.

117. J. P. Stern, *Hitler: The Führer and the People* (London, 1975), pp. 39, 82, 85–86, 88–91; Sir N. Henderson, *Failure of a Mission: Berlin, 1937–1939* (London, 1940), pp. 70–71; Barden, *Nuremberg Rallies*, pp. 113–20, 125, 133–34; S. Morley, *"A Talent to Amuse": A Biography of Noel Coward* (Harmondsworth, 1974), p. 193.

118. Wheeler-Bennett, *King George VI*, pp. 199, 215, 254, 302–4, 371–81; F. Donaldson, *Edward VIII* (London, 1976), chs. 6–8.

119. The Times, *Crown and Empire* (London, 1937), p. 184.

120. Frost, *Coronation*, p. 136.

121. Battiscombe, *Queen Alexandra*, p. 302; Tanner, *Recollections of a Westminster Antiquary*, p. 67.

122. Nicolson, *King George the Fifth*, p. 92.

123. J. Pope-Hennessy, *Queen Mary, 1867–1953* (London, 1959), pp. 519–20.

124. R. Lacey, *Majesty: Elizabeth II and the House of Windsor* (London, 1977), p. 78; Wheeler-Bennett, *King George VI*, p. 151.

125. Longford, *House of Windsor*, p. 94.

126. D. Marquand, *Ramsay Macdonald* (London, 1977), p. 774.

127. The fullest account of this is given in The Times, *Hail and Farewell: The Passing of King George the Fifth* (London, 1936).

128. J. Dimbleby, *Richard Dimbleby* (London, 1977), pp. 227–29; L. Miall, ed., *Richard Dimbleby: Broadcaster* (London, 1966), pp. 75–76. For popular reaction to the death of the king, see: Ziegler, *Crown and People*, pp. 84–96.

129. Norris, *Farewell the Trumpets*, p. 498.

130. Briggs, *The History of Broadcasting*, vol. 4, *Sound and Vision*, p. 470; Martin, *The Crown and the Establishment*, p. 15.
131. Rodgers, *Commemorative Souvenirs*, pp. 38–43.
132. E. G., Coronation, Planting Committee, *The Royal Record of Tree Planting, the Provision of Open Spaces, Recreation Grounds and Other Schemes Undertaken in the British Empire and Elsewhere, Especially in the United States of America, in Honour of the Coronation of His Majesty King George VI* (Cambridge, 1939).
133. L. N. and M. Williams, *Commemorative Postage Stamps of Great Britain, 1890–1966* (London, 1967), pp. 9, 25–40; T. Todd, *A History of British Postage Stamps, 1660–1940* (London, 1941), pp. 211, 214, 215, 217; H. D. S. Haverbeck, *The Commemorative Stamps of the British Commonwealth* (London, 1955), pp. 89–94.
134. R. Rose and D. Kavanaugh, "The Monarchy in Contemporary British Culture," *Comparative Politics*, 8 (1976): 551.
135. Lacey, *Majesty*, p. 245; Ziegler, *Crown and People*, p. 198; A. Duncan, *The Reality of Monarchy* (London, 1970), p. 95.
136. Morris, *Farewell the Trumpets*, pp. 545–57; Dimbleby, *Richard Dimbleby*, pp. 370–75; B. Levin, *The Pendulum Years: Britain in the Sixties* (London, 1972), pp. 399–407; R. Crossman, *The Diaries of a Cabinet Minister*, vol. 1, *Minister of Housing, 1964–66* (London, 1975), pp. 141–43, 145.
137. Ziegler, *Crown and People*, p. 84.
138. D. C. Cooper, "Looking Back in Anger," in V. Bogdanor and R. Skidelsky, eds., *The Age of Affluence, 1951–64* (London, 1970), p. 260; L. Harris, *Long to Reign Over Us?* (London, 1966), pp. 18, 52.
139. Briggs, *Sound and Vision*, pp. 457–73; Dimbleby, *Richard Dimbleby*, pp. 223–39.
140. Lacey, *Majesty*, p. 208; E. Shils and M. Young, "The Meaning of the Coronation," *Sociological Review*, new series, 1 (1953): 80.
141. Ziegler, *Crown and People*, pp. 131–37.
142. Miall, *Richard Dimbleby*, pp. 145–46, 157, 161, 167; Dimbleby, *Richard Dimbleby*, pp. 225–52, 326–30.
143. For an account of television coverage of royal ceremonial, see: R. Baker, "Royal Occasions," in Mary Wilson, et al., *The Queen: A Penquin Special* (Harmondsworth, 1977), pp. 105–27.
144. *Daily Mirror*, 8 June 1977.
145. Ziegler, *Crown and People*, p. 176.

8

RICHARD WORTMAN

Moscow and Petersburg: The Problem of Political Center in Tsarist Russia, 1881– 1914

The concept of political center, discussed above by Clifford Geertz, raises interesting questions when applied to societies containing diverse and even conflicting symbolic traditions. In such cases, ceremonial activity defining the political center may clash with the expectations and beliefs of parts of society and cast doubt on the sacredness of the existing political system. The last decades of the Russian autocracy reveal such a situation of symbolic uncertainty, which both reflected and influenced the political strife of the era. A change in the values and traditions the autocracy celebrated made the nature and location of the political center problematic. The definition of symbolic political center inevitably affected the prestige of the capital, the administrative and political center of the empire. The tsar, by depriving the capital of his personal aura, gave sanction to a historical and symbolic tradition that in many respects was at odds with the government through which he ruled. His ceremonial activity gave visual expression to the old problem of the two capitals—Moscow and St. Petersburg—and created uncertainties about the very nature of Russian autocracy.

"St. Petersburg is the fundamental symbol of imperial Russia," Vladimir Weidlé wrote.[1] Peter the Great had bestowed the overwhelming force of his personality on his city, and his successors continued to reside in the capital, and lead its ceremonies and celebrations. St. Petersburg was the residence of the emperor, and the ceremonial life of the capital centered on his person. As absolute monarch, he represented the incarnation of secular power engaged in the strengthening and advancement of the nation. At the great occasions of the capital, he appeared in pomp and splendor, the exemplar of the values of the social and political elite.

The Imperial Court was the ceremonial center of the administration. Those who had achieved high rank witnessed or participated in the ritual life of the imperial family in the Winter Palace. The principal ceremonies— the imperial processions, the New Year and Easter functions, the blessing of the waters—were visible expressions of the shared concerns and the bonds of personal fealty that united the tsar with his officialdom.

The parade fields were the ceremonial center of the military. There the tsar bestowed his attention upon his troops and gave them inspiring gestures of supreme approval. They in turn gave him rousing exclamations of loyalty, and performed virtuoso displays of posture, marching, and riding. The officers who stood or rode by his side felt a common lot and shared military ethos with the emperor. The tsar knew all personally and addressed them with the familiar *ty*, encompassing them in the charmed circle of his associates. "For all of us," a guards officer living in the provinces wrote, "Petersburg was the enchanting residence of the Tsar. And everyone who traveled to Petersburg was considered one of the elect, who could expect the happiness of being close to the Tsar."[2]

Imperial ceremonies had a secular emphasis: They celebrated the tsar's worldly preeminence. Even when the occasions were religious, attention focused on the celebration rather than the occasion, on the imperial figures rather than the religious services performed on that day. It was the procession from the imperial chambers to the palace church that displayed the tsar and his family on their way to worship in the palace church. At Easter, the greetings in the Winter Palace and the great balls provided the moments of imperial grandeur, not the services themselves. The emperor worshiped in a relatively modest setting. Then he reigned like a demigod over the festivities.

St. Petersburg was the emperor's city and the emperor was a visible presence in its streets. Nicolas I and Alexander II walked or rode through the capital without a convoy, until 1879 when revolutionary terrorism put Alexander's life in danger. The security and inviolability of the emperor in his city were signs of his preeminence. Invulnerable among his subjects, he could openly confront them. The mythology of autocracy extolled the emperor's accessibility. The tsar, strolling through the capital or in the gardens of the capital, met an unfortunate and set his grievances right.

The coronation remained the principal ceremony of Moscow. Since Peter the Great, it expressed the continuity between the old and new capitals. It enacted what Geertz describes as the ruler's taking possession of his land; the all-Russian emperor took possession of his Muscovite heritage. Though the church ritual remained faithful to the Moscovite original, the trappings—the regalia, clothing, and festive events—were those of Petersburg, unveiled in their greatest splendor to dazzle the old capital. The coronation marked the old capital's recognition of the preeminence of the new.

Nonetheless, Moscow retained the image of national capital. Both cities were called "capitals" and Moscow the first or original capital (*pervoprestol'naia stolitsa*), where the throne had been initially located. The emperors and empresses paid homage to Moscow on gala visits, when the court revealed its sumptuous panoply in the cathedrals and palaces of the old capital. But these visits were also reassertions of Petersburg's primacy. The social and religious events expressed the autocrat's connections with the national heritage. The court's departure left feelings of emptiness and abandonment that confirmed Moscow's secondary position. Prince Shcherbatov caught this sense when he personified Moscow as a forsaken widow. Her sovereigns' presence only expressed their displeasure. "No sooner do they arrive in the city which is the ancient capital of their forefathers than they hasten to leave it, in order to return merrily to the shores of the Neva."[3]

After the Napoleonic invasion, Moscow became the center of patriotic and romantic sentiment. The rebuilding of the capital and the intellectual development of Moscow accompanied a new national pride reflected in all aspects of Russian culture and thought. The existence of two capitals troubled the awakened national consciousness. "Two capitals cannot flourish equally in one and the same state just as two hearts cannot exist in the human body," Pushkin wrote.[4]

During the 1840s and the 1850s the question of Russia's capital became the subject of extended debate between the Slavophiles and Westernizers. The Slavophiles defended Moscow as the true capital. "Moscow is the capital of the Russian people," Constantine Aksakov declared. "Petersburg is only the residence of the emperor," suggesting that in Russia, the presence of the ruler was not sufficient to establish the political center.[5] They emphasized Petersburg's alienness and impermanence. Ivan Aksakov called it "the negative moment of history" which "cannot create anything *positive* in the Russian sense." A return to the positive was possible only through "the negation of Petersburg as a political principle."[6] Alexander Herzen, before he fell under Belinskii's influence, felt similar misgivings. For him, Petersburg was a city that "had neither a history nor a future," that each autumn awaited "the squall that would submerge it," a reference to the legend that Petersburg was doomed to sink into the swamp from which it had arisen.[7] Conservative intellectuals like Vasilii Zhukovskii and Michael Pogodin frequently expressed their preference for the old capital, which they thought represented the true center of the nation.[8] "The heart of Russia" was the common phrase for Moscow.

The emperors also showed recognition of Moscow's national character. In the eighteenth century, Peter the Great and Catherine the Great often visited Moscow to celebrate victories. Nicholas I's trips to Moscow were occasions for displays of national sentiment. Nicholas's appearances at the Kremlin cathedrals and other shrines were described at length and extolled in the official press. But the recognition was fleeting, and the visits served as much to display the western character of the Moscow elite as the national sentiments of the court. Thus in 1849, Nicholas decided to spend Easter week in Moscow—the only occasion of an imperial visit for the holiday in the nineteenth century. But the principal reason for the emperor's presence was the dedication of the new, neoclassical, Kremlin palace. And the principal event, in the eyes of all except nationalist writers like Pogodin and Shevyrev, was the great masquerade at the palace of Governor-General Zakrevskii. Indeed, Nicholas showed his contempt for the unguarded expressions of national taste that accompanied his visit. He remained true to the western institutional and military values that centered in Petersburg.[9]

During the reform era, political conflict began to disturb the quiet of St. Petersburg. Alexander II and Maria Aleksandrovna increasingly regarded the city with distaste and preferred the solitude of their rural palaces. In 1858, Alexander wrote to his mother of his wish to get away from the capital, "whose atmosphere is more or less gangrened." In 1861, he referred to "the gangrened population of the capital" in a letter to his sister. The empress warned her son, Grand Duke Vladimir, of "the bad influences of idle and dissolute youth, which swarm in Petersburg."[10]

At the same time, conservative nationalist writers depicted Petersburg as the symbol of all destructive western influence. Constantine Leontiev, writing of the decomposition of "Petrine models," asserted that the "sooner Petersburg becomes something in the nature of a Baltic Sebastopol or a Baltic Odessa, the better it will be, I maintain, not only for us but probably also for so-called humanity."[11] Leontiev dreamt of Constantinople as capital. Alexander III's tutor, Constantine Pobedonostev, felt uncomfortable in Petersburg and expressed his preferences for Moscow. As tsarevich, Alexander III associated with the "Russian party" in Moscow and supported its nationalist and protectionist program. He felt ill-at-ease in the court life of the capital. He wrote to Pobedonostev in 1880 of his longing "to be far from all the vileness of city life and especially Petersburg."[12]

But until the beginning of the 1880s, these sentiments remained private and did not affect the ceremonial activity of the members of the imperial family. They continued to appear at reviews, balls, and receptions and remained visible in the streets of the capital. Only in the last two decades of the nineteenth century did the emperor begin to withdraw his presence from the capital. At this point, Petersburg, which had never enjoyed the reputation of national capital, began to lose the aura that attached to it as residence of the tsar as well. There took place a shifting of allegiance, as the emperor, appearing as Russian tsar, increasingly associated himself with the old capital and the national feelings it evoked.

The turning point in this respect was the assassination of Alexander II at the Catherine Canal in Petersburg on 1 March 1881. The murder of the tsar, as he rode to his weekly review of the guards of the capital, destroyed the image of Petersburg as the emperor's own city. No longer could he appear in its streets as if in an olympian enclave. With the assassination, the sense of the tsar's inviolability died as well, much as it had in France with the execution of Louis XVI.[13] The emperor was no longer visible or accessible in his capital. Alexander III retreated to the suburban palace of Gatchina, which, surrounded by cordons of guards, became the imperial residence. The tsar came to be referred to as "the prisoner" (*uznik*).

But more than the tsar's security was jeopardized. The act represented a profanation of the imperial city. Petersburg became in the eyes of some "a defiled, disgraced and indecent place for the residence of the Sovereign." There were suggestions, especially in the Moscow press, that the capital be moved to Moscow.[14] But they were hardly taken seriously in official spheres. Petersburg remained the capital, but it was Petersburg without the signs of its preeminence, divested of its charisma. The ceremonial acts and events that distinguished the capital lapsed or lost their symbolic force. The tsar became increasingly suspicious of the administration, regarding bureaucrats as well, with their legalistic and practical preoccupations, as threats to his authority. The capital ceased to appear as the political center even as the administration became larger, more assertive, and unyielding. The blocks of massive government edifices were deprived of their sacred aura once the imperial favor became ambiguous. Then Petersburg began to lose its reason for existence. It became a phantasmic presence in the world of the symbolists, a signifier without a signified.

Alexander III preferred a simple life of solitude in the country. The descriptions of him, chopping wood early in the morning at Gatchina, wearing a checked Russian shirt and Russian boots, playing with animals and children, presented the tsar as "of the same rough texture as the great majority of his subjects."[15] Like Peter the Great, he broke with the established culture of the elite and, by taking on features of the common man, withdrew his support from its pretensions. His open impatience with the amenities and trappings of court functions was a public repudiaton of the capital and its values. "Not loving external glitter, superfluous luxury, and blinding splendor, the late sovereign did not live in the Great Winter Palace," a columnist of *Moskovskie Vedomosti* wrote after his death.[16] But Alexander did not follow Peter's example and impose his own cultural mode. Rather he withdrew into his solitary, simple, private life, and participated, albeit half-heartedly, in the social and ceremonial functions of the capital.

Alexander III conscientiously resumed the events of the social season after the years of revolutionary crisis. But it was the empress who was the spirit of these occasions. A charming and convivial hostess, Maria Fedorovna loved to dance and socialize, while the emperor preferred to withdraw to a game of cards. Alexander was an awkward and forbidding presence, who intimidated his intimates and did not seek their affection or admiration. "His manner is cold, constrained, abrupt, and so suggestive of churlishness as often to deprive spontaneous favors of the honey of friendship for the sake of which they are accorded," a correspondent wrote.[17] He immediately curtailed the military ceremonials in Petersburg that had remained prominent events during his father's reign. He discontinued the popular Sunday reviews of the guards in the Manege and the spring parades. Occasions for drill became increasingly infrequent, and owing to the new, drab, Russian style uniforms that he introduced, not especially stirring.[18]

Nicholas II also made no secret of his dislike of Petersburg. He longed to move the capital, though he had Yalta and not Moscow in mind.[19] In the first years of his reign he endeavored to live at the Winter Palace and carry on the traditional social obligations of emperor. But he too felt ill-at-ease in public, and the Empress Alexandra abhorred public occasions and had none of her mother-in-law's social grace or charm. She immediately discontinued the empress's small dinners for members of the court, which had kept the imperial family in touch with court society.[20] The imperial family spent increasingly prolonged periods at Tsarskoe Selo.

Nicholas II, unlike his father, loved the parade grounds and felt in his element among the officers' corps. He resumed the spring parades and replaced the simple Russian style uniforms of his father's reign with new imposing ones reminiscent of earlier splendor. But his association with the military was, for the most part, not visible in the capital. He joined the officers in their regimental breakfasts and dinners. The center of military ceremony shifted from the capital to the camp at Krasnoe Selo, where maneuvers and parades united the tsar with his elite troups in a holy ceremony, followed by brilliant social occasions.[21]

But even when military exercises and celebrations took place in the capital, the mood had changed. The *champs de mars*, the scene of the great parades and popular entertainments, now had a mortuary atmosphere about it. "It is surrounded by objects calculated to bring back recollections of the saddest nature," the English military attaché noted.[22] A hundred yards from the northeast corner was the votive chapel on the site of Karakazov's attempt on Alexander II's life. To the southeast was the Engineering Castle, where Emperor Paul, the father of two nineteenth-century emperors, had been murdered. To the southwest, a chapel and later a "temple" was erected on the spot of Alexander's assassination, worshiped as a sacred shrine to his martyrdom. Petersburg had become the scene of the emperors' mortality not their immortality, recalling their tragedies rather than their triumphs.

Moscow, "the holy city," represented the traditional religious values that the ideologists of autocracy now extolled. Constantine Pobedonostev, chief procurator of the Holy Synod, emphasized the role of the Russian Orthodox Church in the preservation of the authority and prestige of autocratic government. He named the principal statement of his political views *Moscow Collection* (*Moskovskii Sbornik*—the English translation is entitled *Reflections of a Russian Statesman*). After the assassination, attempts were made to give Petersburg something of the appearance of Moscow. Alien, western influences were to be dispelled, the capital was to be resanctified by making it more like Moscow, by Muscovitizing Petersburg. The first expression of this tendency was the "temple" built to consecrate the site of Alexander II's assassination on the Catherine Canal. The official announcement for the architectural competition specified that it was to be in the "national" style. The architects submitting projects followed the earlier official definition of "national," decreed by Nicholas I, that is the classical, neo-Byzantine manner of the Assumption Cathedral in the Kremlin. But Alexander III was displeased and declared that the temple should be built in the "style of the time of the Moscow tsars of the seventeenth century."

The architect, Alfred Parland, like the others in the competition, understood what Alexander meant—the flamboyant national architecture of the sixteenth and seventeenth centuries, or, more specifically, Vasilli the Blessed. Parland accordingly drew up his plans for the Temple of the Resurrection of Christ or, as it came to be called, the Savior on the Blood, as a copy of Vasilli the Blessed. Its multicolored intricate decorations and mosaics introduced a strange contrast to the other great cathedrals of the capital—the Kazan Cathedral and St. Isaacs, both replicas of St. Peter's in Rome. The effect in the neoclassical city was less than felicitious, creating what one authority described as "a troubling dissonance."[23] (See fig. 8.1.)

The interior itself was a strange cultural amalgam. The design followed not the warren of Vasilli the Blessed, but the traditional open cruciform space of the Byzantine cathedral. The walls were covered by frescoes, among them works of Victor Vasnetsov and Michael Nesterov. The pavement stained with the emperor's blood was kept under a flamboyant canopy in seventeenth-century style. The enormous donations allowed no expense to be spared for a temple which "surpasses all the churches of Petersburg in its sumptuousness." It was illuminated by 1,589 electric lights and even equipped with steam heat.[24]

Nicholas II shared his father's taste for a national style in architecture and introduced more Muscovite motifs into the Petersburg landscape. He had the new neoclassical building of the School Council of the Holy Synod remodeled into the Alexander Nevskii Temple-Monument in memory of Alexander III. (See fig. 8.2.) The architect, Pomerantsev, made over the right side of the building in imitation of an old Russian church at Borisoglebsk. The neoclassical lines and symmetrical disposition of windows were now decorated with an old-Russian portal, mosaic frescoes, and tracery. Five onion-form cupolas and a tent-style steeple rose above the flat rectangular roof. Inside, paintings with "a religious-moral meaning" depicted the lives of Nevskii, St. Sergei, and other princes and saints of old Russia.[25] The Tercentenary Cathedral, dedicated in 1914, was an explicit and exact copy of Rostov church architecture of the seventeenth century. At Tsarskoe Selo, Nicholas had the Fedorov Cathedral built for the empress in imitation of the Annunciation Cathedral in the Kremlin, though with seventeenth-century elements to give it a more national appearance.[26]

Nicholas also tried to bring Moscow into his own life and the life of the Petersburg court. If his father's national persona was the peasant-tsar, Nicholas's was the Muscovite tsar wearing the vestments and performing the Byzantine ceremonies of the seventeenth century. Like his father, he enjoyed reading about Russia's early history. But lacking Alexander's

Fig. 8.1. The Temple of the Resurrection of Christ on the Blood (Khram Vaskresenie Khristova na Krovakh), St. Petersburg, 1883–1906. From A. A. Parland, *Khram Voskresenie Khristova* . . . (St. Petersburg, 1907). Slavonic Division, New York Public Library, Aster, Lenox, and Tilden Foundations.

Fig. 8.2. Alexander Nevskii Temple-Monument, St. Petersburg. K. Korol'kov, *Tsar-mirotvorets, Imperator Aleksandr III* (Kiev, 1904).

practical disposition, he was given to imagining himself in roles and situations of the past, especially when political difficulties began to multiply. Muscovite autocracy came to represent for him the ideal polity that existed in harmony with all classes of the population. It was a fantasy of government free from conflict, the ruler obeyed and loved by his subjects.[27]

For his model, Nicholas looked to Tsar Alexei Mikhailovich, the most tranquil tsar, who could rely on his own judgments without struggling against the heads of administrative institutions or challenges from political movements. He appropriately chose the name Alexei for his son. The minister of interior, Sipiagin, artfully played upon and encouraged Nicholas's predilections. He had the minister's chambers in the neoclassical building of the ministry redesigned to resemble the Hall of Facets in the Kremlin. He longed to receive the tsar with Muscovite ritual and hospitality. When Nicholas accepted his invitation, he ordered an elaborate Russian feast with a gypsy orchestra from Moscow. The day before the event was to take place, Sipiagin was felled by an assassin's bullet.[28]

The most spectacular recreation of the seventeenth century was the gala costume ball of 1903. Nicholas viewed this as no mere masquerade, but as a first step toward restoring Muscovite court ritual and dress. Seventeenth-century attire was mandatory. Museums were searched for pictures, artists and couturiers were hired to make costumes at enormous cost. Courtiers came as boiars, *okol'nichie*, and other service ranks of Muscovy. The ladies wore seventeenth-century gowns studded with their ancestral jewels. The officers of the guards were dressed as *strel'tsy*, the musketeers of old Russia. Nicholas wore a brocaded processional robe and crown of Alexei, Alexandra a gown brocaded in silver, a miter, and a huge emerald pendant surrounded with diamonds.[29]

"The court looked very pretty filled with ancient Russian people," Nicholas wrote in his diary. The event was so huge a success that it was repeated for the dowager, who had been abroad, and members of the diplomatic corps, who attended in their usual evening dress. A deluxe two-volume album was published with photographs of all the guests in their costumes, identified with their twentieth- and seventeenth-century ranks. But the court regarded the ball as little more than an enchanting diversion, and the forbidding expense of adopting Muscovite dress discouraged further experiments of this type. Soon after, the Russo-Japanese War and then the revolution of 1905 brought a halt to all social and ceremonial life in the capital.[30]

Petersburg remained impervious to Muscovite influence. To express their attachment to Moscow, Alexander III and Nicholas II visited the old capital. There they sought to enter communion (*obshchenie*) with what they viewed as the faithful masses of the Russian people. Alexander III first envisaged a Zemskii Sobor, an assembly of 3,000 to 4,000 deputies, most of them peasants, which was to meet with the tsar in the Church of the Redeemer in Moscow. Pobedonostev and other advisers, however, quickly discouraged this scheme. Instead, the communion was to be expressed in ceremonial form. The tsar, visiting the shrines of the Kremlin, received the adulation of the faithful, which replaced institutional expressions of support for autocracy.[31]

The first of these visits took place only a few months after Alexander III's accession. In July 1881, during the maneuvers at Krasnoe Selo, the tsar abruptly announced his intention to travel to Moscow. At the Kremlin, where he bowed to the people and received the traditional greetings of the estates, he demonstrated his unity (*edinenie*) with the first capital. He declared, "The Late Little Father expressed his gratitude many times to Moscow for her devotion. Moscow has always served as an example for all of Russia. I hope this will be true in the future. Moscow has attested and now attests that in Russia, Tsar and people comprise one, concordant [*edinodushnoe*] whole."[32]

The gratitude to Moscow for its devotion contrasted with the disdain Alexander had shown toward Petersburg. The acclaim he received in the Kremlin on this and subsequent visits was taken by the devotees of autocracy as a national mandate. On the steps of the "red porch" in the Kremlin, the tsar heard thunderous hoorahs, the ringing of bells, a salute. He bowed in acknowledgment. Voeikov, an officer of the Uhlans, indicated the great significance of the gesture. "This is a custom unique to the world—the autocratic tsar bows to his faithful subject people. This custom is the sacrament of the communion of the tsar with his people." Such rhapsodic accounts as well as prints of the highlights of the tsar's visit appeared in popular periodicals. The cover page of *Vsemirnaia Illiustratsiia* showed Alexander and the empress receiving the acclaim of the crowd before the Assumption Cathedral in the Kremlin.[33] (See fig. 8.3.)

From Moscow, Alexander traveled through the old towns along the Volga "from the most ancient times consecrated by devotion to Russia, where after the great troubles of the XVII century, true Russian people elected the Romanov house to the throne." The tsar now sought to renew the original mandate of 1613, to root his rule in the feelings of the people of the Russian heartland. He followed the itinerary that he had taken three times as tsarevich. He visited Nizhnii-Novgorod, the gathering point of the militia of 1612, and Kostroma, the location of the Romanov *votchina* where Michael and mother were in hiding in 1613. The jubilation, Voeikov wrote, provided the tsar with a sense of popular, national support. "He drew from these outpourings of the people, these historical shrines alive with their past, the necessary strength and faith to pacify and uplift the Russian State, preserved and given to him by God."[34]

Alexander on this and subsequent trips was no longer the sovereign proceeding through his land to take possession of it by displays of grandeur and majesty. Rather, he returned to the historical center in order to reveal his connection with the old monuments and symbols, once the new had become treacherous and threatening. He was expressing his sense of belonging to the Muscovite origins of the Russian empire and distancing himself from its Petersburg phase. St. Petersburg the symbol of rational

Fig. 8.3. Imperial Procession of Tsar Alexander III from the Assumption Cathedral, July 17, 1881. From *Vsemirnaia Illiustratsiia,* 1881, no. 658, p. 137.

power containing the disorderly elements of Russia had lost its force as a source of authority. The tsar rather found justification for his rule in the elemental devotion of the simple people of Russia to their sovereign and to the order and might that he represented.

The coronation of the tsar, taking place in Moscow, now became a central symbolic event, declaring the new national, religious sense of authority to Russia and the world. The official accounts of Alexander III's coronation in 1883 stressed the national and popular character of the celebration. They presented it as far more than the traditional conferral of God's blessings on the tsar's rule. The Church now represented the Russian people. The coronation was "a general-national event which expressed the historical union of the Sovereign with his State, his vow to the Church, that is to the soul and conscience of his people, and finally the union of the Tsar and people with the Tsar of tsars in whose hands rests the fate of both tsars and peoples." The rhetoric of mutual affection between tsar and people dominated the official explanation of the evolution of the coronation. The people's attitude toward the tsar had remained unchanged since the sixteenth century, it emphasized. "The people saw and see in him the bearer of its moral consciousness, its conscience and faith."[35]

The events surrounding the coronation emphasized the new importance of Russia's Muscovite heritage. For the occasion, Tschaikovsky composed a cantata, *Moscow*, based on the romantic historical poetry of Apollon Maikov. The work, which has not found a place in the symphonic repertory, was performed during the Coronation Banquet in the Hall of Facets. It sung the glory of the Muscovite princes and tsars who had united *Rus'* and overcome the Tartars. The *bogatyr'*, symbolizing Russia, was addressed by "people of God of all countries, of eastern countries."

> For all eastern countries, you, now,
> Are like the rising star of Bethlehem,
> A prophesy about Moscow, Your Moscow
> Two Romes Fell,
> The Third Stands
> There will be no fourth.[36]

The gala performance at the Bol'shoi Theater included the first and last acts of Glinka's *Life for the Tsar*, the latter showing Tsar Michael's entry into Moscow in 1613. At Alexander II's coronation, it had been *L'Elisir d'Amore*.

Alexander III's coronation received massive publicity both in Russia and abroad. For the first time, foreign correspondents were admitted to the coronation services in the Assumption Cathedral. They described the grandeur and excitement of the ceremony to an international audience. The London *Times* correspondent, Lowe, wrote, "The solemn strains of the national anthem, the joyful pealing of the bells, the thunder of the swiftly served cannon, the surging sea of spectators, and the loud and continued cheers, all produced a scene that can never be forgotten by those who witnessed it." At night, "the city went almost mad with Monarchical joy." The correspondent for the *Standard* sensed the meaning of the event. "Peter's town may rule for a time, but Moscow still remains the center of national life and some day may with greater right become the capital of the Russian tsars."[37]

In subsequent years, conservative publicists in Moscow stressed Moscow's contribution to the evolution of the Russian state. For them, Moscow's feminine character, rather than the masculine ruthlessness of Petersburg, represented the source of the state spirit. Moscow's self-abnegating love assured the tsar's complete obedience. "Surrounding their cradles with tender care, caressing their childhood and days of youth, Moscow conveyed from clan to clan the love for the generations of its tsars, transferred from clan to clan the harmonious ideas of the state principle [*gosudarstvennost'*], the precepts of her wise first-service.[38]

The final and most spectacular visit of Alexander III to Moscow took place after his death, when his coffin was borne along its streets on the way from Yalta to Petersburg. The elaborate and emotional celebration appealed to the national taste for mourning. An English observer wrote, "If a poetic or artistic genius depicted the incarnation of death on earth, he could create nothing more artistic or harmonious than what was presented in the days of mourning."[39] Throngs watched in grief and awe as the funeral procession passed through Moscow to the tolling of its many bells, beating of drums, and the strains of the funeral march. "The whole people, like a single person, bared their heads, as the holy dust of the deceased Emperor approached," the *Vsemirnaia Illiustratsiia* correspondent wrote. "The picture was majestic. From all sides one heard sobbing and weeping."

Most significant was the presence of the tsar's body in the old capital. He lay in state, not in the Winter Palace, as had his predecessors, but in the Archangel Cathedral near the princes and tsars of Moscow. Courtiers and common people filed by and paid their last respects to the tsar, whose coffin was held in a "gorgeous catafalque all glittering with gold." The conservative and official accounts emphasized the national character of the devotion of all classes of the population to their tsar. "And in this mixing of tears, shed over the grave of the deceased tsar, the great mysterious unity of the Russian people was consummated with its great beloved tsar, which is inaccessible to the ordinary mind."[40]

Constantine Pobedonostev, not usually given to emotional transports, was inspired by the sight of the tsar close to his pre-Petrine forebears. The coffin lay "in the heart of Russia" near "the early leaders of the Russian land." The "orphaned people" mourned them all. They also mourned "the most tranquil tsar, Alexei." Pobedonostev took the comparison further with his last respects to his pupil. "Farewell, Pious, Kind to the people, most tranquil, Tsar Alexander Alexandrovich!"[41]

But the body of the tsar had to be removed to Petersburg for burial. It was done with some haste, for the embalming had been performed poorly and decomposition had begun. By the time it had reached Petersburg, the body had been covered with powder, making the tsar's face almost unrecognizable. The stench became so acute that the guards at the Peter-Paul Cathedral had difficulty completing their duty.[42]

The Petersburg procession, though joined by an impressive array of notables and members of the imperial family, lacked the spirit of Moscow's. Few people appeared on the street and the procession moved fitfully and irregularly.[43] The gloomy Petersburg October day depressed feelings: "a line of route lugubrious with the hangings of undertakers' woe, and dismal with slush and mud, and a drizzle from a sullen, leaden-hued sky." A correspondent from Moscow took the murky weather as a sign of Petersburg's "rottenness," borne on a western wind. The onlookers, respectful and reverent, did not display the feelings of devotion evident in Moscow. Uncertainties about the shift of superiors under the new tsar made official concerns paramount and diminished the effect of the bereavement.[44]

The Petersburg ceremonies featured the westernized elite of the court and European royalty. Alexander III was laid to rest amidst the neoclassical magnificence of the capital, mourned by the imperial family, the highest officers and officials of Petersburg, foreign princes, and heads of state. An English correspondent described the effect. "A thousand glimmering candles were reflected in the silver wreaths, the majestic brocade of the canopy, and the star-spangled breasts of the uniforms, producing a scene of such splendor as is seldom witnessed." After Nicholas and Maria Fedorovna paid their last respects, the cathedral was filled with sobbing. "Many gray-bearded heads bent in silent grief, in many eyes unaccustomed to tears, great tears glistened. Many knees were bent and many of those praying, in the uniforms of the highest ranks, covered their faces with their hands so that their neighbors would not be witnesses to their grief."[45] Played to a foreign audience, the final obsequies blessed the all-Russian emperor, the representative of international royalty, the tsar's European self. The French lavished attention on their new ally, sending more than 5,000 memorial wreaths, many of them in silver. The French delegation brought 10,000 bouquets of artificial flowers, tied with the tricolor, affixed to which were pictures of Alexander and President Carnot with the legend, "united in sentiments and death."[46]

Moscow was to be the site for a monument to Alexander built from donations from the population. "Of course, only the heart of the Russian land is the place for an *all-national* [*vsenarodnyi*] monument. In the focal point of Russia should stand the monument to the One Who in his ideal image tied our past with the future, Who resurrected the ancient precepts of the Moscow gatherers and organizers of *Sacred Rus'*." Moscow contained the shrines of the great tsars of the past. "Where but among them should the monument of the greatest of their descendants and successors stand resplendent—a monument that should become a new symbol of Holy Russia, a new Russian shrine?"[47] The statue, finally placed before the Redeemer Cathedral in 1909, showed Alexander III, huge and austere, on his coronation throne, wearing a crown and holding orb and scepter. It was the only statue of a Russian emperor as the annointed of God.

For Nicholas II, Moscow symbolized pure autocracy, free from the constraints that had accompanied the development of a bureaucracy and educated public opinion. It was, in his mind, a historical alternative to the institutions and officials that thwarted his will in the capital. It was medieval Moscow that he envisioned, the Moscow of churches, monasteries, tolling bells, and religious processions. Modern Moscow of course would intrude on these images. The Khodynskoe field disaster after the coronation, the gruesome assassination of his uncle, Grand Duke Sergei, governor-general of Moscow, provided unpleasant reminders of the present. But these could be forgotten. In Moscow, the tsar could appear as religious leader of his people, performing the sacraments that consecrated his authority. Nicholas's visits to Moscow were frequent during the first years of his reign. Interrupted by the revolution of 1905, they were resumed once he and his advisers regained confidence in the stability of society in the years preceding the First World War.

To emphasize his religious mission, Nicholas began to visit Moscow for Easter, the major holiday in the Orthodox calendar. In March 1900 he traveled to Moscow to observe Easter in Moscow, the first imperial visit during Easter since Nicholas I's in 1849. The celebration was surrounded by considerable publicity. Besides the usual newspaper reports, the government published an account that was sent free of charge to the 110,000 subscribers of *Sel'skii Vestnik*, the organ of the Ministry of Interior. The volume drew explicit connections with seventeenth-century Muscovy. Nicholas had come to Moscow "by sacred precept of our native ancient times" to spend Easter "in close union with the faithful orthodox people, as if in sacred communion with the distant past . . . with that past when Moscow was 'the capital town,' when the tsar and Moscow Patriarch lived there, when the life of the first capital was an uninterrupted and undeviating observance of the Church Statutes, and the example of such a life was the Moscow Tsar himself."[48]

The official account described the ceremonies and processions of the Lenten and Easter seasons in old Moscow, along with the emperor's and empress's part in the services. The climax was the great Easter night procession to the Church of the Savior. At midnight, the emperor, in the uniform of the Preobrazhenskii Regiment, and the empress, in a white Russian dress and *kokoshnik* studded with gems and pearls, followed the leading court ranks from the Kremlin Palace to the church. Behind them were members of the tsar's suite, other members of the court, and the ladies of leading Moscow families. The city was brilliantly lit. Worshipers crowded into the Kremlin cathedrals. The clock on the Savior Gate struck midnight. A cannon salvo burst from Tainitskii Tower. The Ivan the Great tower began to ring, and its sounds were echoed by all the "forty times forty" bells of Moscow.[49]

In a rescript to the governor-general of Moscow, his uncle Sergei Alexandrovich, Nicholas spoke of the realization of his "intense wish" (*goriachee zhelanie*) to spend Holy Week and Easter in Moscow, "among the greatest national shrines, under the canopy of the centuries-old Kremlin." Here, Nicholas declared, he had found his communion with his people, "with the true children of our beloved Church, pouring into the temples" and a "quiet joy" filled his soul. Sharing the Easter holiday with the worshipers gave him a spiritual mandate. "In the unity in prayer with My people, I draw new strength for serving Russia, for her well-being and glory."[50]

These sentiments were not feigned. He announced loudly that he felt at home in Moscow, calm and confident. In a letter to his mother he described his joy preparing for Holy Communion in the Kremlin cathedrals. He and Alexandra had spent their days visiting them and reading about Muscovite history. "I never knew I was able to reach such heights of religious ecstasy as this Lent has brought me to. This feeling is now much stronger than it was in 1896, which is only natural. I am so calm and happy now, and everything here makes for prayer and peace of the spirit."[51]

Nicholas observed Easter in Moscow again in 1903. *Moskovskie Vedomosti*, the conservative nationalist daily, extolled the visit as a demonstration of the unity of the people with the tsar, in contrast with the divisiveness it described in Petersburg. An editorial asserted that the tsar encountered not the destructive spirit, but the constructive force, "with which Moscow created Russia." The Kremlin recalled Moscow's mission. "Here, among the national shrines of the Kremlin, one's lips involuntarily whisper, 'This is the Third Rome. There will be no fourth."[52]

In the midst of worker unrest, the newspaper printed reports of the workers' spontaneous enthusiasm for the tsar, which were reprinted in a volume published in 1909. A series of articles by the worker F. Slepov related what were purportedly his and his comrades' feelings. The workers, Slepov wrote, brought Nicholas bread and salt. They were so happy that "they felt like flying." When the tsar passed them along the boulevard, they went delirious with joy. "The land, it seemed, shook with joyous enthusiasm. And, as if unwilled, a rapturous cry escaped from the heart. Like an electric current, it ran through all. Tears wetted many eyes. Many people crossed themselves."[53]

Moscow was the tsar's true home. As the crowd dispersed, Slepov overheard such remarks. "Look how close by he passed. Why doesn't he stay longer and live in Moscow? What is Petersburg? Moscow is better." Most Muscovites felt the same way. "Moscow is the heart of Russia and therefore dreams that the Tsar will bestow upon her the joy of as long a stay as possible in the Kremlin, with its Russian shrines so revered by the people." The tsar also was happy, like a "father, finding himself among his children, seeing them after a long absence."[54]

Not surprisingly, the editors of *Moskovskie Vedomosti* drew the same conclusions. They expressed regret that "our old Moscow cannot, as it did in ancient times, surround the tsar on days of his imperial labors, as at the times of holiday meetings." Petersburg could not provide "the tranquil, clear, national setting for governmental work that exists here in old Moscow, within the walls of the sacred Kremlin, in the center of native Russia, which can conceive only of age-old Russian foundations [*ustoi*]."[55] The conservative Petersburg daily *Novoe Vremia* contemptuously dismissed these claims as another futile appeal to "reduce the work of Peter the Great to nothing." The author of the column confidently observed that "the Petersburg period of Russian history has already lasted for two-hundred years."[56]

The Russo-Japanese War and the revolution of 1905 terminated the tsar's Easter visits to Moscow. The bloody events in Moscow, especially the December insurrection, made the old capital as forbidding a place for the tsar as the new. But in Moscow the revolutionary events did not have the symbolic impact they did in Petersburg. The Moscow insurrections left the holy places untouched. Moscow might be physically threatening for the tsar, but its shrines remained inviolate. The events in Petersburg, on the other hand, discredited and dishonored the sacred places of the autocracy, particularly the Winter Palace. The first episode took place at the ceremony of the blessing of the waters on 6 January 1905. The tsar joined by members of his suite, courtiers, and high-ranking officials went out to the Neva to watch the Metropolitan perform the ceremonies. The ladies were watching, as was the custom, at the windows of the Winter Palace, when a shot shattered several of the panes. An investigation failed to reveal foul play, but the mishap remained a mystery and served as an ill-omen.

Three days later, a crowd of workers approaching the palace peacefully, to ask the tsar for peaceful rectification of their grievances, were massacred. "Bloody Sunday" made the official residence of the tsar a symbol of brutal inhumanity and exploitation, a sign not of the refinement but the barbarism of Russian autocracy. Finally, the reception of the members of the First Duma in the Winter Palace, in April 1906, became a spectacle of mutual incomprehension and rebuff. The tsar appeared in a stiff formal imperial procession, organized, it was said, by the empress herself. The deputies of the Duma wore everyday clothes to emphasize their distance from the monarchy. The speech from the throne outraged the deputies. The political struggle had conquered the ceremonial center of the Russian Empire.

After the revolution, the emperor and empress resided at Tsarskoe Selo under heavy guard and did not venture into the capital. Their aloofness from the social life of Petersburg rankled in high society, Alexandra's continued refusal to give debutant parties arousing especial ill-will. The failure to perform the ceremony of the blessing of the waters caused consternation among the common people of the capital, who believed that the prayers purified the water. They blamed the outbreaks of cholera occurring from 1908 to 1910 on the suspension of the ceremony. The blessing was resumed in 1911, the same year Nicholas and Alexandra made their first appearance at the Mariinskii Theater since the revolution.[57]

Nicholas, to be sure, also remained wary of Moscow, which had been a center of the liberal and revolutionary movement in 1905. Only in April 1912 did he venture into the city, for the unveiling of the monument to Alexander III and the opening of the Alexander III Art Museum. The mood was tense. Expecting trouble, the authorities tightened security measures and increased arrests. The police interrogated the entire consular corps about foreigners in the capital. The guards regiments entering the capital were met with cries of "butchers, Praetorians, tsarists," in reference to their bloody suppression of the Moscow insurrections. The tsar stopped the procession to pray at the spot where his uncle, the hated Grand Duke Sergei, had been blown to bits. Moscow society was hostile to the empress, who, worried about the heir's health, remained particularly inaccessible and failed to appear at the opening of the museum. Even the meeting with peasant elders, which Nicholas usually performed well, was uneasy and strained. A right-wing journal contrasted the visit to Nicholas's joyous reception in 1903.[58]

But the atmosphere in Moscow changed quickly. Once the conservative monarchical forces rallied to his support, Moscow again became the center of displays of dedication to the sovereign. It was there that the spiritual bond that he sought reappeared. That very summer, in August 1912, Nicholas entered Moscow to tumultuous ovations, after the festivities commemorating Borodino. Nicholas, himself, was inspired by the religious services on Red Square. Then, the Moscow nobility staged a ceremony of devotion, where they, and provincial marshals of the nobility, presented the tsar a patriotic banner. Samarin, the Moscow marshal, read an impassioned declaration pledging to defend him as the nobility had defended Alexander I one hundred years before. The declaration addressed Nicholas as an "absolute" monarch. The mood in the hall was elated and adoring. The empress was moved to tears.[59]

The Borodino celebrations and other displays of support in the provinces confirmed Nicholas's sense that the Russian people persisted in their devotion to him. As the Duma became increasingly assertive, despite its conservative composition, and his ministers lost his trust, the image of a national autocracy became compelling. After 1905, his official statements frequently used the word *Rus'* instead of *Rossiia*. Official literature began to present the seventeenth century as the most important period of the foundation of Russian autocracy, diminishing the role assigned to Peter the Great. It depicted the seventeenth century as an era of national unity, when tsar and people shared common goals, and autocracy appeared in its ideal form, of personal spiritual leadership of the nation. The authors often suggested the seductive parallels between the two centuries: both began with social and political troubles, and those of the twentieth, like the seventeenth, would be resolved by a renewed, popular autocracy. Moscow became the symbol as well as the monument of this image of the past—an example of Michael Bakhtin's notion of "chronotope," as Katerina Clark has shown for the Soviet period.[60]

This theme ran through the celebrations of the three-hundredth anniversary of the Romanov dynasty in 1913. The tercentenary, the first commemoration of the dynasty's beginning in 1613, acknowledged its Muscovite sources of political legitimacy. The celebrations themselves cast significant doubts upon the symbolic role of Petersburg. The first part of the celebrations, marking the election of Michael Romanov, by the Zemskii Sobor, took place there in February. It was an incongruous setting indeed. A historical celebration meant to affirm continuity took place in a city symbolizing discontinuity. The rectilinear plan of the capital exemplified European symmetry and rationality. The rather sparse decorations, provided by the Petersburg city government, were Venetian in inspiration and clashed with the religious, national tenor of the celebration. The monarchist press made caustic comments about the everyday look of the capital, the unrelieved impression of its severe barrack style. "We were promised a spectacle, but we got only sadness." The appearance of the city should have been transformed. It should have taken on a "fantastic, legendary garb. Then the people would be in a gay mood, would, for a while, shed their everyday cares and feast on spectacle, which in our dull time is needed more than ever."[61]

Nicholas and Alexandra's unconcealed aversion to the capital and its elite revealed how little it represented the center of political life for the monarch himself. Nicholas remained perfunctory and aloof from the capital elite and the estate representatives visiting from the provinces. There were few crowds cheering political support, only the somber figures of members of the Union of the Russian People and the Union of the Archangel Michael, organizations that had lost most of their popular backing. Many of those devoted to the monarchy left the celebrations disappointed and disgruntled.[62]

If the February events revealed the capital's loss of political charisma, the second part of the celebration taking place during May in the Volga region and Moscow, revealed the tsar in his own element. Following the route of Michael's journey from Kostroma to Moscow in the spring of 1613, Nicholas received an enthusiastic response. The Moscow celebrations, commemorating Michael's entry into the city, took place at the site of the events, and evoked thoughts of the past. A Russian observer wrote, "Places sanctified by centuries, the golden cupolas of the Kremlin, near which the imperial cortege stopped, the harmonious tolling of the Moscow bells and the triumphal meeting of the crowned Romanovs at the gates of the Assumption Cathedral amidst the glittering vestments of the clergy— everything gave special meaning to the celebration I saw and deepened the general impression."[63] In the Kremlin cathedrals and on the Red Porch, Nicholas again joined in the rituals and paid homage to the symbols of Muscovite autocracy. He visited the tombs of the early Romanovs. At their graves, and before the icons of the Mother-of-God, he sought the sources of his authority in the divine grace and popularity of the Muscovite tsars, rather than in the spirit of power and transformation that had animated Peter and his successors.

The acclaim of the population contrasted to the apathy of Petersburg. "The mass emotion this visit engendered was overwhelming," Bruce Lockhart recalled.[64] Some observers found the response less spontaneous than that along the Volga, but one thought it "deeper and stronger." It was a "wonderful hymn of mutual love," which showed that "not she, not the citizens of the white-stone city were guilty of the disorders of 1905." The receptions, balls, and dinners radiated a warm, cordial spirit. "There is good reason," he concluded, "for Moscow to be called the heart of Russia."[65]

Most important, Nicholas and Alexandra were impressed with reception they received during the May celebrations. They believed that the enthusiasm was genuine and that the Russian people persisted in their religious devotion to the throne. It confirmed that, despite the passage of time and the appearances of change, Russia remained attached to the political principles of three centuries before. Emboldened by such a vision, Nicholas contemplated and proposed a curtailment of the Duma's prerogatives, in effect an abrogation of the October Manifesto. But even the reactionary cabinet that he had appointed refused to consider such a step.[66]

Nicholas's final and perhaps most moving display of attachment to Moscow took place in the summer of 1914 as Russia was preparing to embark upon war. Both capitals gave the tsar fervent demonstrations of support. But the sense of the ceremonies, as well as the nature of the sentiments evoked, differed markedly. Nicholas's appearance in Petersburg at the Winter Palace on July 20 lasted a few hours. He arrived along the Neva and was rushed through the crowds to the palace. At the religious service, he repeated Alexander I's famous vow that he would not make peace as long as one of the enemy was on the soil of the fatherland. It was a highly formal occasion, limited to important officials, officers, and court ranks. After a priest read the manifesto, Nicholas addressed the assembled officers as "the whole army, united in nation and spirit, strong as a granite wall," and received a wild roar of approval. Then he and the empress went out onto the balcony to meet the crowds filling the vast palace square. The throng fell to their knees and sang the national anthem. The emperor crossed himself and wept.[67]

But the Petersburg ceremony, though stirring, was brief and fastidious. Nicholas visited the city, held a court ceremony, blessed the army, confronted the people. Then he returned to Tsarskoe Selo. In Moscow the visit was extended and the ceremonies were more inclusive. He entered the city on the traditional route along Tver' Boulevard, riding in an open carriage to popular acclaim. In the Kremlin Palace, he received not only high officials but representatives of the estates. He addressed not the army but the nation. "In your persons, the people of the first capital, Moscow, I greet the Russian people, loyal to me, I greet them everywhere, in the provinces, the State Duma, the State Council, unanimously responding, to rise amicably and cast aside discord for the defense of the native land and Slavdom."[68]

The scene of Nicholas bowing from the Red Porch to the frenzied crowd on the Kremlin Square impressed the foreign visitors with the power of Russian national sentiment. The English ambassador wrote that "the heart of Russia voiced the feelings of the whole nation." His daughter felt that she was no longer in the twentieth century. "This was the old Moscow of the Tsars. Little Mother Moscow, threatened and besieged over and over again, and yet always miraculously emerging from her smoking ruins!" The French ambassador also felt himself transported back beyond the eighteenth century and admired "the frantic enthusiasm of the Muscovite people for their Tsar." The tsarevich's tutor, Gilliard, thought that the people of Moscow were "so anxious to keep the tsar as long as possible that they mean to hold him here by manifest proofs of their affection."[69]

On the subsequent days, the tsar visited the shrines of Moscow, hospitals, and the stores of medical materials provided by the Merchant's Bureau and the zemstvo. He met the assembled mayors of major towns. Finally, he visited the Trinity Monastery, where he was blessed by the Miracle Icon of the Visitation of the Virgin, which had accompanied Russian campaigns since 1654.[70]

Nicholas returned from Moscow inspired by the fervor of the reception. He felt a new confidence and closeness to his people. He believed that the country had united behind him and submerged their political differences.[71] His vision confirmed, he was less likely than ever to bow to political compromise. But the quest for legitimacy in the religious culture of Muscovy could hardly bolster his political position. Nicholas remained the all-Russian emperor reigning over institutions centered in Petersburg. He remained a product of Petersburg culture who was most at ease in guards' uniform and among the elite regiments of the capital.

The two traditions coexisted, integrated neither in ideology nor in ceremony, epitomized in their chronotopes, two capitals, each impugning the symbolic appeal of the other. Petersburg, "the basic symbol" of imperial Russia, had lost the favor of the tsar, and with it, its aura of preeminence. Moscow radiated the charisma of the political heritage cherished by the tsar, but had no tsar. The very glorification of Moscow had insurgent implications, casting doubt on the institutions in Petersburg that governed the empire. Many leading officials felt Nicholas betraying the interests of state for mystical delusions that could be exploited by men like Rasputin.[72] Upholding values and pursuing goals at variance with those of his ruling elite, the tsar himself became a force for disorder in the final years of political crisis. His vision of the past precluded a unified effort by monarchists and conservatives to preserve the old regime, leaving the field to the opponents of autocracy.

In a monarchy, the locus of the monarch is the political center. In early twentieth-century Russia, there were two such loci, betraying the autocrat's own ambivalence about the heritage, nature, and goals of the state. If symbolic forms can confer the aura of the absolute and command reverence, then symbolic confusion can just as well dispel the sacred spirit that surrounds power for its loyal adherents. By 1914 not only did the autocracy face widespread and vocal political opposition. In the course of the previous decades, it had become increasingly ambiguous what exactly Russian autocracy signified.

Notes

1. V. Veidle, *Zadacha Rossii* (New York, 1956), p. 213.
2. Col. Paul Brunelli, "Moia letopis'," unpublished manuscript, Hoover Archive, p. 14.
3. Mikhail M. Shcherbatov, "Petition of the City of Moscow on Being Relegated to Oblivion," in Marc Raeff, ed., *Russian Intellectual History: An Anthology* (New York, 1966), p. 53.
4. Quoted in M. Perkal', *Gertsen v Peterburge* (Leningrad, 1971), p. 158.
5. Aleksandr Gertsen, *Byloe i dumy* (Moscow, 1962), 1:470; on the evolution of

the Petersburg myth in general, see N. Antsyferov, *Dusha Peterburga* (Petersburg, 1922); a recent analysis of the problem is Sidney Monas, "Petersburg and Moscow as Cultural Symbols," in Theophanis George Stavron, ed., *Art and Architecture in Nineteenth-Century Russia* (Bloomington, 1983), pp. 26–39.

6. Nicholas V. Riasanovsky, *Russia and the West in the Teaching of the Slavophiles* (Gloucester, Mass., 1965), p. 66.

7. A. I. Gertsen, *Sobranie sochinenii* (Moscow, 1954), 2:34.

8. See for example M. Pogodin, *Istoriko-kriticheskie otryvki* (Moscow, 1846), pp. 131–59; V. A. Zhukovskii, *Polnoe sobranie sochinenii* (St. Petersburg, 1902), 12:155.

9. N. P. Barsukov, *Zhizn' i trudy M. P. Pogodina*, vol. 10 (St. Petersburg, 1896), pp. 220–53.

10. Alexander II to Alexandra Fedorovna, April 20, 1857, Ts.G.A.O.R., 728-1-2496, p. 65; Alexander II to Olga Nikolaevna, October 8, 1861, Ts.G.A.O.R., 728-1-2612a, p. 4; Maria Aleksandrovna to Vladimir Aleksandrovich, November 16, 1871, Houghton Library, bMS Russian 26, p. 35.

11. Konstantin Leontiev, *Against the Current* (New York, 1969), pp. 208–9.

12. "Pis'mo Tsesarevicha Aleksandra Aleksandovicha k K.P. Pobedonostevy," in *Starina i Novizna* (St. Petersburg, 1902), 5:1.

13. Michael Walzer, *Regicide and Revolution* (Cambridge, Eng., 1974), pp. 5, 13–14, 35–42.

14. V. V. Voeikov, "Poslednie dni Imperatora Aleksandra II i votsarenie Imperatora Aleksandra III," *Izvestiia Tambovskoi Uchenoi Arkhivnoi Kommissii*, Vyp. 54 (Tambov, 1911), p. 102; F. A. Wellesley, *With the Russians in Peace and War* (London, 1905), pp. 90–91.

15. Charles Lowe, *Alexander III of Russia* (New York, 1895), p. 322.

16. S. Petrovskii, ed., *Pamiati Imperatora Aleksandra III* (Moscow, 1894), pp. 318–19.

17. Lowe, *Alexander III*, p. 330; Vera Galitzine, *Reminiscences d'une emigrée* (Paris, 1925), pp. 70–71.

18. B. V. Gerua, *Vospominaniia o moei zhizni* (Paris, 1969), 1:81.

19. A. Mosolov, *Pri dvore Imperatora* (Riga, n.d.), p. 16.

20. Carl Graf Moy, *Als Diplomat am Zarenhof* (Munich, 1971), p. 208.

21. Allan K. Wildman, *The End of the Russian Imperial Army: The Old Army and the Soldiers' Revolt (March–April 1917)* (Princeton, 1980), pp. 6–7; P. N. Krasnov, *Pavlony* (Paris, 1943), pp. 51–73.

22. Wellesley, *With the Russians*, pp. 32–33.

23. *Khram Voskresenie Khristova sooruzhennyi na meste smertel'nogo poraneniia v boze pochivshego Imperatora Aleksandra II na ekaterinskom kanale v S-Petersburge* (St. Petersburg, 1907), p. 2; Louis Réau, *Saint Petersburg* (Paris, 1913), pp. 67–68.

24. *Khram Voskresenie Khristova*, passim; Réau, *Saint Petersburg*, p. 68; Grigorii Moskvich, *Petrograd i ego okrestnosti* (Petrograd, 1915), p. 103.

25. K. Korol'kov, *Tsar'mirotvorets, Imperator Aleksandra III* (Kiev, 1904), pp. 57–60; *Niva*, 1901, no. 13, p. 259.

26. *Niva*, 1914, no. 5, p. 97; Alexandre Spiridovitch, *Les dernières années de la cour de Tsarskoe selo* (Paris, 1928–29), 2:253–62; "The Feodoroff Imperial Cathedral in Zarskoe Selo," typescript in New York Public Library, Slavonic Division, p. 135.

27. L. G. Zakharova, "Krizis samoderzhaviia nakanune revoliutsii 1905 goda," *Voprosy Istorii*, no. 8 (1978): 130–32; A. A. Polovtsov, "Dnevnik," *Krasnyi Arkhiv*, no. 3 (1923): 99–100; Alexandre Iswolsky, *Memoires* (Paris, 1923), pp. 271–72.

28. Zakharova, "Krizis," pp. 130–32; S. E. Kryzhanovskii, *Vospominaniia* (Berlin, n.d.), pp. 192–93, 206–8.

29. Grand Duchess Maria Georgievna, "Memoirs," manuscripts in personal collection of David Chavchavadze, pp. 129–32; V. N. Voeikov, *S tsarem i bez tsaria* (Helsinki, 1936), pp. 38–39.

30. Zakharova, "Krizis," p. 131; Maria Georgievna, *Memoires*, p. 132; V. N. Voeikov, *S tsarem*, p. 39; *Al'bom kostiumirovannogo v bala Zimnem Dvortse v fevrale 1903 g.* (St. Petersburg, 1904); Mosolov, *Pri dvore Imperatora*, p. 18.

31. P. A. Zaionchkovskii, *Krizis samoderzhaviia na rubezhe 1870–kh—1880kh godov* (Moscow, 1964), pp. 450–60.

32. *Vsemirnaia Illiustratsiia*, 1881, no. 656, p. 102.

33. Ibid.

34. V. V. Voeikov, "Poslednie," pp. 151–54.

35. *Opisanie sviashchennogo koronovaniia ikh Imperatorskikh Velichestv Gosudaria Imperatora Aleksandra III i Gosudaryni Imperatritsy Marii Fedorovny* (St. Petersburg, 1883), pp. 2–3.

36. Ibid., p. 27.

37. Lowe, *Alexander III*, pp. 70, 74–75; V. S. Krivenko, ed., *Koronatsionnyi sbornik* (St. Petersburg, 1899), p. 151.

38. E. Poselianin, *Iasnye dni; 17 oktiabria; 29 aprelia, 28 oktiabria* (Moscow, 1892), p. 18.

39. Lowe, *Alexander III*, pp. 247–49.

40. Petrovskii, *Pamiati*, pp. 86–88.

41. Ibid., pp. 88–89.

42. A. V. Bogdanovich, *Tri poslednikh samoderzhtsa* (Moscow-Petrograd, 1924), pp. 182–83.

43. Ibid.

44. F. Dukhovetskii, *Dve nedeli v Peterburge; Vospominaniia torzhestva pereneseniia i pogrebeniia tela Imperatora Aleksandra III i svetlogo dnia brakosochetaniia* (Moscow, 1894), pp. 6, 23–24, 60; Lowe, *Alexander III*, pp. 296–98.

45. Lowe, *Alexander III*, p. 301; Dukhovetskii, *Dve nedeli*, pp. 38–39.

46. Lowe, *Alexander III*, p. 300 n; Korol'kov, *Tsar' mirotvorets*, p. 57.

47. Petrovskii, *Alexander III*, p. 375.

48. *Tsarskoe prebyvanie v Moskve v aprele 1900 goda* (St. Petersburg, 1900), pp. 23–24.

49. Ibid., pp. 53–55.

50. Ibid., pp. 55–56.

51. Zakharova, "Krizis," p. 131; Edward J. Bing, ed., *The Secret Letters of the Last Tsar* (New York, 1938), p. 137.
52. *Moskovskie Vedomosti*, March 30, 1903, p. 1.
53. Ibid., *Moskovskie Vedomosti*, March 29, 1903, p. 1; April 1, 1903, pp. 2–3; *Russkii tsar' s tsaritseiu na poklonenii Moskovskim sviatyniam* (St.Petersburg, 1909), p. 25.
54. *Moskovskie Vedomosti*, April 1, 1903, pp. 2–3; *Russkii tsar'* . . . , p. 26.
55. *Moskovskie Vedomosti*, April 16, 1903, p. 1.
56. *Novoe Vremia*, April 18, 1903, p. 3.
57. V. N. Voeikov, *S tsarem*, p. 40; *Russian Court Memoirs, 1914–1916* (New York, n.d.), p. 41; Meriel Buchanan, *The Dissolution of an Empire* (London, 1932), pp. 27–29; Sergei Zavalishin, ed., *Gosudar' Imperator Nikolai II Aleksandrovich* (New York, 1968), pp. 229–30.
58. Spiridovitch, *Les dernières*, 2:230–31; R. H. Bruce Lockhart, *British Agent* (New York, 1933), p. 73; Bogdanovich, *Tri poslednikh samoderzhtsa*, p. 501.
59. Spiridovitch, *Les dernières*, 2:264–67; Bing, ed., *Secret Letters*, pp. 272–73; Lockhart, *British Agent*, p. 74.
60. These tendencies are the subject of my article in manuscript, "The Romanov Tercentenary of 1913 and the Historical Imagery of Russian Autocracy"; on chronotopes see Katerina Clark, "Political History and Literary Chronotope: Some Soviet Case Studies," in Gary Saul Morson, *Literature and History: Theoretical Problems and Russian Case Studies* (Stanford, forthcoming).
61. *Novoe Vremia*, February 23, 1913, p. 14; *Moskovskie Vedomosti*, February 24, 1913, p. 2.
62. Spiridovitch, *Les dernières*, 2:317; A. N. Naumov, *Iz utselevshikh vospominanii 1868–1917* (New York, 1955), 2:234.
63. Naumov, *Iz utselevshikh vospominanii*, 2:236–37.
64. R. H. Bruce Lockhart, "Preface," in Bing, ed., *Secret Letters*, p. 10.
65. E. E. Bogdanovich, *Istoricheskoe palomichestvo nashego tsaria v 1913 godu* (St. Petersburg, 1914), p. 163.
66. Geoffrey A. Hosking, *The Russian Constitutional Experiment* (Cambridge, Eng., 1973), pp. 201–2; A. Ia. Avrekh, *Tsarizm i IV Duma* (Moscow, 1981), pp. 114–15.
67. Maurice Paléologue, *An Ambassador's Memoirs* (New York, 1925), 1:50–52; *Novoe Vremia*, July 21, 1914, p. 4; Spiridovich, *Les dernières*, 2:482–83.
68. *Moskovskie Vedomosti*, August 6, 1914, pp. 1–2; V. N. Voeikov, *S tsarem*, pp. 104–5.
69. Sir George Buchanan, *My Mission to Russia* (Boston, 1923), 1:214–15; Meriel Buchanan, *Dissolution*, p. 103; Paléologue, *Memoirs*, 1:93, 95; Pierre Gilliard, *Thirteen Years at the Russian Court* (New York, 1970), p. 114.
70. *Moskovskie Vedomosti*, August 9, 1914, p. 2; V. N. Voeikov, *S tsarem*, p. 106.
71. Gilliard, *Thirteen Years*, p. 122.
72. See for example V. N. Kokovtsov, *Iz moego proshlogo* (Paris, 1933), 2:154–56, 170–72; Iswolsky, *Memoires*, pp. 284–98; Spiridovich, *Les dernières*, 2:356–57, 401–2.

PART FIVE

Symbolism, Politics, and Everyday Life: Colonial Virginia and Industrial Germany

9

RHYS ISAAC

Communication and Control: Authority Metaphors and Power Contests on Colonel Landon Carter's Virginia Plantation, 1752–1778

15. Saturday

Excessive hot day and no rain as yet. Such are the Seasons I have had to crop in ever since 1751, always on violent extremes. I can't but take notice of the death of my little Canary bird, an old housekeeper having had it here 11 year this month and constantly fed it with bread and milk, and I wish the heat of this weather did not by Souring its food occasion its death, for it sung prodigeously all the forepart of the day. At night it was taken with a barking noise and dyed the night following, vizt, last night. I know this is a thing to be laught at but a bruit or a bird so long under my care and protection deserves a Small remembrance.[1]

The matter-of-fact recording of harsh punishments is missing, but otherwise this entry serves well to illustrate the character and consistency of the text at the center of this study: its dramatic reporting of climate and crop prospects; its preoccupation with diet and the disorders of the body; its turning back on itself in time; and, above all, its defensiveness, justifying a laughably feminine lapse into sensibility by the invocation of the duties of patriarchal lordship—offsetting the sorrowing description of a dying bird with the idea of enduring, inclusive "care and protection."

This essay is about diverse ways of acting out conflicting conceptions of patriarchal and paternalist roles as envisaged and reported in the diary of a mid-eighteenth-century Virginian gentleman. Themes of power, ideology, and legitimation will be traced as they appeared in that plantation

275

society. Reversing the perspective of Filmer and Locke, the analysis will explore how conceptions of the government of the kingdom relate to ideas about the regulation of the household and the estate. The focus will be on perceptions of justice and the exercise of authority in the context of the family—an entity then considered to comprise both the master's kin at the great house and those who were his so-called slave dependents.

Questions about ways of imagining and acting out the role of the planter intersect with questions about both the patriarchal character of the Anglo-American plantation system, and the changing ethos of the family in Anglo-American society. Eugene Genovese's whole interpretation of the worlds the slaves and planters made is built around a conception of an ambiguous bargain between these two constituent classes in the plantations of the antebellum South.[2] For all his illuminating insights, however, the concept of paternalism that covers this framework of relationships is of uncertain application to any particular time and place, because of the wide-ranging eclecticism with which the sources are collated in its construction. Exploring the patterns of relationship on an actual plantation at a particular time should contribute toward a more historically located understanding. This is especially important because family life (an essential component of the patriarchal concept) was changing in profound ways during the two-and-a-half-century duration of chattel slavery on the North American continent. The dates of the diary used here, and the circumstances of the diarist, enable this to be at least a pilot study of the kinds of accommodation required in a plantation household whose master was exposed to cosmopolitan influences. Sensibilities were changing markedly in the upper ranks of English society through the eighteenth century. Lawrence Stone has proposed the term *affective individualism* as a key to understanding corresponding remodeled patterns of domesticity, and this essay is a single-instance study of changing sensibilities in the "family."[3]

Customs, rituals, symbols, ideologies, and forms of legitimation have a public aspect that calls for patient review and interpretation, but behind these lurks always the matter of power. This is probably the most mysterious and elusive aspect of social life, especially when the actual setting is the slave-based plantation. The study that follows will search, though it can never resolve, the enigma of how some people are forced to accept a very harsh and unequal distribution of valued goods. Central to systems of control, though by no means constituting the whole of them, are the definitions, the claims, and the enforcement methods of the ruling group. What follows is a set of soundings in the diary (1752–78) of Colonel Landon Carter of Sabine Hall, a slavemaster who was almost obsessed with law, reason, and justice. First to be examined are indications of the character of his law and his justice, and then the terms of his slaves' acceptance of it are explored. Lastly (as attention fastens on the metaphor of fatherhood), trends in familial values and associated control systems will be considered.

Law, Rule, and Reason

It was a winter's day at the meeting place of the General Assembly in Williamsburg, Thursday, February 27, 1752. Colonel Landon Carter was among the eighty-four newly elected burgesses who had already declared their character as Protestant Hanoverian Sons of Britain by taking "the Oaths . . . of Allegiance and Supremacy, and . . . the Oath of Abjuration" as well as subscribing "the Test." At the vice-regal command, they now constituted themselves as a House by choosing and presenting a speaker. Next, again by command, they attended at the Council Chamber, where the newly arrived lieutenant governor, Robert Dinwiddie, made the customary colonial equivalent of the speech from the throne. He referred to his royal commission, to his "Sense of the Importance of the Trust," and to his "Solicitude to discharge the same"; he assured the assemblymen that it would be his "Inclination and Endeavour, to cultivate . . . Virtues of a Social Nature"; he celebrated his "Affection" for the "Gentlemen" before him, recalling his former residence in Virginia, when he "had mingled in Scenes of domestic Felicity," experiencing "the endearing Reciprocations of Friendship." The House of Burgesses was urged to "consider what Bills may be . . . necessary, for promoting the public Quiet, . . . securing Property, . . . extending Commerce, establishing the Peace, Safety, and Regularity of an equitable and well order'd Government." In conclusion, addressing again the whole Assembly, he recommended to the gentlemen that they should, in their work, "diffuse a Spirit of Benevolence, and Unanimity, . . . the Vital Principles of public and private Happiness." By those means, he concluded: "you will deserve the paternal Affection of his Majesty; and . . . be intitled to the Favour of Almighty God, who, that we might consider each other as Brethren, has not disdain'd to be called the Father of us all."[4]

The lieutenant governor had offered a deliberately conventional view of a politics in accordance with the spirit of the age. The receptiveness of his audience is revealed by the reply in kind that Landon Carter carefully drafted for the Burgesses. The House gave "cordial Thanks" for his Honour's "affectionate Speech," declared themselves "truly sensible of his Majesty's Paternal Care"; and promised that, reassured by reflection on his Honour's "social Virtues," they would attend to such "Grievances, . . . Irregularities, and . . . Defects as shall appear to obstruct the Public Tranquility," hoping at the same time "to obtain . . . the Favour of that Omnipotent Being, who hath not disdained to be called the Father of us all."[5]

The exchange between governor and burgesses amply sounded and reechoed notes conveying the profound resonances between themes of power and ideology in the state and in the family. The ancient formula for authority—divine patriarchy—was still invoked, but already it had been transposed in a most revealing way. Although the lieutenant governor referred to "God" directly, he imagined Him in an abstract, distanced way, and stressed the divine "Spirit of Benevolence"—that is, he associated the deity with a humanitarian set of imperatives for social action. In case the point should be missed, His Excellency went on to explain that the divinity "has not disdained to be called the Father of us all," with the intention that human beings "might consider each other as Brethren." The signs of a two-way process of sentimentalization of conceptions of family roles and of images of authority will be later examined in more homely contexts than that constituted by a vice-regal address. For the moment attention is directed to the initiation of Colonel Landon Carter as a legislator, and to some significant features of his conceptions of law, reason, and government as revealed in his parliamentary diary. It is clear that this methodical, self-improving gentleman undertook the keeping of such a record largely in order to help him master the rules and procedures of the Assembly.

A complex attitude to law and custom is revealed in the diary. On the one hand he esteemed legal knowledge highly and had prepared himself thoroughly for this first session. He had studied manuals of parliamentary procedure so carefully that, in answer to a ruling from the Speaker on what was "a standing order of the House of Commons," he could confidently declare that "he never read [of] any such." Yet he was also resistant to legal formalities and to the lawyers who seemed to thrive by obscuring issues behind the technicalities of their calling. He perceived "the Lawyers" as a distinct group in the House who would tie the rest in knots if they were not contained. He took pride in answering them "close" and meeting the "distinctions made" upon his arguments, point for point.[6]

The squire's straightforward approach was immediately and continuously in evidence. In cases where the substance of authority could be sustained by a simple amendment of a return, made at the table by the clerk of the House, he spoke against the practice of ritually summoning before the bar those county sheriffs who had made informal election returns. He also opposed the ruling that "limitted the petitioners" against improper elections "to particulars in their Charges"; Landon wanted instead to give them "Liberty" to make use of all "the relevant evidence." He successfully protested against a "Crye for rejecting . . . as soon as read" a petition for a ferry that had been before a previous assembly. "I thought otherwise, vizt. that Public Conveniences ought always to be considered." His two most evident triumphs were speeches arguing forcefully that the common good should outweigh legal niceties. He proudly recorded that he urged this so forcefully in one instance that some of the lawyers "changed and Came Over." When a maze of uncertain procedural rules and customs seemed to stand in the way of sound judgment, he "answered All and declared against law obligatory on Parliaments[:] that Precedents and orders made were only demonstrations of what was done heretofore and no farther directory of what was to be done than as they came within the bounds of Good reason and Justice." At bottom he preferred a commonsense, each-case-on-its-own-merits position, as can be seen in his continuation of the last-quoted argument: "We could not be thought reflecting on the dignity of the house by Contradicting former orders[,] for every order was Governed by its own Circumstances, and unless the Journals had minuted every Circumstance" no man could properly "call it a Contradiction"—or, indeed, hold precedents binding.[7]

This tendency to favor ad hoc judgment was tightly restrained in Landon Carter's jurisprudence from lapse into mere arbitrariness. He had a very strong sense of rules and propriety. In a startling action for a newcomer, he made this strictness felt when, during his sixth day in the assembly, "on the Sitting of the House [he] moved that the Chair might admonish the members . . . that the rising and going out confusedly upon an adjournment was contrary to the Rules of Parliamentary decency." On another occasion he urged cutting through the procedural thicket of precedents, but concluded by arguing that "it was clear [that] . . . the Law had directed" what was to be done; and as long as that was so, "the law was the directory." Repeatedly he took his stand on the bedrock of *known rules*. It becomes clear in the course of a number of bitter contests that one of his main grounds for disliking lawyers was their penchant for making distinctions and finding ways to dissolve the solid certainties of the law when their own purposes might require it.[8]

The squire's sense of "Good reason and Justice" as applied to cases, and his insistence on law, rights, and rules of conduct, worked together to motivate a powerful and constantly renewed impulse to resist the development of concentrations of power within the public realm. (The pattern of value orientations manifest in Landon Carter's burgess journal is very much the one associated with what has been called the "Country ideology." But since party labels were abhorrent to this man, who esteemed independence and the light of reason above all, it is better to identify him merely with the broad Anglo-American tradition that celebrated the independence of the landowner, especially the gentleman. In this cluster of ideas we can see how conceptions of law and lawmaking were embedded in more continuous patterns of everyday life.) By the end of his first week in the House he had successfully prevented its standing Committee for Claims from assuming certain regulatory powers over expenses incurred in the counties; he jealously maintained the independent discretion of the local authorities, insisting that, "as the Courts do always Levy the same on the People they must be the best Judges whether the Charge was extravagant." His conception of government was indeed profoundly judicial, and he showed the same jealousy of the House's encroachment on the adjudicative work of its own committees. When Edmund Pendleton, one of "the Lawyers" and a manager of the burgesses, moved "that the Committee [for Privileges and Elections] might be instructed to proceed on Certain Bonds inserted in the Complaints," Landon "opposed . . . alledging it was a mere simple Rule in the Power of the Committee," and that he was "not for having the Committee in those things Circumscribed, for that would be making it Appear ridiculous." He gave the managers a little homily on judicial correctness and the impropriety of prejudging from "Supposition"—the argument that time would be saved was all very well "in the mouths of Gentlemen who Accustomed themselves to read only one side of the Question," but judicially it was indefensible. To his great satisfaction, the diarist felt able to record that "Mr. Attorney and the other Lawyers chewed the Expression over and endeavoured to return it, but they could not."[9]

In sum, Landon Carter had a view of law and authority that was magisterial. Furthermore, the content of his notions of government derived, as might be expected, very much from his own long experience—shared with the great majority of his fellow burgesses—as a justice of the peace. He had a liking for law as certain rule (rather than intricate technicality), and this was coupled, almost paradoxically with a readiness to judge cases according to circumstances.[10] But there was a different context in which Colonel Landon Carter, his fellow burgesses, and many of the voters in the counties they represented, acted simultaneously as lawmakers and judges. The focus of this essay, like that of the diary on which it is based, now shifts from the provincial legislature to the plantation domain of which the diarist was the ruler.

Sabine Hall and Plantation Justice

Neither a detailed map of Landon Carter's domains nor a tabulation of the demography of his dependents can be presented here. What follows immediately is a sketch, adequate for present purposes, to indicate the social setting of the episodes that are to be presented and commented on in the remainder of the paper.

The master of Sabine Hall was a widower in his forties when the first of the surviving fragments of his diaries was inscribed. With interruptions, the record continues from that time until a few months before his death in December 1778, when he was sixty-eight. Living in the Hall with him were his youngest daughters, Judith and Lucy, and his eldest son, Robert Wormeley Carter, alias "Robin," who was, in the colonel's own phrase, "heir-apparent" to this family seat. In an unusual arrangement, the son had with him a family of his own—his wife, Elizabeth Beale Carter, and four children, Landon Jr., George, Lucy, and "baby Fanny." The old man believed that his daughter-in-law constantly encouraged his son to defy him, and that their children were being ruined by indulgence and the denial of his right, as head of household, to discipline them.

Also resident at the Hall were an Anglo-Virginian staff that included a clerk-accountant, a housekeeper, and an apprentice estate-manager, Billy Beale who, as he learned the business, acted as an "overlooker" of all the operations. Close under the master's eye were a home-quarter overseer and a slave staff of more or less responsible aides—Nassau, the master's attendant and surgeon; Toney; Talbot; Johnny the Gardner; their wives, offspring, and others. Surrounding the Hall at varying distances were the Home, the Mangorike, and Fork Quarters—small Afro-Virginian settlements from which (with much sending of workers to and fro as needed) the fields belonging to each were cultivated. The Home and Mangorike quarters had white overseers; the Fork was under a black "foreman." In all, it seems that the number of mature men and women workers was somewhere between 40 and 50, indicating a slave population approaching 100 in the neighborhood of Sabine Hall. Beyond that there were some seven distant quarters operated under quasi-lease arrangements, with which this essay is not concerned. The able-bodied workers among the slaves were kept engaged in tilling the soil incessantly; they plowed it, hoed it, and dunged it, in order to keep it in production. On the 350 or so cleared acres, Landon would raise some 280,000 tobacco plants and 300,000 corn plants, each in its hoed-up hill. He also sowed more than 150 acres of wheat, oats, peas, beans, and barley. The plowing, hauling, and manuring all made the estate's herd of cattle a vital resource, a matter for the master's most anxious concern.

This plantation certainly had its "court" and its "magistrate." The "law," however, could only be made known in the course of continuous struggles between slaves who were attempting to secure (or extend) their "rights" and the master attempting to assert his will. The configurations and their ambiguities may be sensed in the following episode:

Yesterday Gri. Garland by Letter made a complaint against Rob. Carter's Weaver who he had catched at his house; he had constantly lost his fowls and was at last told of this man's going there to his woman and though he could not prove it, did suspect that William and his wench must be concerned about it, and he only desired the man might be corrected for it. As a magistrate I ordered him as Constable to give him 25 lashes and send him home. This morning by accident I ask after this man and was told he was sick. I ordered him to come to see me; he came out and there in a most violent passion swore he would not be served so by me or by anybody for he daresay I was glad to have people murdered. I ordered him to be tied. He rushed in, bolted his door, and as the people were breaking in to him he broke out of the window and run off. I sent after him and rode about; when I came in he was at my door; and there before John Selfe [the overseer] told me I was not his master and his master would not have let him be served so, nay, that I would not dare to have done it, on which I gave him a stroke with my switch and he roared like a bull, and went on with his tongue as impudent as Possible so much as J. Selfe told him he ought to be made to hold his tongue. I then had him carried to a tree, and at last he humbled himself; but I fancy it was only the fear of another whipping, but he only got three cuts and was forgiven for this once.[11]

The indignant slave first assailed Landon Carter's human decency, declaring him to be one who "was glad to have people murdered," and then, in the second confrontation, he challenged the legality of the colonel's exercise of a master's jurisdiction over him, he being the slave not of the old man but of the son and heir.

One can see more deeply into the negotiation processes that constituted plantation law, in an earlier diary entry where no disputed jurisdiction was involved:

[April] 25. Friday. . . . My man Bart came in this day. He has been gone ever since New year's day. His reason is only that I had ordered him a whipping for saying he then brought in two load of wood. . . . This he still insists on was the truth. Although the whole plantation asserts the contrary, and the boy with him. He is the most incorrigeable villain I believe alive, and has deserved hanging, which I will get done if his mate in roguery can be tempted to turn evidence against him. Bart broke open the house in which he was tyed and locked up; he got out before 2 o'clock but not discovered till night. Talbot is a rogue. He was put in charge of him. I do imagine the gardiner's boy Sam, a rogue I have suspected to have maintained Bart and Simon [another runaway] all the while they have been out.[12]

The development of this episode arose from a proferred exchange, which was at first accepted but which shortly after met with violent hostility in return. Bart's initial "gift" lay in an artful assigning to his master, Landon Carter, of the estimable role of fair judge in appeal. We can readily see how the primary form and meaning of the encounter were shaped by this opening move. Bart evidently "came in" of his own accord, went directly before the master, and initiated a rehearing of charges made against him nearly five months before. He insisted that the defense he then offered "was the truth." Wherever this approach actually took place, Bart's opening, by casting Landon Carter as judge and himself as appellant against wrongful conviction and unjust sentence, traced in the circle of the developing interaction a metaphor of the courtroom. The master could have instantly disallowed the judicial metaphor by ordering the runaway seized and whipped. Indeed, had he done so he would only have been insisting on the carrying out of his own earlier orders. Landon Carter's immediate response, however, further filled out the proposed metaphor by calling witnesses (or by recalling their former testimony). A retrial appeared to be granted. Clearly, Bart's intention was that his innocence should be formally established by the process, the sentence against him quashed, and these circumstances allowed in extenuation of his four-and-a-half-month withdrawal of labor and obedience.

Despite the fact, however, that the master's initial response implied acceptance of Bart's definition as a point of departure for proceedings, things did not turn out as the returned runaway had designed. Bart was apparently isolated by Landon Carter's lineup of witnesses, who testified against him—whether under duress or not we cannot tell. Furthermore, the master was judge in his own cause—such is the nature of slavery—and so the encounter was terminated when Landon Carter, angered at the slave's refusal to yield to his overbearing insistence, gave Bart as prisoner into Talbot's charge, to be "tyed and locked up," himself turning to enter a vengeful judgment in his diary-cum-court-record.

The master's anger is instructive in a number of ways. We may see in it the manner in which power and meaning jangle together in the clashes of this dramatic interaction. Bart's definition of the situation constituted a power play, creating the forms of action we have seen. He might, of course, have opened with a feigned or real confession, with contrition, and with a plea for mercy. Yet even under pressure the slave refused to switch to such a groveling line, though the master evidently urged it upon him by the way he handled the citation of the witnesses. In his course of action Bart was not only adhering to his own initial definition (a man on trial may persist in asserting his innocence), but also he was laying claim to independent social personality, itself a form of power. This last particularly provoked the master's wrath, in turn revealing clearly how he had come to redefine the situation. The sequel showed that he was right to feel threatened. His will in the matter and his animosity to the prisoner were clear to all, yet, although the fact that Bart "broke open the house in which he was tyed and locked up" was known "before 2 o'clock," it was "not discovered [i.e., reported to the master] till night." We must assume that Bart's escape was connived at, if not actively assisted, by those who knew when it occurred. Landon Carter, then, had overbid his hand in this power play. The runaway had come in freely and proferred his master a worthy role as judge, with the opportunity to make a dignified retreat. Bart had, however, received in return a forced demonstration of his social isolation; he was given rough treatment and dark threats of worse to come. Yet Bart was indeed a "person"; he was not isolated, but rather endowed with manifest social power. He had no need to submit to the crushing of his social personality for his influence was such that he could not be held a prisoner in the close little world of Sabine Hall when it became clear that his offer of terms was not to be accepted. Bart was able to step once more outside the metaphoric framework of "plantation law," which he himself had evoked, and resume the life of an outlaw, free-booting in the woods.

In Bart's powers as a person (including his ability to open granaries and stores to supply extras to a needy people) lay the roots of Landon Carter's humiliation. In the end the whole neighborhood came to know how outlawed runaways had been concealed in the colonel's kitchen vault while his militia (i.e., poorer neighbors called from their crops) were out hunting for them.

The master's imprudent anger is further significant in another way. Taken in conjunction with a great deal we know about the self-defeating anger to which Landon Carter was prone (with his close kin, as well as with his slaves), it suggests that the meaning of the encounter with Bart is not adequately rendered if it is taken simply as a retrial upon appeal, followed by judicial confirmation of sentence, imprisonment, and escape. The strong emotion evident in the master's entry concerning the hearing was properly incompatible with the role of stern judge that was implicit in the definition of the situation as he first accepted it. Tracing the course of the encounter, we see how rapidly Landon Carter was moved implicitly to redefine the action. In place of the courthouse metaphor with which Bart had opened, he began passionately to act out another, that of the outraged "father" whose will must prevail in the settlement of disputes within his household.

The episodes involving William the weaver and Bart the wood hauler may be profitably compared in the context of the simultaneously operating judicial and patriarchal metaphors. In the first-named of these, the man on trial, William, when threatened with a flogging on an already flayed back, submitted and was "forgiven." Bart's case was more explicitly a forensic affair, with the slave setting up Landon as judge, where William denied him that or any legitimate role. Most revealing, however, was the demand of Landon Carter, as the master in both these episodes, that allusions to courts of law through claims to rights be abandoned and replaced by acceptance of sovereign power. The inducement offered, of course, was the possibility of clemency once a show of submission had been made. Patriarchy, even for a man like Colonel Carter who identified so strongly with the role of a judge in law, was ultimately a matter of will first and the grace of mercy afterward. For this he paid a price. The slaves' sense of both the form and substance of right is clear enough. William, and others in his position, submitted to power only for the moment. Clearly one of the major causes of "running away"—the withdrawal of labor—was an outraged sense of justice denied.[13]

Conflicting images of rightful authority and clashing definitions of the situation might be resolved by the display of the master's power, as in

William's ordeal, or by a demonstration of his powerlessness, as in the triumph of Bart; these are dramatic indications of disjunctions and contrarieties in the control system of the plantation. But there were also the "revelations" that are so much a feature of the diary. Frequently, matters assumed by the diarist to be on a certain footing turn out in time to be far otherwise. The structure of the community made for a turbulent flow of information. This was amplified by the cultural gulf between the master and his "people" at the quarters, and was added to by the complex alliance and support systems they sustained. It was compounded by the master's own way (already noticed) of conducting "hearings." But a breakdown-of-communications model of plantation organization will not do. There had to be an implicit bargain securing a measure of "acceptance" from the slaves and imposing obligations on the master.

The slaves knew they had to be given "care and protection." The master was obsessed with this, as can be seen in his constant anxiety over the corn crop that provided the staple diet of the people at the rate of one peck per adult per week. "God be merciful or we perish for bread." One might see this in terms of profit accounting—what he did not grow he must buy—and surely that was part of his concern, but ultimately he had a more inclusive outlook, an intense identification with the endeavors of the community he directed. Consider this rare but revealing expression of a momentary sense of well-being: "5. *Saturday*. A heavenly day, Such is the great goodness and Mercy of God to give a prospect of food and raiment to the labours of mankind." Landon was likewise deeply involved with matters of health, and preoccupied with his role as healer. Sickness and medicine too were channels of communication and control. One familiar aspect can be seen in the "sickness" of William the weaver, by which he brought his case before the master, but there is much, much more. The slaves often came to Landon Carter for treatment, and when sickness persisted beyond his applications of the violent remedies of the day, they expected him to summon the doctor for more. Even when he doubted the practitioner's capabilities, he would comply "because it is the duty of a Master." His sense of the cumulative weight of all such obligations pressing upon him gave rise to utterances that are striking epitomes of the notion of the white man's burden, both in the plaintive tone and the inversion of the truth: "Although I have many to work and fine land to be tended, I hardly make more than what cloaths them, finds them tools and pays their Levies. Perhaps a few scrawney hogs may be got in the year to be fattened up here. If these things do not require the greatest caution and frugality in living I am certain nothing can do."[14]

The slaves showed by their actions that they saw matters in a very different light. Their "acceptance" of the bargain upon which the system necessarily rested did not amount to passivity, any more than the deference exacted from them meant that they defined themselves as their "superiors" did. The plantation organization was a framework—are not all social arrangements?—within which a struggle for advantage was relentlessly pursued.

The diary in part resembles the annals of a guerrilla war. Landon Carter was forever learning of raids and depradations. Some were easy pickings: "There never were such thieves on my Plantation before. Not a melon of any kind can be kept"; or, a little more doubtful: "A young bull killed one steer and lamed another yesterday. The people, it seems, eat the Steer. I wish it may Not be a contrivance"; but mostly it was an intermittent siege of storehouses that no amount of vigilance seemed able to protect. Careful accounting governed the process, monitoring the stocks of corn and the issue of standard rations. In this and other respects the diary is not only a record of communications and controls but was a part of the control system itself. But always subsequent checks revealed unaccountable deficiencies and provoked outbursts that only expressed the limits of the master's power. After more daring robberies it might be found that a cornhouse had actually been broken into by a runaway such as Bart. More commonly, ways of borrowing the keys seemed to be found.[15]

Once, when the colonel was having his well cleaned out, he found himself reviewing a little archaeology of villainy. The recovered artifacts pointed to a covert subeconomy on the plantation. The diarist already knew enough of it to interpret the signs with perfect confidence:

Abundance of trash, mud and things tumbled and thrown in, Particularly a Plow gardiner Johnny stole 3 years ago and offered to sell that and another to Robin Smith, who, being a Penitant, Advised him to go and Put it where it might be found; but Johnny being suspected got whipped for them and threw them both into the Well as he told Robin Smith. I fished and got up one, but the other could not get till now.

Found also the 2 bows of a pair of handcuffs, but the bolt we could not find. Joe had been Ironed in them and got his little brother Abraham to swear he saw black Peter take them, and carry them behind the Kitching; but the rascal threw them into the well, and I do suppose sold the bolt. A good whipping both Joe and Johnny shall have and Abraham for lying tomorrow.

The master knew the acquisition of liquor from a neighboring small planter, Robert Smith, to be the motivation behind these bolder depradations. There was, clear to his view, a fatal nexus in all this. Landon Carter lived too early even to have the opportunity to apply the later English saying for intoxication—"the quickest way out of Manchester"—and there is no indication that he ever considered whether getting drunk might not have been the readiest escape for slaves. Perhaps, for different reasons, we should also be wary of such an interpretation. Beyond sour comments that he would not keep plowhorses because the slaves ride them about at night, the diarist revealed nothing about occasions at the quarters—about the forms of celebration there, to which drinking was no doubt an essential accompaniment. Liquor and the theft needed to acquire it were integral to the life of the plantation community. The meanings for the Afro-Virginian slaves remain obscure; for Landon Carter (and no doubt for all of his kind) these were important confirmatory signs of the incapacity of the slaves and so of the legitimacy of slavery and the power of the master that it entailed. "I never rightly saw into the assertion that negroes are honest only [even?] from a religious Principle. Johnny is the most constant churchgoer I have; but he is a drunkard, and a thief and a rogue. They are only [honest] through Sobriety, and but few of them."[16]

Another means readily available to the slaves for adjusting the "bargain"—for carrying on their struggle for advantage—was their effective control of work input. "I have always observed it when any work is in a hurry you will have abundance of lazy fellows unwilling to go about it." For instance, at the time of the very arduous hanging of the crop to cure in the tall tobacco houses: "I commonly see if people can't be sick to lay up with the rest, they find out a way of disabling themselves."[17] The master, of course, would take reprisals, so that "whippings" to make slaves "pay" for their neglect were routine. (These were usually imposed in "judicial" fashion, in the form of a sentence to be "executed" the next day. Sometimes the wording suggests faintly some sort of hearing or trial.) The "bargain" within which withholding and penalties occurred was an extremely harsh one to our view, as can be seen by this set of rules spelling out the master's expectations and his manner of enforcement:

I discovered this day what I never knew before, nay what I had positively forbid years ago, but negroes have the impudence of the devil. Last year the suckling wenches told the overseers that I allowed them to go in five times about that business; for which I had some of them whipt and reduced it to half an hour before they went to work, half an hour before their breakfast; and half an hour before they go in at night. And Now they have made the simpletons believe I allow them to eat their morning's bit. So that a wench goes out to bake for that, then they must have time to eat it, then another bakes for their breakfast. But these things I have forbid upon their Peril.[18]

Even with, or perhaps because of, such harsh imposition, the cultural norms of the larger society—the work styles and rhythms of the slaves and the Anglo-Virginian common planters—set limits to what could be exacted. A master such as Landon Carter had to depend for supervision on overseers who seemed to have little more interest in maximizing production than the slaves. A constant conflict over ways of working was set up by the same compulsive diligence that is expressed in the diary itself. This conflict was greatly intensified by the squire's commitment to experimental agriculture after the manner of Jethro Tull—"farming" he called it, in contradistinction to "planting." The "diary" is indeed a conglomerate of genres, but the bulk of it is a farmbook of the kind needed for the application of natural philosophy to husbandry. In this respect the diary was itself again a powerful instrument of control. In an early approximation to time and motion procedures Carter would count and measure work performances and try to make the hands keep at the top of their capabilities, or at least—"by my book"—to refute their assertions. "I thought I should catch Manuel; he pretends the river field was as much work again this year as it was last year [that is, twice as much], but I told him it was bare 2 rows and 1/3 more."[19]

The interpretation of Southern slaveowners as profit-maximizing exponents of work discipline thus finds a case in point in Landon Carter, but not much *general* support. It is very clear from the singularity of the diary itself, and from its internal evidence, that Landon Carter was at odds with his fellows. As Professor Jack P. Greene has powerfully demonstrated, he was a man who had formed his values and style in a self-disciplined rejection of the "easiness" he observed everywhere around him.[20] Full-blown patriarchalism, embodying more intimacy and sharing of values between ruler and ruled, would probably have manifested itself in less measuring and driving, and a more relaxed acceptance of the pace and work habits of the "family" of workers. Even Landon Carter, however, showed an ultimate resignation to the ways of his "people." Bonds of patriarchy constrained him despite his struggles to be free of them. This was apparent in the sense of the weight of responsibility already noted. It appeared also in the occasional largesses: "[April] 26. Thursday . . . Tomorrow, please God, every bit of my cornfield fences shall be compleatly righted. On Saturday the people shall have a holiday to draw the Seine . . . or what they please"—or a feast: "Killed a beef this day for my negroes." Perhaps his pride of patriarchy was boosted by the note that the beast was "honestly worth £5," but having noted the cost, he could not help assessing the benefit (or lack of it) two days later: "I see clearly that the giving this beef this year will be of full as bad consequence as it had been [in] years before;

for I did not observe one hand imployed in the pea Patch with any show of diligence."²¹

The master too was bound in to the system—as is clearly shown by his continuance of a custom he considered to be of "bad consequence." His entrapment is even more apparent in his repeated judgments against, and his continued employment of Manuel, his plowman-teamster. There are many entries and only a selection can be given. Behind Landon Carter's very explicit condemnatory typification of Manuel, one must seek to discern his typification of himself—of himself as revealed in his descriptions of his own dealings. Early (July 28, 1758) we get an indication of the master's dependence on the man: "My oats only finished getting in this day. Manuel's leg broken and the Election had made it late." Intimations of a complaint that will become a tirade appear in 1766 (the same year we learn that Manuel was a grandfather): "I find that it is not so much the obstinacy of my steers that won't break to drawing kindly[,] as the Villany of Manuel concerned."²² Between this entry and 1770, only a few pages of diary survive to cover the spring months. It was then that the heavy work demanded from oxen, weak from the winter, rendered the care of these valuable creatures a matter of critical importance. In the cold, wet March of 1770 we find reckonings preparing against Manuel:

9 Friday . . . .

The cattle that have died this year are 8 in Lawson's penn, 5 in Dolmon's, and 2 steers killed in the same place by Mr. Manuel and the Boy Kit. They were ordered to drive them to the fork to be raised where they had plenty of food and they drove them through the same marsh in the Corn field where each mired and died. When people can do this notwithstanding they have a plain level main road to be sure correction can never be called severity.

14. Wednesday

This weather that threatened us ever since the last good day came on in the night with hail rain and wind so that our old fields are as much afloat as ever they were and I do suppose such a violent check to the poor Cattle that were just beginning to lick themselves and grow chearful as it were upon the juices of the buds that I almost dread to hear of more deaths amongst them. And to mend the matter one of my draught Oxen well fed this whole winter with Corn, Pea vines, Rye straw, spelt straw, and wheat straw, the night before last broke his neck intirely by Manuel's carelessness. He fed the Creature and then turned him out of the Cowyard and I suppose going naturally in search of grass it stepped into the ditch or gully and so broke his neck. This is the third draught Steer put to a violent death by that cursed villain. The two former for the sake of a short cut in stead of being drove along the road to the fork where they were ordered to be taken care of. They were drove first one over the marsh where it mired and died. My orders were to whip that boy severely for it but this did not deter Manuel for above a month afterwards, the other steer being ordered to the Fork for the purpose of a plenty of food, he drove him over the same marsh where he mired and died. Certainly for these things no justice can be done without a most severe correction.

On Tuesday, March 27, the charge sheet was added to as the record of this plantation "trial" shows:

Ball yesterday found some shelled Corn as well as eared Corn in Manuel's quarter with one of my bags. Thus has that rascal made good my suspicion either of not giving all the Corn he was allowed to the Oxen he drove to the horses or else [he] has robbed me of [such] Corn as he brought from Mangorike. I have contrived that he shall not fail of a good whipping. He pretends the bag Bart brought to him and he found the Corn amongst the shucks in the Tobacco house but this is a presumptive lie. I thought it to be impossible that those Creatures should look so poor when they had all along been so well fed.

On Thursday, April 26, the explosion came:

Mr. Manuel has at last compleated every scheme that he might have in hand to ruin me. Before this winter came in I was possessed of 8 oxen, 4 of them well used to the draft and 4 newly broke. In a little time he contrived that 3 of them should mire and die only because he would not see 4 of them when spelled drove to the fork to be rested along the road over the dam but suffered a rascally boy to drive them over the marsh where they mired. The other he contrived to lame. I constantly allowed 2 bushels of ears besides fodder to feed those 4 that were worked every day they did work and I am certain from the honesty of Ball [the overseer] they had this food. But now, as they were but 4 to work, two horses were allowed to go before them that I might spell them two and two. For my horses I constantly gave half a bushel of shelled Corn every day they worked. In a little time Manuel consigned two of those horses to death and so he has continued behaving till last week when I wanted to Cart out my dung I had neither horses nor Oxen to carry a loa[d]. He proposed breaking 2 more. I gave him leave on Friday. Now although his wife was the Cowkeeper he never troubled himself to direct her to keep them up in the penn and on Saturday morning came so late from his night revellings they were turned out. He took me two hands half the day but could not get them up. On monday with the same two hands and another he yoked a pair and was

tuesday, and wednesday all day walking them about as he pretended and this day
he turned one of them out. It did nothing but lie down and when I saw the other in
a yoke with one of the old Oxen, that creature he pretended was so sullen, it would
not draw. This is too much to bear. However I kept my temper and resolved to sell
Mr. Manuel. He was once a valuable fellow, the best plowman and mower I ever
saw. But like the breed of him he took to drinking and whoring till at last he was
obliged to steal and robbed my store of near half the shirts and shifts for my people
besides other things. For this I prosecuted him and got him pardoned with a halter
round his neck at the gallows. For a while it had some good effect but returning to
his night walking he turned thief as before killed beef which was found upon him
but no proof of the property to be had. He again escaped. Since then by means of
the same practices he has killed me 20 or 30 horses and as many draught oxen. He
sleeps now [not?] at night and must do it in the day and to make up his work by
one barbarity or another he has as certainly killed these Creatures as ever he has
been concerned with them and now I will part with him.[23]

This rich narrative, its plot, characterization, and retrospections, all require close study that cannot be given here. At this point it is necessary
merely to underscore the customary commitment to this old slave that is
implicit in the passion with which Landon argues to himself that they
must be parted—and which becomes explicit when we find Manuel at
work on May 25, in charge of a resuscitated team, carting dung as usual,
or satisfying his master on June 19, that he "shall go on much faster [with
the plowing] now having got his Oxen into a better way of turning." The
strength of the connection is only further demonstrated by a petulant
entry for July 11 (again in the language of the court order) that Manuel has
not lived up to his promises "to be done [in] the River side field. . . .
Therefore my long taken resolution shall shortly be put in Execution."
Again the sequel shows that Manuel plowed on. The very next day the
master played that trick, catching Manuel out by quoting the diary against
him. In the continued plowing and the "game" we see the squire's continuing relationship with the man who exasperated him so. In the spring of
1771 (February 25) a familiar pattern recurred: "It seems another of Manuel's oxen has died at the Fork [Quarter,] which makes three that have
died. And I do suppose all for want of care, this is so great a rascal." But
still he was kept on, to be whipped in 1773, it being presumed that he
"broke open the door" to let out his daughter—who had earlier run away
in protest at a punishment Landon had ordered.[24] And so, we may assume, it would have gone on, a troubled series of manifestations of power
and obligation in the painful yet enduring patriarch-dominated plantation
community. (In the event, History intervened. It was Manuel who broke

the tie, running away to Lord Dunmore in 1776. Having put himself out from under Landon's protection, he may indeed have been sold away to Carolina as the diary entry resolved he should be.)[25]

Patriarchy and Fatherhood

Ancient configurations of lordship—cycles of command, duty, transgression, and chastisement—appear in the long relationship with Manuel. At many points in the diary, however, Landon Carter's extensive self-explanations and justifications give insights into what may be distinctive new patterns. The actual content of the patriarchal metaphor in any time and place must ultimately be related to fatherhood, as then and there imagined, perceived, and practiced.

Landon Carter's diary certainly contains very troubled explorations of the requirements of the paternal role. Monday's reflections on some of the occurrences of Sunday, September 10, 1775, reveal a great deal. First, the squire of Sabine Hall reviewed the climate and the current "heat of bilious complaints" and "the Numbers that are laid up." The only person with the skills to assist the master's "endeavours after humanity" was his slave surgeon, Nassau, "who has not been sensibly sober one evening since this day fortnight" (for which no diary entry survives). Then the diarist was led to trace a narrative of this slave's outrageous delinquency in the life-and-death errand on which he was sent, going on to record Nassau's defiance and his ultimate submission. The episode seems to be concluded when the master bestowed on the unworthy slave a forgiving "father's" pardon, "out of humanity, religion, and every virtuous duty," but it is evident that there was a complicating sequel. Landon had been exercised during these two days by other stirrings of his paternal feelings. His troubled state arose from an encounter early on the previous day with one of his daughters. Judith had eloped with Reuben Beale (brother of Landon's son's wife), after her father "wrote to her . . . to bid her never see [him], if she is ever to go into the way of her Amorato." Now, on the same day as he detailed his dealings with Nassau, Landon reported that:

Yesterday I walked up to my daughter Judith in the church, though I at the door, to ask her how she did and she hardly took notice of me. At Night, I received a letter from her which from one of less sense might be overlooked, but from her it carried all the Airs of a Species of revenge because I would not take her offending husband into favour. My son who cannot get [yet?] help Piping to his wife's affections, endeavoured much to get this unaccountable man [Reuben Beale] restored, Pretending more contrition in him that I dare say he will ever shew on the occasion[,] . . . Robin [Landon's son] would have had a mild tender answer written. But I [wrote to] put her in mind of her behaviour and in answer said that, although it would be condescending to her [un]dutifull [behavior] and set a bad example to disobedient Children, Yet she and her husband might come where they pleased and stay as long as [they] would at S[abine] Hall, only declaring I would accommodate myself to such a trial if possible. Thus my God have I suffered myself to destroy thy divine order in governing this world; but thy religion is not only full of forgiveness but of the Social Virtue of forgetting injuries, though against the texture with which thou has made man and all for that grand and adorable end of a truely Social Virtue. We are thy imperfect beings in points of right and wrong; but I beseech thee let this not be imputed to me as a crime. I have laboured and can only justify myself by the means of the word possibly imperfectly conceived by me. And, if it is not too offensive to thy Justice in Mercy, save us all.

During the disciplining of Nassau, Landon had spoken of a God implacably wrathful toward those who despised His Holy Word. Now he agonized whether he was not bound by that same Word to be as implacable toward those who persisted in disobedience against a father's God-given authority. He partially resolved this dilemma by reflecting (as he had done in Nassau's case) on the divinely taught qualities of "Mercy" and "forgiveness." This solution drew, of course, on deep Christian traditions that counterposed penitence and redemption to transgression and punishment. But the language in the diary entry has strong traces of more complex meanings not so long established in Christian doctrine. The double narrative of the entry for Monday, September 11, had begun with the diarist preoccupied with his "endeavours after humanity," and it came to crucial turning points not simply in the discourse of traditional Christian orthodoxy, but indeed by a declaration that he acted "out of humanity" (in the case of Nassau), and with a twice-stated explanation that he was concerned for "Social Virtue" (in the justification of his concession to his daughter and son-in-law). He had ventured uneasily to overturn the divinely required enforcement of patriarchal authority "in governing this world" for the sake of an aspiration for benevolent human order that he hoped was also sanctioned by the doctrine of forgiveness as conveyed in the Word.[26]

Landon was explicit in equating "Principles of order and society" with "duty to Parents . . . within the scripture rule," and in projecting the patriarchal regime into the cosmic realm so as to receive it back legitimated as divine law. "How can you love God," he once imagined himself asking his defiant son, "whom you have not seen, and despise Parents who you have seen?"[27] But while this form of legitimation remained important, there were contrary tendencies within this father's conception of authority in the family—contrary to the extent that following one rather than the other might be "imputed . . . as a crime." There was command, with inexorable punishment for the disobedient; and there was the tenderness that reaches out to appeal to the affections.

We may see a little further into this complex by reviewing yet other episodes in the Sabine Hall "family." Landon Carter had a grandson of the same name. He was born in 1757, eldest son of the colonel's eldest son, Robert Wormeley Carter, and Elizabeth Beale Carter, both of whom lived with him at Sabine Hall. The record of their lives together is interspersed with recurrent quarrels. One only is selected for comment:

I made it my business out of duty to talk to this Grandson and namesake, and set before him the unhappiness he must throw everybody into as well as himself, for he must be dispised by all his relations. At first he endeavoured to avoid me, and went away. I bid him come back; he pretended to be affraid that I wanted to scold at him. I told him no, it was my concern that made me earnest to advise him to imploy his good sence which god had blessed him with, and not to sacrifice that to a temper which must in the end make him miserable. At last he seemed to listen, and indeed shed tears at what I said. I hope in God then he will learn to behave better.[28]

How to interpret this? Much of it falls within the expected patriarchal framework—the "duty" undertaken, the appeal to honor lest this heir of the squire's heir "be dispised by all his relations"—even the "tears" of repentance. Yet there are many signs that reinforcement of traditional forms of familial authority is not what this record is most about. First, it can be discerned that this conversation was not an "audience" with the master of the Hall. The fourteen-year-old boy had not come obediently in answer to a summons, but rather the old man had had to go out of his way and to give assurances of his kindly intentions before he could secure a hearing. The grandfather's words did not evoke a fixed order of commandments graven as Law, but appealed for feelings to be considered. The reference was not to the sin-leading-to-damnation of dishonoring his father(s) and mother, but to "the unhappiness he must throw everybody into as well as himself" if he persisted in not controlling "a temper which must in the end make him miserable."

Only two instances can here be cited to suggest that such a nonpatriarchal approach to communication and control, mixed to be sure with customary patriarchal modes, extended beyond the circle that we call the family. Nassau was both his master's body servant and his surgeon-aide in the care of the sick.

[September 23, 1773]. . . .

I have been obliged to give Nassau a severe whipping this day. He has been every day drunk ever since Mulatto Betty was taken ill, and had like to have died with inflaming his bile, for he fell down in an instant and had I not been here to prevent the doses of laudanum, he must have gone; I gave him a Vomit of Ipecacuana which eased him instantly. The next day his blood was so inflamed, he was obliged to be blooded. And yet he will drink; he can't say he can't help it, because he could help sending for liquor. I have threatened him, begged him, Prayed him, and told him the consequences if he neglected the care to one of the sick people; that their deaths through such want of care must be an evidence against him at the great and terrible day, talked a great deal to him in most religious and affectionate way; and this day by day; and yet all will not do; he seems resolved to drink in spight of me, and I beleive in order to spight me. He knows he never gets a stroke but for his drinkings, and then he is very sharply whipped; but as soon as the cuts heal he gets drunk directly. I am now resolved not to pass one instance over and think myself justified both to God and man. I confess I have faults myself to be forgiven, but to be every day and hour committing them, and to seek the modes of committing them admits of no Plea of frailty; I hope then I may still save his soul.[29]

There is a great deal in this passage, but attention is here only called to the inclusion of persuasion by appeal to the feelings. To be sure "whipping," "threatening," invocation of "the great and terrible day," and a determination to impose punishment implacably for every transgression predominate over the begging, talking in an "affectionate way," and the request for regard to others. Nevertheless these other elements are unmistakably present, and they recur in the diary narratives. Other small indicators of an indecisive shift from unalloyed patriarchal lordship can be seen in one of the diarist's occasionally repeated phrases in comment upon the death of a slave whose life he had tried to save with his medical skills: "as a *human creature* I had all imaginable care taken of him" (my emphasis). Perhaps too much should not be made of it, but I would attach significance to the invocation of a universal benevolence and common humanity (rather than of his patriarchal obligation to protect his dependents), which appears as part of a pervasive pattern in the ethos communicated by the diary.[30]

Conclusions

As Landon Carter adapted his diary to his changing situation, it moved from being a parliamentary journal to being an estatebook or farmbook and thence became an increasingly personal record. From out of its complex forms a number of images and representations of authority and power have been traced in this essay. We have seen how, in the high ceremonial of government, both governor and the gentlemen planters of the Assembly invoked not only divine fatherhood but also a "Spirit of Benevolence" and an ethos of "paternal Affection." They felt this appropriate in an age where the "Inclination . . . to cultivate . . . Virtues of a Social Nature" was to be celebrated in public as well as private spheres. We have seen the preference of Landon Carter as a legislator, acting in the county-bench paternalistic tradition, both to have a secure basis in the law (as certain "directory") and to claim wide powers of discretion (since "every order was Governed by its own Circumstances"). We have seen the careful balance between "law" (with its concomitant idea of "rights") and discretion overturned by the explicit metaphor of fatherhood in that same legislator's dealings on the plantation—a shift that made strategic aspects of the relationship between slave and master into a constant struggle over the definition of the situation. The slaves sometimes overtly, and often covertly, negotiated for their entitlements, taking what they could get, while the master strove to keep relations on a patriarchal basis in which submission was the prime condition. Repeatedly he would hold out to them the possibility of their receiving a father's clemency once their obedience was ritually affirmed.[31] We have seen how the master's endeavors to establish and maintain dealings on this footing were complicated and compromised by his own self-legitimation as a lord who owed his people care and protection. (His very view of their dependence and congenital incapacity obliged him to bear with them, and so entitled them to indulgences.) Finally, we have seen how the conception of fatherhood was changing, with the inclusion of the newer language of humanitarian sensibility alongside traditional concerns for repentance and forgiveness.

Through all these representations of authority there runs, as a recurrent theme, a certain alternation between the imperatives of fixed rules and the appropriateness of judgments addressed to the particularities of cases. This alternation itself heightened and reinforced the role of the patriarch. Both the invocation of the law and the discretionary judgment (including the granting or withholding of mercy) emphasized the power of the dominant figure to rule. A model drawn from sociolinguistics will illuminate the processes of communication of authority and power here. In the terminology of Basil Bernstein, the strong patriarchal role can be associated with a "positional" system.[32] Where very marked rank, age, and gender distinctions define for different persons highly particularized roles, each with its clear duties and entitlements, the verbal component of communication may be "restricted." Much of the content of the message in such circumstances is carried by implicit knowledge of the persons from whom it originates and those to whom it is directed—its "positional" aspect. In contrast to this, Bernstein's model identifies a sociolinguistic system of opposite tendency, where a framework of fixed roles, obligations, and rights, if not less present, is less taken for granted. In this domain, the communication must be verbally "elaborated" so as to establish the relevant identities of those involved—typically, personal needs are articulated and the anticipated or desired feelings of the recipients are addressed. As "positional" modes of communication were of the essence to traditional patriarchy, so "elaborated codes" were increasingly pervasive with the advance of the cult of "sensibility."[33]

Landon Carter appears as a man caught up in profound contrarieties. From his early upbringing in the household of an old-fashioned patriarch, and from his secondary socialization under the influences of humanitarianizing cosmopolitan culture, he was pulled strongly in opposite directions.[34] On the one hand the disobedient must be punished in order not to destroy the "divine order in governing this world"; on the other hand those in his household must be taught to understand his feelings, to respond with appropriate emotions of their own, and so to act humanely. The project of manipulating persons by reference to inner states has been glimpsed in Landon's remonstrance "in an affectionate way" with his slave Nassau, and seen more clearly in his almost pleadingly intimate advances to his wayward grandson, setting before the boy "the unhappiness he must throw everybody into as well as himself." Above all, this approach to the social world is writ large in the diary itself. Much of the eloquence of the document derives from its character as a retreat for the contemplation of hurt feelings. The encounters that went awry because others refused to return the emotional responses that Landon had scripted for them were all rehearsed on the page—an ex post facto manipulation of the situation that was in turn projected forward when he contemplated the impact of his writing after his death: "let who will read it . . . and after I am gone let such people clap their hands upon their hearts. . . . Let them reflect."[35]

A sociolinguistic model of a spectrum of communication systems between an intense "positional" mode at one extreme and an explicitly "elaborated" mode at the other, provides a tool to think with, a means to explore more than just the particular forms of communication and control, of authority and power, that appear through, and are embodied in, Landon Carter's diary. This rich document is as exceptional as its writer was eccentric, yet very general patterns of relationship and currents of cultural change are discernible in the episodes described. When the diary and the social microcosm to which it refers are reviewed with the aid of Bernstein's concepts, important questions are raised both in the history of the politics of the family and in the history of "the family" as the framework for plantation slavery in Virginia and North America generally. The work of Jan Lewis shows that the current of "sensibility," which runs through Landon Carter's recording of his life, later became a torrent of sentiment in the personal writings of succeeding generations.[36]

The transfer of upper- and middle-class sensibilities from the metropolis of the mother country to the provincial extremity of a southern colony has important implications for our understanding of the history of the family. On the socioeconomic side of the question, direct explanations of these changes by reference to "structural" transformations commonly associated with the industrial revolution seem to break down, since "affective individualism" was rapidly assimilated into the slaveowners' world where basic socioeconomic relationships remained locked in agrarian patterns of lordship and bonded labor.[37] On the cultural-hermeneutic side, it can be recognized that while the "feelings" have had a central place in the history of the family at least since Ariès published his momentous history of childhood, neither Ariès nor those who have followed him, have sufficiently attended to the nature of the actual phenomena at the heart of their enquiry.[38] The study of "the feelings" is necessarily the study of *expressions* of feeling, and so must begin with conventions, genres, and languages. An explicit or implicit sociolinguistic theory is indispensable. Whether or not the controversial Bernstein model proves useful in the developing history of the family and of slavery remains to be seen, but for the moment reference to it is intended to draw attention to the variable and highly meaningful relationship between forms of verbalization and the social systems of which they are an integral part.

On the plantations, where the forms of family life interlocked with those of slave-based production, it seems that elaborated "sensibility" and its romantic intensification contributed to what Willie Lee Rose has styled "the domestication of domestic slavery."[39] Patriarchy was sentimentalized into paternalism; the postures to the world and the experiences of life of whole generations were accordingly reoriented.[40] The particular forms of communication—the control attempted and the resistance returned—that have been traced from Landon Carter's diary may stand thus not only as explorations in the mysterious rites of power but as a set of closeup views of a particular once-widespread system of domination—plantation slavery—in the early stages of a major transformation.

Notes

1. Landon Carter, *The Diary of Colonel Landon Carter of Sabine Hall, 1752–1758,* ed. Jack P. Greene (Charlottesville, Va., 1965), vol. 1, p. 216. The introduction to this edition provides an analysis not only of the ideology and worldview of Landon Carter but of the political culture of his age. This essay was and is a key contribution to our whole understanding of that subject; it has been republished separately as Jack P. Greene, *Landon Carter: An Inquiry into the Personal Values and Social Imperatives of the Eighteenth-Century Virginia Gentry* (Charlottesville, Va., 1965).

2. Eugene D. Genovese, *Roll, Jordan, Roll: The World the Slaves Made* (New York, 1974), see especially pp. 3–7, 70–86. The complexity of the social-cultural dynamics of the plantation world considered as a "family" system have been superbly opened for consideration by Herbert Gutman, *The Black Family in Slavery and Freedom, 1750–1925* (New York, 1976). For a similar close analysis of a single antebellum plantation see Drew Gilpin Faust, "Culture, Conflict, and Community: The Meaning of Power on an Antebellum Plantation," *Journal of Social History,* 14 (1983): 83–97.

3. Lawrence Stone, *The Family, Sex and Marriage in England 1500–1800* (New York, 1977).

4. *Journals of the House of Burgesses of Virginia, 1752–1755; 1756–1758,* ed. H. R. McIlwaine (Richmond, Va., 1919), pp. 3–5.

5. Ibid., pp. 8–9.

6. Landon Carter, *Diary,* ed. Greene, vol. 1, pp. 72, 81, 73.

7. Ibid., pp. 69, 76, 81, 75.

8. Ibid., pp. 73, 75.

9. Ibid., pp. 73, 81, 82.

10. Aspects of these questions are dealt with in A. G. Roeber, *Faithful Magistrates and Republican Lawyers: Creators of Virginia Legal Culture, 1680–1810* (Chapel Hill, N.C., 1981).

11. Landon Carter, *Diary*, ed. Greene, vol. 2, p. 845.

12. Ibid., pp. 290–91. The interpretation following the quotation of the episode arising from Bart's return is quoted and adapted from Rhys Isaac, "Ethnographic Method in History—An Action Approach," *Historical Methods*, 13 (1980): 51–53.

13. I am construing here in terms of cultural metaphor what is brilliantly dealt with in essentially social-psychological terms (under the very valuable rubric, "role performance") in Gerald W. Mullin, *Flight and Rebellion: Slave Resistance in Eighteenth-Century Virginia* (New York, 1972), pp. 67–82.

14. Landon Carter, *Diary*, ed. Greene, vol. 2, p. 754; vol. 1, pp. 348–97.

15. Ibid., vol. 2, p. 712; vol. 1, pp. 588, 301, 329.

16. Ibid., vol 2, p. 843.

17. Ibid., vol. 1, pp. 426, 508.

18. Ibid., p. 496.

19. Ibid., vol. 2, p. 687; vol. 1, p. 442.

20. Genovese, *Roll, Jordan, Roll*, pp. 285–325; Jack P. Greene in Landon Carter, *Diary*, ed. Greene, vol. 1, pp. 13–27.

21. Landon Carter, *Diary*, ed. Greene, vol. 1, pp. 396, 494, 496.

22. Ibid., vol. 1, pp. 306, 296.

23. Ibid., pp. 366, 367–68, 376, 396–97.

24. Ibid.

25. Manuel (who had, no doubt, already learned of the governor's offer of freedom to rebels' slaves who would rally to the royal standard) went off with eight others when they heard that HMS *Roebuck* was in the Rappahannock River. They set off on the night of June 25, 1776, after robbing Landon's son, grandson, and others of guns and valuables—but not the old squire, who evidently thought a certain patriarchal divinity had hedged him and his chamber that night. They left in a periauger (small boat), were chased ashore by a patrol, and eventually recaptured. Even after this act of Manuel's putting himself out of Landon's protection, the angry master had to enumerate in his diary all that he had done for the ingrate to prove that *now*, at last, "to Carolina he shall go if I give him away." Ibid., vol. 2, pp. 1051–55, 1109–10.

26. Ibid., vol. 2, p. 941. For a fuller discussion of the dealings with Nassau see Isaac, "Ethnographic Method," *Historical Methods*, 13 (1980): 52–53.

27. Landon Carter, *Diary*, ed. Greene, vol. 2, p. 736.

28. Ibid., vol. 1, p. 578.

29. Ibid., vol. 2, p. 778.

30. Ibid., vol. 1, p. 589; vol. 2, pp. 651, 664. For an insightful preliminary study of the emergence of humanitarian sensibilities see Norman S. Fiering, "Irresistible Compassion: An Aspect of Eighteenth-Century Sympathy and Humanitarianism," *Journal of the History of Ideas*, 37 (1976): 195–218.

31. For a very perceptive discussion of the patriarchal-patronage implications of the power to pardon, see Douglas Hay, "Property, Authority and the Criminal Law," in Douglas Hay et al., eds., *Albion's Fatal Tree: Crime and Society in Eighteenth-Century England* (New York, 1975), pp. 17–63, esp. pp. 40–49.

32. Basil Bernstein, *Class, Codes and Social Control*, vol. 1, *Theoretical Papers* (London, 1972). The clearest outline-cum-adaptation for general purposes is to be found in Mary Douglas, *Natural Symbols: Explorations in Cosmology* (New York, 1972), pp. 42–54. The model is adapted in a somewhat different way in Dell Hymes, *Foundations in Sociolinguistics: An Ethnographic Approach* (Philadelphia, 1974), pp. 38–39. For another historical application of the Bernstein model to the history of the family, see Hans Medick and David Sabean, "Call for Papers: Family and Kinship, Material Interest and Emotion," *Peasant Studies*, 7 (1979): 139–60.

33. For a fine analysis of a seemingly affectless and very position-oriented system of communications in the diary of a patriarch that contrasts very strikingly with Landon Carter's, see Michael Zuckerman, "William Byrd's Family," *Perspectives in American History*, 12 (1979): 253–311.

34. For strong indications concerning the regime maintained by Landon's father see Louis B. Wright, ed., *Letters of Robert Carter, 1720–1727: The Commerical Interests of a Virginia Gentleman* (San Marino, Cal., 1940). On Landon's extended education in England, and on his cultural values generally, see Greene, *Landon Carter*, pp. 1–2 and passim.

35. Landon Carter, *Diary*, ed. Greene, vol. 1, p. 359.

36. Both the large sweep and the finer details of the change in the character of correspondence and diaries expressing personal feelings is superbly dealt with in Jan Lewis, *The Pursuit of Happiness: Family and Values in Jefferson's Virginia* (Cambridge & New York, 1983), pp. xiii–xiv, 209–15, and passim.

37. See Stone, *Family, Sex and Marriage*, esp. pp. 257–69, and Lewis, *Pursuit of Happiness*, pp. 216–20.

38. Philippe Ariès, *Centuries of Childhood: A Social History of Family Life*, trans. Robert Baldick (New York, 1962). For a study of family feeling in Landon Carter's region that is perhaps insufficiently attentive to the changing conventions controlling the writing of letters and diaries, see Daniel Blake Smith, *Inside the Great House: Family Life in Eighteenth-Century Chesapeake Society* (Ithaca, N.Y., 1980). Stone, *Family, Sex and Marriage*, p. 227, broaches the question of literary conventions and the tracing of the history of "feeling." This is a lead that must be systematically followed. See Lewis, *Pursuit of Happiness*, pp. xiv–xv.

39. Willie Lee Rose, *Slavery and Freedom*, ed. William W. Freehling (New York, 1982), p. 18. I owe a great debt of gratitude to Professor Rose for both personal encouragement and proferred wisdom on the subjects explored in this essay.

40. See Lewis, *Pursuit of Happiness*, pp. 221–22.

10

ALF LÜDTKE

Organizational Order or Eigensinn? *Workers' Privacy and Workers' Politics in Imperial Germany*

"Politics" traditionally refers to the formulation, achievement, and sustained *organization* of collective interests. Generally, events and expressions are considered political if they consolidate or challenge prevailing patterns of economic or state power. Forms of expression that do not meet these criteria are usually labeled as "private."

Concerning the history of working-class politics under the Imperial Reich, this distinction implies that historians should focus primarily on the Social Democrats and on the socialist trade unions.[1] Normally, the efforts of these organizations—to criticize, transform, and (even more) reform the Reich's semiabsolutism and the class system—are deemed to have been the only political efforts of the wage-earning masses. The assertion of needs by those who never joined the unions or the Social Democratic Party (SPD)—or, for that matter a Catholic workers' association— or who dropped out of such organizations, is perceived, by definition, as "prepolitical" if not nonpolitical.

The same kind of observation holds true for the analysis of political forms and rituals. Political expression usually refers to practices, legitimations, or presentations made by the state or by political parties. A *conditio sine qua non* of this type of political expression is the use of conspicuous symbols (like the red flag) and of slogans from party conventions, the latter usually formulated by leading party or union officials. Study of political rhetoric, meanwhile, is confined to the evidence contained in parliamentary debates or in newspapers.

Accordingly, demonstrations, parades, riots, and other forms of popular "rough" politics appear, in the academic view, mainly as nonpolitical events.[2] An example is the Berlin beer boycott of 1894, an incident that joined trade unionists and the majority of the unorganized workers in the nation's capital for more than six months. In the historians' records, the boycott is filed away as an exotic episode, if not as a nonpolitical "economic war" (Eduard Bernstein).[3] So are events like the violent Berlin housing riots of 1872.[4] These enormous and determined popular manifestations seemingly lacked the qualities of true political action: what, after all, did the beer boycotters or housing rioters know or care about genuinely political matters—that is, about the long-term effects their actions would have on existing modes of domination and distribution? Finally, and most important to our purposes in this essay, workers' ordinary postures and gestures in face-to-face exchanges with policemen or supervisors, the so-called insubordinate stubbornness or insolence of workers and their dependents—all this seems to have been nothing more than the private expenditure of hope or anger.

This brief sketch should indicate that a distinct notion of politics is implied in the traditional view. Such a view legitimates—indeed, necessitates—the existence of a relatively independent leadership to guide the diffuse and supposedly nonpolitical masses. That is to say, the traditional view perceives the masses as nothing but "objects" who do not pursue interests and needs of their own. The complex or antagonistic aspirations of these people are belittled; neglected is the intense perseverence of working-class men and women, their abilities to endure hardship, to be respected, to enjoy life—goals stimulated and molded by individual and collective action.

In contrast to this traditional formula, I propose to examine the articulation and expression of both individual and collective needs as forms of political behavior. My focus will be on the total spectrum of expressions and daily assertions by individuals as well as by different groups and classes. I will emphasize not simply the ways in which people tried to raise demands or resist the demands of others, but also those modes of self-reliance whereby (in theoretical terms) people reappropriated these constraints and pressures—the specific, even peculiar, practices whereby individuals handled their anxieties and desires. I wish to transgress and then blur the usual boundaries between political and private.

Let me offer a few examples of what such blurring can teach us. Meat was not part of workers' daily diet in Imperial Germany: if, by some good fortune, a pork chop or rib was available, the wage-earning males in a given household got the lion's share, if not all of the meat. The implied scorn of wage-working (and house-working) women and girls—even the bite of hunger they suffered—was not, however, simply a family matter.[5] Slowness in demanding a general suffrage, quite apart from the readiness of men and women to accept or justify lower wages for women, relied on and, in part, stemmed from precisely this kind of daily patriarchalism. In turn, the generally accepted or publicly approved standards of appropriate treatment of male wage earners, and of men generally, reinforced seemingly "private" forms of discrimination against women and "others." Thus, public perceptions about the fair apportionment of society's resources were reconstituted in private and intimate interactions as well as in public and organized ones. Politics was always at stake.

Efforts to counter offenses and demands, to change the proportions, and to redefine the terms of behavior were political as well. Put somewhat differently: the creative reappropriation of the conditions of daily life implied a striving for time and space of one's own. Workers' self-presentation and clothing offer an example of this. Workers in top hats and white shirts—the demonstrative wearing of a ceremonial outfit at work—turned a symbol of festive celebrations (or, perhaps, of conspicuous privacy, as in the ceremonial dress of mourning) into a political articulation. Rudolf Wissel recalled such an action—"scandalous" to both mates and officers— as having taken place during the May Day celebrations of a small group of Social Democrats at an imperial shipyard in 1889. Those participating employed, even proclaimed, their own self-reliance.[6]

Self-reliance was expressed in other ways as well. "Horseplay" or fooling around—not caring, at least for a time, about the expectations of supervisors and fellow workers—was closer to home for most factory workers. In all such cases, the search for the political in seemingly private actions and expressions demands that we come to terms with the intricate connections between the spheres of production, reproduction, and consumption in working-class life. At the same time, meanwhile, we must recognize that expressions of self-reliance—commonly known as *Eigensinn*—could not abolish the sphere of organized formal politics.[7] To be sure, some formal political impositions—taxes and tariffs, police regulations, and draft notices—could simply be ignored or evaded. But repeated and refined demands by state officials could be expected to follow; if anything, in the nineteenth century, the power of official bodies (like the police and welfare agencies) to intercede in private life increased. To understand the politics of private life—and of self-reliance, *Eigensinn*—we must attend to all of these matters. To begin, let us survey the complex, heterogeneous patterns of formal organization among German workers, with special reference to a specific group, the turners and other machine construction workers. With these patterns in mind we can then better interpret the multiple meanings of *Eigensinn*.

The turners and other machinists only reluctantly participated in their trade union, the "free" (that is, socialist) Deutscher Metallarbeiterverband (DMV), founded in 1891 following the expiration of the repressive antisocialist law of 1878.[8] Except in the big cities like Berlin, an average of three out of four workers stayed outside the union.[9] Even after a rapid increase in membership between 1903 and 1906—which saw the union almost double in size—and despite further, though much less spectacular, growth after 1909, two out of three metalworkers either never participated in the union, or did not renew their initial membership. The inverse was true in Berlin, a center of big industry and machine production: after 1906, two out of three metalworkers were listed as union members—but this remained an exceptional case.[10] More important, membership in the union was not directly related to membership in the Sozialdemokratische Partei Deutschlands (SPD).[11] Even in Berlin, no more than 16 percent of the total union membership joined the party; among the metalworkers, the figure was about one-third.

These figures should be used with extreme caution; at best they may indicate some general trends. People's motives and the dynamics of historical process are only very crudely mirrored in such statistics. However, a comparison with the total national figures for party and union membership, respectively, points to some interesting conclusions about the *variations* in workers' organized participation. Between 1903 and 1913, the membership of the socialist trade unions tripled: in 1913, almost 2.5 million union members were counted.[12] (Over the same period, the size of the industrial workforce roughly doubled, from 4 million to almost 9 million.) The party, however, only doubled its membership, claiming 1,080,000 enrolled members in 1914. If one breaks these figures down according to short-term periods, the discrepancies between union and party enrollment are even more striking. In particular, the growth phase of 1903 to 1906—a time of economic boom—led to a membership increase of 90 percent for the unions, but only about 38 percent for the party. In all, metalworkers generally seem to have been overrepresented in terms of union participation, even though only a minority played a continuous active role; in Berlin, meanwhile, participation in both the DMV and the SPD far exceeded national norms. At the same time, membership in the DMV by no means led workers into the SPD.

The important point here is that workers' attitudes toward various organizations differed considerably according to the character of specific branches of industry, as well as according to local or regional conditions.[13] If we take a second factor into account—the multiplicity of sociocultural milieus—the heterogeneity of the working class becomes all the more apparent.[14] A good example is in one of the centers of the Prussian province of the Rhine, Düsseldorf.[15] Large-scale metal production began and then expanded in Düsseldorf after the 1870s. The social and political identity of the native working class, however, remained defined by its "Catholic" setting. Not surprisingly, prior to 1914 the Düsseldorf Social Democrats were successful only with newly arrived immigrants and younger workers. To be sure, the party recruited some Catholic workers, mainly those who, unlike most of their coreligionists, had learned skilled occupations on the job. Moreover, the constant flow of immigrants, and the rise of a new population of first-generation Düsseldorf workers, changed the town's sociocultural complexion. Nevertheless, native workers clung to the Catholic Church, especially to its social organizations, the Zentrum, the Katholische Arbeiterverein, and the Christian Union.

A third factor—gender—makes the pattern of organization seem all the more complicated. Women participated in the unions to a far lesser degree than men. In 1903, 20.8 percent of all the Reich's male workers were union members, while only 4.4 percent of the female workers were so registered.[16]

Obviously, different socioeconomic and sociocultural contexts affected workers' readiness to participate in those organizations that claimed to represent their interests. However, it is important not to perceive these different contexts as static structures, segmented like a layer cake. Likewise, it is important not to interpret the growth of these organizations in linear terms. Friedrich Engels made this mistake in the early 1890s, convinced that the Social Democracy would increase year by year until it outnumbered its opponents, in a more or less automatic process.[17] Before the decade was out, it was clear that Engels's prediction was erroneous. In part, the diverse, nonlinear trends of organizational development were connected to different experiences in particular branches of industry, as well as differences of sociocultural milieu. Above all, however, the level of organization remained tied to economic movements; that is, the years of economic upswing (1894–1908, 1903–1906, 1908/09–1912) show the most marked increases in membership figures and growth rates.[18] Organizing efforts seemed to pay off more during periods of economic upswing than during slumps; conversely, to defend wages and work conditions in times of constraint—especially when laid-off comrades increased the pressure to submit to lower wages and deteriorating conditions—was more difficult, making the SPD and the unions appear far less attractive. While different groups reacted very differently to organizing efforts, their behavior also varied in accordance to general economic movements that cut across differences within the working class.

Concerning the practices, connected experiences, and expectations of workers, these figures lead us in two directions:

First, in the long term, the socialist organizations far outdrew other unions and workers' organizations. Cooperative or "yellow" organizations (*Werkvereine*) remained at the margin. Except in certain areas of the country, the same held true for the Catholic organizations; even from 1911 to 1913, at their peak, the Christian unions lagged far behind the socialist unions, with 350,000 members as compared to the socialists' 2.5 million.[19] As we have noted, meanwhile, the socialist unions were relatively more successful in recruiting members than was the SPD. So were a variety of other nonparty socialist organizations, ranging from those like the cooperative shopping associations (*Konsumvereine*) that tried to help workers manage their daily lives, to diverse clubs that offered workers a new kind of "free" time and space—groups like the bicycling association (Radfahrer-Bund).[20]

Second, participation in various organizations—including the socialist unions—remained something of an auxiliary feature of workers' lives, for men and women alike. Certain groups of skilled workers, as well as workers with artisanal backgrounds like the turners—that is, workers who sustained an idea of themselves as "labor aristocrats"—did, to be sure, take union membership as a kind of obligatory requirement of their position. Yet even then, those who accepted formal organization did not display a *mechanical inclination* toward organization and sustained or militant participation. In this connection, it is important to note the changing attitude of workers through the life cycle. To return to our main example: after the late 1890s, most machine construction workers appear to have *joined* the DMV, but most of them also withdrew or "let it go" after one or two years. At least outside of Berlin, two out of three never showed up again, never paid any dues after the first few months, and thereby allowed their names to be scratched from the union rolls. Nor did the machine construction workers show any great inclination for spectacular collective action or strikes, as compared with such groups as the miners, dockers, construction workers, and the much-less-organized textile workers.[21]

These cross-cutting conclusions—on the relative importance of the socialist unions but the secondary place of all organizations in workers' lives—beg further explication. Above all, however, we should not interpret them to mean simply that workers were complacent, inactive, or apathetic unionists. The metalworkers, for example, at least in the big cities, went on to become the most militant adversaries of the SPD's support for the war, and of the related prowar stance of the central board of trade unions, from 1914 to 1918. The turners, meanwhile, formed one of the core groups of shop stewards who agitated the great antiwar strike of ammunition workers in the winter of 1917, and who went on to play important roles in the revolutionary movement in the fall of 1918.[22] To begin to understand how this could have been so, we are forced to look beyond the arena of "formal" politics and union participation, to see how workers—and metalworkers in particular—expressed their hopes and fears in other ways. We must, that is, examine the many ways in which these workers practiced and understood self-reliance, *Eigensinn*, if we are fully to comprehend their active participation in the distribution and redistribution of resources and "life chances" (Max Weber)—if, in other words, we are to understand how they behaved "politically." As we shall see, the case of the turners makes clear that attentive militancy was by no means confined to formal organizations like unions and parties. To spend time, money, and energy in supporting a union or party—to add "organizational activity" to the many tasks of daily survival—was, in fact, just one among many ways in which workers could assert their needs and interests. To understand these other forms of assertion, however, we must try to interpret workers' lived experiences and "informal" expressions, both in and out of formal organizations. Let us begin by taking a closer look at life on the shop floor.

On the job, factory workers did not simply operate their tools and machines, or cooperate with each other in various ways—they also, literally, lived together, for long hours at a time. This physical contact, this "being-together-in-the-same-place," must be related to the rest of life on the shop floor, to those endless uncertainties that constantly molded workers' experiences: unpredictable variation of wages, the risk of accidents or of being laid off, and so on. Let us start by considering a quotation from a participant observer among the metalworkers, Paul Göhre, a Protestant pastor who stayed anonymously for six weeks with roughly 120 turners and drillers in a machine construction workship in Chemnitz (Saxony). Göhre recalled: "The cooperation at work led to continuous and frequent contact and immediate exchange. These contacts were especially lively between immediate colleagues and people of the same work-group, who worked under the same foreman. Almost unintentionally these contacts became close and intimate. Every occasion to chat or engage in conversation was used."[23]

It seems, however, that nonverbal exchanges and physical contacts were more important than conversation. Göhre noted that:

> More than anything else these people teased one another, scuffled and tussled—indulged in horseplay, where and whenever it seemed possible. People looked for friends, and acquaintances; clay was thrown at someone who passed by, the slipknot of his apron was untied from behind, the plank of a seat was pulled away while a fellow worker took a break, someone's way was blocked unexpectedly or they "pulled someone's leg." But, to be sure, especially favored among older workers at the end of the week was another form of horseplay: "beard-polish." Shaving was a once-a-week affair, a common practice among workers, and was performed usually Saturday night or Sunday morning. By the end of the week, the worker whose beard had grown in would grab the head of a chap with more tender cheeks, lips, and chin, and would rub his face against the youth's face, a process which of course had a quite painful result. Before the victim realized just what had happened to him, the wrongdoer had already disappeared. Even less pleasant was another practical joke, which I—fortunately enough—had to experience only once. A worker is leaning against a post, taking a break; for no particular reason two of his co-workers recognize him, a look of understanding passes between them—and one of them approaches the leaning one from behind, claps him tight with his arms while the other takes the face of the immobilized victim in his black, dirty hands and slowly pulls his moustache to either side, pressing his thumbs against the face of the harassed workmate. This joke is, as I can testify, very painful. . . . Among those who knew one another nobody was excepted. Even age made no difference."[24]

Such was the intense and continual nonverbal social exchange that took place between those who worked and—at least part of the time—lived together.

These brief interludes of "being-by-oneself-and-with-one's-workmates" were most commonly carried out by means of body contact, including physical violence. Workers did, to be sure, express and reaffirm *Eigensinn* by walking around and talking, by momentarily slipping away or daydreaming. Primarily, though, their outbursts of self-reliance took the form of reciprocal body contact and horseplay—simultaneously "being-by-oneself" and "being-with-others," neglecting but not directly interfering with the continuing work process.

The struggle for control of one's own body—which involved at once a demonstration of manual dexterity and physical skill and the cultivation and preservation of social relationships—required an obvious display of physical force. In this way these interactions expressed and reaffirmed the patriarchal social hierarchy and displayed alleged male behavior.[25] Basically at stake, however, was the workers' *reciprocal* appreciation, recognition, and encouragement. There was nothing personal to the physical victimization; everyone on the shop floor knew that, next time, the "victim" was likely to be one of the other "players." Simultaneously these interactions can be read as reconfirmations of factory experiences in which all participants shared—of being "bound tight" and "fixed on the spot," being marked and made dirty—being exposed to external manipulations whose perpetrators, at least temporarily, were beyond control of the victims. Violent physicality in this context might have been one moment in an endeavor "to-be-let-alone" *and* "to-be-by-oneself-and-others." In sum, these interactions and expressions were not meant primarily as direct resistance to demands "from above"; instead, with these outbursts, workers established a space of their own.[26]

It is important to note, in this connection, that this form of social intercourse did not occur during officially conceded breaks. Rather, the workers reappropriated bits of the very time that formally was designated as working time. They made it their own by frequently neglecting or breaking the imposed time schedule. Their chatting with each other, their walking around, the repeated horseplay—these were illegal breaks. As such, these incidents created multifaceted and ambiguous situations. Resistance to the foreman or boss could be and was practiced during these intervals. But simultaneously, even more intensely, these moments involved taking distance, not only from domination at the work place but also from fighting or resisting the imposed and experienced restrictions of one's own needs and interests—a kind of immediate joyful *dépense*,[27] taken without any calculation of "effects" or "outcomes." The workers, then, were "by themselves" when they actively neglected the consequences of their social intercourse, at least momentarily. *Eigensinn* happened in isolated (though constantly repeated) moments; in these reappropriated situations the workers created, expressed, and fulfilled their own needs. And the "meaning" as well as the "function" of these moments of *Eigensinn* was twofold: workers could "be alone" as well as with their buddies.

Obviously, *Eigensinn* did not immediately counter, let alone overthrow, the system of capitalist production. Judged by the usual standards of "resistance" and "accommodation," *Eigensinn* might appear as nothing but evasion from (and, perhaps, compensation for) daily toil—a rather marginal aspect of workers' alienation. However, such a functionalist interpretation is far too abstract. It completely misses the potentiality that workers' practices, and *Eigensinn* in particular, might contain. Ignored are the facets of agency that are intricately connected with "passivity" or even with "apathy" and "acceptance." Put somewhat differently: workers' self-willed distancing from the demands of supervisors and from the pressures of the work process without directly fighting them certainly could connote individualistic, even hostile neglect of one's own workmates. Simultaneously, though, by (inter-)acting and expressing themselves on their own terms, workers could keep at a distance the constraints of the factory as well as those of the daily struggle for survival before and after work; in this way, capacities for individual or collective action could be developed. Here, again, in its double meaning, *Eigensinn* signified and expressed the peculiarities of workers' politics: a striving for "being-by-oneself" *and* "being-with-others."

Two very broad propositions can be developed on the basis of this brief look at *Eigensinn*, both of them connected to the "political" components of the daily lives of "immediate producers" (Karl Marx).

1. Workers did not pursue their interests in a strictly "instrumental" way; nor did they act "politically" in the sense of striving for a change of the mode of production.[28] Such idealizations follow an inappropriate, one-dimensional model of politics and fail to grasp the ambiguities, intertwinings, and contradictions of interest with *Eigensinn*. What is overlooked, in short, is the "mode of life" of those concerned.

2. At least in more developed industrial capitalist societies, divergent, perhaps separate, and even contradictory political arenas—"public" and "private"—can be discerned. However, the "politicization of the private" by interconnected assertions of interests, needs, and *Eigensinn* in face-to-face relations is misread if it is taken as "privatization of politics." The "daily" politics of the time do not show a tendency toward depoliticization. On the contrary, they reveal various forms of redistribution of material and emotional resources as well as of (life-)time and (life-)chances. Such forms implicitly relativized the arena of formal politics; in other words: the "self-willed" politics of the so-called dominated put state-centered politics into perspective.

Let me develop these propositions in turn.

Concerning 1:

In the context of their daily politics, workers did not easily distinguish between social obligations and *Eigensinn*, between material interests and individual needs. Nor did social obligations and self-reliance fall into the kinds of neat analytic boxes employed by scholars. Above all, it is important not to conflate the pursuit of interests with the kind of purposeful, instrumental behavior and attitudes usually stressed by historians and others. For example, workers who strove to achieve some ideal of "respectability" should not (as is commonly done) be interpreted as the captives of some pale reflection of petit-bourgeois aspirations, or as the victims of some distorted form of class consciousness. Respectability offered the workers a standard of their own, drawing on very distinct experiences—a standard that nurtured their efforts to earn a living,[29] but was never disconnected from the workers' own daily uncertainties and insecurities, or from their own hopes for a better future. In this connection, various endeavors to survive by illegal means—the unlawful appropriation of food, coal, or wood—were not perceived by workers as some violation of respectable norms.[30] At all events, success—that is, survival, material and social improvement—fostered not submission but that particular demonstrative pride visible in encounters with neighbors and workmates, as well as in confrontations with those Marx called the "commissioned and noncommissioned officers" of the workshops. This was the pride that, in various ways, lay behind the workers' assertion of "self-will" in their daily politics.

These daily politics were in no way fixated on resistance or on any determined stance against demands, constraints, or repression. Various forms of self-will were ubiquitous: again and again, *Eigensinn*—as tenacious as it was effortless—could be detected in daily life, in associations with colleagues, friends, and relatives, and most often in loosely organized groups—playing sports (especially gymnastics, soccer, and bicycling), singing, fiddle and banjo playing, drinking with buddies (for men), Kaffee Klatsches (for women). In big cities like Berlin and Hamburg around 1900, the attractions of leisure industry further expanded the scope of these self-willed activities.[31] Single people or small groups visited big "beer palaces," leisure parks, and the cinema *(Kintopp)*, or strolled in the department stores (Hermann Teitz, Karstadt) and along the brightly illuminated big boulevards. All of these places had become accessible by public transportation, especially the tramways or special railway systems (S-Bahn, Berlin, Hamburg).[32] Always, the attraction was the chance to be with and for one's self only. Threats from rulers and their agents, from policemen, superintendents, or foremen, were out of sight and could—for a time—be forgotten.

Concerning 2:

In terms of the politicization of private life, it must be recognized that interference from above was an integral part of the private *mode of life* of the workers and their families. Rigorous daily enforcement of order in the home as well as in the factory, on the streets and in schools and offices, was part of everyday life.[33] Workers had to be aware of the constant efforts of supervisors, masters, and foremen to control their activities and expressions, not only at work; simultaneously, in the settlements and housing projects of the big companies, superintendents constantly surveiled the level of noise or the regularity of cleaning; they even controlled the reading of newspapers. In the Krupp housing projects, at least in the 1880s, bringing home the social democratic newspaper was punishable by firing and immediate eviction from the company flat. Moreover, at the Krupp works at Essen, and at another big company, the Gutehoffnungshütte works at Oberhausen, state and local policemen were directly incorporated into the factory settlements.[34] Officers lived among the workers and were partly paid by the corporations. The inhabitants had to deal with the daily display and intervention of these policemen; although visibly of state authority, they simultaneously represented and executed both corporate and state domination.

These experiences with the physical violence of the state and private policing were interconnected with a masked form of violence from above: *violence douce* (P. Bourdieu). It is insufficient to limit ourselves, here, to the overtly repressive features of state and corporate policies. Control strategies and practices were linked to legitimations and activities that aimed, ostensibly, to improve conditions of life of those concerned, but that also aimed to control workers' habits. Local authorities (and increasingly, from the 1890s on, state officials and the state administration) developed programs to improve the nutrition, housing conditions, and the education of the industrial proletariat;[35] these policies provided programs to feed poor children or to allow and to support mutual benefit savings or construction associations; special attention was paid to encouraging workers to cultivate individual garden plots. At the same time, official efforts at improvement involved various forms of policing.[36] Vagrants were chased and arrested; "mad" people were increasingly detained in special institutions; compulsory education was enforced by the police, at least in the towns and cities.

At stake in all of this was not simply a combination of violent and manipulative means by which the dominant classes enforced obedience. "Progressive" reforms did not simply reflect the "bourgeois" character of social improvement, or represent a totalizing of bourgeois norms and standards. Obviously, "imposed" standards of cleanliness[37] or education in many cases matched the immediate interests and needs of those who were "policed." To be clean and to be educated, after all, could open up real prospects for a better life. Electricity in streets and homes, sewage systems in the cities, medical check-ups for the young, all alleviated the burden of daily reproduction; no one had to feel ashamed of using these public services. Such efforts cannot simply be put down as a pale reflection of a "hegemonic culture."

Put slightly differently: interventions from above framed, even molded, the daily chores and pleasures of workers and their families; even then, however, getting by within that frame involved far more than accepting and coping with given conditions. Dealing with everyday demands and pressures—to say nothing of unexpected turns of fortune—created possibilities for distancing, for fighting back, or for turning government intervention to personal uses; above all, while workers lived within the constraints imposed by others, they also reframed and reorganized their conditions; they re-created and (re-)appropriated work and nonwork, fulfilling order and demands but also displaying *Eigensinn*: they made their lives, toilsome as they were, their own. And through their refusals, recreations, and self-willed actions, they shared in a common endeavor to erase any division between the private and the political.

One example—and result—of this kind of distancing was the separation of the broad and diffuse masses from the arena of centralized politics, both those of the dominating classes and of the opposition SPD. Evidence of this separation can be found, after 1900, in the membership fluctuation and turnover rates mentioned above: only a limited number of the original membership remained within workers' organizations. Even more impressive evidence was the vitality of various unorganized or spontaneous movements, like the one that surfaced in January 1906 in the course of an SPD-led demonstration for the general suffrage in Hamburg,[38] or in the September 1910 in Berlin-Moabit, triggered by rapidly increasing food prices.[39] In both instances, the bourgeois and socialist newspapers charged that "disorderly" people, mostly casual laborers and unemployed, had taken over; once in command, these disorderly elements moved from demonstrating to ransacking and plundering, without any discipline—even "revolutionary" discipline. The self-willed politics of the unorganized were, quite simply, incomprehensible to those who deemed themselves the truly political leaders of the people. At the same time, many of the supposedly popular movements of the era actually testified to the separation of the masses from formal political organization. The various popular self-mobilizations in response to government initiatives after 1890 (notably in response to colonial policy and naval rearmament) were in fact largely restricted to (petit) bourgeois opinion makers and organizations.[40] It is doubtful whether many industrial workers (or workers in general) participated at all.

But we may take this particular point a step further. The separation of political arenas not only distanced workers from formal organizations; it was also a feature of organized workers' experiences *within* these organizations. To understand how this was so, let us return to formal workers' politics—this time to forms of social interaction within the socialist organizations.

For organized workers, the separation of political arenas mirrored the practices and expectations of "their" party leaders. The hierarchical organization of internal party processes, and even more their public appearances, made this clear. When the SPD mobilized its adherents, its demonstrations all too quickly resembled military parades.[41] The "use value" of marching in a row and of keeping up with the front rank seems to have been overwhelmed by the "surplus value" of a militaristic structuring and organizing of the masses: such military practices infiltrated the party functionaries' very notion of alternative social organizations; even more, they influenced the daily practices of the rank and file. There was a military terminology congruent with this: according to the written and spoken rhetoric of the party establishment, the "revolutionary army" or the "battalions of the revolution" marched forward.[42]

The separation of arenas was further epitomized during the delivery of public speeches (Fig. 10.1). The speaker(s) faced the crowd; the crowd's role was to listen quietly, not to argue with the speakers;[43] if a discussion did follow the speech, both speaker and audience looked forward to its becoming a *gemütliche*, an easygoing, even cozy, chat. Not only did reformist functionaries or bureaucrats like it this way; so did one of Germany's leading radical intellectuals and authors, Rosa Luxemburg. Ironically enough, convivial and relaxed talks "after the event" reaffirmed the very distance between leading (or speaking) persons and the ordinary

Fig. 10.1. Socialist open-air meeting, c. 1910. From Eduard Bernstein, *Geschichte der Berliner Arbeiterbewegung* (Berlin, 1907–10).

rank and file.[44] Of course, direct communication with the leaders was possible—but generally, leaders preferred to keep it limited to informal talk, off the record.

In general, the meetings offered workers something rather different from their ostensible formal political purposes. Indeed, it is not clear whether much of the audience partook of the meetings' formal aspects— whether those toward the back of the crowd could even hear the speakers.[45] Rather, the meetings offered social contacts as well as a live show, a spectacle, a sport of attack and defense (a sport that was especially intense on those occasions when a nonsocialist or an antisocialist was permitted to address the crowd).[46] The audiences, as contemporary photographs attest, were largely composed of men (Fig. 10.1), for whom the comradeship of fellow workers may have been much more important and meaningful than "understanding" the text of the distant (and distanced) person on the rostrum. The appeal of the meeting was not, meanwhile, denied to women. In her autobiography, Adelheid Popp, one of the earliest and most active female Social Democrats, repeatedly recalled attending rallies, from the 1870s onward; as she put it, the women listened attentively, even devoutly, to the proceedings, carefully following the speaker's remarks, sometimes holding their breath.[47] Popp's recollections suggest that she and her fellow Social Democrats were involved in far more than the fulfillment of an obligation; rather, they were taking part in an enjoyable display of their convictions and loyalties. So the other men and women preserved in contemporary photographs seem to have taken the meetings as a kind of mixture, as a declaration of their loyalties and a Sunday outing, to be attended in proper Sunday clothes.[48]

Beyond these festive features, meetings and assemblies contained more meanings still. Not the least important was the opportunity to demonstrate competence and fitness in one of the traditional fields of the educated: rhetoric and its appropriate performance. Nikolaus Osterroth, a Catholic miner who turned relatively late in life to the SPD, left a very detailed and lively report of how workers strove to become respected speakers.[49] It was of little importance to succeed in offering a consistent flow of substantive points, Osterroth noted; far more important was an ability to impress the audience. The crowd admired a man who did not mind standing and forcefully making a point, one who was able to overcome his anxiety—the reddening of his ears, the sweat under his collar— to speak up. Osterroth failed catastrophically at his first attempt to speak; he earned warm applause, all the same, just for having tried; consequently, he tried again.

In terms of successful organization, party functionaries were well aware of the importance to the rank and file of personal impressions, if not face-to-face contacts, with well-known members of the party establishment. Successful training of speakers was and remained a decisive step in the promotion of rank-and-file members within the party hierarchy. The party published handbooks of advice to speakers; in 1908 Eduard David, one of the most prominent Social Democrats, edited a manual of more than 100 pages.[50] At least one-fourth of the book contained very detailed information on how to overcome *Lampenfieber* and avoid the impression of having lost one's lines—in general, how to give the audience the feeling that the speaker was a tough guy who was not going to be fazed, whether by hostile people in the audience or by any technical problems with the stage or the hall.

Speakers, in turn, expected a disciplined audience. To be sure, conspicuous discipline—at meetings and demonstrations, but also in local party life—might have been strange to people who were used to a day-laborer's or migrant laborer's settings. Most of these workers had experienced very different forms of social intercourse and exchange within their peer groups. However, artisanal or skilled workers, especially second-generation working-class people, greatly appreciated any visual display of discipline. This could range from extremely punctual execution of the local library regulations to sober and well-dressed appearance at meetings and militarylike order at big demonstrations.[51] In part, such displays evoked old memories: to behave oneself, to keep silent and obey orders, were fundamental principles of childrearing in respectable working-class families. In their autobiographies, workers usually refer to being taught, as youngsters, to keep still in church, when they had to participate either in the Lutheran *Konfirmandenunterricht* or in the Catholic preparatory course for communion. Repeatedly mentioned, in this context, was the harsh treatment of disorderly students in school; likewise, the brutal discipline meted out during compulsory military service appears, in the autobiographies, as a necessary humiliation, which "made real men" of young soldiers. Considering these experiences, all of the political organizations relied on comprehensive personal histories of internalized norms of well-ordered conduct in public, and strict discipline vis-à-vis "representatives" (which usually meant vis-à-vis superiors).

This common experience of being corrected and disciplined in front of others helps explain party discipline; it may, however, also explain an apparent irony—the extent to which young men, many of them sons of respected SPD members, were attracted to niches of nondiscipline, centered on self-defense, which were built into the otherwise well-ordered organizations. Parties, mutual relief associations, and unions always faced physical as well as verbal attacks from opponents and competitors. Above all, the SPD but also the Center Party (and their affiliated associations) were furiously denounced and assaulted by the ruling classes and state agencies. State repression and wide-ranging hostility of many of the "good citizens" in most cases restricted or forbade direct counterattacks against police; such was not the case, however, regarding competing political groups. For instance, in the western provinces of Prussia members of the Catholic organizations attacked "invading" Social Democrats: the prevailing group had to show and to prove who was "master of the place."[52] In Saxony or Hamburg, Social Democrats would have claimed "older rights" and attacked "newcomers." In any case, to youngsters these attacks turned into legitimized opportunities to fight the opponent gang from another neighborhood or the next village.

Thus, *Eigensinn* could be practiced and experienced by pushing for discipline, by adopting a "respectable" comportment—but also by physically fighting opponents and rivals. Even more, these very different ways of behaving might not have been perceived as antagonistic or reciprocally exclusive: either way, autonomous and self-determined behavior, at least its male version, was claimed and expressed. Simultaneously, adults could reimagine, even revive, their own adolescence by witnessing the self-willed actions of their (or others') children, while the children were reminded of their fathers' conspicuous discipline and of the disciplining that they themselves would one day undergo.

Eigensinn, then, penetrated, in various degrees, into the socialist organizations that supposedly represented the workers. Simultaneously, other organizations preserved various "particularist" forms for the pursuit of self-will. Tied to these "particularist," "down-home" needs and interests were various associations for mutual support and relief. These associations were efforts to establish separate supply networks split off from the constantly expanding consumer markets in town and in the countryside. People endeavored to achieve a self-willed control over those market segments that seemed to impinge most directly on workers' daily reproduction. Shortly after 1900, tens of thousands joined and participated regularly in cooperative grocery stores. The big cities were the centers of these co-ops—in Hamburg 73,000 people had joined the Konsum by 1913; the unions of Hamburg registered 143,000 members the same year[53]—but in smaller towns and in the countryside as well as in "mixed" areas like Baden and Württemberg workers also joined in considerable numbers.

What is important to note here is that many of these local associations and clubs were not organized from above or by some outsider but on the spot, by the very people who joined them. Completely on their own, the membership set up sporting clubs, savings associations, and cooperative shopping organizations (dubbed "potato clubs").[54] In all cases, the members articulated and sustained their need to be distant from the demands of others and their self-willed interest in organizing for their own survival. Even more, these extended networks of communications and of mutual help did not exclude individualized forms of daily reproduction and of relaxation. For example, in the industrial villages near Duisburg in the Ruhr, workers kept up, even replanted, their own subsistence gardens.[55] In part, these efforts were stimulated by local administrators and state officials, who offered cheap land and advice on how to farm. The workers, however, took advantage of these state interventions for their own purposes, for their individual use, profit—and fun.

In all, much like the leisure clubs mentioned earlier, the consumer associations aimed at far more than their declared goals; above all, the members constantly reconstituted, experienced, and, simultaneously, were attracted to what might be called the "inner face" of these organizations. Put slightly differently, members reappropriated, at least to a certain degree, the organizational frame. In and by these daily practices, people employed—and allowed for—forms of *Eigensinn*.

Thus, two rather independent spheres of proletarian *Eigensinn* can be discerned. One was immediately and intricately tied to social relations at work and social space in the neighborhood. The second sphere of *Eigensinn* developed in the "inner face" of formal organizations. Those who joined and stayed with these organizations displayed and experienced *Eigensinn* of their own.[56]

If we are to avoid simple moralization, it is necessary—indeed unavoidable—to distinguish between the various political arenas thus far discussed. For investigative purposes, the distinction in industrial capitalist societies between private and *Eigensinn* politics on the one hand, and state-centered or formal politics on the other is in no way obsolete. We should of course be aware that in making this distinction we emphasize the—surmised—*function* of various forms of politics rather than the perspective of those concerned. Still, the separation of political arenas was functional for the protection of existing positions and structures of domination. This applied not only to the dominators, and their shifting "alliances,"[57] but also to the leaders of oppositional organizations, such as the SPD of 1914.

By looking at the functions of this separation of arenas, and by understanding the uses dominating groups, including labor leaders, made of this separation, we may more clearly understand existing forms of hegemony. By hegemony, I mean that process of permeation throughout society of unspoken cultural and ideological patterns, which makes the dependence of the dominated appear as necessary or irrevocable.[58] For example, the bourgeois-classical "education," as it was imitated by the educational efforts of the labor movement, contained multifaceted tendencies of accommodation to the dominant culture. Implicitly, these educational programs reinforced bourgeois and patriarchal structures;[59] though they were stimulated by humanitarian motives, these motives did not impinge on actual practice: instructors behaved rudely and seemed to enjoy treating their disciples in an authoritarian manner. Or, to take another example even closer to home for wage workers—in demanding a "just" wage, workers ceased to debate the legitimacy of the structure of capitalist wage labor.

But this is only one side of the coin. The demonstrative silence of the proletarian masses in state and organizational politics often corresponded to an intense political sensibility and militancy, indeed to active "self-will," in the factory or the office, in the tenement house and on the street— a fact overlooked if we simply examine the hegemonic functions of formal institutions and organizations. Even more, such articulations by the dependent and dominated expressed the ways in which they interconnected politics, the "private" sphere, and *Eigensinn*. Upon closer examination, what becomes visible is not a separation of different arenas, but a contiguous simultaneity of private "small joys" in daily practice. Involved, here, was an alternative vision of what life should be like for oneself and for all mankind. That is to say: the fact that workers ignored the arena of state and party politics does not mean that they had no concept of an alternative political and social organization but only that such concepts remained close to peculiarly "private" and "self-willed" politics.

Revealing examples of such alternative visions are contained in the responses of over five thousand miners, textile workers, and metalworkers to a questionnaire sent out in 1910 by the theologian and social reformer Adolf Levenstein. One of Levenstein's questions asked the workers to outline their hopes and wishes for the future. Many expressed the wish to "eat as much as I want," to own a microscope, and at the same time to see the "godly spark" or, at least, to achieve the "prevention of war" throughout the world.[60] Organized workers depicted their utopia in a different way: far more than others, they tended to focus on the quality of future politics, and on the particular features of the "state of the future" (*Zukunftsstaat*)—a term that figured prominently in the speeches and writings of party leaders.[61] Many rank-and-file members shared this concern. For example, in 1893, more than 700,000 copies of Bebel's speeches on the

Zukunftsstaat were printed and sold within a few months. In the following years, similar pamphlets appeared from time to time and, at least according to the figures on printed copies, were well received by a considerable number of party and union members. In all cases, the extinction of the state was the most prominent feature of the organized workers' predictions about the society of the future.[62]

Given the experiences organized Social Democrats and union members tended to have with the police and the courts, it is not surprising that they followed the more conventional lines of "political" thinking. Talk of the state of the future certainly evoked, among organized workers, all sorts of recollections, of unpleasant, if not brutal, treatment by police or military patrols during May Day parades, funerals, "political" demonstrations, and strikes.[63] In this sense, they connected private experiences with public politics. Still open to question, though, is whether the organized workers simultaneously held to the kind of views mirrored in the Levenstein questionnaire material, connecting forms of *Eigensinn*, private life, and politics, and thereby aspiring to a domain of their own. The public postures of union officials certainly did not hint at any concealed longings for a total reversal of the private and the political (Fig. 10.2). Instead, they conveyed an accommodation to the dominant set of values—values of an increasingly "bourgeois" society. But the values and aspirations of the membership—all the ways in which ordinary unionists may have connected "public" politics, "private" politics, and *Eigensinn*, have yet to be worked out.

Two modes of *Eigensinn*—self-reliance—emerged before the eve of World War I. On the shop floor and in working-class neighborhoods, "being-by-oneself-and-with-others" had become an experience that offered satisfaction as well as a sense of individual and collective identity. Workers marked off—or at least claimed—space and time of their own. In a parallel way, organized workers developed a distinct mode of *Eigensinn* precisely by experiencing organized collectivity on a daily basis. This latter form of *Eigensinn* seemed, at least in some respects, consciously at odds with what the organized workers considered the insolence or naiveté of the unorganized. Both organized and unorganized workers, however, tried to separate their activities from commercial forms of consumption and reproduction: they hid their distribution of daily provisions and leisurely pleasures from the rest of the world. At the same time, *Eigensinn* politics, as well as the self-willed assertions of organized workers within their organizations, remained separate from the arena of formal or state-centered politics.

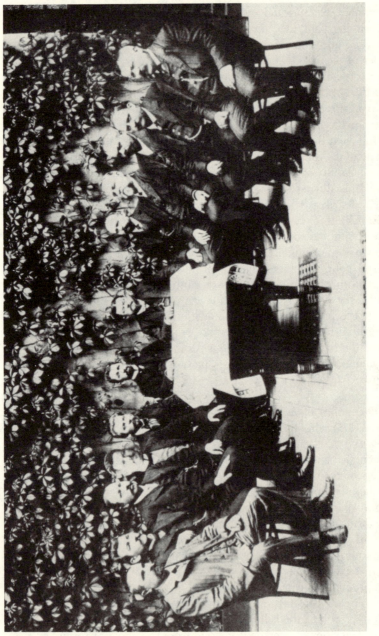

Fig. 10.2. Board of the Trade Union Commission of Berlin, c. 1910. From Eduard Bernstein, *Geschichte der Berliner Arbeiterbewegung* (Berlin, 1907–10).

In August 1914, the demands of the dominant cliques and classes to support the war immediately affected all of Germany. Those who practiced *Eigensinn* politics, whether in or out of official organizations, did not recognize the implied change: with the onset of war, the impact of formal politics could no longer be concealed or hidden; rather, it would be experienced more directly and more brutally than ever before, as sons, husbands, and fathers were sent off to the slaughter. The social and human costs of being dominated became obvious on a scale previously unknown, as the wounded limped in the streets and the lists of the war dead lengthened. The vast majority of proletarians, however, maintained that it was still possible to distance themselves from formal politics, even when they themselves cooperated with state agencies on a day-to-day basis. Marching to war did not, in itself, seem to violate a fundamental disinterest in government affairs or block self-willed pursuit of personal needs and interests. The situation was different only for those workers tied to the network of socialist organizations, many of whom shared the feeling that the outbreak of the war offered them a singular chance to prove the seriousness of their political endeavor.

In all, the *Eigensinn* politics of both the unorganized and the organized, rooted in the specific experiences of "being-on-their own," could, in moments of acute crisis, lead in different, ambiguous directions. In its most common forms, *Eigensinn* politics did not impinge on the arena of formal politics. Conspicuously, in August 1914—and again, in the spring of 1933, when the Fascists seized power—state officials and top-ranking party functionaries were able to rely on this separation and distancing. In both cases, it may appear as if the *Eigensinn* politics led the workers to lose their cause. Yet *Eigensinn* had its ambiguities—for it was the very self-willed actions of those in the socialist organizations that helped spawn the antiwar resistance of 1917 and 1918 and the ensuing revolutionary actions— and, we should add, helped some organized workers survive the fascist terror.

Notes

This paper pursues themes on working-class life and politics that I presented to the Davis Center Seminar, Princeton, in the spring of 1982.

1. Cf. G. Roth, *The Social Democrats in Imperial Germany* (Totowa, 1963); D. Groh, *Negative Integration und revolutionärer Attentismus* (Frankfurt, 1973); G.

A. Ritter, *Staat, Arbeiterschaft und Arbeiterbewegung in Deutschland* (Bonn, 1980), esp. pp. 33ff., 69ff. More attention to collective actions outside the Social Democratic Party is paid by E. Lucas, *Zwei Formen von Radikalismus in der deutschen Arbeiterbewegung* (Frankfurt, 1976). Recently this focus has been questioned in at least some studies on local settings and particular branches of industry, which use a notion of politics closer to the one I am trying to develop. See F.-J. Brüggemeier, *Leben vor Ort. Ruhrbergleute und Ruhrbergbau 1889–1919* (Munich, 1983). Other organizations that addressed themselves to (industrial) workers have been neglected so far—as well as forms of workers' participation in these organizations. Some exceptions are to be found in the local studies noted below. A general overview of the Christian Unions, i.e., one important part of the Catholic "camp" (being almost as influential among factory workers as the socialist unions—at least in some areas) is provided by M. Schneider, *Die Christlichen Gewerkschaften 1894–1933* (Bonn, 1982); on the Catholic Zentrum Party see E. L. Evans, *The German Center Party, 1870–1933* (Carbondale, 1981). The role of Catholic organizations in the life-course of Catholic workers around Neuss and Krefeld (both close to Düsseldorf) has been scrutinized in a stimulating manner in a recent work by D. Linton, "Imperializing Laboring Youth: The Transformation of the Socialization Framework in Germany, 1871–1918" (Ph.D. diss., Princeton University, 1983).

2. In much current research, strikes figure primarily as a field of activity in which workers made a series of transitions to the "political"; see K. Tenfelde and H. Volkmann, eds., *Streik* (Munich, 1981), passim.

3. See E. L. Turk, "The Great Berlin Beer Boycott of 1894," *Central European History*, 15 (1982): 377–97; W. K. Blessing, "Konsumentenprotest und Arbeitskampf," in Tenfelde and Volkmann, *Streik*, pp. 109ff.; E. Bernstein, *Die Geschichte der Berliner Arbeiterbewegung* (Berlin, 1910), vol. 3, pp. 324ff.

4. A. Lange, *Berlin zur Zeit Bebels und Bismarcks* (Berlin/GDR, 1972), pp. 134ff.

5. Several similar examples are mentioned in H. Rosenbaum, *Formen der Familie* (Frankfurt, 1982), p. 413.

6. R. Wissell, *Aus meinen Lebensjahren* (Berlin, 1983), pp. 43ff.

7. The term *Eigensinn* is derived from a passage of "thick description" that the popular philosopher Ch. Garve published in the 1790s. He was commenting on dependent peasants in Silesia, their gestures and behavior toward the lord: "Part or even a consequence of their [i.e., the peasants'] insidiousness is a certain *Eigensinn*, which makes the peasant distinct when he is embarrassed or when some prejudice has become deep-rooted in him. . . . As his body and his limbs get stiff the same apparently happens with his soul. He, consequently, becomes deaf to all propositions that are made to him." Ch. Garve, "Über den Charakter der Bauern und ihr Verhältnis gegen die Gutsherrn und gegen die Regierung," in Garve, *Popularphilosophische Schriften*, ed. K. Wölfel (Stuttgart, 1974), vol. 2, pp. 799–1026, 859ff. I have tried to elaborate the notion of *Eigensinn* in "Cash, Coffee-Breaks, Horseplay: '*Eigensinn*' and Politics among

Factory Workers in Germany around 1900," in M. Hanagan and C. Stephenson, eds., *Class, Confrontation, and the Labor Process: Studies in Class Formation* (Westport, Conn., 1984).

8. A history of the DMV has yet to be written. Main aspects, however, are discussed in the biography of a local and later regional functionary, Hans Böckler (who became the first president of the United Trade Unions after the Second World War); see U. Bordorf, *Hans Böckler: Arbeit und Leben eines Gewerkschafters von 1875–1945* (Cologne, 1982).

9. See the painstaking study of fluctuating union membership by K. Schönhoven, *Expansion und Konzentration, Studien zur Entwicklung der Freien Gewerkschaften im Wilhelminischen Deutschland 1890–1914* (Stuttgart, 1980), esp. pp. 110, 132ff., 148ff., 167ff., 193ff. The fruitfulness of further regional breakdowns of general data is shown by F. Boll, *Massenbewegungen in Niedersachsen 1906–1920* (Bonn, 1981), pp. 45ff.

10. These and the following figures on Berlin are from D. Fricke, *Die deutsche Arbeiterbewegung 1869–1914* (Berlin/GDR, 1976), pp. 718ff., 731. A similar level of organization among metalworkers is indicated by figures on the areas of Hanover and Braunschweig—both, like Berlin, major urban centers. See Boll, *Massenbewegungen*, pp. 45, 55ff.

11. On party membership see Fricke, *Arbeiterbewegung*, pp. 240ff. The figures on the unions are from Schönhoven, *Expansion*.

12. The basis of my extrapolation is a table in G. Hohorst et al., *Sozialgeschichtliches Arbeitsbuch*, vol. 3 (Munich, 1975), p. 67.

13. The spectrum of organizations includes, of course, the Christian ones as well as the corporation-sponsored "yellow" antistrike associations. On the Christian, i.e., Catholic Unions, see M. Schneider, *Die Christlichen Gewerkschaften*, passim, esp. pp. 767ff. (and on variations according to branches or regions, pp. 221ff., 290ff.). The "yellow" organizations were somewhat attractive to workers who ranked (themselves) as "skilled" workers. In total numbers, though, the membership remained by far below 5 percent of the socialist union's membership until 1914; in early spring of 1914 roughly 100,000 had enrolled, as compared to 1.5 million in the socialist unions, cf. K. Mattheier, *Die Gelben* (Düsseldorf, 1973), p. 324. On the functions of these corporation-prone associations from the employee's perspective, see H. Homburg, "Externer und interner Arbeitsmarkt: Zur Entstehung und Funktion des Siemens-Werkvereins 1906–1915," in T. Pierenkemper and R. Tilly, eds., *Historische Arbeitsmarktforschung* (Göttingen, 1982), pp. 215–48; see also Boll, *Massenbewegungen*, pp. 68ff.

14. This approach has been proposed and outlined by M. R. Lepsius, "Parteiensystem und Sozialstruktur: Zum Problem der deutschen Gesellschaft," in W. Abel et al., eds., *Wirtschaft, Geschichte und Wirtschaftsgeschichte* (Stuttgart, 1966), pp. 371–93.

15. M. Nolan, *Social Democracy and Society: Working-class Radicalism in Düsseldorf 1890–1920* (Cambridge, 1981), pp. 42ff., 113ff.

16. Schönhoven, *Expansion*, p. 114. On the participation—or at least the enroll-ment—of women in the SPD, and on cooperating women's associations be-fore the new "Law of Associations" of 1908, see G. Losseff-Tillmanns, ed., *Frauen und Gewerkschaften* (Frankfurt, 1982), p. 154. In 1914, 17 percent of the 1 million SPD members were women while the unions counted only 10 per-cent women among their members—but the absolute figures indicate that many more women joined the unions than the party: 250,000 to 170,000 party members. The peculiarities of regional developments of women's work and women's participation in the (socialist) unions are shown by Boll, *Mas-senbewegungen*, pp. 61ff. (see also pp. 48ff.).

17. F. Engels, letter to Bignami, February 13/26, 1877, in *Marx-Engels Werke (MEW)* (Berlin/GDR, 1962), vol. 19, pp. 89ff.; ibid., "Interview" (March 1, 1893) in *MEW*, vol. 22, p. 547. See H.-J. Steinberg, *Sozialismus und deutsche Sozialdemokratie* (3d ed., Hanover, 1972), p. 68.

18. See Schönhoven, *Expansion*, 125ff.

19. Cf. Schneider, *Die christlichen Gewerkschaften*, pp. 767ff. The growth rate of the Christian Unions was, until 1913, similar to that of the "free" or socialist unions. The quantitative ratio between both remained, however, about 1:8 (the latter representing the socialist unions). Unlike the socialist unions, the Christian ones suffered from a dramatic loss of members after 1913; until 1914 they lost about 40 percent of their 350,000 members.

20. H. Wunderer, *Arbeitervereine und Arbeiterparteien: Kultur- und Massenor-ganisationen in der Arbeiterbewegung (1890–1933)* (Frankfurt/New York, 1980).

21. See D. Geary, "Identifying Militarism: The Assessment of Working-Class Attitudes towards State and Society," in R. J. Evans, ed., *The German Work-ing Class 1888–1933* (London/Totowa, N.J., 1982), pp. 220–46, 233ff.; Lucas, *Zwei Formen*, p. 147. Miners' strikes and also, more generally, the contexts of miners' work and daily resistance are analyzed in F.-J. Brüggemeier, *Leben vor Ort*, while Brüggemeier discusses miners of the Ruhr area. The peculiarities of the Saar region are meticulously depicted by H. Steffens, "Arbeitstag, Arbeitszumutungen und Widerstand: Bergmännische Arbeitserfahrungen an der Saar in der zweiten Hälfte des 19. Jahrhunderts," *Archiv für Sozial-geschichte*, 21 (1981): 1–54. On the dockers see the case study on Hamburg by M. Grüttner, "Basisbewegung und Gewerkschaften im Hamburger Hafen seit 1896/97," in W. J. Mommsen and H.-G. Husung, eds., *Auf dem Wege zur Massengewerkschaft* (Stuttgart, 1984), pp. 152–70.

22. On motivations behind and forms of militancy in the context of workers' antiwar activities during the World War 1914–18 see the memoirs of one of the most active turners in this period, R. Müller, *Vom Kaiserreich zur Republik* (Berlin, 1924); on the revolutionary actions, see G. Högl, *Gewerkschaften und USPD von 1916–1922* (Phil. Diss., Munich, 1982).

23. P. Göhre, *Drei Monate Fabrikarbeiter und Handwerksbursche* (Leipzig, 1891), pp. 76f.

24. Göhre, *Drei Monate*, pp. 77f.

25. For the general importance of this dimension see P. Willis, *Learning to Labour: How Working Class Kids Get Working Class Jobs* (2d ed., New York, 1981), esp. pp. 43ff.

26. This is discussed in much more detail in my article "Cash, Coffee-Breaks, Horseplay."

27. G. Bataille, "Der Begriff der Verausgabung," in his *Das theoretische Werk* (Munich, 1975), vol. 1, pp. 9–31.

28. On political struggle under Kaiserreich's "half-absolutist pseudo-constitutionalism" see H.-U. Wehler, *Das deutsche Kaiserreich 1871–1918* (2d ed., Göttingen, 1975), p. 63.

29. Even "labor aristocrats" had to rely on extra earnings to feed their families. A statistic from Chemnitz indicates that, in 1900, 58.8 percent of the "skilled metalworkers" could not feed a household of two adults and three children (the figures for construction workers and for textile workers were 81.6 percent). Not only unpaid domestic labor, but also women's wage work and wage work of the children, as early as possible, remained a basic economic need for sustaining one's family; cf. Rosenbaum, *Formen der Familie*, p. 399. It should be mentioned, however, that most of the workers tried to earn some extra money by selling self-made items (e.g., toys), by doing repairs (e.g., clothes or coaches), or by day-laboring (as waiters, guardsmen, or the like). And everyone tried to get overtime; see Göhre, *Drei Monate*, p. 15.

Subsistence farming or, for that matter, gardening also contributed substantially to the daily nutrition of working-class families. Even in the 1930s more than 60 percent of the families of industrial proletarians who lived in small towns or villages relied on "evening" farming. This was by no means simply a rural phenomenon: in big cities as well, husbands grew potatoes, beans, and peas on small plots, fed pigs, goats, and rabbits (to be sure, the latter mostly tended to by the wives); in 1939, 25 percent of urban families enjoyed these supplies from their own garden or plot. See J. Mooser, "Familienarbeit und Arbeiterfamilie," in W. Ruppert, ed., *Arbeiterkultur* (Munich), forthcoming.

Daily survival was fundamentally dependent on wages. The enormous and constant variations from paycheck to paycheck and, thus, the severely restricted calculability of cash income is discussed in my piece "Cash, Coffee-Breaks, Horseplay."

There is still another side to this problem: perspectives and reality of old-age poverty including its effects on the respective adults; cf. H. Reif, "Soziale Lage und Erfahrungen des alternden Fabrikarbeiters in der Schwerindustrie des westlichen Ruhrgebiets Während der Hochindustrialisierung," *Archiv für Sozialgeschichte*, 22 (1982): 1–94.

30. That such was the case is borne out by the constant pilfering of goods from the Hamburg dockside; see M. Grüttner, "Working-Class Crime and the Labour Movement: Pilfering in the Hamburg Docks, 1888–1923," in Evans, ed., *The German Working Class*, pp. 54–79.

31. D. Mühlbert et al., *Arbeiterleben um 1900* (Berlin/GDR, 1983), pp. 61ff, 151ff., 160f.; A. Lange, *Das Wilhelmnische Berlin* (2d ed., Berlin/GDR, 1980), pp. 78, 82ff., 96.

32. AG Berliner S-Bahn, ed., *Die Berliner S-Bahn* (Berlin, 1982), pp. 59ff., 191ff.

33. K. Saul, *Staat, Industrie, Arbeiterbewegung im Kaiserreich* (Düsseldorf, 1974); for the 1880s see also the poems in H.-J. Steinberg, ed., *Mahnruf einer deutschen Mutter* (Bremen, 1983), which were submitted to the paper *Der Sozialdemokrat* for publication but never published.

34. Cf. *Wohlfahrtseinrichtungen der Fried: Kruppschen Gubstahlfabrik zu Essen zum Besten ihrer Arbeiter und Beamten* (Essen, 1883), p. 24. Historisches Archiv der Gutehoffnungshütte/Oberhausen Nr. 20015/4, fol. 8, letter to the Mayor of Oberhausen, Schwartz, of Sept. 4, 1869.

35. There is only one comprehensive study (see n. 40) on the "reform" policies put forward and pursued by state and local authorities; however, local and regional state archives, e.g., Essen and Düsseldorf, contain numerous files on, for instance, the improvement of vegetable growing or pig raising (and so forth).

36. Cf. A. Funk, "Die staatliche Gewalt nach Innen" (Habilitationsschrift typescript; Free University of Berlin/Dept. of Political Science, 1982; forthcoming in book form, Frankfurt, 1985).

37. On the improvements in health care and public services, measured in terms of decreasing infant mortality, see R. Spree, *Soziale Ungleichheit vor Krankheit und Tod* (Göttingen, 1981).

38. R. J. Evans, "'Red Wednesday' in Hamburg: Social Democrats, Police and Lumpenproletariat in the Suffrage Disturbance of 17 January 1906," *Social History*, 4 (1979): 1–31.

39. H. Bleiber, "Die Moabiter Unruhren 1910," *Zeitschrift für Geschichtswissenschaft*, 3 (1955): 173–211. See also Boll, *Massenbewegungen*, pp. 134ff.

40. G. Eley, *Reshaping the German Right* (New Haven/London, 1980), pp. 118ff.

41. See the proud notation the Social Democratic Düsseldorf *Volkszeitung* made of the May Day parade of 1903: "Many a bourgeois made a bewildered face as he saw the lively Reds parade by like a brigade of soldiers"; quoted by M. Nolan, *Social Democracy*, p. 138. A report on the May Day parade in Solingen, 1903, described the development of the proletarian movement into a "proletarian army" that had been made visible by the parade; see P. Friedemann, "Feste und Feiern im rheinisch-westfälischen Industriegebiet 1890–1914," in G. Huck, ed., *Sozialgeschichte der Freizeit* (Wuppertal, 1980), pp. 165–85, p. 167. See also B. Emig, *Die Veredelung der Arbeiter: Sozialdemokratie als Kulturbewegung* (Frankfurt/New York, 1890), p. 233. On funeral parades (which self-evidently required solemn conduct) see Bernstein, *Berliner Arbeiterbewegung*, vol. 4, pp. 354ff.

42. See, for instance, J. Dietzgen's article "Dass der Sozialist kein Monarchist sein kann," *Der Volksstaat*, Aug. 13, 1873, quoted by C. Stephan, *"Genossen, wir dürfen uns nicht von der Geduld hinreifen lassen!"* (Frankfurt, 1977), pp. 282–

93, 290f. A systematic content analysis of W. Liebknecht's or, even more, of August Bebel's speeches—or of those of other leaders or speakers—remains to be done. On Bebel, the long-standing leader of the SPD, see H. Bley, *Bebel und die Strategie der Kriegsverhütung 1904–1913* (Göttingen, 1975), pp. 76ff.

43. This seems to hold at least for the large number of local organizations that were not located in the urban centers of big industry; see, on the case of Göttingen, A. v. Saldern, "Arbeiterkultur in sozialdemokratischer Provinz (1890–1914)," in P. E. Stüdemann and M. Rector, eds., *Arbeiterbewegung und kulturelle Identität* (Frankfurt, 1983), pp. 10–34, esp. pp. 29f. Immediately after the expiration of the anti-Socialist repressive laws (1890) discussions tended to be extensive, especially in industrial centers like Chemnitz/Saxony; see Göhre, *Drei Monate*, p. 90.

The way one of the leading and most vigorous speakers (Rosa Luxemburg) mentioned meetings and her speeches makes clear that usually there was not much discussion: people admired her because she triggered lively debates; see R. Luxemburg, *Gesammelte Briefe* (Berlin/GDR, 1982), vol. 2, pp. 27–36 (spring 1903), 195f. (October 1905).

44. This split is mirrored in the recollections of a party newcomer from the 1890s; see O. Krille, *Unter dem Joch* (2d ed., 1914; Berlin/GDR, 1975), pp. 94ff.; see also his poem on an election rally, published in 1904, ibid., pp. xxxi f.

45. Cf. R. Luxemburg, *Gesammelte Briefe*, pp. 27ff., 175f. (esp. on the rush which was implied for a speaker who had to speak at three or four rallies on one day).

46. See, for instance, the quoted poem by Krille, on an election rally around 1900. See also Krille's recollections of the first time he attended a Social Democratic meeting, in his *Unter dem Joch*, pp. 94ff. The importance of collective singing is discussed by V. L. Lidtke, "Lieder der deutschen Arbeiterbewegung, 1864–1914," *Geschichte und Gesellschaft*, 5 (1979): 54–82. See on Catholic organizations N. Osterroth, *Vom Beter zum Kämpfer* (2d ed., 1920; Berlin/Bonn, 1980), pp. 63ff.; R. Kiefer, *Sozialdemokratische Arbiterbewegung in der Stadt Neuss vom Sozialistengesetz bis zum Ersten Weltkrieg* (Reinbek, 1982), pp. 89ff.

47. A. Popp, *Jugend einer Arbeiterin* (reprint, 7th ed., 1915–22; Berlin, 1977), pp. 74ff. One element of the fun that meetings could stimulate were arguments or disputes with opponents, as referred to in Luxemburg's letters; see Popp. Skepticism of any widespread interest in lectures on general topics of political strategy and debate is strongly articulated only in the context of women's education in and by the party, at least in Berlin after 1910/11; see J. H. Quataert, *Reluctant Feminists in German Social Democracy, 1885–1917* (Princeton, 1979), pp. 198ff.

48. G. Korff, "Volkskultur und Arbeiterkultur. Überlegungen am Beispiel der sozialistischen Maifesttradition," *Geschichte und Gesellschaft*, 5 (1979): 83–102; Borsdorf, *Hans Böckler*, pp. 55ff. (on May Day in Fürth/Bavaria, 1901); on the

difficulties inside factories see H.-J. Rupieper, *Arbeiter und Angestellte im Zeitalter der Industrialisierung: Eine sozialgeschichtliche Studie am Beispiel der MAN 1837–1914* (Frankfurt, 1982), pp. 200f. On the assemblies commemorating the March 18 revolt in Berlin of 1848 and the Paris Commune of 1871, see B. W. Bouvier, *Französische Revolution und deutsche Arbeiterbewegung* (Bonn, 1982), pp. 377f.

49. Osterroth, *Vom Beter zum Kämpfer*, pp. 72ff.; more generally this point is made by F. Brüggemeier, "Soziale Vagabondange oder revolutionärer Heros," in L. Niethammer, ed., *Lebenserfahrung und kollektives Gedächtnis* (Frankfurt, 1980), pp. 193–213.

50. E. David, *Referenten-Führer* (Berlin, 1907), pp. 85ff. Lectures and talks implied direct if not face-to-face contact. The importance of the latter is underlined in the analysis of the Social Democrats' recruitment patterns during the Imperial Reich by J. Loreck, *Wie man früher sozialdemokrat wurde* (Bonn/Bad Godesberg, 1977), pp. 197f., 229f.

51. Saldern, "Arbeiterkultur," p. 27; J. Belli, *Die rote Feldpost unterm Sozialistengesetz* (9th ed., 1912; Berlin/Bonn, 1978), p. 67; Göhre, *Drei Monate*, p. 89; as an aspired (and acclaimed) standard assumed by C. Hillmann, *Die Organisation der Massen* (Leipzig, 1875), pp. 48, 51.

52. Dahlem, *Jugendjahre*, pp. 133ff. For another report (by W. Reimes) see G. Bers, ed., *Arbeiterjugend im Rheinland: Erinnerungen von W. Reimes und Peter Trimborn* (Wentorf, 1978).

53. On Hamburg see V. Böge, "'Werkzeug des Umsturzes' oder Instrumente reformorientierter Arbeiterpolitik? Die Gründung der Volksfürsorge in Hamburg 1912–14," in A. Herzig et al., eds., *Arbeiter in Hamburg* (Hamburg, 1983), pp. 387–404; on Remscheid and its established working-class culture see Lucas, *Zwei Formen*, p. 63. In the new settlements at Duisburg-Hamborn (housing imported workers from the rural east) local merchants could successfully block any such attempts; see Lucas, *Zwei Formen*. On support of daily survival in the Catholic milieu, see Kiefer, *Sozialdemokratische Arbeiterbewegung in der Stadt Neuss*, pp. 90f.

54. Workers employed by the Krupp Company set up several of these associations mostly to save enough money to get reductions each fall from potato-growing farmers and peasants; see Historisches Archiv Krupp, WA 41/74-364, passim (on clubs founded in 1887, 1889, and 1890).

55. Lucas, *Zwei Formen*, pp. 69ff.

56. More generally, this interpretation of *Eigensinn* may call into question H. Bausinger's notion of "zig-zag" loyalty, used to describe a simultaneous loyalty to the party of the proletariat *and to* the nation-state, the Imperial Reich. A majority of working-class Germans may, in fact, have had only a very limited sense of "loyalty" to either, in accordance with their disinterest for *any* sort of "formal," state-centered politics. See H. Bausinger, "Verburgerlichung—Folgen eines Interpretaments," in G. Wiegelmann, ed., *Kultureller*

Wandel im 19. Jahrhundert (Göttingen, 1973), pp. 24–49.

57. See D. Abraham, "Corporatist Compromise and the Re-Emergence of the Labor/Capital Conflict in Weimar Germany," *Political Power and Social Theory,* 2 (1981): 59–109 (included is an analysis of the Kaiserreich patterns).

58. One example is the steadily increasing number of openly anti-Jewish and anti-Semitic jokes in popular Social Democratic papers, especially the *Wahre Jacob,* after about 1890; see R. Leuschen-Seppel, *Sozialdemokratie und Antisemitismus im Kaiserreich* (Bonn, 1978), pp. 242ff., 259ff.

59. On the "clearly antifeminist" positions (and actions) of "the" male working class see Quataert, *Reluctant Feminists,* pp. 153ff.; on complementary aspects of ideological debate and open organizational conflict between men and women in the SPD after 1908 see S. Richebächer, *Uns fehlt nur eine Kleinigkeit* (Frankfurt, 1982). For most women, "politics" was and remained confined to parliamentary politics and long-term planning of society's future; see the lecture of a (female) textile worker's union functionary, M. Hoppe, *Zur Arbeiterinnen-Frage* (Berlin, 1910), pp. 13f.

60. A. Levenstein, *Die Arbeiterfrage* (München, 1912).

61. V. R. Calkins, "The Uses of Utopianism: The Millenarian Dream in Central European Social Democracy Before 1914," *Central European History,* 15 (1982): 124–48, 134ff.

62. F. Boll, *Massenbewegungen,* pp. 151–87; cf. Boll, *Frieden ohne Revolution?* (Bonn, 1980), pp. 100–119.

63. *Berichte der Sozialdemokratischen Partei Deutschlands* (Sopade), vols. 1–7 (Frankfurt, 1980).

Contributors

SEAN WILENTZ is Assistant Professor and Philip and Beulah Rollins Preceptor in History, Princeton University.

CLIFFORD GEERTZ is Harold S. Linder Professor of Social Science, Institute of Advanced Study, Princeton.

RALPH E. GIESEY is Professor of History, University of Iowa.

SARAH HANLEY is Associate Professor of History, University of Iowa.

TEOFILO F. RUIZ is Associate Professor of History, Brooklyn College, City University of New York.

JOHN ELLIOTT is Professor in the School of Historical Studies, Institute of Advanced Study, Princeton.

MAURICE AGULHON is Professor of History at the University of Paris I (Panthéon-Sorbonne).

DAVID CANNADINE is Fellow and Lecturer in History at Christ's College, Cambridge.

RICHARD WORTMAN is Professor of History, Princeton University.

RHYS ISAAC is Reader in History, Latrobe University.

ALF LÜDTKE is a research fellow (M.P.I.) at the Max-Planck-Institut-für-Geschichte, Göttingen.

Index

Volumes in the Shelby Cullom Davis Center Series